P9-CQI-261

A RESEARCH PRIMER

for

PASTORAL CARE

and

COUNSELING

Larry VandeCreek
*with the Research Committees of
the American Association of Pastoral Counselors
and
the Association for Clinical Pastoral Education*

Journal of Pastoral Care Publications, Inc.
1988

A RESEARCH PRIMER FOR PASTORAL CARE AND COUNSELING

by
Larry VandeCreek

© 1988
Journal of Pastoral Care Publications, Inc.

ISBN 0-929670-00-0

Printed in the United States of America
on acid-free paper

Contents

LINCOLN CHRISTIAN COLLEGE AND SEMINARY

80367

Acknowledgments

Fifteen years ago I could not have written a book about empirical research. This fact testifies that I am indebted to many who have helped me develop new interests and learn new skills. Primary among them are my colleagues in the Department of Family Medicine at Ohio State University. Family Medicine, itself struggling to establish a scientific basis, has provided an ideal culture in which I could develop. My debt extends to many, but Larry Gabel merits special mention. To him I took my early research efforts, and he taught me basic scientific and mathematical principles. He and I have not published anything together, but his influence lies behind the efforts which have gone into this book.

Some years after I began to do reserach my file drawers were filled with data and rejection letters from editors. Then I learned of Gayle Carpenter and her technical writing skills. She taught me how to write, a skill I had not learned until that time. I owe much to her.

I would not have written this book, however, without the encouragement of my colleagues on the Research Committee of the American Association of Pastoral Counselors. Their vigorous response to my initial suggestion served as the immediate context and catalyst. Dick Augspurger, John Carr, Dick Fisher, and Clyde Getman, the publication subcommittee, have made suggestions, read drafts and provided helpful criticism. To them I am also indebted.

Finally, I am indebted to the Journal of Pastoral Care Publications, Inc. and to Orlo Strunk, Jr., its Managing Editor. Their interests have stimulated my energy as well as my hope that research in pastoral care and counseling will begin to make the contribution of which it is capable.

—LARRY VANDECREEK, D.MIN.

*In science, I missed the factor of meaning;
and in religion, that of empiricism.*

—C. G. Jung

Introduction

Why write a book about research in pastoral care and counseling? Equally important, why read such a book? Let me respond to these questions thereby setting the stage for the chapters which follow.

Ministers who specialize in pastoral care and counseling constantly rub shoulders with professionals in peer disciplines who possess an empirical scientific literature. By "empirical" I mean research which describes its subject matter by using numbers and by conducting statistical tests. Other types of research exits, and they are valuable. These include the recording and classification of observations as well as the vast historical and literary research which has characterized much of the work in the religious and theological literature. These research efforts must never be neglected. Empirical research, at least as defined and described in this book, takes the next step by increasing objectivity and exactness through the use of numbers and statistical tests. These processes determine more precisely the differences between various observations, classifications, or relationships.

Pastoral care and counseling specialists produce a minuscule amount of such work. Most of the existing empirical literature in pastoral care and counseling is contained in graduate degree dissertations. Only a few current books and journal articles are empirical. The rest consist of observations, opinions, subjective impressions and theory-building discussions. Ministers practicing pastoral care and counseling have not produced an active empirical research tradition.

So what? Is empirical research in pastoral care and counseling really necessary? Can't we get along without it? Will empirical research help us? That depends on our goals for pastoral care and counseling and our sense of responsibility in the professional world. We do not need empirical research if pastoral care and counseling is to live off the good will of others, funded by hospitals and mental health sources because we "hopefully do some good." We do not need empirical research if we are never asked to justify our role and existence in scientific institutions and professional communities. Empirical research is unnecessary unless we want to know more about ourselves in a concrete way. It is also unnecessary if we are satisfied with and confident about the *status quo*.

The primary reason for producing a scientific literature comparable to that of our peer professionals is, quite frankly, that we have a moral obligation to do so. We possess a moral obligation not only to discover whether we are helping our clientele and patients, but also to determine whether some of our efforts are more helpful than others, whether religious interventions of one style or another are helpful or hurtful. The truth is that we do not know whether we heal or hurt, at least we do not know as clearly as we could or in ways which are meaningful or convincing to our scientific contemporaries. Some pastoral specialists would say that we know the answers to these concerns from professional experience and informal feedback. I will not engage here in epistemological arguments about how or whether we know these answers. I will simply state the fact again that the empirical data are not in our books and journals. For that reason, we need to be concerned about whether we are "pulling our weight" as a profession in this scientific age.

This leads to an even deeper issue, again one with moral implications. As a profession we are living off the discoveries and insights of other professions. Since Anton Boisen's contribution to clinical health care ministry during the 1920s, we have made observations, and developed theories as well as clinical styles of ministry for chaplaincy and pastoral counseling, but little more. We have been unable to put the capstone in place. That is, we have not built an empirical research tradition which tests our observations and theories. Our theory-building has been admirable, but we simply do not know if these theories work. There are, of course, a few exceptions, a few empirical studies which have been published in scientific journals.

The problem is even deeper than that. It is true that we have not discovered new and unique interventions for the problems of the persons with whom we work. But have we even tried? Have we, as professional groups, taken our pastoral "equipment" into the hospital or counseling room and, after developing appropriate questions and theoretical frameworks, even tried to test them in some objective fashion? Little evidence exists that, as a profession, we have consistently tried to do that. That, I believe, makes us morally culpable. As members of our respective organizations we have been too ready to make a living on existing, borrowed insights and practice patterns, and not ready enough to test our own insights. Consequently, we can legitimately be seen in the scientific world as a "do nothing" profession which has failed to make a contribution to knowledge in a scientific age. We are, as a profession of clinical ministry, unable to point to solid empirical contributions of knowledge to the academic community or to our other colleagues in the practice of ministry.

Why is this so? The first reason is that many chaplains and pastoral counselors work in institutions which do not support research. These institutions or centers are primarily service oriented. Beyond that, however, it seems that we either do not want to make such a contribution (not seeing the importance of it), or do not know how to carry out rigorous scientific work. I believe the latter is the primary reason. My conversations with chaplains and pastoral counselors as well as with journal editors reveal that much research exists, but it lacks scientific strength. The purpose of this book is to enable increasingly competent empirical research. Some benefits may also accrue to those who, already skilled in research, do not currently understand its importance in the scientific professional world.

This book stands in a tradition of similar efforts by others. In 1976 Samuel Southard wrote *Religious Inquiry*[1] which discusses in a less rigorous manner many of the technical questions addressed in this book. In 1984 Richard E. Davies wrote *Handbook for Doctor of Ministry Projects*.[2] It is more detailed and statistical than the present book, neglecting the personal struggles involved in research work which I address in the first section. Thus, this book stands between these two, addressing personal and professional struggles but also insisting on scientific rigor.

Increased empirical research will not bring utopia to pastoral care and counseling, however. At least two dangers exist. The first is that, despite our increased efforts, we perform such work poorly. Poor research work is worse than none at all. Poor work creates faulty conclusions, erroneous claims, and disdain in the broader scientific community. The second danger is that we may place too much confidence in science, that we begin to worship at its altar, implying that nothing is true unless it is demonstrated at a p value below 0.05. These two temptations are real and must be resisted, but we certainly cannot justify abstinence from scientific work because the temptations are too great.

So although this book is a primer, a starter, it is not therefore simple. I have sought to address the root issues involved in our neglect of empirical research in order to cultivate it. I have deliberately addressed the more subtle and attitudinal issues of "doing research" since these are not addressed elsewhere for the religious professional. I briefly address such technical subjects as the management of variables and the use of statistics. I leave this technical side of research underdeveloped because research consultants can make suggestions directly applicable to specific projects. Such information can also be obtained in other books. From my point of view, learning mathematics and statistics is less important than learning to identify and use a consultant.

I have concluded with a chapter on writing about the results of research for journal publication. It encourages the use of a technical writing consultant. My efforts are confined to describing the discipline of writing a journal article and to demonstrating that good writing is hard work.

Section 1

Personal and Professional Struggles

Research work, like all other endeavors, is carried out within the context of our personal and professional questions. These questions, in comparison to those we have about the technical research process, cut more deeply into our efforts to carry out a project. We begin to ask why we are trying to do research, why we find it so difficult, what we need to accomplish in order to be successful, and what the rewards will be. Such questions need satisfactory answers if we are to be productive.

In this section I seek to address some of these questions. I suggest that a long historical relationship exists between religion and science which makes empirical research difficult for ministers. This relationship is characterized by such factors as a lack of education in and experience with the sciences as well as a classical conflict between theology and science. After responding to these concerns, I suggest in Chapter 3 that we are more scientific than we think and that foundations are already laid for our research efforts. Personal and professional struggles need not hobble us.

Chapter 1

Why Ministers Don't Like to do Research

So you are interested in doing some research! Welcome to an exciting process!

Oh—you are not so interested? You are reading and thinking about research because your institutional staff is pushing for research? You are reading this because you are part of a degree program which requires research? I understand. In one way or another, many of us have experienced that. At some point I too was dragged kicking and screaming into doing research. I have survived. And not only have I survived, I have actually learned to like research. I like answering the questions, uncovering the facts. If you enjoy learning how people work, you can enjoy doing research too.

My goal is to help you understand enough of science and its processes so that you can do a good job in answering your particular research questions. This increased understanding can save you anxiety, time, and effort as you make your way through the scientific process. So again I welcome you to an exciting process. I challenge you to make it interesting and eye-opening. I challenge you to learn how the research process works, how science works. This learning will put you more clearly in touch with some of the fundamental motifs of our culture and its determination to be scientific.

Perhaps you are still not sure you have the time, interest, or inclination to learn the research process. I have no quarrel with that. You have some good reasons for skepticism, fear, and doubt. The very word "research" itself can be intimidating. It can also be confusing because the word has a variety of meanings. I will use the word "research" to mean systematic and intentional inquiry into a problem which produces results in the form of numbers, although other valid forms of research exist. I also mean that findings will be made available to a professional or academic community, usually through presentation or publication. This is a difficult task.

Research is a foreign and difficult task for most ministers and they are hesitant to undertake it. I maintain that their hesitation is well-founded rather than silly or idle. It is present for very good reasons. In the remainder of this chapter, I will explore three concerns and four misconceptions about science so that you can begin to think about their influence upon you. Only then can you move ahead. I will discuss the historical relationship between science and theology, an additional reason for hesitation, in the next chapter.

CONCERN I

When you, as a minister, begin to explore how you might conduct some research, you step into a very different world than that to which you are accustomed. In this new world, the rules are different than those which prevail in the religious community. This gives rise to the first reason for hesitation.

I want you to think back to your educational experiences in high school. In those formative years, you were finding your niche in the subject areas of greatest interest to you. Usually this niche was established as you were rewarded for good work, and this reward in turn created further interest. The increased interest generated energy. The energy generated more attention to the area of study. A reinforcement cycle was created and you began to settle into in-depth study. For some persons, this reinforcement cycle focused on mathematics, for others it was chemistry or physics. For others, however, it was history or religion or English or foreign languages. In a vague way, the students of the sciences could be distinguished from those in the humanities. At the college level, this division between the sciences and the humanities continued. As more and more focus upon your area of concentration was demanded, you moved further away from other subjects and their ways of thinking.

This process was not absolute, of course. History majors still took courses in the sciences, but probably with increasing reluctance. Chemistry majors took courses in the arts and humanities, but probably only because they were required. This process was part of a continuing struggle to find a vocational place. Many students changed majors, some even moving back and forth between the sciences and the humanities, but gradually the sorting process happened and all found a place.

Since you are now in ministry, you probably settled into the humanities, gradually leaving the sciences behind. In so doing, you left behind not only the study of specific content such as chemistry, physics, or mathematics, but also a way of thinking about the world and what is important in it. Persons with education and interest in both the sciences and the humanities can occasionally be found, but they are exceptions.

My point is this: doing research requires you to move back toward the perspectives of the sciences and mathematics. If you liked science and mathematics in your educational work and understood something of that mentality, then moving into research may be easier for you. If you have little or no exposure to science, the research perspective will be harder to explore. In either instance, your limited exposure is probably one source of your hesitation about research. I want to facilitate that process of understanding the science and research world.

CONCERN II

A second concern plays a role in your hesitation about doing research. This additional factor is your personality, what excites you and keeps your interest, compared to what you regard as dull, uninteresting, and mundane. Many believe that research work is the latter: dry and dull as dust. This can be true, but the real issue is more complex.

In doing research, a determining factor related to personality is the ability to be curious and to ask questions. In short, you need to venture beyond traditional, conventional ways of thinking in order to challenge assumptions and to ask new questions. Later in this book, I will discuss more extensively your need for a skeptical and critical mind as you do research. For now, you need to reflect on and search for that part of your personality which wonders if things are really the way they seem, that part which seeks to break down the whole into its parts so that they can be more clearly known.

The inquiring, searching part of your personality may be difficult to find. As noted earlier your education may not have helped you develop it. Some people also seem to possess more searching, skeptical characteristics than others. Recently, I finished a Myers-Briggs Type Indicator study of pastoral counselors in a four state region. This instrument was chosen because other researchers have given it to thousands of people and typical characterizations of specific vocations, including parish clergy, have been compiled. The results from parish clergy studies as well as the new pastoral counselor study indicate that critical thinking typically is not the pastor's primary strength. Rather, pastors are caring, intuitive, supportive persons who emphasize the need for faith and hope rather than skepticism and critical thinking.[1] Your supportive, caring characteristics may be evident to you. You will do much better in your research work, however, if you can discover and use your critical and skeptical faculties.

How can these faculties be developed? Let me suggest a simple, straight-forward methodology. Later in this book we will suggest ways in which a critical question can be developed into a research project. At the moment, my concern is to help you explore areas by asking questions.

The methodology I suggest is this. As you go about your daily routine you have contact with problems, both personal and organizational. Select problems which possess some urgency and begin to be curious about them. Having taken this first step, ask: "Why is this a problem?" "What is the difficulty here?" As you explore these questions, you will begin to get behind assumptions and behaviors. This encourages exploration and searching, the foundations of research.

CONCERN III

Like educational experience and personality, a third concern which may contribute to your hesitation about research has deep roots. Simply put, this factor is the feeling that research is not part of the clergy role, that doing science is secular, and that paying attention to data, numbers, and statistical tests is contrary to the serious calling of ministry. Ministry, you may assert, cares for the spiritual, for the soul, for God's action in the world, and for the lives of God's people. Research pays attention to none of these, it may seem to you, and involves ministers in activities quite outside their calling.

This stance toward ministry and research may be helped by openly discussing it with others. The role binding which excludes research is only true in limited ways. For example, exegesis and hermeneutics are orderly, scientific processes involving research although they usually do not involve mathematics. However you choose to deal with this factor, it can be a highly significant variable in making you feel uncomfortable with research.

In addition to these concerns about science and research, ministers have other reasons for hesitation concerning research. These reasons, which arise from stereotypes and misconceptions about science and research, have profound influence on us. I will conclude this chapter by discussing four of these misconceptions.

MISCONCEPTION I:

I must become a scientist in order to carry out research.

A scientist is an awesome figure in our culture. The name brings with it images of persons whose theories and data have revolutionized our world. Conversely, the word may also evoke images of the "absent minded professor" who secludes himself or herself in a laboratory, far away from the realities of life. These misconceptions can either intimidate or offend us.

These images are true of few scientists, however. Most are usually quite typical educated persons, making their livelihoods by using relevant methodologies in specific scientific areas. In many ways ministers are already scientists. Like most educated persons today, they try to think about problems and processes in a rational way, and so in a limited manner they already engage in the scientific process. The challenge to conduct a research project creates an invitation to engage in an additional technical process. This process leads to increased thoroughness and to more careful technical measurement which can in turn produce increasingly discriminating results.

If they wish to publish their work, then their studies must reflect the level of technical sophistication in the field. They will, for example, experience difficulty publishing case studies (a relatively simple scientific process) in a discipline which is already publishing quantitative measurement data. Conversely, a researcher will likely have equal difficulty publishing double blind placebo controlled studies (a highly sophisticated method) in a discipline which has not yet examined its subject matter through case studies.

You do not need to become a world famous scientist in order to carry out respectable research. Rather you need to observe your own scientific processes and know the level of sophistication in the field you wish to study. These matters point to the next misconception.

MISCONCEPTION II:

I must understand the scientific method to undertake research.

This misconception is parallel to the preceding discussion. Those of us who have not majored in the sciences but remain influenced by introductory courses still often carry the fantasy that a single grand immutable method lies behind all discoveries.

Scientific process is carried out with a great diversity of methods. Competent scientific studies can be done in a variety of ways, although each must pay attention to central underlying principles. The methods of the social sciences are not those of the organic fields. A specific scientific method is always the product of the basic principles of that scientific field as they are applied to the subject matter. Scientists who study human beings must respect the process of informed consent, something about which astronomers, for example, do not need to worry. Astronomers and other physical scientists, therefore, possess unique freedoms in their work. Their subject matter creates its own limitations, however. While the human sciences can directly examine, converse with, and touch their subject matter, astronomers must be content to only look at their subjects from afar and can examine only the products produced by their light. Those who study animals do not have all the constraints of working with humans, but neither can they interview their subjects or study their verbal problem solving processes. In all of these fields, scientific methods must accommodate to the subjects which are studied and this invites creativity of method.

This creativity, however, must be as true as possible to the basic principles of the scientific field. Fundamental is the need to utilize as much objectivity as possible so that findings can be defended without relying on our subjective hopes, wishes, and impressions. Methods frequently used to achieve as much objectivity as possible include the following: operational definition of terms; the use of quantitative rather than qualitative measure (hence the use of numbers); the careful recognition and control of bias and variables which influence results; the need to be skeptical, questioning, and careful in the interpretation of results; and the need to replicate studies to determine if someone else in another setting produces the same results.

MISCONCEPTION III:

I must definitely prove my answer in order to claim credible scientific results.

The stereotypes of science are interdependent and I hope you are gradually calling them all into question. With regard to this misconception, it is important to know that science cannot prove anything in a final way. The methodology is incapable of final proof, a fact which will be discussed further in the following chapters. At this point in the discussion, it is important to know that scientific methodologies are used to determine the likelihood that results are not simply random. Random results are useless because they are unreliable; a second identical study could produce opposite findings if the results are random. The more unusual the results, the more likely it is that they are not due to random chance. Science has quantified this in the "p value." A "p value" of 0.05 indicates that there is a 5% chance or less that these findings are due to random chance. A second identical study by someone else which produces equivalent results will further confirm the findings and increase confidence in the face of scientific skepticism.

Consequently, your scientific duty is to produce as competent a study as possible within the limitations of subjects, time, money, and energy, and to interpret the findings carefully. Science, technically speaking, never *proves* anything. Our call as scientists is not to offer "proof" but to produce technically competent studies which suggest conclusions and which can be replicated by others. When the conclusions reached in several studies support each other, skepticism is gradually subdued.

MISCONCEPTION IV:

I must endure a technical, boring, difficult process in order to complete research.

This misconception can contain a grain of truth. The research process is a careful, technical one. Regardless of the specific methods, it uses step-by-step processes which honor underlying principles. The rest is misconception.

Yet you may say, "I never endured anthing so boring or difficult as the process of doing research for my degree." It is important to note that many who say this have usually gone through the scientific process only once. And it is a miserable and difficult process for everyone the first time. Blind to the difficulties to be confronted just around the next turn, you are constantly frustrated by new problems. During this first research process, you are usually short on time, money, and patience when repeatedly confronted or challenged by faculty adivsors. In the face of all this, it is easy to give up on the process, defend the results as best you can, and promise yourself never to get entangled in all this again because it required endurance beyond your reserves.

Unfortunately, we are tempted to stop, right after having come through the worst. Having gone through the process once, you find that it becomes easier. The road map is clearer; the sense behind the process is more apparent. You can now move through the process more quickly and easily, continuing to refine your understanding. And if you are nurtured, encouraged, and guided during the first experience so that the results are exciting, then the process becomes self-perpetuating. The second, third, and fourth projects further and further unravel the mystery of the problem you are studying.

That is the excitement of science and research. The facts become clearer; the undiscovered facts become a gigantic, engrossing mystery deserving of the best detective using the most sophisticated methods. Now compelled to discover the truth behind this problem, you move onward until you know the facts as clearly as possible, dispensing with fiction. Boredom is gone in that compelling rush toward the truth. The basic principles of science become second nature and the challenge is to design more and more sophisticated methods to reveal the truth as clearly as possible. The adventure of the search, the hunt, has set in and it will not let you go until you know more! Caught up in this process, you begin to reap the benefits and excitement of research.

In conclusion, further thought and reflection about these factors may make it clear why you are hesitant about research. No doubt some of the hesitation has to do with educational experience, with your personality style, with perceived conflicts regarding appropriate clergy behavior, and with various misconceptions about science. I wish to reflect further about these matters by briefly discussing the history of the relationship between religion/church and science/research in the next chapter. In that discussion, it will become clear that the church has been uncomfortable with science for centuries, and an awareness of this historical background may help you understand and overcome your hesitation.

Chapter 2

Understanding the Historical Background: Struggles Between Science and Theology

The church and the clergy have struggled long and hard with their relationship to science, and consequently your hesitation concerning research possesses deep historical roots. This chapter briefly recounts the history of that relationship to help you identify the early precursors of your concerns. At the same time, the discussion should help strengthen your grasp of the history of science.

The ancient church fathers were very hesitant about science. Scientific ideas influenced their world intensely, although these ideas seem primitive now. Augustine was the first whose thoughts about science had lasting influence. He thought of scientific knowledge as spiritually barren and misleading. "Nor dost Thou draw near," he wrote, "but to the contrite in heart, nor art Thou found by the proud, no, not though by curious skill they could number the stars and the sand, and measure the starry heavens, and track the course of the planets."[1] He subsequently argued in *The Trinity* that theology must be regarded as *sapientia* (wisdom) in contrast to *scientia* (knowledge), the term he reserved for the sciences. This knowledge, he argued, was derived from transitory, temporal things and led to nothing unless it was combined with wisdom from theology. Philosophy too was a kind of science and needed the wisdom of theology.[2] Since philosophy was the most important science of the day, Augustine worked hard to draw it together with theology. Augustine's point of view became the foundation for theology's position as "queen of the sciences," a view which stood for centuries.

The next major change occurred in the 13th century, bringing a redefinition of the relationship. The pre-eminence of theology was disintegrating. The new science in the West was increasingly independent, and theology's relationship with science began to be re-evaluated. As universities emerged with their scientific curricula, theology needed to demonstrate a scientific character in order to be included in the new intellectual world. This was a crucial test for theology.[3]

Thomas Aquinas defined theology as a science, thereby adjusting its Augustinian foundations. Aquinas, borrowing Aristotle's model, taught that theology was a "derived science," and demonstrated its scientific character by working with the Scriptures and the Creeds. The scientific process for theology was a deductive one which drew specific theological truths out of these raw materials. Theology entered university curricula largely on the basis of Aquinas' argument.[4]

Other theologians (like some today) were not convinced that theology was a science, among them Duns Scotus, Alexander of Hales, and Bonaventure. They argued that theology was a practical matter aimed at producing qualities of love and respect in human beings. Despite their argument, they were overshadowed by Aquinas and his Aristotelian arguments.

The Reformation re-emphasized theology as a practical matter. Martin Luther did not see theology as a science, and, with John Calvin, he spoke strongly against the Scholastics, the theological scientists of the day. Both Luther and Calvin viewed theology as the practical study of the relationship between God and human beings. Calvin's *Institutes of the Christian Religion* was in fact the first comprehensive theology which was not grounded in Aquinas' scientific, Scholastic metaphysics of essences. Torrance claims that this characteristic was so distinctive that modern theology began with his work.[5] Be that as it may, both Luther and Calvin stood in opposition to the concept of theology as a science by virtue of their stance against the Scholastics and by virtue of their efforts to make theology more understandable to the ordinary citizen.

The interrelationship between theology and science after the Reformation was complex, in part because theological pluralism abounded, and in part because science and its influence grew rapidly. The 17th and 18th centuries were so heavily influenced by science that theologians once again began to argue that theology needed to be classified as a science if it was to maintain any intellectual respectability and influence. Friedrich Schleiermacher, for instance, defined theology as a practical science and identified it as a study of Christianity.[6] In the subsequent decades this definition produced a number of theologies dependent upon Schleiermacher, all of which taught that a study of the history of Christianity was the heart of theology.

In 1893 Wilhelm Dilthey wrote *Einleitung in die Geisteswissenschaften,* which introduced the study of human life as scientific subject matter, and which has become a classic in the history of science.[7] Ernest Troeltsch explored theology's relationship to the human sciences as they were introduced by Dilthey. Troeltsch's early work interpreted religion as a psychological process which focused on the beautiful, the good, and the divine, all ideal contents as opposed to sensory perceptions. These, said Troeltsch, all came to expression and influence in religion and were at the core of theology's scientific study. Troeltsch's work during his life gradually moved from an individually oriented psychology of religion to a broader analysis of historical structures and their meaning. This scientific attention to meaning also became a major focus of the human sciences.[8]

With or without theology, the sciences experienced their own problems, particularly in the struggles between the human and the natural sciences. Methods used with inorganic substances could not be transposed directly into the study of humans. Experimental methods were limited and humans were not as predictable or consistent as the materials of the natural sciences. Nonetheless, the human sciences grew and gave primary attention to human interaction and meaning. H. G. Gadamer and J. Habermas argued in this regard that the human sciences were necessary as a separate group of disciplines because natural laws could not work with or characterize the presence of meaning. They suggested that human meaning was the content of the human sciences and theologians such as Troeltsch and his successors went on to suggest that this was also true of theology.[9]

The entire scientific endeavor was challenged by philosophers who came to be known as logical positivists. They argued that true science was composed of statements whose accuracy could be tested and whose truth was logically demonstrable. Early positivists, such as Carnap, argued that true propositions made assertions about reality and these assertions could be proven on the Principle of Verification. This principle essentially held that statements could be believed only after they had been scientifically tested and verified by results. He, along with others, attacked theology and allied disciplines on the basis that their propositions could not be shown to be either true or false. They charged that theology was not a science at all. Its assertions were meaningless because they did not actually describe reality in a way which could be tested or proved.[10]

The viewpoint of logical positivism was refined by Karl Popper. He believed that the Principle of Verification was faulty because scientific laws themselves could never be more than hypotheses. Popper pointed out that science could never claim total verifications of a hypothesis because it could not possibly analyze every case of, or every situation pertinent to, the hypothesis. The hypothesis, technically speaking, remained unproven as long as a single instance of the phenomena under study remained unexamined. He declared that knowledge, therefore, should be built on the Principle of Falsification. This principle argued that, since not every instance of a problem under study could be examined, the scientist should make a fair and objective selection of existing cases and test them. If no case was found which falsified the hypothesis then it could be regarded as verified, as estahblished. Popper believed that this approach was more reasonable and would still separate true knowledge from speculation and mythology.[11]

Popper used this argument to criticize not only theology but other sciences which had difficulty using logical methods to test and prove their conclusions. Education, psychology, and social work felt the sting of his critical analysis. These disciplines soon took steps to mimic the deductive sciences and thus defend their status. Carefully planned scientific projects which used statistical analyses began to appear in their journals.

Popper's Falsification Principle was brought to the attention of the theological community by Anthony Flew, who wrote a much-debated essay in which he concluded:

> Now it often seems to people who are not religious as if there was no conceivable event or series of events the occurrence of which would be admitted by sophisticated religious people to be sufficient reason for conceding "There wasn't a God after all" or "God does not really love us then" . . . . I therefore put . . . the simple

question, "What would have to occur or to have occurred to constitute for you a disproof of the love of or existence of God?"[12]

You can see the problem. Flew defined the methodology according to the Principle of Falsification. How could the religious community set its particular problems in this form? This was an enormous challenge. Scientists were disdainful, provocative, and proud. Sweeping claims were made. The church and theology were put on the defensive until some clarity evolved.

One part of the challenge was to determine whether the scientific approach possessed any relevance to theology at all. Did scientific methodology possess a model at all usable to theology? Many theologians tried to build a new place for theology using scientific processes as much as possible. They employed hermeneutical principles from the disciplines of history and philosophy in order to create a contemporary, defensible theological science.

Pannenberg, among others, contributed to this endeavor in *Theology and the Philosophy of Science*. He asked how theological statements could be evaluated. What kind of evidence, if any, could be used in the evaluation? For Pannenberg the emergence of these questions went hand-in-hand with the realization that the scientific viewpoint had infiltrated our entire view of reality and that "the early Christian witness and the historical figure of Jesus belongs to an age which for us is past, and so their relevance to the present can be assessed only as an act of interpretation." This focus on the problem underlined the importance of hermeneutics:

> The solution of the hermeneutical problem must try to determine whether the primacy of God and his revelation over all that is human and relative . . . can, through reflection on its self mediation in the process of Christian tradition, be stated in such a manner that, although of course it still requires faith, it does not require the possibility of basing theology on an *arbitrary* venture of faith.[13] (emphasis added)

Thus, hermeneutics was charged with the task of devising methods to refute the charge from positivism and the opinion common among secular society that what someone believes does not matter because all beliefs are equally valid (or invalid). Hermeneutics was to demonstrate that the content of faith was not arbitrary. In accepting this task, theology sought to build a hermeneutical methodology and a theological system which qualified as a science.

Other theologians worked at the problem in a different way. They held that while decisive falsification of theological statements was not possible, there was evidence for and against specific beliefs. Basil Mitchel presents this point of view in a remarkable parable.

> In time of war in an occupied country, a member of the resistance meets one night a Stranger who deeply impresses him. They spend that night together in conversation. The Stranger tells the partisan that he himself is on the side of the resistance—indeed that he is in command of it, and urges the partisan to have faith in him no matter what happens. The partisan is utterly convinced at that meeting of the Stranger's sincerity and constancy and undertakes to trust him. They never meet in conditions of intimacy again. But sometimes the Stranger is seen helping members of the resistance, and the partisan is grateful and says to his friends, "He is on our side." Sometimes he is seen in the uniform of the police handing over patriots to the occupying power. On these occasions his friends murmur against him: but the partisan still says, "He is on our side." He still believes that in spite of appearances the Stranger did not deceive him. Sometimes he asks the Stranger for help and receives it. He is then thankful. Sometimes he asks and does not receive it. Then he says, "The Stranger knows best." Sometimes his friends, in exasperation say, "Well, what would he have to do for you to admit that you were wrong and that he is not on our side?" But the partisan refuses to answer. He will not consent to put the Stranger to the test. And sometimes his friends complain, "Well if that's what you mean by his being on our side, the sooner he goes over to the other side the better."[14]

This parable illustrates that evidence for and against the partisan's viewpoint exists. The evidence is indecisive, however, because the partisan takes a faith stance and explains the evidence in a way compatible with his faith.

This brief discussion illustrates the struggle between theology and science for nearly two millennia. Your own concerns about the world of science may, in fact, be part of the aftermath of these historic confrontations. In the eyes of many religious persons, science has been the enemy, challenging the very foundations of belief. However, fundamental changes have occurred within the philosophy of science as positivism has begun to crumble, and these changes merit attention. The new philosophies of science are more moderate and more compatible with the tasks of the life sciences and theology. You may find the contributions of Michael Polanyi and Thomas Kuhn helpful.

As early as 1946 Polanyi was insisting that science was highly diverse and not created by a simple rationalistic process as the positivists had supposed. He argued that the intuition, presuppositions, and faith of the scientist are fundamental to discovery. He pointed out that science needs to be understood as a community of inquirers held together by a common faith. This faith is not in the exercise of the scientific method, but rather in a discipline imposed upon by scientists themselves in the interest of discovering an objective, impersonal truth. The essence of this faith is that such truth exists and can be found by disciplined research and study. This faith is fundamental, intertwined with the entire scientific milieu of the culture, and can be defended only by further statement of the scientist's faith. Polanyi insists that "we have no clear conception of how discovery comes about," noting that "either you know what you are looking for, and then there is no problem; or you do not know what you are looking for, and then you are not looking for anything and cannot expect to find anything."[15]

This dilemma has not been as powerful for him as its initial impact would imply because he acknowledges a creative rhythm in scientific work. His description may apply to your own experience:

> In the course of any single experimental inquiry the mutual stimulus between intuition and observation goes on all the time and takes on the most varied forms. Most of the time is spent in fruitless efforts, sustained by a fascination which will take beating after beating for months on end, and produce ever new outbursts of hope, each as fresh as the last so bitterly crushed the week or month before. Vague shapes of the surmised truth suddenly take on the sharp outlines of certainty, only to dissolve again in the light of second thoughts or of further experimental observations. Yet from time to time certain visions of the truth, having made their appearance, continue to gain strength both by further reflection and additional evidence. These are the claims which may be accepted as final by the investigator and for which he may assume public responsibility by communicating them in print.[16]

In a later work Polanyi develops this philosophy of science further. He states that the "complete objectivity as usually attributed to the exact sciences is a delusion and is in fact a false ideal." In its place he offers the concept of "personal knowledge" which explores the dimensions of doubt and commitment in scientific endeavors. This personal knowledge involves "a coherent system of superior knowledge, upheld by people mutually recognizing each other as scientists, and acknowledged by modern society as its guide." Thus, he concludes that this superior knowledge includes "all that is coherently believed to be right and excellent by men within their culture."[17]

Polanyi's description of the scientific process, indeed his definition of science itself, is very different from the positivists. To him, science is an interpretive process, a process of providing a framework for facts rather than a process which verifies or falsifies statements. The framework itself is based on assumptions accepted *a priori*.

Polanyi's point of view is not new. He reiterates an older point of view which was never completely submerged during the era of the positivists. Francis Peabody wrote about medicine during the heyday of the positivists. His famous essay "The Care of the Patient" is a classic statement of that point of view:

> It is rather fashionable to say that the modern physician has become too scientific. [Was the care of this patient] . . . too scientific or was it not scientific enough? The popular conception of a scientist as a man who works in a laboratory and who uses instruments of precision is as inaccurate as it is superficial, for a scientist is known, not by his technical processes but by his intellectual processes; and the essence of the scientific method of thought is that it proceeds in an orderly manner toward the establishment of truth.[18]

Thomas Kuhn's viewpoint is rooted in a historical perspective and is compatible with Polanyi's. Kuhn argues that a limited number of world-shaking scientific revolutions have taken place and that each revolution has introduced a new paradigm, a new way of thinking. Each new paradigm completely restructures a particular field of science and, once it is widely accepted, suggests the questions which demanded further research. This further research creates a "normal science" which says Kuhn, is "a mopping up operation . . . [which] engages most scientists throughout their careers." This "normal science" is further described by Kuhn as paradigm-dependent.[19]

Kuhn's philosophy posits that, in the course of time, this

paradigm-dependent research not only turns up data which explains and elucidates the paradigm, but also data which challenges the paradigm. In this way, the limitations of the paradigm become more evident until finally it is so weakened that a new structure is suggested which accounts for data in a more creative and exciting way. An historical example will make his concept clearer:

> Today's physics textbooks tell the student that light is photons, i.e., quantum-mechanical entities that exhibit some characteristics of waves and some of particles. Research proceeds accordingly, or rather according to the more elaborate and mathematical characterization from which this usual verbalization is derived. That characterization of light is, however, scarcely half a century old. Before it was developed by Planck, Einstein, and others early in this century, taught that light was transverse wave motion, a conception rooted in a paradigm that derived ultimately from the optical writings of Young and Fresnel in the early nineteenth century. Nor was the wave theory the first to be embraced by almost all practitioners of optical science. During the eighteenth century the paradigm for this field was provided by Newton's *Opticks*, which taught that light was material corpuscles. At that time physicists sought evidence, as the early wave theorists had not, of the pressure exerted by light particles impinging on solid bodies. These transformations of the paradigms of physical optics are scientific revolutions, and the successive transition from one paradigm to another via revolution is the usual developmental pattern of mature science.[20]

Kuhn also believes that this movement from paradigm to paradigm is not a cumulative acquisition of knowledge which leads to a better and better "fit" between nature and knowledge. Science, according to Kuhn, does not progress. He points out that it is not intrinsically better to believe that light is photons rather than transverse wave motion. Rather, he suggests, the contemporary theory explains current facts as we know them and fit our common sense about the world. And the genius of the scientist, he said, is expressed in the ability to see the facts in a new light. The genius of Antoine Lavoisier, who discovered oxygen, was that he "saw oxygen where Priestly had seen dephlogisticated air and where others had seen nothing at all."[21]

Another example from Kuhn illustrates that the essence of science is the ability to see the world in a new way, and thus it is a highly subjective process:

Since remote antiquity most people have seen one or another heavy body swinging back and forth on a string or chain until it finally comes to rest. To the Aristotelians, who believed that a heavy body is moved by its own nature from a higher position to a state of natural rest at a lower one, the swinging body was simply falling with difficulty, constrained by the chain, tortuous motion and a considerable time. Galileo, on the other hand, looking at the swinging body, saw a pendulum, a body that almost succeeded in repeating the same motion over and over again *ad infinitum.* And having seen that much, Galileo observed other properties of the pendulum as well and constructed many of the most significant and original parts of his new dynamics around them . . . All of these natural phenomena he saw differently from the way they had been seen before.[22]

Kuhn believes that the faith of the scientist plays a key role in these paradigm changes. Paradigms are not subject to proof and are highly prized by adherents in part, of course, because most of their work is paradigm dependent. Changes in scientific points of view, therefore, come about through long years of struggle. He repeats Max Planck's comment that "new scientific truth does not triumph by convincing its opponents and making them see the light, but rather because its opponents eventually die and a new generation grows up that is familiar with it."[23]

This chapter has reviewed the historical relationship between theology and science, noted theology's attempt to shape itself into a science, and concluded with a summary of two contemporary philosophies of science. These contemporary perspectives move away from the rigid narrowness of positivism and view science as a broad social and intellectual phenomenon based upon many assumptions about the world. The scientist seeks to be objective within the confines of these assumptions. This perspective is more compatible with pastoral care and counseling and may be more encouraging to you. If you find yourself continuing to think about science as proving the truth in an absolute way, then remember the perspectives of Polanyi and Kuhn. Science is composed of a community of scholars who ask you to join with them in answering questions by using accepted, disciplined methodologies.

Chapter 3

Moving Ahead: Concerns at the Beginning

We need to push forward, beyond the issues of hesitation and history. This chapter will discuss the fundamental ingredients and attitudes which shape research work. The discussion is divided into three parts: 1) the ways in which you are already scientific, 2) assumptions of the scientific researcher, and 3) research pitfalls.

YOU ARE ALREADY SCIENTIFIC

Research work requires a scientific process and this realization can be frightening. "What do I know about the scientific process?" you ask. Being scientific is not as strange as it seems, however. You are already scientific simply by your participation in Western culture even though you may not have conducted research projects. Scientific attitudes are so much a part of the fabric of your culture that you scarcely recognize them. How can you become aware of this fundamental scientific stance?

Imagine yourself living in an illiterate, prescientific culture. Such a culture could be found in ancient history or in a current primitive tribe. In this culture neither reading nor writing would exist. Knowledge would consist of what was remembered from generation to generation. It would be as fragile as life itself because if the only "knower" died, then the knowledge would disappear. Books would not be available; no dictionaries or libraries would exist. Much energy would be devoted to day-to-day survival and to remembering the available knowledge.

As Walter J. Ong has pointed out, the memory process

would rely upon thinking memorable thoughts. This would be accomplished by creating mnemonic patterns involving highly rhythmical, patterned language dominated by verbal formulas and memorable sayings. This language process would encourage memory at the expense of exact details,[1] and attention to clear, accurate factual observation would be minimal. "Objectivity would not be valued because," as Ong has noted, "knowing means achieving close, empathic, communal identification with the known. Knowing means getting into and with that which is rather than the objectivity we scientific persons have come to assume."[2] And, since meaning and interpretation are understood in this way, the facts and events would be edited and rearranged to ease the burden of memory and to promote the perceived meaning. If you imagine yourself in such a culture, you realize that science would be practically impossible. You also realize how implicitly scientific you are.

The development from a prescientific into a scientific culture required centuries of struggle. The essence of this process was the development of the ability to distinguish between subjective impression and objective observation, a cornerstone of science. Two illustrations will make clear that this development occurred much later in human history than is often assumed.

The first illustration arises from St. Luke's management of historical materials as he wrote his Gospel and the Acts. Many scholars agree that Luke, as a physician (thus scientist) and historian of his day, created some problems for us in his management of materials. Various difficulties exist and these are described in standard critical New Testament studies. Many of these difficulties, however, are rooted in St. Luke's emphasis upon meaning rather than factuality. He did not distinctly separate facts and meanings. Nor could we expect him to do this because this distinction had not yet been clearly developed. Martin Dibelius comments on these phenomena:

> The ancient historian does not wish to present life with photographic accuracy, but rather to portray and illuminate what is typical, and his practice of aiming at what is typical and important allows the author of *Acts* partly to omit, change or generalize what really occurred. So it is that, where he sometimes appears to us

today to be idealizing and describing what was typical, he was really trying to discharge his obligation as a historian.[3]

If you find this perspective ridiculous or unique, it is a measure of how scientific you have yourself become, all the while forgetting that this scientific mentality is very new in the history of humanity. The historian's task in the New Testament period was not first of all to put down a chronological sequence of events. St. Luke wrote, indeed, that he was setting forth "an orderly account"[4] but this seems to refer not so much to a factual and chronological order as we think of it today as to a meaningful logical or even theological order. Principles of scientific objectivity had not yet been developed.

A second example is even closer to modernity. Once again, the careful reporting of observed events will be missing and your response to this will demonstrate how scientific you are. The 14th century Black Plague which swept through Europe arrived in Sicily late in 1347, carried by infected sailors from seaport to seaport. Once it was discovered in a city, the citizens would make valiant efforts to combat the disease. Their usual choice of intervention was to parade religious relics in the streets while reciting litanies, hoping by this means to drive away the evil spirits who brought the disease. This was itself an unscientific process, but that is not the point of interest here. Rather, a historian of that period recounted the procession of priest and people in Messina, Sicily, carrying with them holy water and the relics of St. Agatha. The historian's narrative of the events on that day notes that

> while the whole population was thus processing around the streets, a black dog, bearing a drawn sword in his paws, appeared among them, gnashing with its teeth and rushing upon them and breaking all the silver vessels and lamps and candlesticks on the altars, and casting them hither and thither. . . .[5]

The factuality of this statement, written by Michael of Piazza in approximately 1360, is doubtful. Today, most will doubt that a black dog appeared carrying a drawn sword in his front paws while walking on his two rear legs. Most will doubt that because they have never seen it happen, but even more so because it contradicts contemporary expectations concerning dogs. The important point, however, is that Michael of Piazza did not seem to be concerned about such an unscientific, erroneous observation in 1360. He appears not to be concerned with the possibility that others would laugh at and dismiss his account as ridiculous. Indeed, he did not need to be concerned about this because the need for critical, accurate observation had not been established even then. As in the previous example, the author was so interested in making a point, in rendering an interpretation of the tragic and lethal plague that he reversed fact and interpretation by placing meaning before accurate observation of events. Many additional examples could be cited, examples in the 20th century.

How strange this inversion of fact and interpretation seems. Today it is very clear that the facts come first. "Get the facts straight" you say, "and then interpret them." Such an attitude is a demonstration that you are deeply scientific, that the foundations for understanding research are already present.

In conclusion, you are more scientific than you realize. The foundations are in place even though you may not have completed college science courses or cultivated a skeptical, critical attitude in your professional work. You know that facts need to be observed and data collected before you begin interpretation. You know that assumptions and biases are important because you can easily see your results the way you want to see them, neglecting obvious alternate interpretations. You know all that and more as a product of growing up in a scientific culture. With these basics in place, you can adopt the additional assumptions necessary for scientific activity.

ASSUMPTIONS OF THE SCIENTIFIC RESEARCHER

The aim of the previous section was to demonstrate that you are more scientific than you first thought. You realize that careful observation precedes interpretation. Conducting your own research project builds upon that realization. This section will expand your basic awareness to include three assumptions which are fundamental to the research process. Many others exist because the research perspective is an integrated world view.

These assumptions, however, are basic and hopefully will en-courage you to explore further details of the research process.

*Assumption I: The world and human experience are more
complicated than they appear*

This fundamental assumption of science is widely accepted in our culture. Today we assume that the world and life possess a "depth" which does not meet the eye, which is not immediately apparent. The scientific process digs into this depth so as to discover more about it. Telescopes look outward into space and microscopes look inward into the smallest elements of matter. Life experiences are examined by psychotherapy as well as the social and behavioral sciences.

The assumption that the world and experience contain "depth" is, in itself, not a unique assumption of science. Ancient prescientific cultures all assumed a depth complicatedness to reality. Gods and demons were behind every event, present in every hill and tree, and constantly active. Their understanding of this depth, like ours, controlled and directed much of life.

The scientific mentality responds to this depth in its own unique way because research seeks to take everything apart. Conventional research methodologies ensure careful work and reliable evidence upon which to base conclusions. Adherence to these scientific rules and methods is the scientific process.

Fundamental issues between theology and science arise at this juncture. Both religion and science seek to find and describe the truth concerning this "depth." Many have argued that these two are enemies, partly because their methods and assumptions differ, but this argument is an over-simplification. In the past, religion shared the methods of the prescientific world. As dis-cussed in Chapter 2, religion had its struggles with science as it developed, but parallel struggles were taking place in other fields as they opposed science. The struggle between religion and science has been particularly difficult because both deal with basic assumptions about life and its meaning. In the adjustment process, theology increasingly realized the potential benefits to be gained by more interest in science.

In this adjustment process, theology has also become aware that science is limited by its very methods. Science can not study, at least in mathematical terms, many of the most important elements of personal life, although this is contested by many enthusiasts of science. Consider the following example from personal life.

A scientist returns home from work. This man is a hard core scientist, let us say a physicist or a molecular biologist, even a mechanical engineer. He makes his living by applying scientific principles and he believes strongly in scientific methodologies. He might be tempted to believe that every important part of life can be analyzed by science. On this particular day he hears his three year old daughter crying as he enters the house and he is momentarily worried. Some severe viral infections have attacked neighborhood children and he hopes his daughter is not among them. He moves through the house straight to where his daughter is crying and finds to his relief that her tears originate in a minor concern. He sits down and plays with her for a while, unaware of how scared he had momentarily become and how relieved he now feels.

This story illustrates a simple but core human experience. But how can science study it? How can it study his parental concern for his daughter, his momentary worry, and his sense of relief? Objective data can not be obtained. Perhaps some self-reported measures can be taken of their impact, but these will be at best difficult to obtain and to compare with the experiences of others.

What conclusions can be drawn from this? The church and theology can derive great benefits from attention to scientific study. They can not blindly ignore science, giving blanket endorsement to everything religious, past and present. Conversely, the church and theology should not worship scientific methods. These methods can study the larger and smaller world, but can not detect, measure, or analyze many of the deeper facets of life, the very facets which are at the core of theology. Scientists may devote their professional lives to scientific activity, but their own personal lives will be carried along by assumptions and meanings which can never be tested. These assumptions and meanings possess a religious character because they refer to ultimate foundations and the very character of the world and life. In this way, religion and science are complementary, needing and benefiting from each other.

You can make a contribution to science by the way you put

the world together as a theologian and by the way you take it apart as a scientific person and a scientist. Taking the world apart requires a basic attitude and leads to the second assumption.

Assumption II: A skeptical, critical, questioning viewpoint is necessary concerning this "depth" and leads to increased objectivity.

This second assumption contains two elements: the importance of skepticism and the necessity of objectivity. The "depth" within the world and life is best exposed through a skeptical, critical, questioning stance which then creates objectivity.

Concerning the first element, science assumes that the world and life do not automatically reveal their "depth." In fact, a camouflage hides their true character. A skeptical, critical questioning attitude is required in order to strip away this outer layer of appearances and to discover the truth.

This thorough-going, persistent skepticism may seem strange and new to you. Ministers are taught to exercise acceptance, faith, and belief; science requires doubt and constant questioning. Assumptions in the two fields are reversed.

The purpose of this questioning is to produce objectivity, the cornerstone of science. This is the second element of the assumption. Attaining objectivity requires that you test subjective, vested interests as well as first impressions, becoming aware of biases and erroneous assumptions about your subject matter. Objectivity requires the courage and skill to "see things as they are" rather than the way you would like them to be.

Objectivity is always relative, of course. True, complete objectivity is never possible for the human being. You must always stand somewhere in your own subjective world—you must always assume something. You will always to a certain extent "see through a glass darkly." This incomplete and elusive quality of objectivity does not argue against its role in your work, however. You will never be completely objective, but neither are you completely truthful, honest, caring, loving, dependable, understanding, or respectful. These present challenges. In science, the achievement of objectivity is the challenge composed of reducing bias and resisting the temptation to "jump to conclusions." The rigorous methods of science are directed toward this goal.

As you develop your research work, apply this objectivity first of all to your assumptions about your subject matter. What do you already accept as fact? What are the "hard facts" already produced by solid studies? This concern demonstrates the importance of reading reports of previous studies. Such reading encourages you to grapple with the findings of other researchers and to examine their assumptions. The evidence generated by a study is only as good as the accuracy of the assumptions. If you disagree with a previous researcher's assumptions, the evidence and conclusions will not likely be acceptable because a direct relationship exists between what you assume and what you "discover." When you disagree with another's assumptions, you need to develop and defend your own, thereby running the risk of criticism. Such personal initiative, however, also creates a unique opportunity for new discovery.

Skeptical thinking must be applied secondly to the research methodology you develop for your study. As will be discussed further in later chapters, a methodology is strongest when it generates data through a variety of deliberately formed groups and under controlled situations. Research is strong when skepticism can not discredit the results.

The application of sufficient skepticism to your assumptions and methodology comprises a difficult task. The difficulty lies chiefly in blindness to the process. Charging ahead into data gathering and analysis, the results strip away the blindness when they are confused or meaningless. But then it is too late. The data gathering is completed and the project can not be salvaged.

A personal experience will illustrate the importance of objectivity and skeptical thinking. Twenty years ago the administration of an inner city neighborhood health center sought data from the community concerning the need for expanded services. Forms were constructed and staff members recruited to gather data through personal contacts and interviews. The results were initially confusing because each investigator's data differed. A skeptical review soon revealed, however, that the data from each staff member supported the need for expanded services in his or her particular professional area. Data gathered by physicians documented the need for more medical services; chaplaincy data called for more religious and pastoral counseling services. The list was as long as the professional diversity of the interviewers. The administration threw out the study results. They were useless.

No doubt many factors contributed to this interesting phenomenon. Major problems existed in the foundational assumptions of the study and in its methodology. The planners assumed, probably for financial reasons, that the staff members could collect objective data from personal interviews. The planners assumed that an inner city resident, knowing the professional affiliation of the interviewer, could provide accurate data in a personal interview. However, the results suggest that respondents gave what they believed would be interviewer-approved responses. The planners assumed that staff members could rise above their own territorial concerns and be objective. The results suggest that interviewers contributed to confusing data. Sufficient skepticism was not exercised and objectivity was miniscule.

Assumption III: Science protects and promotes objectivity by emphasizing the need for discussion with and review by experienced research peers.

This assumption emphasizes that research cannot be a solitary, individualized experience, devoid of peer contact. New researchers usually try to establish a wall of privacy and isolation around their work, rationalizing that criticism is unfair or that their ideas may be stolen. In reality, they are usually struggling with their insecurity and feelings of vulnerability as researchers. They may even recount stories of Galileo, Pasteur, and other early researchers who worked alone. Such days are gone; research is now a communal effort. As a result, most funding agencies will not provide grant money to individuals in their own names, and all research within institutions, from established professionals as well as students, is peer reviewed. In some settings where mistakes may be life-threatening, peer reviewers may require investigators to make specific changes in design before they can proceed.

Such communal supervision is not mere bureaucratic intrusion. In performing research, you join colleagues who are devoted to the discovery of facts which clarify the nature of the world and life. This is a disciplined as well as difficult process and collegial review is in reality an essential means of promoting appropriate skepticism and objectivity.

If you are new to research work, some type of consultation or supervision is essential. Ask yourself serious questions when your reluctance and resistance to such contact emerges. Let experienced colleagues help you. No one expects you to have all the answers about your design. No one expects you to be perfect. Put aside your pride as well as fear and explore your ideas with experienced colleagues.

RESEARCH PITFALLS LEADING TO UNFINISHED WORK.

By now it is clear that a research project requires a careful, disciplined process. If you are conducting your first project, you can legitimately expect some problems. Unfortunately, these difficulties sometimes overwhelm the new researcher.

A pastoral counselor tells a story about the screening interview conducted by a graduate program to which he had applied. The program director, having welcomed him, showed him a drawer of student files, one-fourth of which were marked "completed." He added that the remaining three-fourths of the students, having finished the course work, never completed the research. The basic pitfall in research work is the inability to finish the project. While work completion is necessary to acquire gratification and reward, no research is worth the effort if it cannot be finished. Five principal factors contribute to unfinished research.

Diminished Motivation
The lack of motivation to continue with the chosen research area is a major factor. What area do you wish to study? Is it pastoral counselor management of depression, minister malpractice, parish minister satisfaction, pastoral care financial productivity in the hospital, or the effects of sermons? Whatever your chosen area, you must be deeply motivated because only this will carry you through the entire process. A passing, superficial curiosity is insufficient. This accounts for much unfinished research. Difficulties outstrip interests and the entire process falters.

Careful thought and self-examination are required when choosing a research area within which to work. Two suggestions are in order. First, give the selection process some time to mature. Do not make the decision in a day or a week. Ask yourself if your current interest area leads to a deeper, even more fundamental interest. If so, move to the exploration of this deeper interest.

Second, discuss your ideas with colleagues, friends, and advisors. Let them help you with the selection process. You do not need all the answers before raising your interests for discussion. Let them explore new and diverse aspects of your interest. Assume that you can sort out the confusion they create and be the better for it.

An Unrealistic Timetable

A second factor which leads to incomplete work is the failure to set a timetable, at least one which can be realistically met. Some persons begin research with no timetable at all. This simply does not work because everyday duties constantly claim priority. Additionally, few remain interested in the same subject forever or have unlimited time and energy. The research must be completed while your interest lasts. Maintaining this timetable requires personal discipline, the same kind of discipline required by the entire scientific process.

You may suffer from the opposite problem. You may set timetables which are unreasonably short and lead to endless frustration. Such a timetable leaves no room for sorting through confusion and working out problems and delays. Self-knowledge and a realistic look at the work schedule are essential here.

Excessively High Expectations of Impact

A third factor which leads to incomplete work occurs when your positive expectations about the impact of the results are not met. Research work seeks to produce important knowledge. Such knowledge should have impact on the problem. But this expectation becomes a trap when your fantasies about the real and immediate difference your research will create are dashed. Be particularly alert if these fantasies seek to prove a point or create change in persons or institutions. Your single research project will seldom result in such change. The persons or organizations may at best receive your results with interest and ignore their implications. The history of science contains many examples of ignored research results. This lack of recognition leads to researcher burnout if the motivation for the work was to produce a high impact on selected individuals, churches, denominations, hospitals, or counseling centers.

Excessive Vested Interest In The Results

A fourth factor which leads to incomplete work and frustration is research in which you possess vested interests and high stakes in the outcome, stakes so high that you cannot possibly be objective. Suppose you are a chaplain at a health care institution and, when confronted with some administrative skepticism about your contribution to patient care, you decide to conduct a research project. You decide to gather data from patients and staff to answer the skepticism. This motivation itself creates a major problem. You have a vested interest in securing positive results. Suppose the project produces such results. You are relieved. You have solved the problem because you can now demonstrate a contribution to patient care. But you will be surprised. Who will believe the results? Closet skeptics will emerge everywhere. They will doubt the results just because you benefited by them. They will suspect that you lacked the proper objectivity and have indulged in self-promotion.

This vested interest in research can result in more complications still. Let us suppose that the results suggest that the chaplain makes no contribution. Your expectations have not been met. You have generated results which are professionally damaging to yourself. The administration will believe the results because they confirm their initial impression. The research will not be rewarded. You may, in fact, lose your job, and the results may be passed around the country by your administrator. Then other chaplains will become upset and angry at you. Isolated in the proverbial doghouse, you will be professionally punished without realizing your expectations.

From this point of view, you should always ask what could be the worst possible outcome of your research. You should avoid projects in which you are not ready for the worst possible outcome. In this instance, your fantasies concerning the positive impact of your work come crashing down in disappointment as you realize that you have created a no-win situation. In frustration you will be tempted to throw up your hands and give up on research. In reality, the problem lies with selecting a research area in which you possessed excessively high expectations and a vested interest in specific results.

Thus, to return to the original theme, the ability to complete the work is related to the choice of a research area. Your research area needs to be one in which you are deeply interested. Yet you need to avoid those areas where others would suspect you are naturally biased and less than objective. And, practically speaking, do not undertake projects unless you are ready for the worst possible outcome.

Problems With Practical Details

A fifth factor which leads to incomplete work consists of problems with practical details. These problems are inherent in your circumstances, both personal and professional. Some of them, however, are created by not thinking through the project in concrete fashion during the planning stage. One example of this problem occurs over and over and is worth special mention.

As you plan your project, ask whether you can get the raw data needed for the project. Do you have access to the people whom you need as subjects? What stands between you and your subjects? Whose permission will you need? Failure to clarify this issue will result in creation of a splendid project which cannot be completed. Suppose you want to gather survey data concerning the fear of death in seminary and medical students, comparing the two groups. Although a worthy subject, the important detail is whether you have contact with these groups. If not, data gathering will be a nightmare. Seminary and medical deans stand between you and the students. Their respective institutions will have policies which govern access to their students. Even if approval is obtained, only a limited number of busy seminary and medical students will likely respond to a questionnaire. Response rate then becomes a problem, manifest, of course, only after you have invested so much in the project that changes cannot be made.

Other practical problems also exist. Many are unique to specific projects. Most can be spotted when you concretely outline the project step-by-step. Make a detailed list of contacts and actions your project requires. Then talk this over with your colleagues and consultant. What is their experience? Where do they see problems? Constantly ask yourself where complications could arise. This process will greatly increase the likelihood that you can finish the work.

In summary, you are more scientific than you realize. This scientific sense forms a base upon which you can build. This building can take place by paying careful attention to the fundamental assumptions of the scientific process. This disciplined process contains many pitfalls which can result in incomplete work. These pitfalls include insufficient motivation for the project, the lack of an appropriate time schedule, excessive vested interest in specific results, and difficulty in managing practical problems.

How then can you proceed? Perhaps it all seems impossible. You would like to do some research, but it now seems to you that the areas in which you are motivated are also those in which you are too invested to be objective. Perhaps it seems that the worst possible outcome precludes the exploration of those areas in which you are really interested. Perhaps research just seems too complicated.

If these are your sentiments, I am encouraged. Your chances of completing a project have increased. Shortly we will be discussing the technical processes of doing research. These processes, while they may seem strange to you, are cognitive and less subtle than the preceding discussion. If you have appreciated the difficulties discussed, then you have taken a giant step.

Section 2

The Technical Process

Now we turn to the more technical process of research. This process brings its own difficulties to which most ministers in pastoral care and counseling are susceptible. We are more comfortable with intuition and broad sweep of emotions than with technical processes.

In research we must pay careful attention to concrete details. The research process demands careful planning and forethought. Additionally, we must be concerned about subtle biases which can enter into data collection. Statistical management of the data and consequent interpretation require their own careful step-by-step processes. And then there is the required writing out of the results. Word upon word, sentence upon sentence, writing can be a tedious process.

You need to remember that you will not master the research process by reading this book. This is a primer and my goal in these chapters is to help you grasp the logical process of research and the interrelationships between the various steps. Sometimes the two seem to work against each other and you may feel confused when you finish. But even that confusion is a step beyond the lack of knowledge about research with which you may have begun. To help you with the confusion, I will consistently suggest that you identify a research consultant. In the end, learning to do research is like learning pastoral care and counseling—it is best done under supervision.

Chapter 4

Creating the Question

Research, as an answering process, seeks responses to specific questions. As researcher, you develop these questions to narrow your interest area into a manageable study. In empirical research (as described in this book) the questions narrow the subject matter even further because quantitative answers are required. This chapter describes selected facets of this process and then develops an example. Finally, the process by which research questions lead to hypotheses will be discussed.

Science begins its disciplined process by creating research questions. Standing at the head of the scientific process, these questions have a lasting impact upon the project. The roots of research confusion and difficulty later in the project are usually hidden within inadequately defined research questions. This technical process challenges you to move with increasing clarity from a general research interest area to specific research questions and to clarify over and over again exactly what you want to know. This clarification process requires patience and skill over weeks and months of work.

During this clarification process, at least two temptations confront you. The first consists of refusal to engage in the clarification and narrowing process at all. Giving in to this temptation, you simply engage in a research "fishing expedition," gathering little bits of data here and there in a variety of forms and shapes. You exercise little, if any, control, and the methodology produces a hodgepodge of information which cannot be interpreted in a meaningful way. As a novice researcher, you may be gravely tempted toward this "anything goes" approach, often a product of research inexperience. Futile attempts to publish the results usually produce a cure for this temptation. More discipline is needed in order to manage the process, control the variables, and avoid being overwhelmed and confused.

The second temptation invites you to formulate the questions prematurely. This temptation involves grasping any questions which occur to you and making them the focus of study. You avoid the struggle of working through the confusion. This temptation appeals to researchers who believe that any research question is good enough, to those who have procrastinated so long that questions must be developed in a few days, and to all who lack the patience or ability to tolerate and clarify the confusion involved in solidifying a study. This hasty process bears bitter fruit months later as interest lags, doubts overcome energy, and the specter of an unfinished project begins to loom ahead. Avoiding either of these temptations commits you to fight your way into clarity, asking over and over again, "What are my questions? What do I want to know?"

This clarificaiton process will best proceed through conversation with others about your ideas and your confusions. Consulting knowledgeable research colleagues is mandatory here. No one can work through the "mud of confusion" without others who will listen and provide feedback. Most degree programs mandate such consultation with advisors as well as fellow students, and experienced researchers continue to rely upon it.

Reading the literature permits unknown colleagues to be your consultants. These authors describe their questions and how they studied them. They will often raise additional questions for study at the end of their report. And do not forget the skepticism of science—one project by itself is relatively weak. Additional studies by yourself or others are always more convincing. These additional studies confirm the validity of the first study, or, in fact, raise new questions about it.

How can you find this literature? No substitute exists for a good library and librarian. You can start by looking for books, but journals will likely be your best source. Your subject may lend itself to a computerized search of indexed journals. Other references include *Dissertation Abstracts International (DAI)*, *Psychological Abstracts*, *Sociological Abstracts*, and Educational Resources Information Center (ERIC). *Religious and Theological Abstracts* is published four times per year and *Abstracts of Research in Pastoral Care and Counseling* is published annually. Search these and other abstracting publications or bibliographies for important references. This entire process produces some clearer awareness of what you want to study.

Thus, creating research questions demands clear, disciplined thinking which rests on the ability to both tolerate confusion and to clarify, clarify, and clarify again. No substitute exists for carefully exploring every facet related to your potential project. These explorations take you in many directions at once, raise many potential research questions and further refine your thinking. Clear, disciplined thinking gradually helps you clarify all this confusion into one set of questions which epitomizes your interests. This process will become clearer as we develop the illustration begun in the previous chapter.

AN EXAMPLE

In the last chapter, I discussed a research effort devoted to discovering the effects of chaplains upon hospital patients. Let us suppose that, having weighed the risks, you decide to proceed. Now you need to shape this interest into a manageable research question. I will develop only a single question here for the sake of simplicity, but many projects develop multiple, parallel, and related questions.

How can this question be developed? Immediately, an additional concern intrudes, a concern not about developing the question, but about research design. Development of the question and the research design go hand-in-hand even though we are discussing them in separate chapters here. The research question always implies a design, and as you develop the question you need to know two things about research designs. First, a design always implies such practical details as budget, time, space, energy, and skill. You will see how this happens as we develop this research question, and I will discuss it more fully in a later chapter. The second thing you need to know about research designs is that they are ranked according to their power, their capacity to produce convincing data in the face of skepticism. A single case study, for example, is less powerful than data gathered from 100 subjects.

This design concept is important at this moment because you may wish to construct a two group comparison study. Suppose you wish to compare the effects of pastoral care provided by chaplains to the effects of pastoral care provided by parish pastors who visit at the hospital. This requires a two-group design and its power rests with the capability to compare the two groups. You could argue that the pastoral care effectiveness of parish pastors forms a baseline against which chaplaincy work could be measured.

After thinking about this possibility periodically for a few days, you realize that this comparison also poses problems. What would the parish pastors think? Would they think you were trying to make them look bad? If you told them about the project, would they immediately try to do better visitations, thereby introducing a temporary, artificial variable? Would they feel in competition with you, that is, that the project would create a winner and a loser

Additionally, who would collect trustworthy data from patients? Would patients likely tell you the whole truth about these two relationships? You would need to find a way to gather "objective" data. Another potential problem would be that patients could seek to protect their pastors and rank them higher just because they know them and have to return to that religious community. Here another variable emerges. Perhaps this comparison needs to take into account whether the patient likes or dislikes the pastor. Maybe the patient would rank the chaplain higher just because he or she does not like the pastor. But then there is another variable. Maybe the patient's ranking would have a relationship to the type of illness. Perhaps illnesses with social stigmas or highly personal qualities permit more help from the chaplain because the patient wants to keep the pastor out of such highly personal matters. And what about the gender of the chaplain and the patient? That too is likely to be influential. Suppose the study examined the effectiveness of pastoral care from a male parish pastor and a female chaplain.

The possibility of a comparison study generates these as well as other concerns. They do not prohibit the project but an awareness of their presence and influence means that you can take them into account during your further thinking. You must somehow contend with them because you are identifying variables which impact upon the data and your management of them must be described and defended in your report. The motivation to work them out lies in the need to create as powerful, as convincing a study as possible.

Let us suppose that, after thinking it over, you set aside the possibility of a comparison study involving chaplains and parish

80367

pastors. The problems seem too great. You will simply study the effects of chaplains on hospital patients, though a comparison design using chaplains is still possible.

How can this interest area be narrowed? Take the nouns of the phrase, "the effects of chaplains upon hospital patients," and ask as many questions about them as possible. Consider the three nouns and their modifiers one at a time.

"Chaplains"

What chaplains?

-Chaplains only at your institution? What about chaplains at other institutions?

-If others are included, will these chaplains be from both general and psychiatric hospitals?

-Will only staff chaplains be involved? What about chaplains in training?

-Will the staff chaplains involved include only those who have certified training in hospital ministry?

-Will Protestant, Catholic, and Jewish chaplains be involved?

-Will chaplains include only selected Protestant denominations?

-Will the study include both male and female chaplains?

-Will chaplains be included or excluded because of age or length of experience?

"Hospital Patients"

What hospital patients?

-Both male and female patients?

-Both patients with and without church membership?

-Patients regardless of which physician admitted them?

-Emergency room patients who are never admitted to the hospital?

-Healthy mothers and their new babies?

-Patients regardless of diagnoses?

-Only those patients who had at least an initial visit from the chaplain?

-Patients irrespective of the amount of time the chaplain spent with them?

-Patients who live outside the city or county?

-Will data be gathered from family members? If so, which family members would be involved?

These questions raise many new issues, some of which permit a comparison study. Should the project involve more than one institution? Who, as regards chaplains and patients, will be included and excluded from the project? Where will you draw the line? At this stage, research is a process of "drawing the line," of defining and redefining who is included and excluded.

How will "effects" be measured?

> -Higher satisfaction with the hospital experience?
> -Less use of pain medication?
> -Fewer calls to the nurses while in the hospital?
> -An increased healing rate as measured by the length of stay in the hospital?
> -A recognized spiritual significance to illness and recovery?
> -Fewer law suits filed against the hospital?
> -An increased motivation for medical follow-up?
> -A more rapid payment of the bill?
> -A change in life style which promotes health?
> -A greater satisfaction with their physician?
> -An increase in church attendance after dismissal?

As you become aware of all these variables and possibilities, I encourage you think about them as opportunities. Discouragement about complexity will only drain your energy and ignoring complexity will create problems at a later point.

How can you go about making a decision in regard to all these options? First, realize that no right answer exists. The question is, "How do you want to shape your research project?" You can make decisions about all these options as you judge necessary, but you must also be ready to explain those decisions in your report. Your consultants and colleagues can provide help as you seek to clarify your research question. You need to ask yourself as you make these decisions whether you are shaping the question in a way which will so sustain your interest that you can complete the project. Additionally, you will need to ask yourself about the practical details mentioned earlier: Can you get the data, and get it in a trustworthy form? Do you have the time and budget to do the study? Is there support in your setting for this work or will your superiors regard it as a distraction which takes you away from your primary duties? And, are you ready for the worst possible outcome? Under what circumstances will social workers, parish pastors, patients, physicians, nurses, ministers, or fellow chaplains be grateful to or angry at you?

Let us suppose that during a period of time you sort through all these options and questions, moving toward increasing concreteness. You begin to know what you want to study based on your sense of emotional energy for the questions, availability of time and subjects, and existing relationships. For the sake of example, let us assume that your interest in "the effects of chaplains upon hospital patients" takes the shape of the following question: "Are male chaplains more effective than female chaplains in providing pastoral care to female patients in this hospital?" Notice that this question is more concrete: "chaplain" in the original statement has now become "male" and "female chaplains" and "hospital patients" has become "female hospital patients." Notice too that this concreteness requires your willingness to leave some options behind because parish pastors and male hospital patients will not be involved.

More options still must be left behind, however, as further definition, clarity, and power are achieved. Think, for example, about the implications of including all female hospital patients. Much diversity exists within this group, probably too much diversity for a good study. How can the group be narrowed? One solution would be to study a specific diagnostic group such as those with AIDS, cancer, or specific OB-GYN problems. A specification of one group depends, again, upon your interest, upon available subjects, and upon relationships which permit the design. For the sake of illustration, let us suppose that you further define your project as studying the following question: "Are male chaplains more effective than female chaplains in providing pastoral care to female cancer patients?" Now other options have been left behind because all non-cancer female patients will be excluded.

This question still possesses considerable breadth and variation. The issues of chaplaincy training and length of experience are unexplored. Additionally, "female cancer patients" is still a diverse group. Will you be studying women with new diagnoses or terminal cancer patients? Will you further define your study group according to the organ system which is diseased? You will need to make some decision about this in order to reduce the variability within your study. And as you make that decision you need to keep in mind the need for an adequate number of subjects who fall within your chosen diagnostic group during an acceptable length of time.

So once again you narrow your study. Now, for sake of example, your research question becomes: "Are male chaplains with four or more units of CPE training more effective than female chaplains with comparable training in providing pastoral care to deteriorating gynecological cancer patients who have been admitted to the hospital for the second time in twelve months?" Now the ambiguity about chaplaincy training is clarified. A rather discrete patient group has also been identified, presumably with sufficient numbers to provide ample subjects.

Now another consideration comes into view because a difficult problem is hidden in this research question and will be apparent when it is converted into a research design. This last definition of the question moved the study into the realm of the near-terminal patient. How can data be gathered from the very ill, often terminal patients or from patients who die before final data are collected? Unless this question is answered satisfactorily, it will defeat the project. Perhaps the clearest answer to the problem is to impose still further specifications into the design which gather data for a very short, specific period of time.

Whatever the difficulties, benefits also exists in working with this patient group. One of the largest benefits is that the results can probably be generalized to other very ill patient groups. Research is valuable when results from a small group can be generalized to a larger population in a logical way. This generalizing process takes the place of studying every subject, a totally unmanageable task. This current project definition allows you to generalize your findings to other groups, such as all women with a GYN cancer or perhaps to all women who are dying from any chronic illness. Such generalization would need to be argued carefully but this definition of the question provides that opportunity and opens up a larger potential audience and number of journals that might be interested in your work.

The project definition is not yet complete, however. Now you must specify the quantitative aspect of the research question. The concern is, to put it simply, "What do you mean by 'more effective' in your research question? How will 'more effective' be measured?" Again, you can select weaker or stronger quantitative methods, and this choice should be based on the specifics of your situation. I will describe the various methods, from weaker to stronger, constructing for the sake of example a design which seems unmanageable to all except the most experienced researcher with a large budget.

You could gather an evaluation of pastoral care near the end of the data gathering period by inviting the patients to make a written statement which evaluates their pastoral care. You could then simply count those which express appreciation and those which do not and relate them to chaplain gender. The strength of this method is that it encourages free and spontaneous expression. It would be even more effective if the patients' report were anonymous. But this approach also contains many weaknesses. Some patients do not express themselves well in writing and many may neglect your invitation. Some patients may not be able to write, due either to illiteracy or continued incapacity.

Three problems dominate this approach, however. The research question you have chosen involves program evaluation. In the evaluation process, this unstructured design can consciously or unconsciously encourage only the return of testimonials. Testimonials are not really research data because they are advertisements and propaganda. While helpful at some points, these materials will be quickly dismissed by editors and experienced researchers.

This problem is linked to a second. Can you reasonably assume that patients will freely provide an objective evaluation of pastoral care, particularly when no format or structure is provided? Does the average hospitalized patient possess that level of ego strength? Probably not! Instead, patients will provide socially acceptable answers, the answers they think are expected of them. A free-form, written statement would probably praise the work of everyone. After all, chaplains are men and women of God.

The third problem is even greater. What criteria are used by patients when they express their evaluation of pastoral care? Most researchers would argue that in this design, the criteria vary with each patient, making the task of analysis impossible. The research design creates no control on this variable. Patients could praise or disdain their pastoral care using many criteria, including, for example, a shared denominational affiliation, age, choice of words in a prayer, or even the hair style and appearance of the chaplain. Such responses use various criteria and some way must be found to create a uniform basis for evaluation.

If, despite all these difficulties you adopt this approach, the research question becomes: "Do deteriorating gynecological cancer patients undergoing their second admission in 12 months more frequently express written appreciation for pastoral care by trained male or trained female chaplains?" You then select a stronger quantitative methodology by constructing a standardized questionnnaire for patient distribution. The standardization strengthens the quality of the data because all patients respond to the same questions, selecting an answer directly related to quantitative interpretation. If you elect this model, the research question becomes: "Using questionnnaire xyz, do deteriorating gynecological cancer patients undergoing their second admission within 12 months provide more favorable scores for pastoral care by trained male chaplains or trained female chaplains?"

A third methodology, the strongest one, involves using published questionnaires. These questionnaires have been tested and evaluated and their performance has been sufficiently satisfactory to merit publication. In this way you build on the strength inherent in another's work. How can you find an applicable questionnaire? Reading the literature is important because authors tell you what they have used in similar situations and any problems they have uncovered. Additonally, you can look for applicable instruments in *The Mental Measurements Yearbook* or other descriptive sources.[1] Again, consultation with knowledgeable consultants is essential.

As you work on questionnaire selection, think ahead to the time when all the data will be collected and analyzed. At that momemt you will probably wish you had collected more information, used more than one questionnaire so that your research question could be examined from more than one perspective. This is an important insight. Gather as much data as possible, using multiple questionnaires. This effort must be balanced only with the estimated endurance and patience of the subjects. Again, if you identify multiple instruments, their potential contribution must be described in the reseach question.

Many additional variables and options must be investigated as the research question is developed for an actual project. You have probably thought of them while reading. I have been concerned with portraying the process rather than with completeness. The process slowly builds the foundation of the project. Clarity born out of exhaustive, careful thinking will bear fruit.

CREATING THE HYPOTHESIS

Having created the research question, you must now hypothesize the answer. Yes, science is an answering process, but the data are collected and analyzed to confirm or deny your hypothesis. What, in your estimation, is the answer to the research question developed in this chapter? Will the data place more value on pastoral care from male or female chaplains? If you knew the answer, you would not need to conduct the study. You probably have a hunch, however, born out of past patient care experiences or shaped by your reading, thinking, or consultation. This hunch motivates the study.

Yet, the hypothesis is often one which states that no difference will exist between groups involved in the study. This is the classical "null hypothesis." In this instance, the null hypothesis would state that the gender of the chaplain created no statistical significant difference in the evaluation of pastoral care provided to deteriorating gynecological cancer patients who completed questionnaire xyz. When significant difference is uncovered (usually p equal to or smaller than 0.05) then you can report that the "no difference" hypothesis was not confirmed and a difference does exist. We will discuss this further in Chapter 6.

While you are finding your way through this process of creating the question, a process in which everything is connected to everything else, you should expect problems to emerge. Problems emerge both for every first-time researcher and for most who have accumulated extensive experience. These problems lead to confusion and discouragement. Finding your way through the maze of questions is difficult and what seems decided today is confused tomorrow. What seemed clear last week is unclear today. Expect it! This is simply the purifying of the research ideas as your move from conception to planning. You are working your way through the heart of the project. Later problems will emerge, of course, but they will not involve the confusion inherent in the planning process. And remember that this confusion and discouragement is worst in the first experience of research just as when you first learned to preach and to provide pastoral care or counseling. It will get easier with experience.

In summary, your research question needs to be shaped by fundamental principles and your management of situational variables. No single, right way exists. A time period of several months is often required to develop research questions. Give yourself that time for careful planning, knowing that you are writing the script and that future changes will be difficult.

Chapter 5

Seeking to Answer the Question: Research Design

Once again the research task changes. Having tentatively identified the research question and stated the hypothesis, your task now is the construction of a design, a plan, which will test your hypothesis. As discussed in the last chapter, some design questions are already settled by the very wording of the research question. This chapter further refines research design concerns. At points my discussion will be limited because this book is a primer and you can read about detailed, technical matters in other sources.

The principal purpose of a research design is to produce objective data. The scientific approach moves beyond personal impression in order to see its subject matter "as it really is" and the purpose of the design is to accomplish this goal. The best scientific designs do not achieve complete objectivity, however. In 1927, Bertrand Russell sarcastically observed patterns of bias in research reports using animals as subjects:

> One may say broadly that all animals that have been carefully observed have behaved so as to confirm the philosophy in which the observer believed before his obsevations began. Nay, more, they have all displayed the national characteristics of the observer. Animals studied by Americans rush about frantically, with an incredible display of hustle and pep, and at last achieve the desired results by chance. Animals observed by Germans sit still and think and at last evolve the solution out of their inner consciousness. To the plain man, such as the present writer, this situation is discouraging.[1]

This amusing and exaggerated statement contains a grain of truth. Some elements of observer bias always enter into scientific activity. From time to time credible research reports emerge which others cannot duplicate, apparently because subjectivity biased the results.

Bias is a serious problem in theological work, including pastoral care and counseling research because meager or ambiguous evidence invites scholars to project their own assumptions into the data. Albert Schweitzer commented on this problem in the broader field of theology and specifically in New Testament studies. In *The Quest of the Historical Jesus:*

> Each successive epoch of theology found its own thoughts in Jesus. . . . But it was not only each epoch that found its reflection in Jesus, each individual created him in accordance with his own character. There is no historical task which so reveals a man's true self as the writing of a life of Jesus.[2]

The task of the research design is to constrain such biases and to prevent them from completely destroying the reliability of scientific findings.

The capacity of the design to produce trustworthy results is described as its reliability. A design and its data are reliable when the research process produces similar results when repeated in another setting and at another time. Reliability, therefore, rests on a stability in the research situation, a stability in which the data gathering is not victimized by shifting organizational and situational factors. Your research should be undertaken when "business as usual" prevails.

Research designs are built upon the clear identification of variables. A variable is any factor which impacts upon the research subjects with a likely influence upon the results. Such variables must be carefully identified so that their changes can be linked to variations in the results. In experimental research designs, you deliberately create a change in one selected variable (the independent variable) while continuing to track the others (dependent or response variables) to determine the effect of that change. In the research question developed in the previous chapter, you would gather data on many dependent/response variables while deliberately assigning male and female chaplains (the independent variable) to visit the gynecological cancer patients.

Research designs begin with the simple and move to the complex, a process which, as discussed in the preceding chapter, increases their power. A weak design produces data which can be interpreted as supportive of many different conclusions. Stronger, more complex designs eliminate multiple conclusions one by one until a conclusion concerning only your hypothesis remains. The data produced by these more complex designs may or may not confirm your hypothesis but they speak directly to it.

You may conclude from this that research uses only the strongest designs. This is not true. For example, a descriptive design, while lacking power, makes an important contribution when examining a new field of study. This design simply describes the variables and their interrelationship without any determination of cause and effect. Such an effort describes the geography of the interest area and sets the stage for more specialized causative studies.

Additionally, researchers often do not use the stronger designs because they pay an increasingly higher price as design strength increases. This price involves multiple, complex patient groups as well as increased time, personnel cost and numbers of patients. These factors always influence what designs are possible. Your chosen research design, therefore, will be a compromise, using the strongest possible design within circumstantial constraints such as budget, time, and the availability of subjects.

We can use the research question from the preceding chapter to illustrate the movement from a simple to a conmplex design with increasing strength. Do female chaplains deliver better pastoral care to the designated patient group? A descriptive study is weak, simply describing how many chaplains and patients exist, their gender and other related demographic data. The study also describes the number of pastoral care visits made and the related gender data. Such a study cannot, however, answer the question. A design which demonstrates cause and effect is needed.

What design features are necessary to draw conclusions about causation? The first is a two-situation or two-group study. To demonstrate cause and effect, you need to manipulate the chosen independent variable to test for its effect. You need data from a situation in which this manipulation occurs as well as from one in which it does not occur. This provides a comparison and allows a conclusion about cause and effect. This can be accomplished in some situations by a single-group study in which baseline data are gathered and then the selected independent variable is manipulated. You can argue that subsequent

changes in the data were caused by your action. This is particularly true if you withdraw the change, allow the data to
return to baseline and then introduce the change a second time
with the same results. This is described in research literature as
the ABAB design (A = baseline and B = experiment by manipulating the variable).

The other way to demonstrate cause and effect requires at
least two groups. You manipulate the chosen variable in the one
group but not in the other. Since both groups are identical in all
other ways, you argue that data differences between the groups
are due to your action. Either of these two designs demonstrates
cause and effect and often both are used to provide a double
comparison.

The second design feature necessary to demonstrate a
causal connection involves randomness. Randomness insures
that the patient assignment to the groups is not affected by bias,
such as assigning all the difficult cases to one group. In our
example, random selection is used either to assign patients to the
participating chaplains or to assign the chaplains to the patients.
Only this random process will convince editors and the skeptical
reader that sufficient objectivity exists to allow for a conclusion
about causal connections.

Random assignment is accomplished in many ways. You can
use a random numbers table from the appendices of a research
or statistics book. Beginning with 1, simply assign each participating chaplain a number. Then select a column in the table
and, with a list of patients in hand, move downward. When you
come to a number which designates a chaplain, he or she is
assigned the next patient. Think clearly about how this will work
because you should not deviate from this assignment process
once you have begun. Plan what you will do if, for example, a
participating chaplain is ill for several days or takes a vacation.
Other methods which assure randomness include the use of dice
or the coin toss (assuming only two participants). Figure 1 diagrams this two group design. Assuming that the data support
the hypothesis, you can argue for cause and effect.

You will experience some difficulty in arguing a causal connection, however, because the design is relatively weak. When
you describe your results, the skeptics will understand your
design, but will wonder whether any objective evidence exists
that documents the benefits to the patients. You see, it is possible
that female patients simply praise female chaplains more highly

without any pastoral care benefits ever existing. How do you know the patients are describing true impovement? The above design cannot determine whether the patients are in fact improved or are only saying so. What is necessary to create an answer?

FIGURE 1
A Two Group Study With Post Experiment Data
(Random Assignment to Groups)

Group 1
(Female Chaplain)   X X X X X X X X X X 0^1
Group 2
(Male Chaplain)   X X X X X X X X X X 0^1

X represents pastoral care visits; 0 represents data gathering. The number of X's (10) are for example only. 0^1 represents self-report data from patients concerning evaluation of pastoral care.

The design requires an independent, free-standing evaluation of the patient at admission, an evaluation which is repeated at the end of the study. This evaluation provides objective evidence of changes in the patient's status. How can such an evaluation be accomplished? Perhaps the patient can complete evaluation questionnaires or a trained interviewer can talk with the patient in structured interviews. In either case, you must determine the content of this pretest-posttest, construct the instrument or interview, and arrange to manage the process in an objective way. Here, as in all social sciences, this increased power exacts a high price in complexity, time and money. Figure 2 illustrates this design.

FIGURE 2
Figure 1 Experiment With Added Pre-Post
Experiment Evaluator Data
(Random Assignment to Groups)

Group 1
(Female Chaplain) 0^2 X X X X X X X X X X 0^1 0^2
Group 2
(Male Chaplain) 0^2 X X X X X X X X X X 0^1 0^2

0^2 represents pre-post experiment evaluator data.

But now another possibility emerges. As noted above, many studies use not only a pretest-posttest measure or interview but also an untreated group as a second comparison. This additional group, which receives no pastoral care but completes the pretest-posttest, further strengthens the design. Data from this group will allow you to determine the benefits of pastoral care because you are measuring a group which receives none. Data from this group form another baseline, a no-treatment baseline against which the male and female chaplain data can be understood. This strengthens the design because, if the data would support it, you could argue that pastoral care to gynecological patients from male chaplains is better than nothing according to data from the untreated group, but that female chaplains are more effective. If you use this three group design, you must have access to a sufficient patient population of gynecological cancer patients and assignments to each group must still be made randomly. This design is shown in Figure 3.

FIGURE 3

Figure 2 Experiment With Added No-Treatment Group (Random Assignment to Groups)

No-Treatment Group O^2 O^2
Group 1
(Female Chaplain) O^2 X X X X X X X X X X O^1 O^2
Group 2
(Male Chaplain) O^2 X X X X X X X X X X O^1 O^2

At this juncture you may realize that you ought to research the benefits of pastoral care by chaplains generally prior to undertaking this gender oriented project. After all, you say, let's study first questions first. Let's determine if pastoral care makes any difference no matter what the gender of the provider, and then let's study whether one gender is better for some patients than the other. You are accurate in that observation. As so often happens, the most complex research problems attract attention first. Working on these complex problems leads you to realize that prior questions and problems exist. In fact, this gender-related project is premature until you have documented that pastoral care makes a contribution, no matter what the gender of the provider. If you actually planned to carry out this project now, you would set aside this current effort and start with a demonstration of the effects of any pastoral care. When that project was successfully completed, you would return to the gender-related project.

But suppose that while reading the literature, you discover an article reporting the beneficial effects of pastoral care. The design is strong and the results solid. Your present study could build on that effort, and then you could proceed without going back to the basic issue.

The design illustrated in Figure 3 can be strengthened even further. Notice that one group only receives the pretest-posttest while the other two groups receive regularly scheduled pastoral care. Some skeptics will argue that your positive results are caused by the increased attention to the two treatment groups. They will argue that the results do not measure the impact of pastoral care but of chaplains who regularly visit patients and talk nicely to them. Researchers describe these benefits due to increased attention as the Hawthorne Effect.

A stronger design results if you control for the impact of increased attention. You accomplish this control by introducing a behavioral placebo into the no-treatment group which avoids the type of pastoral care tested with the other groups. Planning this placebo requires you to define exactly the nature and structure of the pastoral care. With that definition in hand, you create a design in which the no-treatment group receives attention but not the pastoral care. They receive the same number of visits for the same number of minutes, but only attention must be provided. How can this be accomplished?

Again, no right formula exists, but here are two possible solutions. A specially trained chaplaincy volunteer can visit this group with the same frequency received by the other groups but only "pass the time of day," inquiring about mundane matters and practical details. Another possibility involves chaplains themselves whose visits could include a structured program of Bible reading, recorded meditations, or the playing of hymns with minimum personal conversation. This would provide attention but not the aspects of pastoral care tested in the other groups. If you adopt this strengthened design, the structure looks like Figure 4.

FIGURE 4

Figure 3 Experience With Added Placebo Pastoral Care
(Random Assignment to Groups)

No-Treatment Group	0^2 Y Y Y Y Y Y Y Y Y Y 0^1 0^2
Group 1 (Female Chaplain)	0^2 X X X X X X X X X X 0^1 0^2
Group 2 (Male Chaplain)	0^2 X X X X X X X X X X 0^1 0^2

Y represents placebo pastoral care.

Now look at the design diagram in Figure 4 and begin to imagine how this will work. What problems exist in the design or in practical details? The design can be strengthened by yet one more modification. Will male or female persons provide the placebo pastoral care to the no treatment group? Gender is fundamental to the entire study and confusion should not exist concerning this in the no-treatment group. The design confusion is easily clarified by adding an additional no-treatment group so that one exists for a female chaplain or volunteer and one for a male chaplain or volunteer. Now you have gender matched comparison groups, a design depicted in Figure 5.

FIGURE 5

Figure 4 Experiment With Additional No-Treatment Groups (Random Assignment to Groups)

No-Treatment Group
(Female Volunteer
or Chaplain) O^2 Y Y Y Y Y Y Y Y Y Y O^1 O^2
No-Treatment Group
(Male Volunteer or
Chaplain) O^2 Y Y Y Y Y Y Y Y Y Y O^1 O^2
Group 1
(Female Chaplain) O^2 X X X X X X X X X X O^1 O^2
Group 2
(Male Chaplain) O^2 X X X X X X X X X X O^1 O^2

In this section, I have sought to demonstrate how research designs develop as a result of scientific skepticism. As the designs reflect more and more complexity, they become overwhelming, flooding your abilities, time, budget, available personnel resources, or cadre of patients. At the point of saturation, you must make a decision about how much complexity the project staff, including yourself, can tolerate. An extraordinarily strong research design is useless if it can not be completed. Choose a design you can manage and simply explain the limits you faced in the written report.

The data gathering instrument is part of the research design. Many excellent books are available and I will not describe the process except to note one area of concern. The process of creating a questionnaire involves a decision about how the data will be scaled or classified. Four data classifications exist and they determine what statistical tests can be used in the process of analysis. I will describe these scales from the least sophisticated to the most accurate and useful. Statistical textbooks and consultants can help you with the details of this matter.

A nominal scale, the simplest, collects responses in arbitrary categories. The responses sort or label objects, people, or opinions. For example, people are either church members or non-members. No relative standing within the groups is possible in the nominal scale. Your questionnaire about pastoral care would create a nominal scale response if you asked, "Was pastoral care from the chaplain helpful? Yes or no?"

The ordinal scale not only categorizes but also ranks responses on the basis of their relative standing within the group. Suppose that an item in your research read, "Taken as a whole, how helpful was pastoral care from the Chaplain? Very helpful, fairly helpful, somewhat helpful, not helpful." Now you know more than in the nominal scale. You know the relative positions of the respondents. Those who respond that pastoral care was "very helpful" can be scored higher than those who said it was "helpful."

The interval scale provides more data still. In addition to categorizing data (nominal) into relative position (ordinal), this scale contains equal distance or difference between its units. Thermometer measurement of temperature is a typical example. The difference between 40°and 50° is the same as the difference between 10° and 20° since the units of measurements are consistent.

The ratio scale is the most powerful because, in addition to nominal, ordinal, and interval characteristics, the measurements are taken from a true zero point. Weight measurement provides an example. Not only is the difference between 10 and 20 pounds the same as 40 and 50 pounds, but you know that 40 pounds is twice as heavy as 20 pounds. This observation uses a ratio scale because zero pounds consist of no weight at all. This is not true of the temperature example. Zero degrees is an arbitrary point because, as a matter of fact, it is different for Fahrenheit and Centigrade scales.

Social sciences seldom are able to use interval or ratio scales because their data do not lend themselves to either scale. Constructing ordinal scales is very important, however, because these data will facilitate your analytical process.

One final observation is important. When you complete

your design, perform a pilot project. Give the design a test run with a limited number of subjects, performing data collection and analysis. In this way, you can be assured that the research process will actually work and produce trustworthy data.

In summary, I have repeatedly emphasized two themes in this book. It is time to repeat them. First, do not be surprised if you are overwhelmed by the complexity of building a research design. This task is another point at which you can "sink down in the mud" of confusion and discouragement. I have not described these more elaborate, powerful designs with the assumption that you will immediately understand and use them. Rather, their description here helps you experience the reasoning process which shapes the building of research designs. At the same time, I hope you have grasped something of the interrelatedness of the entire research process.

Second, the use of a research consultant in building a design is mandatory for the inexperienced. Let your consultant help you with advice. Raise your questions. The scientific process involves a point of view which must be caught through experience and struggle. Keep working to capture that scientific methodology by reading but also by talking with a knowledgeable consultant.

Chapter 6

Working With The Data

You have worked long and hard to produce good quantitative data. This effort has focused upon creating numbers which can be concretely analyzed, compared, and interpreted. These data have placed you in a strong position when compared with narrative or testimonial responses. Now the time has come to reap the benefits. The data are collected! Now what must you do?

The clear answer is that you must analyze the data. That can be a larger and more complicated task than first imagined, however. Data come in many different forms and through many different research designs. These characteristics, plus the number of respondents, influence the choice of statistical tests. Consequently, you must continue to talk to your consultant. What test is appropriate for these data? Hopefully this is not your first conversation about data analysis. Wisdom dictates that planning for data analysis takes place during the design phase of the project. If planning has taken place at that time, then your analysis problems are already under control.

In this chapter, I do not plan to describe the various statistical and analytical processes. Many good books are available. Rather, I will describe some selected fundamental mathematical concepts. This will help you get inside the mathematical mind and create an initial common ground between your consultant and yourself. I will discuss Measures of Central Tendency, Measures of Central Dispersion, and the concept of "Statistically Significant Difference."

MEASURES OF CENTRAL TENDENCY

This name is applied to the mean, median, and mode of the data. Fundamentally, they all in their own way describe the center location of the data, the point around which the data cluster. They describe the inward tendency of the results.

The mean is calculated by dividing the sum of the scores by the total number of scores. The median is a point on a measurement scale above which lie exactly half of the scores and below which lie the other half. The mode, a third measure of central tendency, is the value or score which occurs with the most frequency in the data.

Each of these measures is a helpful description of the data, particularly when large variations occur. In your research project concerning gender of the chaplain suppose you gather financial income data from the patients. The data report that 99 subjects report an income of $30,000, but one subject is a millionaire. The mean income for the group is $39,700 but this is misleading because only one subject is above $30,000. The median and mode are more helpful here; both are $30,000, but they conceal the fact that one subject was a milionaire. Thus these multiple mathematical expressions each possess benefits and disadvantages. Despite the versatility of these three Measures of Central Tendency, the mean is the most frequently reported and the basis for additional mathematical calculations.

MEASURES OF CENTRAL DISPERSION

The Measure of Central Tendency describe the various center points of the data, points around which the data cluster. These descriptors by themselves are incomplete and can be misleading because they do not describe the amount of spread in the data. For example, the mean of 50 represents 45 and 55 as well as 25 and 75. This matter is important because while the central tendency measurements describe the center point, some descriptor is needed to depict how representative this mean is of the total data. Clearly a mean of 50 is more closely representative of data values of 45 and 55 than of 25 and 75. The descriptors which describe the data spread are Measures of Central Dispersion.

The range is a natural measure of dispersion. The range is composed of the largest and smallest value in the data set. This simple measure has many disadvantages, the most serious being that it relies completely on two values, the highest and the lowest.

How could all scores in the data set be involved in measuring the dispersion? Such a mechanism would be the counterpart to the mean in the Measure of Central Tendency. The most common approach begins by measuring the deviation of each score from the mean whether it is positive or negative (above or below the mean). This new list of numbers which describes deviation from the mean can be summed and divided by the total number of scores. This sounds familiar because it follows the same procedure as finding the mean. The result of adding this list of deviations from the mean and dividing by the total number of scores produces a "mean deviation."

"Mean deviation" in itself is not useful, however, because the sign (the positive or negative quality) of the number has been ignored. Statisticians find this troublesome and they prefer to change all numbers into positive ones as they work with them. They accomplish this by squaring them. All squared numbers (the number multiplied by itself) are positive. This additional step, therefore, calculates the deviation from the mean and squares that number. These squared numbers are then summed and divided by the total number of scores. This process produces a measure of dispersion called "the variance." From time to time this measure is reported in research articles.

Usually the variance is itself a stepping stone to the most common statistic of dispersion because it has created another problem. When the number is squared, the unit descriptions are also squared (i.e., inches become square inches). This is easily corrected by taking the square root of the variance. Now the original unit of measurement is restored and you have calculated the most common measure of dispersion, the standard deviation. It is frequently reported in data tables with the mean, one representing the Measure of Central Tendency and the other the Measure of Central Dispersion. These two measures become the basis for most of the statistical tests which search for the presence of statistically significant differences.

STATISTICALLY SIGNIFICANT DIFFERENCE

The preceding measurement processes describe characteristics of data in concrete form. Scientists, however, are not satisfied with mere description. They wish to make statements about the effects of experimental actions upon the subjects, particularly that part of the subject's life under study. This is understandable because the statistical descriptions in your results may not represent the next set of subjects because they may be due to chance. The scientist wants to make a statement such as, "The difference between the two groups previous to and following the experimental intervention is of such magnitude that we cannot reasonably ascribe it to chance variation." That statement tells us something about this part of reality and the reader can assume that a second study could logically produce approximately the same results. This is a decided advance over mere description.

Research possesses a mathematical process for determining whether the difference is large enough that it is not likely to be due to a random, chance event. This process determines the "p value" (for probability) and establishes the chance (in the form of percentage) that the difference is just random and thus not to be expected again. Usually the acceptable level is 0.05 (five chances in a 100); then you are in an even stronger position to claim that the difference is due to your experimental intervention. Remember our discussion in an earlier chapter in which we stated that science never proves anything. Here you see the background to that statement. The very structure of the scientific mathematical process describes proof only in terms of probability.

How can this concept be explained further? The first step is to realize that the scientific method always looks for difference but expects to find none. In science the burden of proof is always on the one who states that a difference exists. Consequently, the improved pastoral care to gynecological patients from female chaplains as discussed previously really requires the assumption that no difference will exist between pastoral care given by males and females. This is the traditional "null hypothesis." If a difference is found, particularly at or below the 5% probability limit, then the p value registers your surprise. Thus, the smaller the p value (0.04, 0.03, 0.02, 0.01, 0.009, etc.), the less tenable the null hypothesis and the more likely that the findings are not due to chance. The p value is usually discussed as a confidence level, confidence, that is, that the findings are not due to chance. Therefore, although we seek to establish a gender-linked difference in pastoral care, we work from an assumption that no difference exists until demonstrated otherwise by a p value of 0.05 or smaller.

All of this can be displayed in graphic form. Let us suppose that the gender issue is completely irrelevant and immaterial to quality pastoral care to gynecological cancer patients. If that is so, the responses to your questionnaire from all patient groups would be random and produce a normal distribution curves (Figure 1, p. 70). In that instance, most of the responses would fall in the middle of the range set up in your questionnaire. Few would choose the extreme upper or lower ranges of "very helpful" or "not helpful." In fact, as you see from the normal curve in Figure 1, a predictable percentage of responses would fall in those various ranges if a normal distribution or "bell-shaped curve" were created. Now in order to produce results at or below the 0.05 p-value, a sufficient number of responses from the group with a female chaplain will have to shift to the right or to the left, producing not a bell-shaped curve but a skewed curve as in Figure 2 (p. 70). The exact number of patient responses or the amount of shift required depends on the number of points on the scale and the number of respondents. This is beyond the scope of this book, but the graphic presentation can help you visualize the process. Consult research books for further discussion.

I have discussed Measures of Central Tendency and Dispersion and the concept of Statistically Significant Difference. A grasp of these concepts will provide some common understanding between your consultant and yourself. Items that remain for discussion with your consultant include choice of the appropriate statistical tests and the data arrangement required for analysis. When the test results are back, your consultant can also help you with appropriate interpretation. Ask your questions and let the consultant help you.

In summary, the crowning jewel in quantitative research is data analysis and the appropriate interpretation of the results. All previous work has pointed toward this culmination. Conversely, analysis of results will be no better than the care taken during the rest of the project. With results in hand, you are ready for the final step—writing the journal article. I will address that in the next chapter.

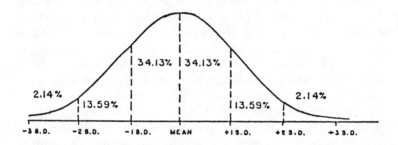

FIGURE 1
A normal distribution as represented by a Bell-Shaped Curve.

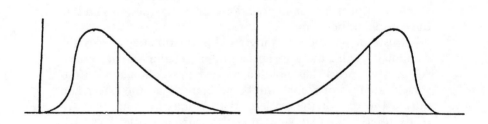

FIGURE 2
*Two skewed curves indicating more extreme
responses than in the normal distribution.*

Chapter 7

Writing the Results

You finished the project! You gained significant insights into your questions. Now other duties demand your attention and you seek relief from the research struggle.

In reality, relief is not at hand! Instead, you face the greatest temptation in your research process, the temptation not to report the project in writing. If you are working in a degree program, you know about the writing task ahead because your advisor and review committee require a written document. The scientific community possesses the same standards. In a strict sense, research becomes research only when published.

The challenge of writing the journal article calls for unique skills. All the skills needed to narrow the interest area into a research question, to design a project to answer the question, to gather and interpret the data, are not what you need now. Now you need technical writing skills. The challenge presented by the need for these skills constitutes the essence of the difficulty and of the temptation to proceed no further. If the writing challenge seems overwhelming, remember that the first experience is always the worst. Even so, experienced researchers believe that writing consumes one-fourth to one-third of the entire energy devoted to a project. Producing good writing is hard work.

This chapter provides resources to cope with this struggle. I will give particular attention to choosing appropriate journals, writing the sections of the research article, and coping with concerns of style and grammar.

JOURNAL IDENTIFICATION

The selection of potential journals must be made before writing begins for two reasons. The first is simple: journals possess different editorial styles and you need to be aware of these differences as you put the manuscript together. Obtain an "Instructions to Authors" statement from each journal in which you are interested and follow the guidelines carefully. Editors typically publish these at least once each year in the journal.

The second, and more complicated, reason for audience identification involves strategy. A painful personal experience will illustrate the importance of this strategy. In my first research project, I studied task importance and time usage among clergy in my denomination. During the study I fantasized that my results would be published in the only denominational periodical. Having completed the project, I sent off the finished product and settled back to await my reward. They rejected my manuscript. They did not publish tables (my submission naively contained many) and my study was not interesting to them. I was crushed and hurt. What could I do now? I had only two alternatives: give up or undertake an enormous rewriting process. The experience taught me a lesson: before writing, identify a broad spectrum of journals to which you can submit your work. This strategy has been successful for me with a recent study which now has been accepted for publication after five rejections. Look through various issues of the journals and identify those which you believe could be interested in your work, making a list. Indexed and abstracted journals usually set higher standards for manuscript acceptance, making them more sophisticated. You should place these journals near the top of your list if you have a strong project.

And now a word about manuscript rejections! Researchers believe that 70% of the manuscripts are eventually published if the author persists. An initial rejection or two is common. Do not take the rejection personally even though that temptation is ever-present. Editors do not insult contributors although the popular press sometimes characterizes them in this way. Take the reviewer's feedback seriously. If no comments are provided, you can request them from the editor. Journals have many reasons for refusing articles. They may have recently accepted or published a similar article. The article, despite your best efforts, may lie outside their interests. Your contribution may have been reviewed by persons who were disinterested in or biased against your subject matter.

Apart from these issues, manuscripts are rejected because

ADORATION MEDLEY

FATHER, I ADORE YOU
Father, I adore you; Lay my life before You.
How I love You!

HOLY, HOLY
Holy, holy, holy, holy,-
Holy, holy, Lord God Almighty;
And we lift our hearts before You as a
   token of our love;
Holy, holy, holy Jesus.

GREAT IS THE LORD
Great is the Lord, He is holy and just;
By His power we trust in His love.
Great is the Lord, He is faithful and true;
By His mercy He proves He is love.
Great is the Lord and worthy of glory!
Great is the Lord and worthy of praise.
Great is the Lord; now lift up your voice,
Now lift up your voice: Great is the Lord!

PRAYER SHEET

CANCER CONCERNS   BEREAVEMENT CONCERNS

MISCELLANEOUS CONCERNS   SICKNESS CONCERNS

JOB CONCERNS   SURGERIES

TRAVEL CONCERNS   CHURCHES TO PRAY FOR

the research design was not carefully planned or executed. Perhaps important variables were not adequately identified or the data were collected in problematic form. Research design mistakes cannot be corrected after the data are collected and you need to find a journal less sensitive to these issues.

If you receive a rejection, be prepared to make any necessary changes and send the article out again within 30 days. Keep the momentum up; keep the manuscript in front of editors.

An ethical issue is also present here. Never send the same manuscript to more than one journal at a time. Editors require that the material not be under consideration elsewhere while they review it.

WRITING THE SECTIONS OF THE ARTICLE

Most research journal articles are composed of four parts: introduction, methodology, results, and discussion. Some journals allow for a conclusion section, and many require an abstract which is placed at the beginning as a summary. Most researchers write these sections separately, welding them together in the latter part of the process.

You can write the literature review first. This review, placed at the end of the introduction and written in past tense, reports relevant findings from other studies. Report your evaluation of and perspectives on these studies along with the research questions which you have explored. Generally, this material requires only a few paragraphs and can be drafted even before data analysis is complete.

The methodology section is often written next. Using verbs in past tense, describe your research design. Make this section strictly a report of relevant activities: you sent questionnaires, interviewed persons, or conducted tests. Carefully describe any unique questionnaires, paper-and-pencil instruments, or equipment you used.

The results section is usually created next. Using present tense verbs, report the number of questionnaires returned, interviews conducted, and the demographics of the respondents. Focus upon the data created by the project. Do not wander into discussion of the results; record thoughts for discussion in note form for that later section. Simply report the findings. Try to limit the number of tables to three or fewer. Journals calculate their costs per page, and tables are expensive because they take up room. Look at sample articles in quality journals and note how specific data are managed by experienced authors.

Most researchers agree that the introduction and the discussion sections are the most important and difficult to write. Many write these sections at this point, relying upon notes they have made for themselves. Both sections are written in the present tense. I will discuss the introduction first.

The introduction must attract the reader's attention. This is usually achieved by statements which convince the reader that your research addresses an important issue or problem. Busy readers scan their journals quickly, spending time only with those articles which catch their attention.

The first introductory sentence is crucial. Make it short and pithy. Choose an active verb and avoid clauses. The best lead sentence is often one which requires no commas. This sentence, which then functions as the topic sentence of the paragraph, is amplified, expanded, and explained in those which follow. After one or two paragraphs, this introduction leads into the literature review.

Read through some introductions in the journals. Some will constitute good writing, but others will be poorly done because some scientists are poor writers. You can practice your writing skills by improving their introductions.

The discussion section presents its own difficulties. Here you discuss your results, linking them to previous studies, noting their implications, and suggesting new research questions for the professional community. This calls for professional discernment and skill in order to illumine the meaning of your findings.

The discussion section often begins with a paragraph which clearly states how the data in the results section answer the research questions. This ties the research report together. The findings entitle you to make some claims, but you must also be alert to unrealistic assertions about them. As a general rule, be conservative in your claims.

After this paragraph, you should comment on important or unusual data characteristics, beginning with that which was presented first in the results section. The discussion section can end by noting limitations implicit in the findings and by raising additional questions for research.

The abstract is written last. Limited to 100-150 words, it can use phrases or sentences from the article, reflecting its four parts. Tell the reader the results in summary form. Avoid statements such as "implications are discussed." Remember that many will only read the abstract, lacking the time for detailed examination of your work.

COPING WITH CONCERNS OF STYLE AND GRAMMAR

Why should you struggle with problems of style and grammar? Simply because good writing will help you publish and because no one writes well without giving attention to these matters. The journal editor and reviewers of your manuscript will be prejudiced against your contribution if reading it is hard work and confusing. They know that poor writing will also tax the subscribers and cause them to stop reading the journal.

Throughout the writing process you confront constant problems of paragraph and sentence construction. All of these problems essentially resolve into the need to communicate the content in clear language without wordiness. This requires a number of skills. First, you must learn to be objective about your own writing. No doubt your first draft looks good to you. You read it over and can make only a few improvements. And yet, it is a first draft. You wonder if it really is that good. How can you lift your own "blindness" to your work?

Here are two behaviors with which you can begin. First, go back to a written draft you created some months ago. The content really does not matter. Read over the draft and begin making changes to improve the style and cut out the wordiness. Notice how you can feel more objective about this writing simply because time has passed. With increased practice, this objectivity can be achieved after you set aside freshly written material for an hour.

The second helpful behavior is simply to dictate a few pages of material for typing. With the transcript in hand, you will soon see the wordiness. Verbal dictation is usually outrageously wordy and the typescript creates an opportunity to identify and reduce this excess.

After you begin this process, I recommend another. Read a few books about technical writing. They will further sensitize you to good and poor writing. Then begin to read journal articles, not necessarily for content, but to examine them for good and poor writing, for clear and confusing grammar. Your future as a good writer rests with the development of that critical eye. And then after you have begun to read critically the writings of others and to struggle with your own, refresh your memory about grammatical construction. In the end, knowledge about parts of speech and old fashioned English grammar make writing easier.

Having described a process by which you can become a better writer, I will make two contributions to this process in the remainder of this chapter. Focusing first upon paragraph construction, I will share the five drafts of this chapter's opening paragraphs. This will help you grasp the process of writing, particularly as it applies to an introduction. Later, I will discuss some problems of sentence construction.

I revised this chapter's two opening paragraphs three times. This redrafting process was my effort to attain my own goals for an introduction. These revisions are reproduced below along with process comments. Here is the first draft of the chapter's opening paragraphs.

FIRST DRAFT

Upon arrival at this point in the research process, you are tempted to be relieved. This has been a difficult process, particularly if it was your first research effort. Perhaps you have gained significant insights into the research question. You are tempted to feel that you are nearly finished.

If your research is part of a degree program, you know that the process is not finished. Now the research project must be written. Even if your work is not part of a degree program, it still needs to be written and reported to the professional community.

I have put something down and that is better than a blank page. Like most first draft writing, however, it is not in finished form and will probably never be published. As I reviewed this first draft material later, I realized that the first sentence did not seize the reader's attention and that the entire tone appeared tentative, in part because the first two sentences used passive verb forms. The two paragraphs were completely rewritten the next day.

SECOND DRAFT

> Relief is at hand! You have finished the project! Perhaps you have gained significant insights into your research question. Now, other duties demand your attention and you are ready to move on.
> In reality, you now stand at the point of greatest temptation, the temptation to take the project no further and to neglect reporting it in the professional literature. Many novice researchers give into that temptation and never complete the project. If your work has been part of a degree program, you know that the project must be described in writing. It is required. That requirement is the standard in the scientific community. Research is not research until it is published.

I have written two new paragraphs although the ideas remain. The sentences in the first paragraph are shorter and capture the reader's attention by commenting on the needed sense of relief. I eliminated the passive verb forms. The second paragraph links this search for relief to the temptation to give up on the publication effort. As in the earlier draft, the paragraph uses the need to create a written document in degree programs as the standard for all research. These paragraphs appear better suited as a chapter beginning and some attention to stylistic and grammatical concerns are appropriate. A few days later some stylistic changes were made.

THIRD DRAFT

> You finished the project! You gained significant insights into your questions. Now other duties demand your attention and you seek relief from the research struggle.
> In reality, relief is not at hand! Instead, you face the greatest temptation in your research process, the temptation not to report the project in writing. You know about the writing task ahead if your work is part of a degree program because your advisor and review committee require a written document. The scientific community possesses the same standards. Research becomes research only when published.

This product appeared at the head of this chapter. Adjustments in this draft included sentence and vocabulary changes. First the statement "Relief is at hand" was moved to the end of the paragraph to create a compound sentence. I felt it was wiser to speak first to the "finished" character of the project and then pick up the sense of relief. Second, the perfect verb forms, "have finished" and "have gained," were reduced to past tense: "finished" and "gained." This shortened and simplified the sentences, increasing their impact.

In the second paragraph, the theme of "relief" was immediately reintroduced and various word changes made. The sentence about novice researchers was dropped because it served no purpose. "That requirement" is was modified to read, "The scientific community possesses." This latter sentence abandons the "to be" verb and substitutes a more robust sentence.

These materials represent the hard work of writing the introductory paragraphs. Equally hard work is needed to produce meaningful materials from the entire first draft.

I will conclude this chapter by addressing the challenge of sentence construction and use an example. The example is a mass of entangled dictated words in the first draft of a semi-annual report to a college president. The president, already aware of the department's ethics grant, is given an up-date in this report. Here is the dictated sentence.

> The ethics grant is in its second year, and while the faculty ethicist provided cannot be guaranteed for continuation, and therefore is unable to attract a full-time person, several of our part-time faculty have combined to provide 20% or more equivalency to give the Department significant increase in teaching effort.

This 50 word sentence, if it can be called that, has multiple problems. Like much dictation, the speaker gets bogged down in clauses and forgets the beginning of the sentence. Most of the sentence is confused and impossible to understand grammatically. No editor would publish it. How can this sentence be reworked into a rigorous, clear, concise statement?

As I have struggled with my first drafts, I have learned not to make small changes. Take the first draft in hand and be ready to completely rewrite the narrative. I often rewrite material in longhand to achieve spontaneous insights concerning sentence structure. This also encourages larger vocabulary usage, resulting in clearer and more rigorous prose. In this first rewriting endeavor, a more clear and meaningful sentence demonstrates success. Here is what the author was trying to say:

> The ethics grant, now in its second year, has stimulated a 20%
> increase in teaching effort from parish-based faculty despite the
> difficulty in filling the grant's full-time faculty position because
> continuation funding cannot be guaranteed at the end of the
> grant.

Many difficulties still exist with this sentence, but the meaning is
clearer. The sentence reports that a grant was received last year
which created a new faculty position, a position which is difficult
to fill because it is temporary. However, the grant has had other
beneficial efforts because it has funded several parish-based
faculty who have increased their teaching time. Their joint
efforts have increased the department's teaching by 20%. The
original sentence used 50 words and unclear grammar; the new
sentence is better writing.

What further refinements are possible? Further work seems
necessary because the concluding phrase of the sentence, "because continuation funding cannot be guaranteed at the end of
the grant," seems a dangling group of words. Perhaps the sentence would be more rigorous if the clause concerning the full-
time position were placed first. This is the result:

> The ethics grant, now in its second year, experiences difficulty in
> filling the temporary full-time faculty position although various
> parish faculty have increased their efforts so that the Department's
> teaching has risen 20%.

This construction of 33 words seems successful because the
sentence is shorter and clearer. A new problem is created, however, because the negative problem with the full-time faculty
position is placed first in the sentence. This order needs reversal
again because positive benefits should be stated first.

The sentence also conveys two thoughts concerning the
grant. Perhaps both clarity and conciseness would be enhanced
with two sentences. This effort produces the following results:

> The ethics grant, now in its second year, produced a 20% increase
> in teaching through the combined efforts of several parish faculty.
> We have not filled the full-time faculty position because con-
> tinuation after the grant cannot be guaranteed.

These sentences are now more readable and manageable. Their shortness allows for more elaboration and flexibility. The positive results of the grant are described first, the unfilled position reported at the end.

These sentences contain 38 words, however. Can other refinements increase the rigor by reducing the wordiness? Two areas invite attention. The first is the parenthetical phrase, "now in its second year," and the double use of the word "not" in the second sentence. Reworking the sentences with this in mind produces these results:

> The second year of the ethics grant supported several parish faculty whose combined efforts produced a 20% increase in teaching. The full-time faculty position remained open because continuation funding is uncertain.

This effort creates a 31 word result. Can this be further reduced for increased economy and clarity?

One phrase still seems loose and wordy, namely, "efforts produced a 20% increase in teaching." The prepositional phrase is unnecessary if reconstructed into "efforts increase teaching 20%." We now have two sentences with rigor composed of 28 words:

> The second year of the ethics grant supported several parish faculty whose combined efforts increased teaching 20%. The full-time faculty position remained open because continuation funding is uncertain.

These two sentences are more clear, concise, and rigorous than the original monstrosity with which we began. Additional changes could be necessary depending upon the syntax of the paragraph in which it appears, but this process helps you understand the hard work which produces good writing.

This rewriting process is exhausting and is another point at which you can become confused and discouraged. All this writing and rewriting, it may seem to you, takes too much time. You may find that your skills are weak and that you possess little experience. In such a situation, remember that approximately one-fourth of the total energy for a project is focused upon the writing process. Also remember that the first time is the worst. Continue to cultivate these skills and writing will become easier.

And now one final word. Send a final draft of the manuscript to a number of your colleagues for review and feedback. Choose those whom you believe can be constructively critical. Never send an article to an editor without this peer review. The journal reviewers will likely give you the feedback you should have gotten from your colleagues, rejecting the article in the process. As noted in the Acknowledgements of this book, selected reviewers read drafts of my work and offered comments.

In summary, writing well is hard work. Everyone who publishes learns these skills by experience or training. A writing consultant can be helpful and save you time and energy. Invite the consultant to review your manuscript when you circulate it to colleagues.

You should be able to obtain feedback from these informal reviews in a couple of weeks. Take it seriously, although you need not adopt all advice given to you. Make these decisions, put the manuscript in final form, and send it to your journal of choice.

But your work may not be finished yet. Many journals accept articles on condition that the authors make some revisions. Make the revisions and return the article as instructed. Usually relief is then at hand. You have finished the project. In due time you will see your name in print. The only remaining task is to circulate reprints to colleagues and others who are interested.

Section 3

A Network of Pastoral Scientists?

What can I say in conclusion? The ancient Greeks developed a dogma which has survived to the present day. They
held that knowledge was good, good for its own sake and for its
practical contribution. Our scientific culture is still heavily invested in that belief. From within that context I have pressed
you, my pastoral peers, to join the scientific community more
committedly and to produce respectable empirical scientific
knowledge. I do so for many reasons, including my belief that
we must make a scientific contribution in this culture if we are to
remain in control of our professional future within health care.
Additionally, I believe we can not maintain our pastoral identity
if we live off the insights of other professions.

We have much to study, to investigate, to understand, and to
research. One example will suffice. A physican colleague excit-
edly approached me recently and told me of a patient whose
medical profile had dramatically improved. Under long term
treatment for a number of chronic conditions, her symptoms
had not only improved but her mood had become lighter and
more hopeful. When the physician inquired concerning these
changes, the patient reported recent life changing experiences,
experiences involving religious components and the awakening
of a nominal faith. "How was this to be understood?" the physician asked me. Clearly the religious experience was benefical and
important to understand. He wanted to know whether the pastoral scientists had studied this phenomenon. What did the
literature say? He wondered if he should expect a relapse.
Should he send the patient to a psychiatrist for evaluation so that
he could understand what had happened? He wondered
whether such experiences as this with all the profound beneficial

effects should simply be ignored by the scientific community. Should the professionals deliberately seek to bring about such life changing experiences in others? I knew this physician did not intent to reduce such profound experiences into a cheap commercialism but sought rather to leave no stone unturned in a passionate quest to help his patients.

I could not tell him about our extensive literature in the pastoral sciences about religious experience and symptom improvement. We know so little. Here is an opportunity for further research. Multitudes of additional challenges await investigation.

So—what can be done if you and I are committed to increasing research knowledge? I was struck by the physician's use of the phrase "pastoral scientist." He helped me become aware that pastoral care and counseling have not cultivated a group of persons who can legitimately think of themselves in that way. Isn't it strange that chaplains and pastoral counselors, all of whom work in a scientific culture and in scientific settings, have not produced persons with these skills! I suggest that such a group is necessary within our ranks. What can be done to create such a group?

Learning research skills by reading books, even this one, will not accomplish that. Admonitions concerning moral obligations to produce scientific knowledge will not produce lasting change. Such change will be brought about by constructing a network of pastoral scientists who band together. Two specific factors are necessary. These factors include the infusion of money into the pastoral research process and the establishment of peer support.

First, pastoral research will increase when you and I are paid to do it. We can not produce quality pastoral research when that task falls outside of our regular duties. We can not produce it during evening hours and on weekends, trying to find energy and excitement when exhausted from other duties. You may be able to produce a dissertation in that way, but it can not be a continuing pattern. Pastoral research efforts must be incorporated into the daily funded tasks of chaplains and pastoral counselors if they are to succeed. And this requires financial support.

If we work for institutions which prize research, they will provide basic funding by encouraging us to include pastoral research in our regular work week. Other chaplains and pastoral counselors who work for more service oriented institutions will need to work harder to secure this support.

Funding support for research can never come wholly from within employing institutions, however. Substantial funding must be obtained through grants and contributions. This implies the identification of potential sources, the creation of proposals, and the publication of results in such ways so as to encourage further work.

Second, pastoral research will increase when a network of professionals provide peer support, guidance, and recognition. Research cannot be carried out alone because scientific activity is a social as well as an intellectual activity. This network of professionals would need regular meetings with opportunities for reporting results, rewarding the best work, stimulating new ideas, and constructing new projects. Such a network of professionals could begin meeting at national conferences to discuss their interests. The Research Committees of national organizations such as the Association for Clinical Pastoral Education, the American Association of Pastoral Counselors, and the National Association of Catholic Chaplains could organize such network meetings. Or perhaps the Joint Council for Research in Pastoral Care and Counseling could sponsor such a network as part of its co-ordinating activities. The potential for such a network must be explored if pastoral scientists are to flourish.

In summary, you can make your contribution to pastoral research. With sufficient experience, you might even become comfortable calling yourself a pastoral scientist. This book has sought to encourage, support, and inform you in that endeavor. You will also need mutual support in a community of researchers. Creation of such a community will require that we band together in some type of network. In this way pastoral scientists will develop and mature, making significant contributions to pastoral care and counseling.

References

Introduction
1. Samuel Southard, *Religious Inquiry* (Nashville, TN: Abingdon Press, 1976).
2. Richard E. Davies, *Handbook for Doctor of Ministry Projects: An Approach to Structured Observation of Ministry* (Lanham, MD: University Press of America, 1984).

Chapter 1
1. Larry VandeCreek, "An Analysis of an American Association of Pastoral Counselors Membership Committee and Its Actions." *Journal of Pastoral Psychotherapy,* 1987, Vol. 1, No. 2, pp. 3–17.

Chapter 2
1. Augustine, *The Confessions of Saint Augustine.* trans. Edward Pussey (New York, NY: Pocket Library, 1957), p. 66.
2. Augustine, *The Trinity.* trans. Stephan McKenna (Washington, DC: The Catholic University of America Press, 1963).
3. W. Pannenberg, *Theology and the Philosophy of Science* (Philadelphia, PA: Westminster Press, 1976).
4. Thomas Aquinas, *Summa Theologia.* trans. Thomas Gilbey (New York, NY: McGraw Hill, 1964), Vol. 1, pp. 1-2.
5. T. F. Torrance, *Theological Science* (New York, NY: Oxford University Press, 1969), p. xiii.
6. F. Schleiermacher, *Brief Outline of the Study of Theology.* trans. T. N. Tite (Richmond, VA: John Knox, 1966), pp. 19-27.
7. W. Dilthey, *Einletung in die Geisteswissenschaften* (Leipzig, Germany: Dunchker and Hujbolt, 1883).
8. For a review of Troeltsch's work, see W. Pannenberg, *Theology and the Philosophy of Science,* pp. 103-116.
9. *Ibid.,* pp. 103-116.
10. R. Carnap, *Logical Foundations of Probability.* 2nd ed. (Chicago, IL: University of Chicago Press, 1963).
11. K. Popper, *Conjectures and Refutations* (London, England: Routledge and Kegan Paul, 1963).
12. Anthony Flew and Alasdair MacIntyre (Eds.), *New Essays in Philosophical Theology* (New York, NY: Macmillan, 1955), pp. 98-99.
13. Pannenberg, *op. cit.,* p. 277.
14. B. Mitchel, "Theology and Falsification," in A. Flew and A. MacIntyre (Eds.), *New Essays in Philosophical Theology* (New York, NY: Macmillan 1955), p. 104
15. Michael Polanyi, *Science, Faith, and Society* (Chicago, IL: University of Chicago Press, 1964), p. 14.

16. *Ibid.*, p. 30.

17. Michael Polanyi, *Personal Knowledge* (Chicago, IL: University of Chicago Press, 1985), p. 18, 375.

18. F. Peabody, "The Care of the Patient," *Journal of the American Medical Society,* 1927, Vol. 88, p. 879.

19. T. Kuhn, *The Structure of Scientific Revolutions* (Chicago, IL: University of Chicago Press, 1970), 2nd ed., p. 24.

20. *Ibid.*, pp. 11-12.

21. *Ibid.*, p. 118.

22. *Ibid.*, pp. 118-119.

23. *Ibid.*, p. 151.

Chapter 3

1. W. J. Ong, *Orality and Literacy: The Technologizing of the Word* (New York, NY: Methuen Publishers, 1982), pp. 31-36.

2. *Ibid.*, p. 45.

3. M. Dibielius, "The First Christian Historian," *Studies in the Acts of the Apostles* (London, England: SCM Press, 1956), pp. 136-137.

4. Acts of the Apostles, 1:1-4.

5. P. Zeigler, *The Black Death* (New York, NY: Harper Torchbook, 1969), p. 41.

Chapter 4

1. James Mitchell, Jr. (Ed.), *The Ninth Mental Measurements Yearbooks* (Lincoln, NE: Buros Institute of Mental Measurement, 1985).

Chapter 5

1. B. Russell, *An Outline of Philosophy* (New York, NY: Meridian Publishers, 1927), pp. 32-33.

2. A. Schweitzer, *The Quest of the Historical Jesus* (New York, NY: Macmillan, 1948), p. 4.

Index

Author Sketch

Larry VandeCreek is a Diplomate in the American Association of Pastoral Counselors (AAPC) and a Supervisor in the Association for Clinical Pastoral Education (ACPE). He is vice-chairperson and Assistant Professor of Family Medicine at The Ohio State University, Columbus, Ohio; and he conducts research, teaches behavioral science, and functions as a pastoral counselor. He is currently a member of the Research Committee of AAPC and chairperson of ACPE's Research Committee. His research interests include co-operative efforts with physicians investigating the electrical activity of the stomach, studies in grief and loss, and research into various functions and characteristics of AAPC and ACPE.

253.0724
V225

LINCOLN CHRISTIAN COLLEGE AND SEMINARY

80367

How to Do *Everything* with

Microsoft Office Word 2007

W9-BVF-074

Guy Hart-Davis

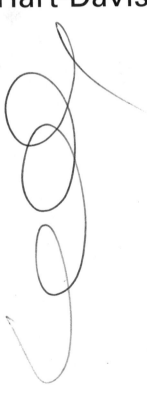

New York   Chicago   San Francisco   Lisbon
London   Madrid   Mexico City   Milan   New Delhi
San Juan   Seoul   Singapore   Sydney   Toronto

LONGWOOD PUBLIC LIBRARY

The *McGraw·Hill* Companies

Cataloging-in-Publication Data is on file with the Library of Congress

McGraw-Hill books are available at special quantity discounts to use as premiums and sales promotions, or for use in corporate training programs. For more information, please write to the Director of Special Sales, Professional Publishing, McGraw-Hill, Two Penn Plaza, New York, NY 10121-2298. Or contact your local bookstore.

How to Do Everything with Microsoft® Office Word 2007

Copyright © 2007 by The McGraw-Hill Companies. All rights reserved. Printed in the United States of America. Except as permitted under the Copyright Act of 1976, no part of this publication may be reproduced or distributed in any form or by any means, or stored in a database or retrieval system, without the prior written permission of publisher, with the exception that the program listings may be entered, stored, and executed in a computer system, but they may not be reproduced for publication.

1234567890 DOC DOC 01987

ISBN-13: 978-0-07-149069-6
ISBN-10:   0-07-149069-8

Sponsoring Editor
Roger Stewart

Editorial Supervisor
Patty Mon

Project Manager
Vasundhara Sawhney,
International Typesetting
and Composition

Acquisitions Coordinator
Carly Stapleton

Technical Editor
Justin Jaffe

Copy Editor
Margaret Berson

Proofreader
Megha Ghai

Indexer
Broccoli Information
Management

Production Supervisor
George Anderson

Composition
International Typesetting
and Composition

Illustration
International Typesetting
and Composition

Art Director, Cover
Jeff Weeks

Cover Designer
Pattie Lee

Cover Illustration
Tom Willis

Information has been obtained by McGraw-Hill from sources believed to be reliable. However, because of the possibility of human or mechanical error by our sources, McGraw-Hill, or others, McGraw-Hill does not guarantee the accuracy, adequacy, or completeness of any information and is not responsible for any errors or omissions or the results obtained from the use of such information.

About the Author

Guy Hart-Davis is the author of more than 40 computer books on subjects as varied as Microsoft Office, Windows Vista, Mac OS X, Visual Basic for Applications, and the iPod. His most recent books include *How to Do Everything with Microsoft Office Excel 2007* and *CNET Do-It-Yourself iPod Projects*.

Acknowledgments

My thanks go to the following people for making this book happen:

- Roger Stewart for getting the book approved
- Carly Stapleton for handling the administration and finances
- Justin Jaffe for performing the technical review and providing helpful suggestions and encouragement
- Vasundhara Sawhney for coordinating the project
- Margaret Berson for editing the text with care and a light touch
- International Typesetting and Composition for laying out the pages
- Megha Ghai for proofreading the book
- Broccoli Information Management for creating the index

Contents

Introduction

The most widely used word processor in the world, Word is the leading application in the Microsoft Office suite. You can use Word to create anything from a shopping list to a thousand-page document with figures, cross-references, and footnotes—not to mention an automatically generated table of contents, table of figures, and index. You can use Word either on its own or together with the other Office applications.

Word 2007 builds on the many previous versions of Word to deliver powerful functionality and many new features along with a slick and easy-to-use interface. If you're new to Word, you've got a large amount to learn. If you're coming to Word 2007 as an experienced user of earlier versions, you've still got plenty to learn, because Word 2007 introduces major changes. But either way, this book will get you up to speed quickly.

Who Is This Book For?

This book is designed to help beginning and intermediate users get the most out of Word 2007 in the shortest possible time. If you fall into either of those categories, you'll benefit from this book's comprehensive coverage, focused approach, and helpful advice. If you're already a Word expert seeking super-advanced coverage, look elsewhere.

What Does This Book Cover?

Here's what this book covers:

- Chapter 1, "Get Up to Speed with Word 2007," shows you how to start Word either manually (for example, using the Start menu) or automatically when you log on to Windows. You'll meet the different components of the Word user interface, including the Ribbon, which replaces the menus and toolbars of earlier versions. After that, you'll learn how to open Word documents and other documents, how to use views and splitting to display documents as you want to see them, and how to get help with Word when you need it.

- Chapter 2, "Create and Save Documents," explains how to create new documents from templates and existing documents, how to save them, and which file format to use when. You'll also learn how to tell Word which folder to use as the default for your documents.

■ Chapter 3, "Navigate, Enter Text, and Use Find," begins by explaining the secret of Word's paragraphs, which is the key to working successfully with text in your documents. Once you know that, you'll learn how to use Word's tools for navigating around your documents; how to enter text via the keyboard or other means, including scanning and speech recognition; and how to move, copy, and delete text. You'll also harness the power of Word's Find and Replace feature for locating exactly what you're looking for and changing it swiftly and easily.

■ Chapter 4, "Format Text Efficiently," is a monster of a chapter that covers the vital topic of formatting in all the depth you need. The chapter starts with an overview that explores the confusing array of formatting methods that Word provides. You'll then learn to apply quick-and-dirty font formatting, paragraph formatting, and list formatting, before moving along to styles and themes, which let you format entire documents quickly and consistently. You'll even learn about language formatting, which you use to tell Word that particular text is in a certain language—or simply that you want the spell checker to leave that text alone.

■ Chapter 5, "Lay Out Pages and Use Headers and Footers," explains how to set up pages so that they look the way you want and how to add headers and footers to your documents. The chapter discusses how to change margins, set page size and orientation, and add line numbering to paragraphs in formal documents. You'll also learn how to place text precisely with text boxes, flowing text from one to another if necessary, and how to align text vertically on the page.

■ Chapter 6, "Spelling, Grammar, Research, and Translation," covers the use of Word's tools for checking and improving your documents. Spell checking is almost universally useful, and Word can perform it either as you type or when you're ready to review your document. Grammar checking is much less useful—and if you use it at all, you will probably want to restrict the items on which Word offers advice. Much more positive is Word's research feature, which lets you consult online references including a thesaurus, and its translation feature—although machine translation requires almost as much caution as grammar checking.

■ Chapter 7, "Add Graphics, Diagrams, and Borders to Your Documents," begins by explaining the different layers that Word uses for positioning text and graphical objects in your documents. Once you've grasped this, you're ready to insert clip art items, shapes, WordArt, and graphics in documents; format, position, and layer drawing objects so they appear correctly; and add borders and shading to objects.

■ Chapter 8, "Print and Fax Documents," shows you how to choose suitable printing options for your Word documents—for example, whether to update fields and linked data or whether to use draft quality. With options set, you'll be ready to print a document the conventional way, print directly from Windows Explorer, or fax a document (if your version of Windows includes faxing capabilities).

- Chapter 9, "Make Word Easier to Use," begins by explaining how to configure essential editing options that confuse and frustrate millions of Word users. You'll learn to tame the excesses of AutoCorrect and harness its power, create new templates and custom styles, and work with "building blocks," Word's new term for prebuilt document parts (such as headers or text boxes) that you can insert to assemble documents quickly. You'll also learn to customize the Quick Access Toolbar and status bar, create custom keyboard shortcuts, and install add-in programs to increase Word's functionality.

- Chapter 10, "Share, Edit, and Revise Documents," brings you up to speed with Word's features for working collaboratively on documents. The Track Changes feature lets you mark the revisions made in a document, so you can easily see what was added, deleted, moved, or reformatted, while the comments feature lets you flag issues in a document without making changes inline. You'll also read how to share documents with your colleagues via a network or send documents to them via e-mail.

- Chapter 11, "Create Tables and Columns," shows you how to lay out tabular data effectively in your documents. The chapter discusses how to create both simple and complex tables, how to apply Word's styles to tables, and even how to perform calculations in tables. You'll also find out how to create "newspaper-style" columns of text, which are useful for newsletter-style document layouts.

- Chapter 12, "Create Bookmarks, References, Footnotes, and Indexes," starts by explaining how to use Word's electronic bookmarks to mark document items you want to access quickly or reference easily. The chapter then shows you how to insert references to bookmarks, headings, and other items; how to create footnotes and endnotes, and easily convert one type of note to the other; and how to create an index for a document. At the end of the chapter, you'll learn how to create a table of contents, a table of figures, or a table of authorities (citations).

- Chapter 13, "Blog and Create Web Pages with Word," gets you working with Word's new blogging feature. Once you've set up Word to use a blogging service, you can create posts and publish them directly from Word. This chapter also discusses how to choose web options to control how Word creates web pages, explains what you need to know about Word's three HTML formats, and shows you how to save Word documents as web pages.

- Chapter 14, "Create Forms to Collect Data," covers how to create electronic forms in Word to collect data. The chapter explains how to plan a form, how to arrange content controls on it and configure them as needed, and how to protect a form against unwanted changes. You'll also read about setting up a form so that it prints only the form data, a useful trick for preprinted forms.

- Chapter 15, "Use Fields to Streamline Documents," introduces you to the possibilities offered by Word's fields. First, you'll learn what fields are, how to recognize them and understand their behavior, and how to insert them in your documents. After that, you'll learn how to edit fields, update fields automatically when you print a document, and lock fields when you want to prevent changes.

■ Chapter 16, "Mail Merge Letters and Much More," shows you how to use Word's powerful mail-merge tools to create form letters, labels, envelopes, e-mail messages, and other merged documents. Creating a main document and specifying a data source is daunting at first, but this chapter shows you how to do both, link the two, insert merge fields in the main document, and then perform the merge.

■ Chapter 17, "Use Outlines and Create Master Documents," explains how to work with outlines and master documents, two tools that help you create and edit long documents more easily. Outline view lets you collapse a document to different numbers of heading levels so that you see only those levels. A master document is a document that contains two or more subdocuments that you can edit either as part of the master document or separately, allowing you and your colleagues to work on the same project's documents at the same time. This chapter also shows you how to create outline numbered lists, which you may need in formal documents.

■ Chapter 18, "Protect Your Valuable Documents," teaches you to use the security features that Word provides for protecting documents. You'll learn how to protect a document with a password for modest security, protect it with encryption for greater security, or apply access restrictions that control which actions a user can take with the document— for example, opening it but not printing it. You'll also learn how to implement restrictions on editing and formatting, apply a digital signature to a finished document to prove it has not changed since you signed it, and remove sensitive or personal information from a document before distributing it.

■ The Appendix lists the keyboard shortcuts you can use to make Word do your bidding without touching the mouse.

NOTE   *Word 2007 runs on Windows Vista and Windows XP. The illustrations in this book show how Word looks with the Vista Basic user interface in Windows Vista. If you're using the Vista Aero user interface, or if you're using Windows XP, your windows will look somewhat different, but everything should function the same.*

Conventions Used in This Book

To make its meaning clear, this book uses a number of conventions, three of which are worth mentioning here:

■ The pipe character or vertical bar denotes choosing an item from the Ribbon. For example, "choose Page Layout | Page Setup | Orientation | Portrait" means that you should click the Page Layout tab on the Ribbon (displaying the tab's contents), go to the Page Setup group, click the Orientation button, and then choose Portrait from the panel that appears.

■ Note, Tip, and Caution paragraphs highlight information you should pay extra attention to.

- Most check boxes have two states: *selected* (with a check mark in them) and *cleared* (without a check mark in them). This book tells you to *select* a check box or *clear* a check box rather than "click to place a check mark in the box" or "click to remove the check mark from the box." (Often, you'll be verifying the state of the check box, so it may already have the required setting—in which case, you don't need to click at all.) Some check boxes have a third state as well, in which they're selected but dimmed and unavailable. This state is usually used for options that apply to only part of the current situation.

NOTE   *This book assumes you're using Internet Explorer rather than another browser. Given that Internet Explorer currently still has the bulk of the web browser market, that's probably a reasonable assumption. But if you're using another browser, you'll see different behavior when you take an action that causes Word to access your default browser—for example, when you CTRL-click a hyperlink in a document.*

Chapter 1

Get Up to Speed with Word 2007

How to...

- Start Word manually or automatically
- Understand the components of the Word screen
- Understand the basics of documents
- Open an existing document
- Open other formats of word-processing documents in Word
- Use views and splitting so that you can view your documents as needed
- Get help with Word

Word is a powerful word-processing application for creating, editing, finalizing, and producing documents of all sorts, from a one-page unformatted note to a thousand-page typeset book. Coming to grips with Word 2007 involves a learning curve, because Word 2007 has a radically different user interface than earlier versions of Word—and indeed different from almost all other Windows applications except for its sibling applications, Excel 2007 and PowerPoint 2007. Even if you're experienced with Windows applications or with earlier versions of Word, plan to spend several hours getting up to speed with this new user interface.

In this chapter, you'll see how to navigate the Word screen and understand its components. You'll learn the basics of *documents* (the files that Word creates), how to open existing documents, and how to use views and windows so that you can see what you need to see. At the end of the chapter, you'll learn how to use Word's built-in help features to find information you need.

Start Word

To start Word, choose Start | All Programs | Microsoft Office | Microsoft Office Word 2007. When it opens, Word creates a new blank document.

When you need to start Word and open an existing document at the same time so that you can work in that document, start Word in either of these ways:

- Choose Start | Recent Items, and then select the document from the Recent Items submenu. (In Windows XP, choose Start | My Recent Documents.)

NOTE *In Windows Vista, if the Recent Items list doesn't appear on your Start menu, right-click the Start button and choose Properties to display the Taskbar And Start Menu Properties dialog box. On the Start Menu tab, select the Store And Display A List Of Recently Opened Files check box, and then click the OK button. In Windows XP, if the My Recent Documents item doesn't appear on your Start menu, right-click the Start button and choose Properties to display the Taskbar And Start Menu Properties dialog box. Click the upper Customize button to display the Customize Start Menu dialog box. On the Advanced tab, select the List My Most Recently Opened Documents check box. Click the OK button to close each dialog box.*

■ Double-click the icon for an existing document in a Windows Explorer window or on your desktop.

NOTE

For instructions and illustrations, this book uses a standard installation of Windows Vista as the operating system on which Word is running. For clarity of printing, the illustrations show the Vista Basic user interface rather than the more highly graphical Vista Aero user interface. If you're using Vista Aero, window borders and title bars will look different, with backgrounds showing through and drop shadows outside the borders. If you're using Windows XP, the user interface will look a little different, but you should be able to follow the instructions easily enough.

Setting Up Officewide Options at First Launch

The first time you launch one of the Office 2007 applications after installing Office, the application prompts you to enter (or verify) your user name and initials, and then choose privacy options in the dialog box that appears.

These are your choices:

■ **Get Online Help area**   Select the Search Microsoft Office Online For Help Content When I'm Connected To The Internet check box if you want to use online help as well as the help files stored on your computer. Online help includes the latest information, so searching it is usually helpful—but if you have a slow Internet connection, you may prefer to search the help files on your computer instead.

■ **Keep Your System Running area**   Select the Download A File Periodically That Helps Determine System Problems check box if you want Office to automatically download a file that helps track system problems. This option is usually helpful.

■ **Make Office Better area**   Select the Sign Up For The Customer Experience Improvement Program check box if you want to let Office collect information about how you use the Office applications, your computer's configuration, and problems Office runs into. Office then connects to Microsoft via the Internet and uploads the information. The information is anonymous, but some people prefer not to provide it. There's no real downside except that Office needs to establish an Internet connection to upload the information—so if you have a dial-up connection, Office causes Windows to dial it.

After the Privacy options, Office displays the "Sign Up For Microsoft Update" screen, recommending that you sign up for Microsoft Update, which automatically downloads and installs new files for Office and Windows when Microsoft makes them available. If you want to let Windows keep itself and Office up-to-date, select the Download And Install Updates From Microsoft Update When Available option button, and then click the Sign Up button. Otherwise, select the I Don't Want To Use Microsoft Update option button, and then click the Finish button. (Windows switches the name of the button in the lower-right corner between Finish and Sign Up depending on which option button you select.)

Start Word Easily and Often

If you start Word more frequently than most other applications, Windows automatically places a shortcut to Word on the "most frequently used applications" section of the Start menu, as shown here. You can then start Word by choosing Start | Microsoft Office Word 2007.

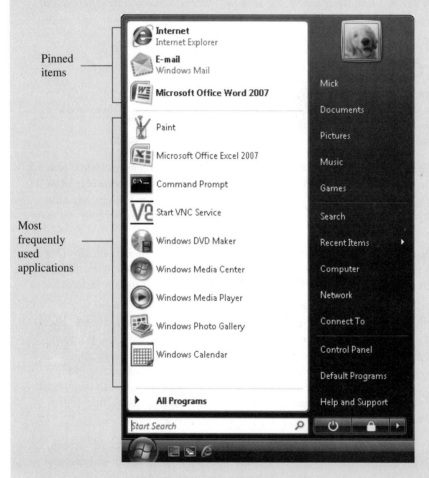

To make launching Word even easier, *pin* Word to the pinned items section of the Start menu, so that it always appears there. To pin Word, choose Start | All Programs | Microsoft Office to display the Microsoft Office folder, right-click the Microsoft Office Word 2007 item, and choose Pin To Start Menu from the shortcut menu. (If a Word icon already appears on the most frequently used programs section of the Start menu, you can right-click that icon instead of displaying the Microsoft Office folder.)

If you use Word in every Windows session, configure Windows to launch Word automatically each time you log on to Windows. The logon process then takes a few seconds longer, but you don't need to launch Word manually.

To make Windows launch Word automatically when you log on, follow these steps:

1. Choose Start | All Programs | Microsoft Office to display the Microsoft Office folder.
2. Right-click the Microsoft Office Word 2007 item, and then choose Copy from the shortcut menu to copy it to the Clipboard.
3. On the Start menu's All Programs submenu, right-click the Startup folder, and then choose Open to open a Windows Explorer window showing its contents.
4. Right-click in the window, and then choose Paste Shortcut from the shortcut menu.
5. Click the Close button (the × button) to close the Startup window.

If you're using Windows in a corporate environment, an administrator may have prevented you from customizing your startup group. If this is the case, you'll need to have an administrator customize the startup group for you.

Understand the Word Screen

When you open Word, it starts you off with a new, blank document (see Figure 1-1). Word displays the insertion point, a slowly blinking vertical line that indicates where text you type will land, at the beginning of the document, so you can just start typing if you're ready to create a document. The Home tab of the Ribbon contains the most widely useful commands, so Word displays it first. The tabs you see here always appear when you start Word, but other tabs appear automatically when you need to use other commands. For example, when you're working in a table, two table-related tabs appear.

Here are the basics of the Word window:

■ **Office Button menu**   Where earlier versions of Word had various menus (such as File, Edit, View, and Format) in the menu bar, Word 2007 has only the Office Button menu. This menu contains some of the commands that used to appear on the File menu in earlier versions of Word. You can open this menu by clicking it or by pressing ALT and then F (ALT, F).

■ **Quick Access Toolbar**   A new feature of Word 2007, the Quick Access Toolbar is a toolbar that provides quick access to the commands represented by the buttons you put on it. (See Chapter 9 for instructions on customizing the Quick Access Toolbar.) When you first start Word, the Quick Access Toolbar appears in its small version, which is positioned to the right of the Office Button menu. You can also display a larger version of the Quick Access Toolbar below the Ribbon instead of the small version. The Quick Access Toolbar at first contains only three buttons: Save, Undo, and Redo.

■ **Ribbon**   Another new feature of Word 2007, the Ribbon is a tabbed bar across the top of the Word window, appearing just below the window's title bar. The Ribbon replaces all the remaining menus and toolbars that previous versions of Word used. Each tab of the Ribbon contains a different set of controls that are linked thematically. Only one tab's contents can be displayed at a time. To switch tabs, you click the text label at the top: Home, Insert, Page Layout, References, Mailings, Review, or View. (If you've used an earlier version of Word, you may mistake the tab labels for menus at first glance, because they appear where menus used to.) Figure 1-1 shows the Home tab of the Ribbon selected, as it is by default when you open a document.

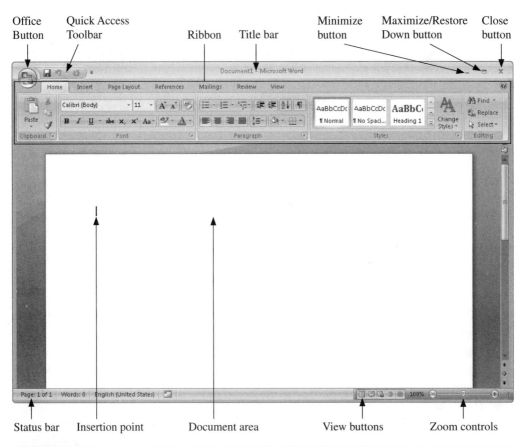

FIGURE 1-1   The Word application window with a document open.

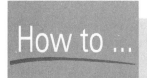**How to ...**

Collapse the Ribbon to Get More Space on Screen

When you need as much space as possible on screen to view a document, you can collapse (or "minimize") the Ribbon to only its labels by double-clicking the label of the tab you're currently using.

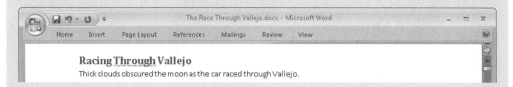

While the Ribbon is minimized, you can click a tab to display the Ribbon so that you can issue a command. Once you've issued the command, the Ribbon minimizes itself again.

Double-click the current tab again to expand the Ribbon back to its normal size when you want to have it displayed again.

- **Title bar**   The title bar shows the document's name and the program's name. When you've just opened Word, and the document's name is Document1, this information isn't much help. But when you've got many documents open, the name helps you distinguish one document from another, or one version of the same document from another. Word uses a separate window for each document you open, rather than opening each document as a smaller window within the main program window (as some other programs do).

- **Minimize button, Maximize/Restore Down button, and Close button**   Use these buttons to resize or close the window. These buttons are standard on most Windows programs, so you're probably used to the way they work: Click the Minimize button to reduce the window to a button on the taskbar, click the Maximize/Restore Down button to flip between a maximized window and a "normal" (nonmaximized) one, and click the Close button to close the window.

- **Status bar**   This bar across the bottom of the window provides a page readout, spell-check status, and other information about the document. Word displays different information on the status bar depending on what you're doing.

- **View buttons**   Click a button to change the view—for example, from Print Layout view (which shows each page approximately as it will print) to Outline view (which shows the document as an outline of different heading levels). You'll learn more about views toward the end of this chapter.

- **Zoom controls** The readout at the left end of the zoom controls shows the current zoom percentage. You can zoom by dragging the slider or by clicking the – (minus) and + (plus) buttons.

- **Insertion point** A slowly blinking thin vertical line, the insertion point marks the point at which characters you type will land in the document.

- **Document area** This area is where you create your document. The insertion point indicates where text you type will appear in the document.

- **View buttons** These buttons let you change quickly from one of Word's five main views to another.

- **Help Button** Click this button to display the Help window, in which you can search for help on any Word topic.

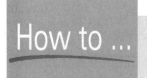 **Work with Task Panes**

Like Word 2002 (which introduced task panes) and Word 2003 (which continued them), Word 2007 uses various task panes—but with major differences from Word 2002 and Word 2003. Here's what you need to know to work with task panes:

- Word 2007 no longer displays the Getting Started task pane when you launch Word. For anyone who's used to closing the Getting Started task pane at the beginning of each Word session, this is a relief.

- Where Word 2002 and Word 2003 display only one task pane at a time but let you switch from one task pane to another by using the drop-down menu of whichever task pane is currently displayed, Word 2007 displays multiple task panes as needed.

- Most task panes appear in the default position, *docked* (attached) to the right side of the Word window. You can drag any task pane by its title bar to any other edge of the window to dock it there if you prefer. Alternatively, you can display the task pane *undocked*, floating freely anywhere in the Word window or outside it, by dragging it away from the side of the window to which it's currently docked.

- You can close a task pane by clicking the Close button (the × button) at its upper-right corner.

- When the task pane is docked, you can resize it by dragging the border on its open side to change its width or depth. When the task pane is floating free, you can resize it by dragging any side or corner.

■ Word displays some task panes automatically in response to actions you take. You can display other task panes manually when you need them. Word makes task panes available only when you can use them and doesn't allow you to display a task pane that's irrelevant to the task you're currently performing.

■ Most of the task panes are available most of the time when you're working in a document in Word, but some are available only for specific files. When a task pane isn't available, it appears dimmed in the list.

Here are examples of common task panes you'll use when working in Word:

■ **Clip Art**   Enables you to search for graphics files organized by collection, file type, and location. You can display this task pane by clicking the Insert tab, going to the Illustrations group, and then clicking the Clip Art button.

■ **Research**   You can search specified encyclopedias, thesauruses, and translation tools for more information about selected words. You can display this task pane by clicking the Review tab, going to the Proofing group, and then clicking the Research button.

■ **Clipboard**   The Office Clipboard can hold up to 24 items copied or cut from any Office application. You can then paste these items elsewhere. You can display this task pane by clicking the Home tab, going to the Clipboard group, and then clicking the Clipboard button (the tiny button, with an arrow pointing down and to the right, at the right end of the bar that says "Clipboard").

Understand Documents and Their Components

Pretty much any work you do in Word involves a document: creating text, editing it, reviewing it, or deleting it in fury.

Almost all documents contain text, but they can also contain various other items, including (but not limited to) the items on the following page.

■ **Headers and footers**   A *header* is an area for information that is repeated at the top of each page—for example, the document's title or page number. A *footer* is an area for information that is repeated at the bottom of each page. You can use either headers or footers or both.

■ **Tables**   A *table* is a frame for laying out text or other items in a grid of rows and columns. Tables are great for arranging complex data.

■ **Pictures, sounds, and videos**   Word lets you insert multimedia objects such as pictures, sounds, and videos in your documents. Sound and videos aren't much use on paper, but they work well in documents for reading online or for web pages.

■ **Graphical objects**   Word lets you insert shapes, charts, diagrams, and other objects, such as WordArt (decorative text made of distorted letters).

Figure 1-2 shows a document that includes several types of components.

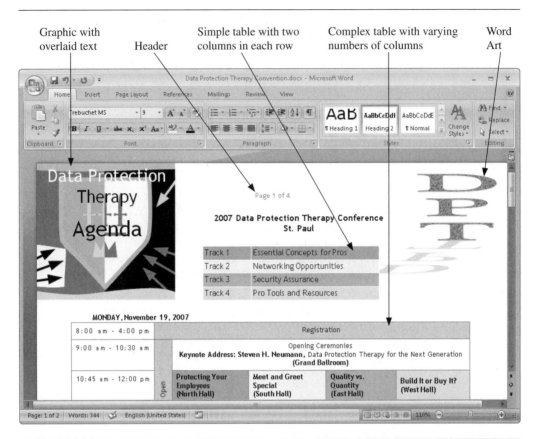

FIGURE 1-2 A document may contain nothing but text, but it can also contain elements such as headers and footers, graphical objects, and tables.

Open an Existing Document

To work with an existing document, you open it. Word lets you open documents in any of three ways:

- From the Office Button menu
- From the Open dialog box
- From a Windows Explorer window or your desktop

Open a Recent Document Using the Office Button Menu

The easiest way to open a document is to choose it from the list on the Office Button menu:

1. Click the Office Button or press ALT, F. Word displays the Office Button menu (see Figure 1-3), which displays a list of the documents you've opened most recently or that you've pinned to the menu.

2. Click the document you want to open.

   ■ If the document is one of the first nine on the list, you can also press the underlined number to its left. For example, to open the first document on the list, press ALT, F, 1 in sequence.

   ■ To see the path for a document, hover the mouse pointer over it for a moment until Word displays a ScreenTip, a little pop-up box containing information.

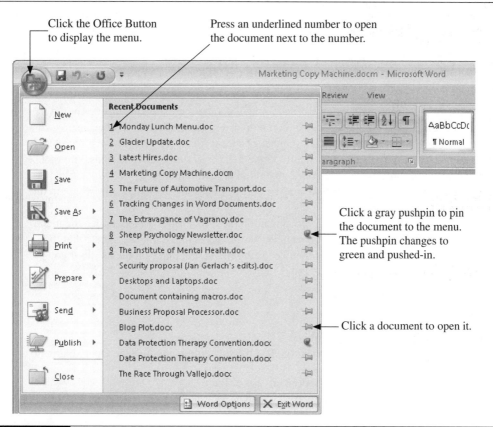

FIGURE 1-3　The Office Button menu contains many of the commands that appear on the File menu in earlier versions of Word.

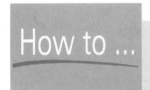

Make the Most of the Office Button Menu

Having your nine most recently used documents on the Office Button menu is handy—but you may find nine is not nearly enough. You can increase the number shown up to 50, and you can *pin* (fasten) particular documents to the menu so that they remain there even if you haven't used them recently.

To customize the Office Button menu, follow these steps:

1. Click the Office Button, and then click Word Options. Word displays the Word Options dialog box.

2. In the left pane, click the Advanced category, and then scroll down to the Display section.

3. In the Show This Number Of Recent Documents box, set the number of documents you want to have on the Office Button menu. You can choose any number between 0 and 50 (inclusive).

4. Click the OK button. Word closes the Word Options dialog box.

When you increase the number in the Show This Number Of Recent Documents drop-down list, Word doesn't add the extra files immediately to the list on the Office Button menu, but rather adds them one by one as you open and close files. This is because Word stores the names only of the specified number of recent files—it doesn't have a secret store of extra filenames that it can add instantly to the list. So if, for security reasons, you reduce the number to 0, someone can't increase that number and immediately see which files you've been working with. (But they may be able to find that information elsewhere in the Windows operating system.)

To make Word keep a particular document on the Office Button menu, open the menu, and then click the pin next to the file's name. Word pushes in the pin to indicate that the document is "pinned" in place, and then keeps the file in that place on the list until you unpin it by clicking the pin again.

Use the Open Dialog Box

If the document you want doesn't appear on the Office Button menu, use the Open dialog box. Follow these steps:

1. Click the Office Button, and then click Open. Alternatively, press CTRL-O. Word displays the Open dialog box (see Figure 1-4).

TIP *You can enlarge the Open dialog box by dragging the dotted triangle in the lower-right corner down and to the right.*

2. Go to the folder that contains the document by using one of these methods:

■ Choose a drive or folder from the Address box at the top of the dialog box.

■ Click one of the buttons in the Favorite Links bar or Places bar on the left of the dialog box.

■ Navigate through the folders in the main box.

3. Click the document, and then click the Open button. Word opens the document.

Click the Recent Pages drop-down button to reveal a list of recent folders.

Click one of these navigation buttons to display a list of folders contained in the folder before the button.

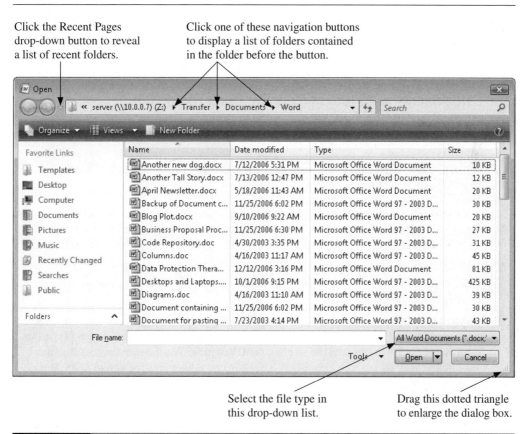

Select the file type in this drop-down list.

Drag this dotted triangle to enlarge the dialog box.

FIGURE 1-4 The Open dialog box lets you open documents that don't appear in the recently used list on the Office Button menu.

Search for a Document

If you're not sure where the document is or what it's called, you can search for it directly from the Open dialog box. Follow these steps:

1. Click the Office Button, and then click Open. Alternatively, press CTRL-O. Word displays the Open dialog box.

2. If you know which folder contains the document, go to that folder.

   ■ Starting your search from the correct folder makes it go faster.

   ■ If you don't know which folder the document is in, at least choose the correct drive rather than searching your entire computer—unless you don't know the drive.

3. Type the search term in the Search box in the upper-right corner of the Open dialog box, and then press ENTER. Word searches the current folder and its subfolders, and returns matching results.

4. If the document you want is listed, click it, and then click the Open button. Word opens the document.

Manage Documents and Folders from the Open Dialog Box

The Open dialog box's main purpose is opening documents, but you can also use it to manage documents and folders. This capability is handy when you find that you need to rename a document that you're about to open: Renaming the document in the Open dialog box saves you having to open a Windows Explorer window for the task. You can also manage documents and folders from the Save As dialog box.

Here's what you can do:

■ **Rename a document or folder**   Click the document or folder, pause, and then click again. Word displays an edit box around it. Type the new name, and then press ENTER.

■ **Delete a document or folder**   Click the document or folder, and then press DELETE (or right-click and choose Delete from the context menu). Click the Yes button in the confirmation dialog box.

■ **Create a new folder**   Navigate to the folder in which you want to create the new folder, and then click the Create New Folder button. The New Folder dialog box opens. Type the folder name, and then press ENTER or click the OK button. Word opens the folder in the Open dialog box, which isn't helpful, as it contains no documents for you to open. But when you're using the Save As dialog box, being able to create a folder and switch to it like this is very useful.

■ **Copy a document or folder**   Right-click the document or folder, and then choose Copy. Navigate to the destination folder, right-click, and then choose Paste from the context menu.

■ **Move a document or folder** Right-click the document or folder, and then choose Cut. Navigate to the destination folder, right-click, and then choose Paste from the context menu.

■ **View the properties for a document** If you're not sure from the name, size, and other attributes visible in the Open dialog box that you've found the right file, right-click it, and then choose Properties from the context menu. The Properties dialog box opens, showing two or more tabs of information about the document. (These are the Windows properties, not the Word properties, which you'll learn about in Chapter 2.)

Open a Document from a Windows Explorer Window

If you know which folder contains the document you want, using the Open dialog box to open the document from Word is easy. But if you need to browse for the document, or search for it, you may find using Windows Explorer easier.

Once you've located the document, double-click its icon or name in the Windows Explorer window to open the document in Word.

If the Open dialog box is displayed in Word, it prevents the document you double-clicked in Windows Explorer from opening. Just press ESC or click the Cancel button to close the Open dialog box, and then the document opens.

Open a Document from Outlook

If you use Outlook as your e-mail program, your colleagues may send you Word documents attached to messages. You have three choices for such a document: You can preview it in Outlook; save it to a folder, and then open it from Word; or open it directly from Outlook. Each method has its pros and cons.

■ **Preview a document in Outlook** Preview the document in Outlook by clicking its title in the message pane. You can't edit the document in Outlook, but you can see enough to decide whether to open the document for editing in Word. Layout elements such as columns, pictures, and text boxes may not appear correctly, so if the document looks wrong, the fault probably lies with Outlook rather than the document itself. The first time you preview a document, Outlook warns you that you should preview only files from a trustworthy source. Click the Preview File button if you want to go ahead. (If you're not sure the source is trustworthy, or if you suspect the file may have been sent by malware rather than by the person who appears to be the sender, check with the sender before previewing the document.)

■ **Save the document to a folder, and then open it from that folder** In the message pane, right-click the attachment's name and choose Save As, or choose File | Save Attachments, and then choose the attachment's name from the submenu. Outlook displays the Save Attachment dialog box. Choose the folder in which you want to save the document, and then click the Save button. Switch to Word, click the Office Button,

Double-Clicking in Windows Explorer Opens the Document in the Wrong Program

If, when you double-click a Word document in a Windows Explorer window, Windows opens the document in the wrong program, it's because the document's file extension (for example, .doc) is associated with a program other than Word. To change the file extension's association back to Word, follow these steps:

1. In the Windows Explorer window, right-click the document you want to open, and then choose Properties from the context menu. Windows displays the Properties dialog box.

2. On the General tab, look at the Opens With readout to see which program is associated with this file extension. For example, the .doc file extension might be associated with OpenOffice.org or WordPad.

3. Click the Change button. Windows displays the Open With dialog box.

4. In the Recommended Programs list box, select Microsoft Office Word.

5. If the Always Use The Selected Program To Open This Kind Of File check box is available, select it.

6. Click the OK button. Windows closes the Open With dialog box, returning you to the Properties dialog box.

7. Click the OK button. Windows closes the Properties dialog box.

Double-click the document in Windows Explorer again. Windows opens the document in Word.

click Open, and then open the document. Use this technique when you want to edit a document or when you need to know which folder the document is in so that you can open, access, and manage it.

■ **Open the document directly from Outlook so that you can read it in Word** In the message pane, right-click the attachment's name and choose Open. The Opening Mail Attachment dialog box opens (as shown here) to remind you that you should open only attachments from trustworthy sources. Click the Open button if you trust the sender. The document opens in Word in Full Screen Reading view and as a read-only document, so you can't save changes to the original file. You can save changes to the document by clicking the Office Button, clicking Save As, and then specifying a different filename or folder in the Save As dialog box.

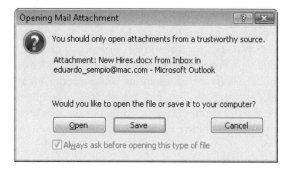

NOTE *When you open a document, Word may display a Security Warning bar below the Ribbon telling you that "Macros have been disabled." If you don't need the macros, click the Close button (the × button) at the right end of the Security Warning bar to close the bar. If you do need the macros, and you're sure they're safe, click the Options button. Word displays the Microsoft Office Security Options dialog box. Select the Enable This Content option button, and then click the OK button.*

Open Documents Saved in Different Formats

All other things being equal, Word is happiest opening documents in the various Word formats. When you select the All Word Documents item in the Files Of Type drop-down list, the Open dialog box shows you the file types explained in Table 1-1.

File Extension	File Type
.docx	Word 2007 format documents
.docm	Macro-enabled Word documents
.dotx	Word templates
.dotm	Macro-enabled Word templates
.doc	Word 97-2003 format documents (or documents from even earlier versions of Word for Windows, or Word for the Mac, or WordPerfect)
.dot	Word 97-2003 format templates (or templates from even earlier versions of Word)
.htm, .html, .mht, .mhtml	Web pages
.rtf	Rich text format files (text with formatting)
.url	URL files (Internet addresses)
.xml	XML documents

TABLE 1-1   Word Document Formats Included in the "All Word Documents" Category in the Files Of Type Drop-Down List

If your documents are in any of these formats, you'll see them immediately in the Open dialog box. To see documents in another format, choose that format in the Files Of Type drop-down list. Word comes with file converters for text (.txt), WordPerfect (.wpd), and Microsoft Works (.wps) files. If you have installed additional file converters, you may be able to open other formats.

If the Files Of Type drop-down list doesn't show the format of the document you want to open, you don't have a file converter for that format. Unless you can get and install a file converter (try searching online for **Word file converter** and the file extension or format), you can't open files in that format. Usually the best solution is to open the document in a program that can open that format (for example, the program that created it) and then save it in a format that Word can open—for example, a Word document format or the rich text format. This is often easier said than done; if you don't have the program, you may need to get someone else to convert the document for you.

After opening a document in another format, save it in the Word Document format if you want to be able to work with it easily in Word in the future. Follow these steps:

1. Click the Office Button, and then click Save As. Word displays the Save As dialog box.

2. Change the filename in the File Name text box if necessary.

3. Choose a different folder if necessary.

4. Choose Word Document in the Save As Type drop-down list.

5. Click the Save button. Word closes the Save As dialog box and saves the document.

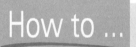

How to ... Display File Extensions

To display file extensions in Windows Explorer windows and common dialog boxes, follow these steps:

1. Choose Start | Computer. Windows displays a Windows Explorer window showing Computer.

2. Choose Organize | Folder And Search Options. Windows displays the Folder Options dialog box.

3. On the View tab, clear the Hide File Extensions For Known File Types check box.

4. Click the OK button. Windows closes the Folder Options dialog box.

To hide file extensions again, select the Hide File Extensions For Known File Types check box.

Convert a Document to Word 2007 Format

Word 2007 introduces a new format for Word documents. Confusingly, the new format is called "Word Document," just as the previous format used to be; the previous format is now called "Word 97-2003 Document." However, the new format uses the .docx file extension rather than the .doc extension that earlier versions of Word used, so you easily can tell the formats apart if you have Windows set to display file extensions. (See the "Display File Extensions" sidebar for instructions on displaying file extensions.)

When you open a document created in an earlier version of Word, Word displays the words "[Compatibility Mode]" in the title bar after the document's name to remind you that the document isn't in Word's preferred format.

If you will use an older document only with Word 2007, you may want to update it to one of the Word 2007 formats so that you can take advantage of all the latest features (such as the XML-based file format). However, if you need to be able to open the document using older versions of Word, you may be better off leaving the document in its current format. You can download conversion filters for Word 2003 and other versions from the Microsoft web site (http://www.microsoft.com) that enable these versions of Word to open Word 2007 documents, but you and your colleagues may prefer not to install these filters on all the computers you use for editing Word documents.

To update the document to the Word 2007 format, follow these steps:

1. Open the document in Word 2007.

2. Click the Office button, and then choose Convert. A Microsoft Office Word dialog box appears, as shown here. The dialog box warns you that the layout of the document may change. Normally, any such changes will be minor.

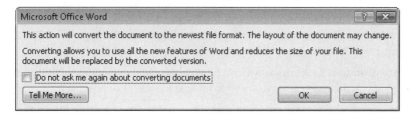

3. Select the Do Not Ask Me Again About Converting Documents check box if you don't want to see this dialog box again.

4. Click the OK button. Word converts the document to the new format and removes the words "[Compatibility Mode]" from the title bar, but doesn't save the document.

5. Click the Save button on the Quick Access Toolbar or press CTRL-S. Word displays the Save As dialog box and selects the Word Document item in the Save As Type drop-down list.

6. Click the Save button. Word closes the Save As dialog box and saves the document.

Use Views, Zooming, and Splitting

To work effectively in a document, you need to see the elements you're creating or manipulating—text, pictures, headers or footers, and so on. Word provides six different ways of viewing your documents: Print Layout view, Full Screen Reading view, Web Layout view, Outline view, Draft view (which used to be called Normal view), and Print Preview.

As their names suggest, the views are designed for different purposes, but you can use them pretty much as you see fit. For example, you might prefer to compose your documents in Print Preview rather than in Draft view or Print Layout view. You can even edit in Full Screen Reading view, which is great for seeing a good amount of a document in an easy-to-read format. This makes editing easier too.

Choose Essential View Options

When you're getting started with Word, spend a few minutes configuring view options to suit your monitor and the way you work. Word comes reasonably well set up for editing in Print Layout view, but you may want to suppress the vertical ruler. Many people find it helpful to turn on text wrapping for Draft view and Outline view and dispose of the horizontal scroll bar (see Figure 1-5). You may also want to display the Style area so that you can instantly see which style each paragraph has. The lower part of Figure 1-5 shows the Style area.

To choose view options, follow these steps:

1. Click the Office Button, and then click Word Options. Word displays the Word Options dialog box.

2. In the Left pane, click the Advanced category, and then scroll down to the Show Document Content area, and then choose whether to wrap text.

3. To make Word wrap text to the full width of the document window rather than to the margins in Draft view or Outline view, select the Show Text Wrapped Within The Document Window check box. This setting helps in two ways:

   ■ If the document's text is too wide to fit in the window, wrapping the text makes it fit, so that you no longer need to scroll from side to side.

   ■ If the document's text is narrower than the window, the wrapping makes the text go all the way across the window, so that you don't have a column of wasted space at the right side of the window.

4. Scroll down to the Display area, and then choose whether to display the horizontal scroll bar, vertical ruler, and Style area:

   ■ If your monitor is wide enough that you don't need the horizontal scroll bar for scrolling from one side of a document to another, clear the Horizontal Scroll Bar check box. (If you've selected the Show Text Wrapped Within The Document Window check box, you won't need the horizontal scroll bar.)

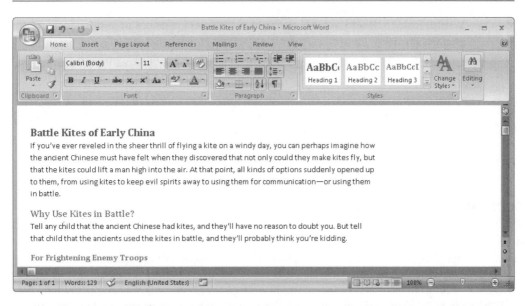

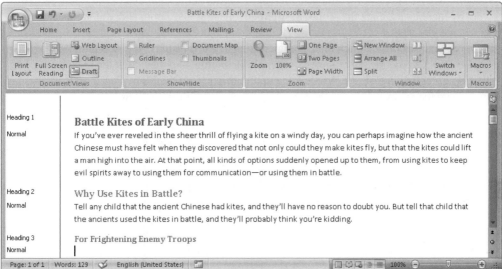

FIGURE 1-5   In Draft view (top), the horizontal scroll bar near the bottom of the window is usually a waste of space, as you'll often find empty space to the right of the text.

■ If you don't want to see the vertical ruler in Print Layout view, clear the Show Vertical Ruler In Print Layout View check box. Unless you need to position text and graphics precisely, the vertical ruler is normally not much use.

■ To make Word display the Style area, set the value in the Style Area Pane Width In Draft And Outline Views box to greater than 0 inches. (Try 1 inch to start with.)

Once you've displayed the Style area, you can adjust its width by dragging the vertical line that separates it from the document area. To close the Style area, drag this line all the way to the left edge of the window.

5. Click the OK button. Word closes the Word Options dialog box and applies the settings you chose.

Zoom the View In and Out

How large a document's text appears on screen, and how easy it is to read, depends on the resolution of your screen, the font and font size, and how far the view is zoomed in or out. Once you've chosen a suitable screen resolution and a font and font size that work for the document, you may need to zoom the view in to make the text appear larger or zoom out so that you can see more of the document at once. Word lets you zoom anywhere from 10 percent (minuscule) to 500 percent (huge).

To zoom in by 10 percent increments, click the + button at the right end of the status bar. To zoom out by increments, click the – button. Alternatively, drag the Zoom slider along its axis to the percentage you want.

For more precise control, click the Zoom percentage. Word displays the Zoom dialog box (see Figure 1-6). Choose the percentage or other option button, and then click the OK button. The Text Width option button, the Whole Page option button, and the Many Pages option button and drop-down list are available only in Print Layout view and Print Preview.

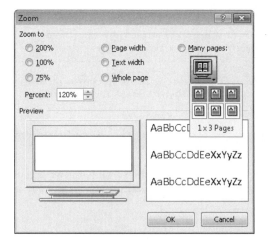

FIGURE 1-6 Use the Zoom dialog box to apply a precise zoom percentage or to make Word display multiple pages at the same time.

Change the View

Word 2007's status bar includes buttons that show you which of the five main views you're using (there's no button for Print Preview). Click another button to switch to that view.

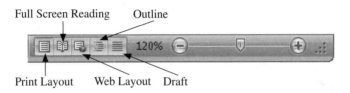

Change Views Using the Keyboard

Clicking the View icons is easy enough, but when your hands are on the keyboard, you may prefer to switch view by pressing key sequences. Table 1-2 shows you the keys to press.

Use the Improved Status Bar

The status bar, the strip that appears along the bottom of the Word window, receives a complete and welcome makeover in Word 2007. In earlier versions, the status bar packed in two page readouts, a section readout, information about the position of the insertion point in layout views, a spell-check status readout, and indicators for macro recording, revision marking (also known as Track Changes), extension mode, and overtype mode.

Word 2007 dispenses with the less useful indicators—but you can put them back if you need them. Instead, you get a simple "Page X of Y" readout (for example, "Page 4 of 27"), a word count, a spelling-check indicator, buttons for changing the view (which you've already learned about), and controls for zooming in and out (see Figure 1-7).

Key Sequence	Switches to This View
ALT, W, P	Print Layout view
ALT, W, F	Full Screen Reading view
ALT, W, L	Web Layout view
ALT, W, U	Outline view and Master Document Tools
ALT, W, E	Draft view
ALT, F, W, V	Print Preview

TABLE 1-2   Keyboard Sequences for Changing the View

How to ... Change the Default View and Zoom to Suit You

Word typically starts you off with a document in Print Layout view at 100 percent zoom. If that suits you, leave it. Otherwise, let Word know your preferred view and zoom. To do so, follow these steps:

1. Start Word. If Word is already running, close it and restart it. You need a blank document open, so if Word doesn't open a new document at startup, press CTRL-N to create one.

2. On the status bar, click the View button for the view you want.

3. Also on the status bar, choose the zoom you want:

   - Click the Zoom In button or Zoom Out button or drag the View slider.

   - For finer control, click the zoom percentage readout and use the Zoom dialog box to choose the exact percentage.

4. Click the Office Button, and then choose Exit Word. Word closes.

5. Restart Word. Even though you haven't "saved" any changes in the conventional sense, Word restarts with the view and zoom you specified.

NOTE *Word 2007's live word count in the status bar is a major improvement over earlier versions. When no text is selected, the Words readout displays the word count for the entire document. When you select part of the document, the readout displays the word count for the selection, a slash, and the word count for the entire document: for example, **25/568**.*

The status bar also displays other controls as needed, as you'll see later in this book.

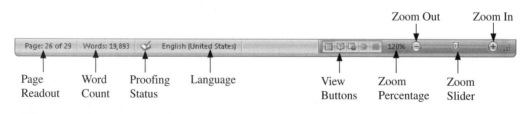

FIGURE 1-7 Word 2007 removes little-used readouts from the status bar and adds the view buttons and zoom controls.

Shortcuts in the Status Bar

You can save time by using the click shortcuts hidden in the status bar:

- Click the Page readout to display the Go To tab of the Find and Replace dialog box. (If you have any of the other position-information readouts displayed—for example, Formatted Page Number, Section, or Line Number—you can double-click these as well for the same effect.)
- Click the Words readout to open the Word Count dialog box.
- Click the Proofing readout to start checking spelling and grammar. (If you've turned off spelling or grammar, Word runs only the check that you haven't turned off.)
- Click the Language readout to open the Language dialog box.
- Click the Zoom percentage readout to open the Zoom dialog box.

Use Print Layout View

Print Layout view (see Figure 1-8) displays your document much as it will look when printed, showing all elements that will print. Print Layout view displays any headers and footers that the document contains, together with any white space at the top and bottom of pages. Turning white space off helps you see each page larger but prevents you from seeing headers and footers.

Use Draft View

Normal view has been Word's standard view since the first Windows versions, but Word 2007 renames this view to "Draft view" and makes Print Layout view the standard view. Use Draft view for composing and editing text when you're concentrating on the content rather than layout.

Draft view (see Figure 1-9) shows as much of the document's main text on screen as possible by leaving out the margins, the headers and footers, and other special items such as footnotes, endnotes, and comments. Draft view displays the document's full contents and most of the font and paragraph formatting. It also displays other items that appear in the text layer of the document, but not items that appear in the drawing layer. For example, if you place a picture in a document inline, so that it's part of the text, it appears in Draft view. If you place the picture in front of the text, or behind the text, it doesn't appear in Draft view, only in the layout views (Print Layout view, Web Layout view, Reading Layout view, or Print Preview).

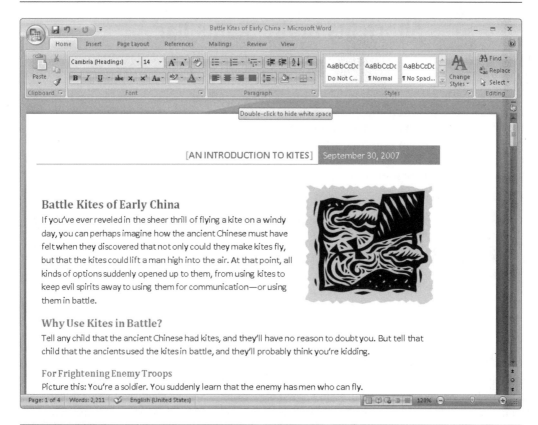

FIGURE 1-8 Print Layout view shows a document page by page. You can toggle the display of white space on and off by double-clicking the bar between pages.

In Draft view, you can display the Style area at the left side of the screen so that you can see the style applied to each paragraph. (See the section "Choose Essential View Options" earlier in this chapter for instructions on displaying the Style area.) You'll probably find the Style area useful when you're checking the formatting in a document.

Use Web Layout View

Web Layout view displays the document approximately as it will appear when saved as a web page:

- Margins, page breaks, and headers and footers do not appear.
- Lines wrap depending on the width of the window and the degree of zoom rather than on the margins.
- Graphics appear in their final positions. Background elements and colors appear.

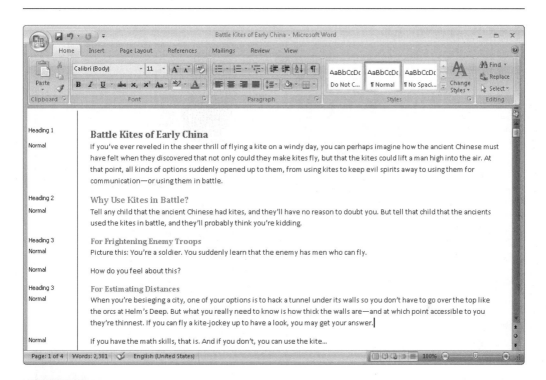

FIGURE 1-9 Use Draft view for composing and editing text when you need to see only inline elements.

Use Full Screen Reading View

Full Screen Reading view (see Figure 1-10) reformats your document to make it easy to read on the screen and displays a minimal set of controls intended to provide only enough functionality for reading. By default, Full Screen Reading view turns each screenful of text into a "page" and displays two pages at a time. Full Screen Reading view doesn't display the true margins or layout elements such as headers and footers.

The View Options drop-down list includes commands for increasing and decreasing the text size, switching between one and two pages, allowing editing (Allow Typing), tracking changes, and viewing comments and changes. The Tools drop-down list provides access to Research tools, a Translation ScreenTip that lets you view an immediate translation of the current word in your chosen language, highlighting, commenting, and Find.

Press ESC or click the Close button in the upper-right corner to move from Full Screen Reading view to Print Layout view. (Even if you were using a view other than Print Layout view before you switched to Full Screen Reading view, Word returns you to Print Layout view.)

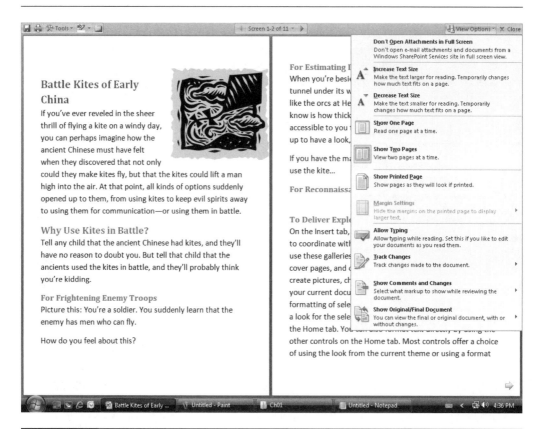

FIGURE 1-10 Use Full Screen Reading view when you need to read a document at a comfortable size on screen.

If you want to see how the document will appear when printed, choose View Options | Show Printed Page. When you're viewing printed pages, the Margin Settings for Actual Page submenu becomes available. Use this submenu to display the margins, suppress the margins, or let Word decide whether to display them (if the text is large enough to read with the margins displayed) or suppress them to make room to display the text at a larger size.

Use Outline View

Outline view (see Figure 1-11) helps you structure and organize complex documents by collapsing your document so that you see only headings of specified levels. For example, you can display only Heading 3 paragraphs and higher-level headings (Heading 1 and Heading 2 paragraphs).

Outline view also includes Word's master document feature, which lets you break up a long document into subdocuments that you and your colleagues can open and edit separately. Chapter 17 discusses how to use outlining and master documents.

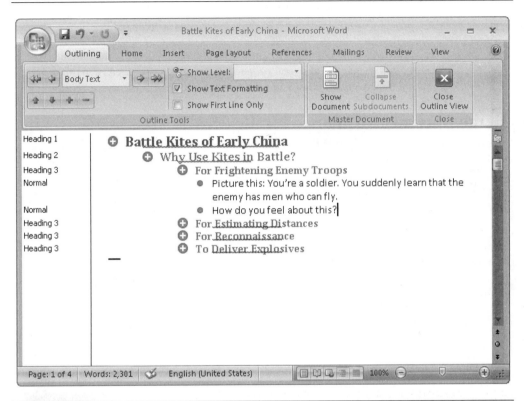

FIGURE 1-11 Use Outline view for outlining and structuring documents and for creating master documents. In Outline view, Word adds the Outlining tab to the Ribbon.

Use Print Preview

Print Preview displays your document as it will print on the current printer. Print Preview hides all the Ribbon's tabs and displays the Print Preview tab instead. You can double-click the Print Preview tab to minimize the Ribbon. Double-click the tab again to restore the Ribbon.

To switch to Print Preview, click the Office Button, and then choose Print | Print Preview. Word automatically changes to Magnifier mode, in which the mouse pointer is a magnifying glass that you can click once to zoom in on the clicked point and click again to zoom out again.

Magnifier mode is handy if you want to use Print Preview simply to make sure that the document is fit for printing. But if you have a high-resolution monitor, you may want to edit in Print Preview as well. To do so, clear the Magnifier check box in the Preview group. Word switches from Magnifier mode to Edit mode, in which you can edit your document as in other views. (To go back to Magnifier mode, select the Magnifier check box again.)

If your monitor has a high enough resolution to display two (or more) pages at a readable size, Print Preview is good for writing and editing. Unlike Print Layout view, in which you can see the end of one page and the start of the next when you scroll down, Print Preview always displays full pages. So when you press PAGE DOWN or PAGE UP, you see the next set or previous set of pages, rather than seeing partial pages. This sounds like a minor difference, but it makes scanning through a long document much faster.

Split the Document Window

If you need to view or work with two parts of the same document at once, you can split the document window into two panes (see Figure 1-12). Double-click the split box at the top end of the vertical scroll bar to split the window halfway down. In each pane, you can display a different part of the document, change the view, or zoom to a different percentage. To move from one pane to the other, click in the pane you want to move to, or press F6.

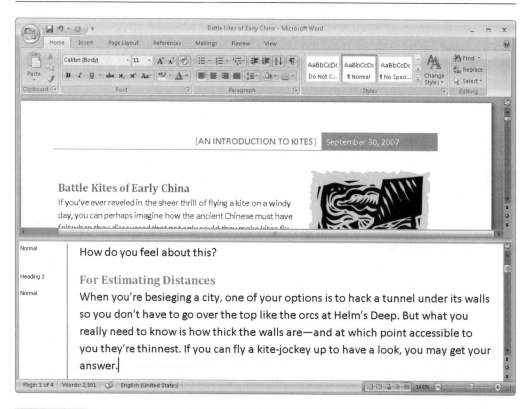

FIGURE 1-12   Split the document window so that you can work in two separate parts of it or use two different views or zoom percentages.

To create a custom split, drag the split box down the vertical scroll bar, or simply drag the split bar up or down the window from its default position. Alternatively, click the View tab, go to the Window group, and click the Split button to display a movable split bar. To position the split bar with the mouse, move the mouse pointer to where you want the split, and then click. To position the split bar from the keyboard, move the bar using the up and down arrow keys, and then press ENTER to fix it in place.

You can remove the split in any of these ways:

- ■ **Mouse**   Double-click the split bar or drag it to the top or bottom of the window.
- ■ **Ribbon**   Click the View tab, go to the Window group, and click the Remove Split button.
- ■ **Keyboard**   Press CTRL-ALT-S.

Open Extra Windows to See More of a Document

When you open a document or create a new document, Word displays that document in a single window. But you can also display additional windows of the same document so that you can see two or more separate parts at once or so that you can work in multiple views simultaneously.

To open a new window, click the View tab, go to the Window group, and click the New Window button. When you open a second window, Word adds :1 to the caption (the text that appears in the title bar) of the first window and :2 to the caption of the second window so that you can tell them apart.

For example, if you have one window open on Document 1, the title bar reads Document 1 — Microsoft Word. When you open another window, the first window's caption changes to Document 1:1 — Microsoft Word, and the second window receives the caption Document 1:2 — Microsoft Word. Subsequent windows you open on the same document receive higher numbers.

To switch from one window to another, use any of these means:

- ■ **Mouse**   Click the window you want or click its Taskbar button.
- ■ **Ribbon**   Click the View tab, go to the Window group, click the Switch Windows button, and then either click the window on the list or press the underlined number next to it.
- ■ **Keyboard**   Press CTRL-F6 or ALT-F6 to select the next window. Press CTRL-SHIFT-F6 or ALT-SHIFT-F6 to select the previous window. (If you have only two windows open, these commands have the same effect.) These commands move you through the stack of all open windows, not just the windows for the active document.

When you close any but the last window of a document that contains unsaved changes, Word doesn't prompt you to save the changes, because one or more other windows remains open: You're closing the window rather than the document. When you close the last window, and so close the document, Word prompts you to save any unsaved changes in the document.

Get Help with Word

To get help with using Word, follow these steps:

1. Press F1 or click the Microsoft Office Word Help icon at the right end of the Ribbon (the question mark icon). Word displays the Word Help window (see Figure 1-13).

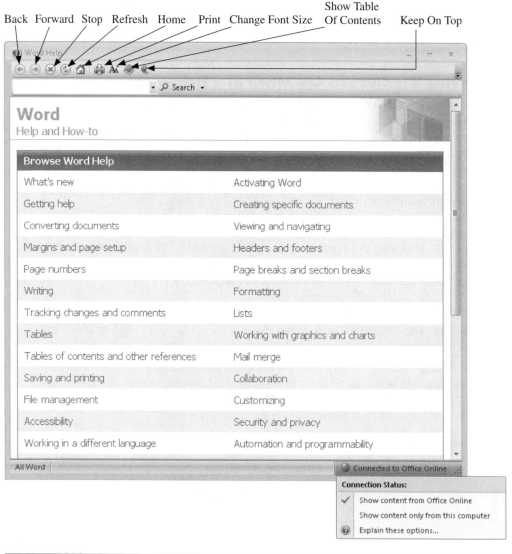

FIGURE 1-13   Use the Word Help window to browse help topics or search for help.

TIP   *You can switch between using Office Online help content and using only the help on your computer by using the drop-down list at the lower-right corner of the window.*

2.   To see what topics are available, click the links in the Browse Word Help list.

3.   To search for help, click in the Search box, type one or more keywords, and then click the Search button. You can confine the search to online content or offline content or to a particular help category either offline or online, by clicking the drop-down button on the Search button, and then choosing an item on the menu (shown here). Click a search result to display the related topic.

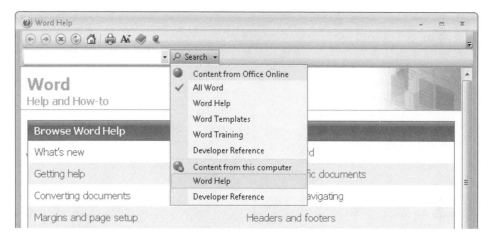

4.   To control whether the Help window appears on top of other windows (such as the Word window), click the Keep On Top button.

5.   When you've finished using help, click the Close button (the × button) to close the Word Help window.

Chapter 2

Create and Save Documents

How to...

- Create new documents
- Save documents
- Tell Word where to keep your documents and which format to use

Now that you know how to navigate Word's interface, you're ready to create documents of your own. This chapter shows you how to create and save documents.

If you're experienced with Windows programs, creating and saving documents may seem as straightforward as breaking an egg—but because Word offers many features and options to let you create exactly the documents you need, you must make many decisions even for creating and saving. To make these decisions, you need to understand the essentials of how Word handles documents and templates, the skeletons on which each document is based. This chapter tells you what you need to know.

To save yourself time and effort down the road, you'll probably want to change some of Word's standard settings when you're getting started. For example, Word presumes you'll keep all your documents in your Documents folder—so if you prefer to use another folder, you'll need to tell Word which folder to use. Word offers plenty of other features that are helpful and time-saving, provided you know where to find them and understand what they do.

Create New Documents

Every document is based on a *template*—a file that's used as the basis for the document. A template can contain anything from simple formatting to a fully formatted and nearly complete document that requires the user to do nothing more than fill in a few fields of information to complete a form. (For example, you might use such a template for a report, for a travel request, or for a performance evaluation.) A template can even include macros written in the Visual Basic for Applications (VBA) programming language that serve to automate the process of completing the document.

When you need a new document, you have several options, which are discussed in the following sections:

- **Create a blank document** You can create what Word calls a "blank document"— a document that contains no text, uses generic formatting that is widely appealing, and has moderate-size margins at the top, bottom, and sides of the page. Just as you can with a blank, letter-size sheet of paper, you can create any type of document in this blank document. Word creates a blank document for you each time you launch Word. A blank document is good when you need to create a new document from scratch, but often you can save time by using one of the other two options.

- **Create a new document based on a template** A *template* is a file that contains preset content, formatting, or both for a document, allowing you to complete the document more quickly. For example, a fax template typically contains the basic layout of the fax, so that you can quickly fill in the recipient, phone number, and message. By using the right template, you can save time and effort.

2

NOTE *Word comes equipped with templates for business letters, faxes, reports, and other common documents. You can download additional templates from Microsoft's Office Online site or create templates of your own (see Chapter 9).*

■ **Create a new document by cloning an existing document**   This technique can save you huge amounts of time and repetitive work. In effect, you use the existing document as a kind of informal template for the new document.

Create a Blank Document

You can create a blank document in any of these three ways:

■ Use the document that Word creates when you launch it.

■ Press CTRL-N.

■ Click the Office Button, click New, click the Blank Document item in the New Document dialog box, and then click the Create button.

Create a Document Based on a Template

A blank document is useful when you want to create a whole document from scratch using Word's standard settings. But frequently you'll want to base a new document on a template that has a particular design or content that will help you finish a document more quickly and with less effort. For example, you can get a jump-start on creating a memo by using a template that contains a standard memo layout with "To," "From," "Subject," and "Date" fields.

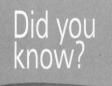
Did you know?

What the Normal Template Is

Word's blank documents may appear not to be based on a template, but in fact they use Word's most important template. This template is called the Normal template, has the file name Normal.dotm, and is loaded at the start of each Word session. (The file extension .dotm represents a template that can contain macros—short programs written in the Visual Basic for Applications programming language.)

When you install Word, the Normal template contains no text, so when you create a "blank" document, it actually is blank. Normally, you'll want to keep the Normal template blank, but you may want to change its margin, font, and paragraph settings so that each new blank document you create is set up the way you want. Chapter 4 explains how to change font and paragraph formatting. Chapter 5 shows you how to change margins and other page-layout settings.

You can also create a new document based on a template—a template that you or your company has created, one of Word's built-in templates, or a template that you download from the Microsoft Office Online web site. See the next section for instructions on downloading templates from this site. See the section "Create a New Template" in Chapter 9 for instructions on creating your own templates.

Create a New Document Based on a Template of Your Own

To create a document based on a template, follow these steps:

1. Click the Office Button, and then click New. Word displays the New Document dialog box (see Figure 2-1).

2. In the Template list in the left panel of the New Document dialog box, choose a template category.

   ■ **Blank And Recent**   This category shows you the Blank Document item, the New Blog Post item, and the templates you've used recently. You'll normally want to choose one from this category.

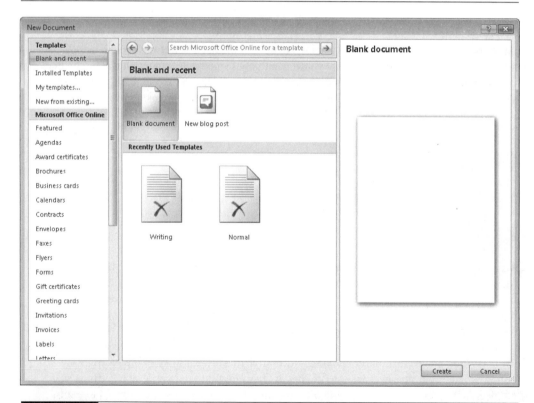

FIGURE 2-1   The New Document dialog box allows you to create a new blank document or template, a document based on a template, or a document based on an existing document.

■ **Installed Templates** This category shows the templates that are installed on your computer. These templates are installed in a shared folder for all Office users and include letters, reports, resumes, and faxes.

■ **My Templates** These are the templates that you've created or installed. Other Office users don't have access to these templates. When you select this item, Word displays the New dialog box (see Figure 2-2). When you first run Word, this dialog box may contain only the Normal template and the My Templates tab. Select the template you want, make sure the Document option button is selected in the Create New area, and then click the OK button.

■ **Microsoft Office Online** These categories let you access a wide variety of templates stored on the Microsoft Office Online site. Click the category to make Word load the templates in the main part of the New dialog box. For example, click the Agendas category to make Word list the available agenda templates. You can then browse the templates and choose the one you want.

3. Select the template you want to use.

4. Make sure the Document option button is selected in the Create New area. (The other option is to create a new template, as discussed in Chapter 9.)

5. Click the Create button. Word creates the document, and you can start working in it.

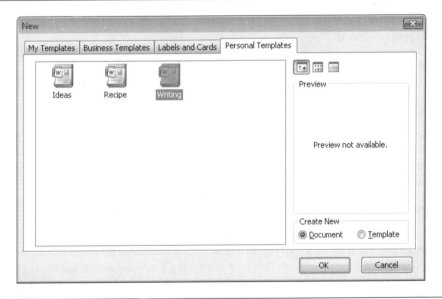

FIGURE 2-2 The New dialog box shows the templates stored in your user templates folder and workgroup templates folder (if you have one).

Find Templates on the Web—But Beware Dangerous Code

Microsoft Office Online is a good source of templates, but you'll find many others on the Web. (Use a search such as *free "Microsoft Word" template*, using the double quotation marks to keep *Microsoft Word* together.)

Unless you have a good reason to trust a site that provides templates (for example, you know the people who run the site, or the site is run by a well-known company), treat all templates as potentially dangerous:

- Templates that use the Word 2007 .dotx file extension are safe, because this file format cannot contain macros (short programs that can take a variety of actions on your computer, including deleting files).

- Templates that use the Word 2007 .dotm file extension contain code written in the Visual Basic for Applications (VBA) programming language. The code is often helpful and may be used by a template to save you time and effort. But the code may be hostile or harmful rather than helpful. You won't know until you install and run the template.

- Templates that use the Word 97-2003 .dot file extension may or may not contain code. You can't tell from the file format.

Until you open the template, you won't be able to tell if the code is useful or harmful. As far as you can, make sure the source is reputable, and check the template with antivirus software before opening it.

Base a New Document on an Existing Document

Often, you can save time and reduce wear on your fingertips by creating a new document based on an existing document rather than creating it from scratch. Word lets you base one document on another in three ways: by using the Save As command, by using the New From Existing command, and by simply copying the contents of one document into a new document.

Create a New Document Using the Save As Command

The easiest way to base a new document on an existing document is to open the existing document, and then save it under a different name. Doing this creates a new document with the same contents as the original document. This way of creating a new document has the slight risk that you'll open the document, make changes, and then save them to the original document rather than to a new document—for example, if someone interrupts you after you open the document.

2

Open the document in one of the ways explained in Chapter 1, and then save it under a new name as described in the section "Save a Document for the First Time," later in this chapter.

Sometimes you'll plan to create a new document this way, but other times, you'll probably open a document, work on it, and then realize you had better save the changes in a new document—for example, in case one of your colleagues needs the original document in its former state.

Create a New Document Based on an Existing Document

Another way of basing a new document on an existing document is to use the New From Existing command. This method of cloning a document eliminates the possibility of your saving changes to the original document rather than to a copy—a major advantage over the Save As command.

To create a new document with the New From Existing command, follow these steps:

1. Click the Office Button, and then click New. Word displays the New Document dialog box.

2. In the Templates list, click the New From Existing item. Word displays the New From Existing Document dialog box, which is a renamed version of Windows' standard Open dialog box.

3. Find the existing document, select it, and then click the Create New button. (The button is named Open until you select a file; it then changes to Create New.) Word creates a clone of the document and opens it.

You can then start working with the document, but it's a good idea to save it first. Click the Save button on the Quick Access Toolbar, press CTRL-S, or click the Office Button, and then click Save. Word displays the Save As dialog box.

Create a New Document by Copying Material from an Existing Document

The third method of basing a new document on an existing document is to copy all or part of the contents of an existing document into a new document. Sometimes you'll actually plan to base a new document on another like this, but more often you'll create a new document and then realize that you can reuse all or part of another document for its contents. To create a document this way, follow these general steps:

1. Create a new document, either blank or based on a template.

2. Click the Office Button, and then click Open. Word displays the Open dialog box. Select the existing document that contains the material you want, and then click the Open button.

TIP   *If you prefer, you can also open the document in another way. For example, open a Windows Explorer window to the folder that contains the document, and then double-click the document to open it in Word.*

3. Select the material you want, and then copy it by pressing CTRL-C or choosing Home | Clipboard | Copy—in other words, clicking the Home tab if it's not already displayed, going to the Clipboard group, and then clicking the Copy button.

To select the whole document, press CTRL-A or choose Home | Editing | Select | Select All—that is, click the Home tab, go to the Editing group, click the Select button, and then choose Select All from the drop-down panel. This book will use this shorter form of describing Ribbon actions from here on.

4. Click the Office Button, and then click Close. Word closes the document you opened and makes the new document active again.

5. Right-click in the new document where you want the material to appear, and then choose Paste from the shortcut menu. Word pastes in the material.

Save Your Documents

When you create a document and start adding content to it, Word stores the document and content only in your computer's memory (RAM) rather than saving it to the hard disk. If Word or your computer crashes, you'll lose the document. (By contrast, some programs—such as Microsoft OneNote and Microsoft Access—automatically save your work for you, so you don't need to save it manually.)

To avoid such loss, save every document as soon as you've created it—and then save it again whenever you've made a change that you don't want to have to make again.

Tell Word Where to Keep Your Documents and How to Save Them

Word assumes that you want to save most of your documents in the same folder, or in subfolders of that folder. At first, Word uses your Documents folder (on Windows Vista) or your My Documents folder (on Windows XP). Documents is the folder that Windows Vista opens when you choose Start | Documents; My Documents is the folder Windows XP opens when you choose Start | My Documents.

In each Word session, Word opens the Open dialog box and the Save As dialog box to this folder at first. If you navigate to a different folder to open or save a file, Word then uses that folder until you change the folder again.

If your computer is part of a Windows network, the network administrator may have set a different folder for you—for example, a folder in your home folder on the server rather than your Documents folder or My Documents folder.

If you want to use a folder other than Documents or My Documents, you need to tell Word which folder. If you don't, you'll need to change folders at the start of each Word session. It's also a good idea to set up Word's AutoRecover feature (which automatically saves information for recovering your files after disaster strikes) and choose several other options related to saving.

How to ... Change the Standard Font in Your Documents

Like all word-processing programs, Word lets you use many different *fonts* (typefaces, or designs of type) to make text appear the way you want it. When you create a new blank document, any text you type appears in the default font, which is called Calibri, at a font size of 12 points, which is a standard size for text in everyday documents (such as letters or reports). Calibri is a new font that's designed to be easier to read on screen than the Times New Roman font that earlier versions of Word used as the standard font—but you may want to switch back.

If you prefer to use another font or size as standard for your documents, change it as follows:

1. Create a new blank document.

2. Type a short sample sentence, and then select it. This text will give you a better preview of the font.

3. Either press CTRL-D, or right-click the selection, and then choose Font from the shortcut menu. Word displays the Font dialog box, as shown here.

4. Choose the font, font style, font size, size, color, underlining, and any other effects. Watch the Preview box to see how your sample text looks with your choices.

   ■ Click the font in the Font list. This list shows fonts in alphabetical order, but it also has a +Body item and a +Heading item at the beginning. +Body makes Word use the standard body font set in the template's theme; +Heading applies the standard heading font. The *theme* is a document-wide formatting scheme (see Chapter 4 for details).

   ■ In the Font Style list, choose Regular (the font's normal appearance) unless you want to use Italic, Bold, or Bold Italic for a different look. Some fonts have only some of these choices—for example, Regular and Bold only.

   ■ In the Font Color drop-down list, choose the color you want. The Automatic item makes Word use a color that contrasts with the background—for example, when the background is white, Word makes the text black. Chapter 4 explains these choices in more detail.

   ■ If you want your standard text underlined, choose the style from the Underline Style drop-down list. Use the Underline Color drop-down list to specify the color for the underline.

   ■ In the Effects area, select the check box for any effect you want to apply—All Caps, Strikethrough, or whatever. Most of these are for display text such as headings or bursts, so you wouldn't normally want to use them for standard text.

5. Click the Default Button. Word displays the confirmation dialog box shown here to check you want to make this change to all documents based on the Normal template—in other words, to all the "new blank" documents you create. Word doesn't change any documents you've created already.

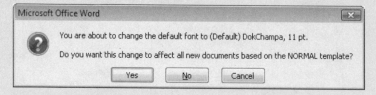

6. Click the Yes button.

From now on, each new blank document you create uses the font formatting you specified. You can apply other fonts as necessary, from the Font dialog box, from the Mini Toolbar (a pop-up toolbar), or from the Home tab of the Ribbon. Chapter 4 explains formatting in detail.

Instead of changing the default font for the Normal template, you can change it for a particular template. To do so, create a document based on that template, and then follow the same procedure for changing the font.

To set your documents folder and set other save options, follow these steps:

1. Click the Office Button, and then click Word Options. Word displays the Word Options dialog box.

2. In the left panel, click the Save category. Word displays the Save options (see Figure 2-3).

3. In the Save Files In This Format drop-down list, choose the file format you want to use.

   ■ Word uses the Word Document (*.docx) format unless you change it. This format is the best choice if other people who need to open your documents use either Word 2007 or a recent version (for example, Word 2003 or Word XP/2002) with an update applied to let these versions read the .docx format. If you need greater compatibility with older versions of Word and with other word-processing programs, choose Word 97-2003 Document (*.doc) instead.

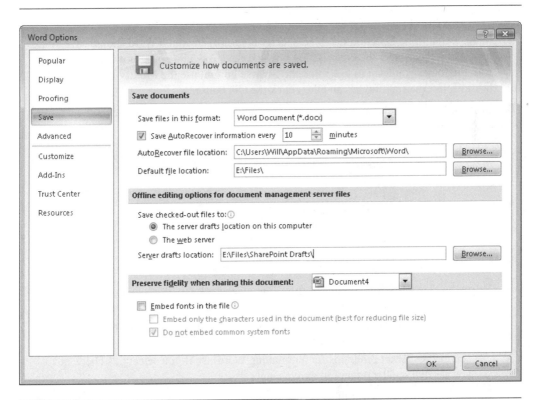

FIGURE 2-3 In the Word Options dialog box, the Save category lets you quickly access the most important save options. The remaining save options are in the Advanced category.

4. Decide whether to have Word save AutoRecover information and, if so, how frequently.

- Word starts you off with the Save AutoRecover Information Every *NN* Minutes check box selected and the interval set to 10 minutes. Every 10 minutes, Word automatically saves an AutoRecover file for each open document in the folder shown in the AutoRecover File Location text box. After a crash, Word restarts and shows you the AutoRecover files that are available. You can then decide whether to save each AutoRecover file (for example, if it contains changes you hadn't saved to the original document before the crash) or discard it.

- AutoRecover can be a welcome safety net, but in most cases, you're better off saving your documents manually whenever you've made any changes worth keeping and forcing Word to make a backup at each save (see step 6 of this list).

- If you decide to leave AutoRecover turned on, shorten the AutoRecover interval to reduce the amount of maximum amount of work you can lose—10 minutes is too much unless you work at the pace of Tsarist bureaucracy.

CAUTION   *AutoRecover files occasionally become corrupted. If this happens, you may lose more work.*

5. In the Default File Location text box, specify the folder in which Word should save your files. This is the folder the Open dialog box and Save As dialog box show first. If this isn't the folder you want to use, click the Browse button, use the Modify Location dialog box to select the right folder, and then click the OK button.

6. In the left panel, click the Advanced category, and then scroll down to the Save section (shown here).

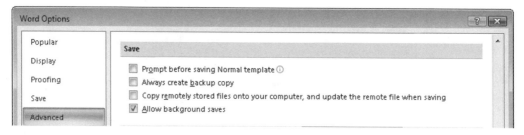

7. Select the Prompt Before Saving Normal Template check box if you want Word to display a message box asking your permission to save changes to the Normal template.

- Word stores many items in the Normal template, including your settings (such as standard font and margins) for blank documents, AutoText entries (boilerplate text), and macros (short programs for automating Word), so if you select this check box, you'll often see the prompt to save changes.

- It's usually best to clear this check box and have Word save the changes to the Normal template automatically without bothering you.

8. Select the Always Create Backup Copy check box if you want Word to save a backup copy of the document each time you save it (after the first time).

NOTE *Word creates the backup copy by copying the last saved version of the document, so the backup isn't* exactly *the same as the current copy. But if you save frequently, the backup remains close enough to the current copy for emergency use.*

9. Select the Copy Remotely Stored Files Onto Your Computer, And Update The Remote File When Saving check box if you work with documents stored on a server to which you're connected via a slow connection.

   ■ For example, you might work in a remote office, connect to the main office via dial-up, and open documents from a server in the main office across the slow connection.

   ■ Saving a copy of the document on your computer and working with that copy eliminates the delay and risk of data loss involved in saving the document across the slow connection.

10. Clear the Allow Background Saves check box.

   ■ A background save is intended to let you resume work more quickly after issuing a Save command, because you can work while Word saves the document. However, background saves make each save take longer and are seldom worth using.

   ■ If you do use background saves, you'll see a pulsing disk icon in the status bar when Word is performing a background save on a large document.

Save a Document for the First Time

The first time you save a document, you must decide which filename to give it, which folder to store it in, and which format to use. You can also add *tags* (extra pieces of information) to the document to help you find it more easily by searching.

To save a document for the first time, follow these steps:

1. Click the Save button on the Quick Access Toolbar; or click the Office Button, and then click Save; or press CTRL-S. Word displays the Save As dialog box (see Figure 2-4).

2. If Word displays the small version of the Save As dialog box, click the Browse Folders button.

NOTE *To access all the features of the Save As dialog box as shown in Figure 2-4, you may need to enlarge the dialog box by dragging the dotted triangle in the lower-right corner down. You may also need to drag the bar that divides the folder browser from the File Name text box upward to reveal the tag area fully.*

3. Navigate to the folder in which you want to store the file.

   ■ You can navigate the folder tree in the Save As dialog box using standard Windows techniques.

   ■ For example, click the Desktop link in the Favorite links pane on the left to display the contents of the Desktop, or use one of the drop-down lists in the Address box to change to a different folder.

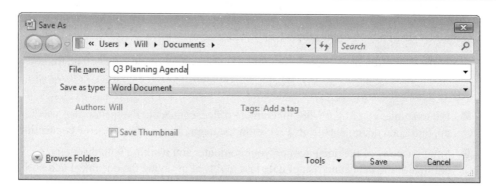

Click one of these links to jump to a different folder.

Click one of these arrows to display a drop-down list showing the sub-folders of the folder before the arrow.

Click the New Folder button if you need to create a new folder within the current folder.

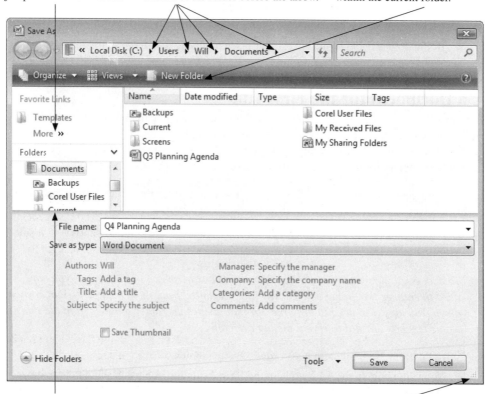

Drag this bar to adjust the size of the folder browser box.

Drag this dotted handle down and to the right to enlarge the dialog box so that you can see more of its contents.

FIGURE 2-4 If you see the small version of the Save As dialog box (top), click the Browse Folders button to display the full version (bottom).

- ■ Type the filename in the File Name text box.

- ■ Word automatically enters the first few words of the document in the File Name box, but you'll often want to change them.

- ■ You can use letters, numbers, most punctuation, and some symbols, but not characters that have special meanings in Windows: asterisk (*), colon (:), backslash (\), forward slash (/), greater-than sign (>), less-than sign (<), question mark (?), vertical bar (|), or double quotation marks.

- ■ The filename, including the folder path to it, can be up to 255 characters long. Usually, you'll want to keep filenames much shorter than this so that they're easy to read in dialog boxes and Windows Explorer windows. Even so, you can easily create detailed names that help you quickly identify your documents.

4. If necessary, change the format for the document.

- ■ The Save As Type drop-down list shows the format that Word will use for the document. Unless you changed the save format (see the section "Tell Word Where To Keep Your Documents and How to Save Them," earlier in this chapter), Word uses Word Document (*.docx), the newest format.

- ■ Use this format unless you need to make sure that users of earlier versions of Word can open your documents even if they don't have the latest document converters installed. In this case, use the Word 97-2003 Document (*.doc) format instead.

5. In the lower part of the dialog box, add extra information to the document to help you find it later when searching in Windows.

- ■ Word adds your name to the Authors readout. To add another author, click your name, and then type it in the box that appears. For example, you might add the name of a colleague with whom you're collaborating on this document.

- ■ When you search for documents, you can search for specific tag information— keywords added to the document to help explain its content. To associate particular keywords with the document, click the Tags readout, which at first shows just a pair of parentheses: (). Type a keyword or phrase. To add another, type a semicolon to separate the new keyword or phrase from the first.

- ■ To give the document a title, click the Title readout and type the title. You might use a title related to the filename or something more descriptive. Similarly, you can assign a subject by clicking the Subject readout and typing text.

- ■ To save a thumbnail picture of each document you create, select the Save Thumbnail check box. Thumbnails help you identify documents visually in dialog boxes and Windows Explorer windows. Thumbnails are most useful when you create documents that look markedly different from one another. If your documents all look the same, thumbnails are of little use. For example, thumbnails of memos that use the same template tend all to look the same.

6. Click the Save button. Word closes the Save As dialog box and saves the document. You can then continue working in the document.

TIP *You can enter any information you want in the tag fields. For example, you might want to put the client's name in the Subject field or designate your manager as the "Author" of the document. You can use the tags freely, but you'll get best search results if you establish a convention and follow it—and preferably have your colleagues follow it too. Word also includes many more document properties in which you can add further information for searching. See the section "Enter Property Information for a Document," later in this chapter, for details.*

Save a Document That Already Has a Name

Once you've saved a document, you can save it again in moments. Press CTRL-S; click the Save button on the Quick Access Toolbar; or click the Office Button, and then click Save.

How frequently you save a document is up to you; but unless you're prepared to lose work or redo work, you should save after making any significant change. Get in the habit of pressing CTRL-S as you finish a burst of typing or an edit—you won't regret keeping your documents saved, and you can use Undo (discussed in Chapter 3) to undo any changes that you decide you don't want to keep.

Save a Document Using a Different Name, Folder, or Format

At any point, you can save a document under a different name, or in a different folder, or in a different format—or a mixture of the three, or all three at once. Here are examples of when you might want to do this:

- **Save a document under a different name** Saving under a different name is an easy way to create a new version of the document.

- **Save a document in a different folder** You can use a different folder to indicate that the document has reached a different stage (for example, that it's ready for review or distribution) or to make it available to your colleagues. Alternatively, you can use Windows Explorer to create a copy and place it in another folder.

- **Save a document in a different format** You can use a different format so that someone with an earlier version of Word, or with a different word-processing program, can work with it. You can also save to a different format to create another type of document. For example, you can save a document as a web page so that you can put it on a web site.

To save a document using a different name, folder, or format, follow these steps:

1. Click the Office Button, and then click Save As. Word displays the Save As dialog box.

2. Do one or more of the following: Type a new name for the document, select the new folder, or choose the new format.

   - If you're saving the document under a new name, type the new name in the File Name box.

   - To use a different folder, navigate to that folder.

   - To use a different format, choose that format in the Save As Type drop-down list.

3. Click the Save button. Word closes the Save As dialog box and saves the document.

Understand the File Formats That Word Can Save

When you open the Save As Type drop-down list, you'll see that Word can save files in a wide array of formats. These formats break down into the following categories:

- **Word documents**   The Word Document (*.docx), Word Macro-Enabled Document (*.docm), Word 97-2003 Document (*.doc), and Word 97-2003 & 6.0/95 - RTF (*.doc) formats are Word-specific formats that allow you to save all the contents of the Word document. Use these formats when exchanging documents with people who use Word. Some other word processors can read these formats, but not always all of the formatting.

- **Word templates**   The Word Template (*.dotx), Word Macro-Enabled Template (*.dotm), and Word 97-2003 Template (*.dot) formats are Word-specific template formats. Use these formats when you create templates for use with Word (see Chapter 9). Use the Word Template format for Word 2007 templates that don't need macros and VBA code. Use the Word Macro-Enabled Template format for Word 2007 templates that *do* need code. Use the Word 97-2003 Template format when you need to create a template that's compatible with older versions of Word.

- **Typeset final documents**   The PDF (*.pdf) and XPS Document (*.xps) formats are for creating final versions of typeset documents. Adobe's Portable Document Format (PDF) is a global standard for distributing final documents electronically in a hard-to-edit format. XML Paper Specification (XPS) is a new format that Microsoft has introduced to rival PDF and has similar capabilities to PDF.

- **Web pages**   The Single File Web Page (*.mht; *.mhtml), Web Page (*.htm; *.html), and Web Page, Filtered (*.htm; *.html) formats are for creating web pages. These formats are based on open standards, and most web browsers and many word processors can read these files successfully. Chapter 13 explains how to create web pages.

- **Text files**   Rich Text Format (*.rtf) and Plain Text (*.txt) are standard formats that all word processors and many text editors can read. Use Rich Text Format when you need to ensure that other people can read and edit a document and you're prepared to lose Word-specific features (such as VBA code) and possibly complex formatting. Use the Plain Text format when you want to save only the text of the document without any formatting and without any objects (such as graphics or charts) the document contains. When you save a document in Plain Text format, Word warns you that you will lose formatting and objects.

- **XML documents** The Word XML Document (*.xml) and Word 2003 XML Document (*.xml) formats use Extensible Markup Language (XML) to save the entire contents of a Word document in a text-based format. XML documents have a defined structure that includes tags that identify the different elements within the document. For example, an XML document that contains a catalog might include tags such as <PRODUCT_ID>, <PRODUCT_NAME>, and <DESCRIPTION>. By using these tags, you could automatically extract the product IDs, names, and descriptions from the document.

- **Works document format** Use the Works 6.0-9.0 (*.wps) format when you need to share a document with someone who has Microsoft Works (a basic software suite that is supplied free with many PCs).

Save a Document as PDF or XPS

One long-standing bugbear of Word users has been the way that a document's layout can change when someone opens it on a different computer than the one used to create it. Even small differences in the fonts available, or in the capabilities of printers used, can turn a document you've spent ages laying out just perfectly into a formatting nightmare.

If you'll be distributing a document to people who don't need to edit it, the best way to keep all formatting intact is to save it as a Portable Document Format (PDF) file or an XML Paper Specification (XPS) document.

Portable Document Format (PDF)

PDF files retain the document's layout both on screen and when printed. Most web browsers can display PDF files, or users can use the free Adobe Reader from Adobe Corporation, which provides versions for all major computer operating systems.

Until Word 2007, creating PDF files from Word has required third-party software, such as Adobe Corporation's expensive Acrobat Professional or the much less expensive GhostScript. Word 2007 takes a giant step forward by letting you save a document as a PDF file without needing any extra software.

You still need third-party software, such as Adobe Corporation's free Acrobat Reader, to open PDF files in Windows Vista.

XML Paper Specification (XPS)

A technology developed by Microsoft to provide a rival format to PDF, XPS is one of the major additions to Windows Vista. The easiest way to think of XPS is as a type of electronic paper for Windows Vista systems. (PDF is the corresponding electronic paper for the Mac, as Apple has built PDF support into Mac OS X.)

2

XPS is an "output-only" format: You export a finished document to XPS to create an "electronic paper" version of the document, rather as you would print the document to create a hard-copy version of it. The resulting XPS file includes not only all the document's visible contents (as the hard copy does) but also hyperlinks that the user can click.

XPS files can also be protected by any Information Rights Management (IRM) restrictions applied to the original document. For example, the IRM might allow only certain people to open the document, or it might expire on a particular date. To view an XPS file, you can use Internet Explorer 7 or a later version.

Get the PDF and XPS Add-Ins

Before you can create PDF or XPS files, you must download and install extra components from the Microsoft web site (http://www.microsoft.com). Follow these steps:

1. In Word, click the Office Button, highlight Save As, and then click Find Add-Ins For Other File Formats. Word launches a Word Help window, which displays the Enable Support For Other File Formats, Such As PDF And XPS topic.

2. Click the Install And Use The Publish As PDF Or XPS Add-In From Microsoft link. Word Help displays the page for this topic.

3. Click the Microsoft Save As PDF Or XPS Add-In For 2007 Microsoft Office Programs link. Word Help opens a browser window to the page on the Microsoft web site.

4. Click the Continue button. You will need to install the Office Genuine Advantage component if it's not already installed on your computer. This component checks that the copy of Office you're using is legitimate rather than pirated. To install this component on Windows Vista, you must authenticate yourself to User Account Control, and then click the Install button in the Internet Explorer Add-On Installer - Security Warning dialog box, shown here.

5. Once you've proved your copy of Office is genuine, click the Download button to download the Save As PDF Or XPS add-in. Click the Run button in the File Download - Security

Warning dialog box (shown here). When the download completes, on Windows Vista you must authenticate yourself to User Account Control.

6. Accept the software license if you want to proceed, wait while Windows adds the feature, and then click the OK button in the message box that tells you installation is complete.

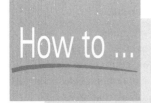 ## Choose Between PDF and XPS

Being able to create PDFs and XPS files directly from Word is great. But deciding which format to use can be tough.

PDF is the established standard electronic document format, and most computers nowadays have PDF-reader programs installed. (Most computer manufacturers include the free Acrobat Reader.) Relatively few computers have Acrobat Professional or another program that allows them to annotate and edit PDFs.

XPS is the new electronic document format and is a part of Windows Vista, so anyone using Windows Vista can open XPS documents by using Internet Explorer. People with older versions of Windows may have to download an XPS viewer from the Microsoft web site before they can read an XPS file.

The recipient of an XPS document can annotate and comment on it but not change its text and content directly. This limitation is useful when you want to prevent the user from changing the document—for example, a contract.

If you simply want to ensure that the recipient can view the file, PDF has the edge. If you create a PDF, you can be pretty sure that anyone you send it to will be able to view it, whereas with XPS, the recipient may not be able to view it. But if you need to ensure that the recipient doesn't edit the file, use XPS rather than PDF.

2

Create the PDF File or XPS Document

To save a document as a PDF file or an XPS document, follow these steps:

1. Open the document and make sure it's fully laid out. Use Print Layout view to verify that the document looks exactly as you want it to and that all the page breaks fall in the appropriate places.

2. Click the Office Button, highlight Save As, and then click PDF Or XPS. Word displays the Publish As PDF Or XPS dialog box (see Figure 2-5).

3. If necessary, choose the folder and type the filename for the document.

   ■ If the dialog box opens in its reduced form, click the Browse Folders button to display the rest of it.

   ■ Because the document will use the .pdf or .xps file extension, it will not overwrite the original document, so you don't need to change the folder or filename.

4. In the Save As Type drop-down list, choose which type of document to create: PDF or XPS Document.

   ■ The first time you open the Publish As PDF Or XPS dialog box, the Save As Type drop-down list displays the PDF item.

   ■ The next time you open the dialog box, this list displays your last choice.

5. Select the Open File After Publishing check box to make your PDF or XPS reader open the file open automatically after Word creates it so that you can check it immediately. If your computer doesn't have a PDF or XPS reader, this check box is unavailable.

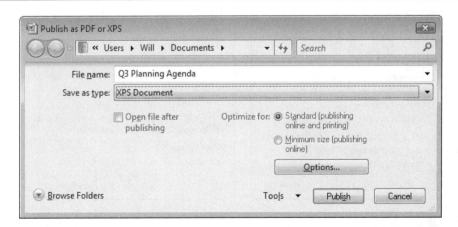

FIGURE 2-5   The Publish As PDF Or XPS dialog box lets you quickly switch between creating a standard-quality file suitable for printing or a minimum-size file for publishing online.

6. In the Optimize For area, choose the quality for the file:

- ■ **Standard (Publishing Online And Printing)** Select this option button if you want to create a file suitable for either printing or publishing online.

- ■ **Minimum Size (Publishing Online)** Select this option button if you want to keep the file size down to a minimum so that the file transfers over an Internet connection as quickly as possible. The resulting file will not look good if printed but will be fine for reading on screen.

7. If you want to use only part of the document, suppress markup, or include nonprinting information in the PDF file or XPS file, follow these steps:

- ■ Click the Options button. Word displays the Options dialog box. Figure 2-6 shows the Options dialog box for PDF files on the left and the Options dialog box for XPS documents on the right.

- ■ **Page Range** In this area, select the All option button to include all pages. Select the Current Page option button to include just the current page. Select the Selection option button to use the current selection (this option is available only if you've

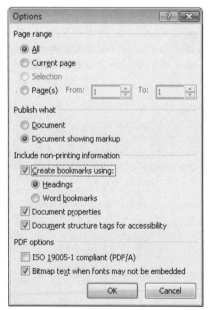

FIGURE 2-6 The Options dialog box controls PDF file or XPS document content and markup settings. You can also choose to publish only part of the document instead of the entire document.

selected part of the document before opening the Publish As PDF Or XPS dialog box). To use a range of pages, select the Page(s) option button, and then use the From text box and To text box to specify the range.

- **Publish What**   If the document contains markup (such as comments or changes made using revision marks), select the Document option button if you want to exclude the markup. Select the Document Showing Markup option button if you want to include the markup.

CAUTION   *Several major governments have embarrassed themselves in the last few years by including sensitive markup unintentionally in documents they've published online. Don't join them.*

- **Create Bookmarks Using**   Select this check box if you want to create bookmarks in the file that allow the reader to move quickly from one item to another. You can then select the Headings option button to make Word create a bookmark from each paragraph formatted with a Heading style or the Word Bookmarks option button to make bookmarks from your Word bookmarks instead.

NOTE   *Chapter 4 discusses styles, and Chapter 12 explains bookmarks.*

- **Document Properties**   Select this check box if you want to include document metadata (such as the document's title, subject, and author) in the PDF. This metadata is sometimes sensitive, so you may want to exclude it from the document.

- **Document Structure Tags For Accessibility**   Select this check box if you want to include document structure tags (such as headings) that the document contains.

- **PDF Options** (PDF files only)   Select the ISO 19005-1 Compliant (PDF/A) check box if you want to create PDFs that meet the ISO 19005-1 standard for long-term document preservation. Such PDFs may not contain audio and video content, and all fonts must be embedded (included in the file). When you turn on this check box, Word makes the Bitmap Text When Fonts May Not Be Embedded check box unavailable. When this check box is available, turn it on to allow Word to substitute bitmap pictures of text when it cannot legally embed the fonts.

- **XPS Document Options** (XPS documents only)   Select the Preserve Restricted Permissions In XPS check box if you want to carry through Information Rights Management (IRM) restrictions from the Word document to the XPS document. This option applies only if you're using IRM in your Word documents. Usually, only large corporations use IRM.

- Click the OK button. Word closes the Options dialog box and returns you to the Publish As PDF Or XPS dialog box.

8.   Click the Publish button. Word closes the Publish As PDF Or XPS dialog box, creates a PDF file or XPS document from the Word document, and then returns you to your document.

If you selected the Open File After Publishing check box in the Publish as PDF or XPS dialog box, the file you created automatically opens in your default PDF reader or XPS reader. Verify that the document looks as you want it to before you distribute it.

Enter Property Information for a Document

As you saw in the section "Save a Document for the First Time," earlier in this chapter, Word running on Windows Vista encourages you to enter some fields of document metadata (data *about* the document rather than actual contents of the document) directly in the Save As dialog box. To make documents easier to identify via searches, and to help the Windows Indexing Service to store the appropriate key information about documents, you can enter property information by using the Properties bar and the Properties dialog box.

To open the Properties bar, click the Office button, highlight Prepare, and then click Properties on the Prepare submenu. Word displays the Properties bar, which contains the Author, Title, Subject, Keywords, Category, Status, and Comments fields, as shown here.

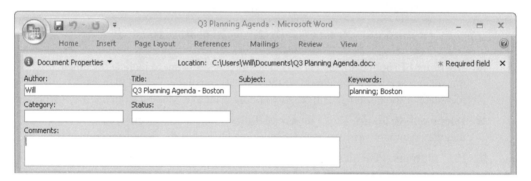

For further properties, click the Document Properties drop-down list and then choose Advanced Properties. Word displays the Properties dialog box. The Properties dialog box contains five tabs, which are discussed in the following section.

General Tab Properties

The General tab contains basic information about the file:

- **Type** The file type—for example, Microsoft Office Word Document.
- **Folder** The folder that contains the file.
- **Size** The file's size in KB.
- **MS-DOS Name** The file name in the 8.3 format—for example, Q3PLAN~1.DOC.
- **Created** The date and time the file was first saved.
- **Modified** The date and time the file was last saved.
- **Accessed** The date and time the file was last opened or saved.

■   **Attributes**   Check boxes indicating whether the file is marked Read Only, Hidden, Archive (set to be archived), or System (Windows considers it a system file).

You can't manipulate any of this information directly on this tab.

Summary Tab Properties

The Summary tab (as shown on the left in Figure 2-7) contains Title, Subject, Author, Manager, Company, Category, Keywords, Comments, and Hyperlink Base fields. Word automatically fills in the author information from the Author property of the template or, if that's blank, with your user name. Word automatically fills in the Company field with the registered organization that's assigned to the copy of Windows you're using.

These fields are self-explanatory except for Hyperlink Base, which enables you to specify the base address for all of the hyperlinks in the document. For example, if you enter **http://www .acmeheavyindustries.com/** in the Hyperlink Base text box, you can then create a hyperlink to http:// www.acmeheavyindustries/com/examples/example1.html by entering **examples/example1.html** rather than the full address.

The Template readout shows the name of the template used for the document—for example, Normal for a "new, blank" document.

FIGURE 2-7   You can enter key information on the Summary tab and Custom tab of the Properties dialog box to make documents easier to identify without opening them.

Select the Save Thumbnails For All Word Documents check box (on Windows Vista) or the Save Preview Picture check box (on Windows XP) if you want Word to save a preview of the document in the file. If the document is visually distinctive, a preview can help you identify it later. If all your documents look much the same, a preview won't be much help.

Statistics Tab Properties and Content Tab Properties

The Statistics tab contains details on when the document was created, last saved, last modified, last accessed, and last printed as well as on the person who last saved it, the revision number, and the total time spent editing it.

The Contents tab provides a list of document contents, such as the document title.

Custom Tab Properties

The Custom tab (as shown on the right in Figure 2-7) contains a variety of predefined properties that you can fill in. You can create custom properties by typing their names in the Name text box. You can also assign to a property the contents of a bookmark in the document. This capability enables you to store the contents of specific bookmarks automatically in the properties and thus have them indexed along with the other property information.

To add a property, follow these steps:

1. Select the property in the Name list, or type a new name to create a custom property.

2. In the Type drop-down list, select the appropriate type for the property: Text, Date, Number, or Yes Or No. This choice isn't relevant if you're linking the property to a bookmark in the document.

3. Enter the data for the property as appropriate:

   ■ For a Text, Date, or Number value, type it in the Value text box. (This text box appears when you have selected the Text, Date, or Number type. When you select the Yes Or No type, Word replaces the Value text box with option buttons.)

   ■ For a Yes or No choice, select the Yes option button or the No option button.

   ■ For information contained in a bookmark in the document, select the Link To Content check box. Word displays a Source drop-down list that lists the bookmarks in the document. Select the bookmark from this list.

4. Click the Add button. Word adds the property and data to the Properties list box. A property linked to a bookmark displays a chain symbol beside it, as the Review Status property in Figure 2-8 does. (If the chain symbol shows a broken link, there's a problem with the bookmark—for example, you may have deleted it.)

To delete a property, select it in the Properties list box, and then click the Delete button.

Chapter 3

Navigate, Enter Text, and Use Find

How to...

- Understand the secret of paragraphs
- Navigate around your documents
- Enter text via the keyboard or other means
- Move, copy, and delete text
- Use Find and Replace

Pretty much any document needs text—and maybe tables, graphics, and a few equations for balance. You can type text using the keyboard, but you can also use a mouse, a stylus and tablet, optical character recognition (OCR), or even voice recognition, depending on your computer and software.

This chapter shows you how to enter text in all these ways; how to move around your documents using the keyboard, mouse, and Word's navigation features; and how to use Find and Replace to find and replace text and formatting in your documents. First, though, you'll learn how Word handles paragraphs, the essential building blocks of documents. This may seem a strange place to start, but it's vital to your using Word successfully and will save you much frustration and confusion in the long run.

Understand the Secret of Paragraphs

The key to working successfully with text in Word is to understand what paragraphs are in Word documents and how Word handles them. This section explains what you need to know.

Understand What a Paragraph Is (in Word)

You know what a paragraph is in a book or newspaper article: a section of the book or article, usually fairly short, consisting of one or more sentences. A paragraph always starts on a new line, often begins with an indent, and frequently has white space before and after it to separate it from other paragraphs.

Paragraphs in Word tend to look like this, although you can format them to look different if you want. But what's important is what you usually don't see—the paragraph mark that indicates the end of the paragraph. This paragraph mark contains the details of the formatting for the paragraph. Every Word document contains at least one paragraph. Even if the document is completely blank, it contains an invisible paragraph character that marks its end.

Each paragraph consists of the paragraph mark (at its end) and all the text or other objects that appear before that paragraph mark but after the previous paragraph mark (or, if it's the first paragraph, the start of the document). When you delete a paragraph mark, the paragraph after the mark becomes part of the paragraph before the mark.

To see where each paragraph ends, you can tell Word to display paragraph marks. To do so, click the Office Button, click Word Options, and then click the Display category. In the Always Show These Formatting Marks On The Screen area, select the Paragraph Marks check box, and then click the OK button. Figure 3-1 shows a blank document with its sole paragraph mark displayed.

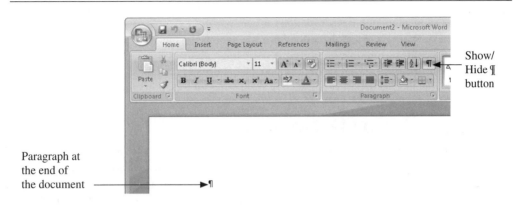

Show/
Hide ¶
button

Paragraph at
the end of
the document ────────▶¶

FIGURE 3-1   Even a blank document contains a paragraph mark at its end. You can't delete
this paragraph mark, which contains the section formatting for the document.

NOTE   *Keeping paragraph marks displayed all the time can be useful, but you may prefer to toggle
them on and off. To display all Word's "formatting marks" (tabs, spaces, hidden text,
optional hyphens, and object anchors), press CTRL-SHIFT-8 or choose Home | Paragraph |
Show/Hide¶.*

Understand What a Section Is

So far, so good. But it gets more complex, because Word lets you break a document down into
sections, invisible divisions in which you can use different layouts, or different headers and
footers, in different parts of the document. Chapter 5 tells you all about sections.

It's Best to Avoid Blank Paragraphs in Your Documents

The easiest way to add extra space between lines of text is to press ENTER twice at the end of
a paragraph. Many people do this, whether they learned to type using a typewriter (on which
adding an extra line this way was standard practice, because each line had a standard height)
or on a computer.

This approach works with Word, but it's not usually a good idea, because it leaves
unneeded blank paragraphs in your documents. A better solution is to add space before or
after each paragraph that needs more space, as explained in Chapter 4.

Each document has at least one section right from when you create the document. You can then break the document up into further sections as needed—for example, if you need to make the first page use a letter layout and the second use an envelope layout.

If a document contains multiple sections, the last paragraph mark in a section contains the details of the formatting for that section. If a document doesn't contain sections, its last paragraph mark contains the details of the section formatting for the entire document.

Navigate Around Your Documents

Rather than starting at the beginning and typing straight through to the end of a document, you'll probably need to move back and forth through a document as you create or edit it. You can move around your documents by using the keyboard or the mouse. To help you get around your documents, Word provides a wide variety of navigation tools, including the scroll bars, the Browse Object feature, and the Find feature.

Navigate with the Keyboard

When you're typing in a document, the keyboard is the easiest means of navigation. Table 3-1 lists the shortcuts that you can use to move the insertion point.

Press This Key Combination	To Move the Insertion Point
←	One character to the left
→	One character to the right
↑	Up one line
↓	Down one line
CTRL-↑	To the start of the current paragraph. If the insertion point is at the start of the current paragraph, to the start of the previous paragraph.
CTRL-↓	To the start of the next paragraph
CTRL-→	To the start of the next word (if there is one) or the end of the current word
CTRL-←	To the start of the current word (if the insertion point is within a word) or the start of the previous word
HOME	To the start of the current line
END	To the end of the current line
CTRL-HOME	To the start of the document
CTRL-END	To the end of the document
PAGE DOWN	Down one screen of text (the amount that fits in the window at its current size)
PAGE UP	Up one screen of text
CTRL-PAGE DOWN	To the next page
CTRL-PAGE UP	To the previous page

TABLE 3-1 Keystrokes and Key Combinations for Moving the Insertion Point

Navigate with the Mouse and the Scroll Bars

To change the position of the insertion point with the mouse, move the cursor to where you want to place it, and then double-click. If you double-click in existing text, Word simply places the insertion point there. If you double-click after the end of the document, Word's Click And Type feature adds blank paragraphs to the end of the document so that there's somewhere for it to position the insertion point. Click And Type may also change the alignment (for example, if you double-click at the right margin, Click And Type changes that paragraph to right alignment) or adds tabs to reach the point at which you double-clicked.

Instead of moving the insertion point, you can scroll the document vertically or horizontally by using the scroll bars. Figure 3-2 shows you how to scroll using the vertical scroll bar. When you have the horizontal scroll bar displayed, it works in a similar way, only for lateral movement rather than vertical.

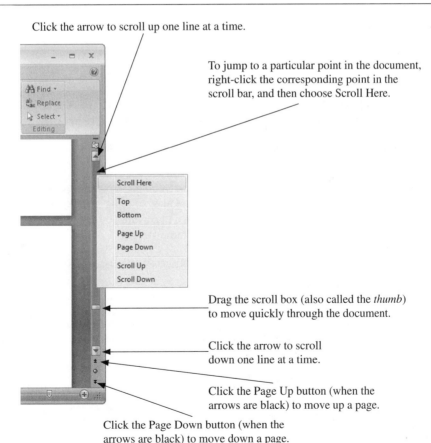

Click the arrow to scroll up one line at a time.

To jump to a particular point in the document, right-click the corresponding point in the scroll bar, and then choose Scroll Here.

Drag the scroll box (also called the *thumb*) to move quickly through the document.

Click the arrow to scroll down one line at a time.

Click the Page Up button (when the arrows are black) to move up a page.

Click the Page Down button (when the arrows are black) to move down a page.

FIGURE 3-2   The vertical scroll bar lets you move up and down the document one line at a time, one page at a time, or in large jumps.

Select Text

To cut or copy text, or to apply most formatting to it, you need to select it first. Word displays a gray-blue highlight over selected text so that you can easily see what you've selected. You can select text using the mouse, the keyboard, or both together.

Select Text with the Mouse

If you can see all the text you want to select, move the mouse pointer to the start or end of the target text, and then drag to the opposite end. You can select sideways, upward, or downward—all work equally well.

Select Text Using Click Shortcuts   Word also offers three shortcuts for selecting with clicks:

- Double-click a word to select it.
- CTRL-click in a sentence to select it.
- Triple-click a paragraph to select it.

How to ... Prevent Word from Selecting an Entire Word at a Time

Word includes a setting that automatically increases the selection by a whole word at a time once you've dragged to select more than one word. If you need to select parts of two words, you can override the automatic selection by holding down ALT while you drag to select.

If you prefer to turn off automatic selection, follow these steps:

1. Click the Office Button, and then click Word Options. Word displays the Word Options dialog box.
2. In the left panel, click the Advanced category. Word displays the Advanced options.
3. In the Editing Options area (at the top), clear the When Selecting, Automatically Select Entire Word check box.
4. Click the OK button. Word closes the Word Options dialog box.

Once you've turned this feature off, you might expect you could ALT-drag to turn it back on temporarily—but you can't.

Select Text Using the Selection Bar   Beyond these click techniques, Word offers quick selection through the *selection bar*, an invisible vertical strip to the left of the leftmost characters in a paragraph. When you move the mouse pointer over the invisible selection bar, the pointer changes from an I-beam to an arrow pointing upward and slightly to the right, as shown here.

Quote for Today

Consider what the Uruguayan expert Nolberto Gruener had to say on the subject of globalization:

Given that we struggle to expand our conception of the local to the regional, and of the regional to the national, even in the latest generations the conceptualization of the global has yet to become truly global rather than merely (and disappointingly) supra-regional.

When the mouse pointer is in the selection bar, you can:

- Drag down the selection bar to select whole lines at a time (as in the illustration).
- Click once to select the line that's level with your click.
- Double-click to select the nearest paragraph.
- Triple-click or CTRL-click to select the whole document.

Add Further Selections to Your Existing Selection   After you've made a selection, you can add further selections by holding down CTRL and then dragging or using one of the click selection techniques described in the section "Select Text Using Click Shortcuts" to make the other selections. Because you're holding down CTRL already, the CTRL-click selection techniques don't work for multiple selections.

Select Text with the Keyboard

Word offers two ways of selecting text with the keyboard. The first way is easy and intuitive, and you'll probably use it most of the time. The second way is odd and awkward at first, but it can come in handy sometimes.

Here's the easy way: Hold down SHIFT while you move the insertion point using the keystrokes shown in Table 3-1, earlier in this chapter. For example, to select from the insertion point's current position to the end of the line, hold down SHIFT and press END. As long as you keep holding down SHIFT, you can continue to change the selection. For instance, after pressing END to select to the end of the line, you could press ↓ to extend the selection down to the end of the next line.

The odd way of selecting text is called Extend Selection. Here's how to use it:

1. Press F8 to start Extend Selection mode. You won't see any change to the Word interface unless you've chosen to display the Selection Mode readout on the status bar. If you have, *Extend Selection* appears in the status bar to the right of the language readout.

2. Press F8 one or more times to select the text you want:
   - The second press selects the word the insertion point is in.
   - The third press selects the sentence the insertion point is in.

- The fourth press selects the paragraph the insertion point is in.
- The fifth press selects the whole document.

3. Alternatively, position the insertion point at the beginning of what you want to select before starting Extend Selection mode, press F8, and then press the character at the end of the selection. For example:

- Press T to select up to the next letter *t*.
- Press the period key to select to the end of the sentence.
- Press ENTER to select to the end of the paragraph.

4. Press ESC to turn off Extend Selection mode.

You now have a selection that you can manipulate as you would any other selection.

Select Text with the Keyboard and Mouse Together

One of the quickest and easiest ways of selecting text is to use the keyboard and mouse together. Click to position the insertion point at one end of the selection, and then SHIFT-click at the other end of the selection. This technique is especially useful for making a selection that requires scrolling to reach the end point: Click to place the insertion point at the beginning, scroll using the mouse, and then SHIFT-click. Don't scroll using the arrow keys or PAGE UP or PAGE DOWN, because those move the insertion point.

Sometimes you may need to select a rectangular block of text without selecting entire lines. To do so, ALT-drag from one corner of the block of text to the opposite corner (see Figure 3-3).

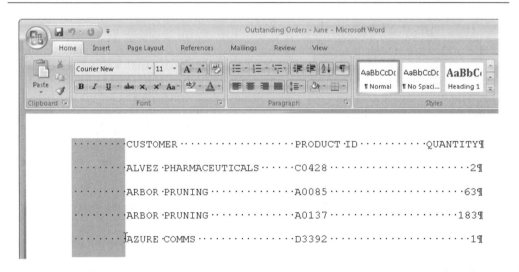

| FIGURE 3-3 | ALT-dragging is an easy way to delete leading spaces used to align text you've copied from a web page or to delete surplus spaces or tabs from a file of database output. |

3

Move Quickly Through Search Results, Tables, Headings, or Other Objects

Moving by page through a document is easy and fast, but often you'll want to move through a document from one object to another object of the same type—for example, from one table to another table, or from one heading to another heading. Word calls this "browsing" and provides the Select Browse Object panel (see Figure 3-4) to let you move quickly among objects.

When you've chosen the object, Word changes the Next button and Previous button to browse by that object, so you can use these buttons to move among objects of that type.

NOTE *From the keyboard, you can press CTRL-ALT-HOME to open the Select Browse Object panel from the keyboard. You can then press ←, →, ↑, and ↓ to move from one browse object to another. Press ENTER to make your current selection the browse object. You can press CTRL-PAGE UP to move to the previous object of that type or CTRL-PAGE DOWN to move to the next object.*

Navigate with the Document Map and Thumbnails

When you're working in a long document, it can be easy to lose track of where the current page appears in the document or where to find the next page you need. Word provides the Document Map and Thumbnails to help you find your way around long documents more easily. You can use only one of these features at a time, as each appears in the same vertical pane at the left side of the window. You can adjust the pane's width by dragging the bar that separates it from the window.

To display Document Map, choose View | Show/Hide | Document Map. Document Map (see Figure 3-5) shows the headings in the document; use it to navigate by heading. Click a heading to jump to it in the document pane. You can expand and collapse the levels of headings that are displayed by clicking the + (plus) and – (minus) signs next to the headings.

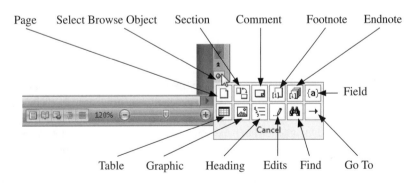

FIGURE 3-4   To move quickly from one heading, graphic, table, or other object to the next, click the Select Browse Object button, and then choose the object from the pop-up panel.

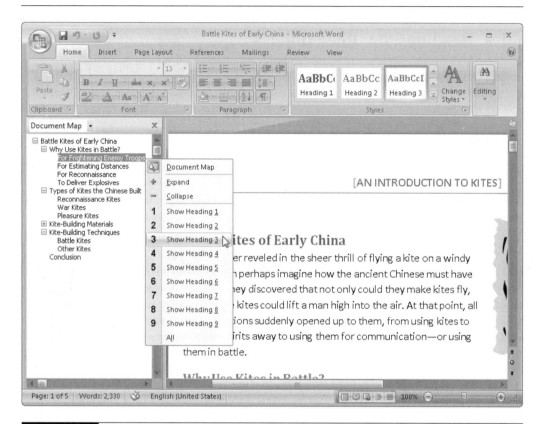

FIGURE 3-5 To control how many levels of headings Document Map displays, right-click in the pane and choose the lowest heading level you want to see from the shortcut menu.

If you find the font in Document Map hard to read, you're not alone. To make the font larger or use a different font, adjust the Document Map paragraph style. See the section "Create Custom Styles" in Chapter 9 for instructions.

To display Thumbnails, click the View tab, go to the Show/Hide group, and then select the Thumbnails check box. Thumbnails (see Figure 3-6) display a thumbnail picture of each page. If you have the Document Map displayed, you can choose Thumbnails in the Switch Navigation Window drop-down list in the Document Map pane's title bar. Thumbnails make it easy to see where graphics, tables, and page breaks are, although you can't read headings at conventional font sizes.

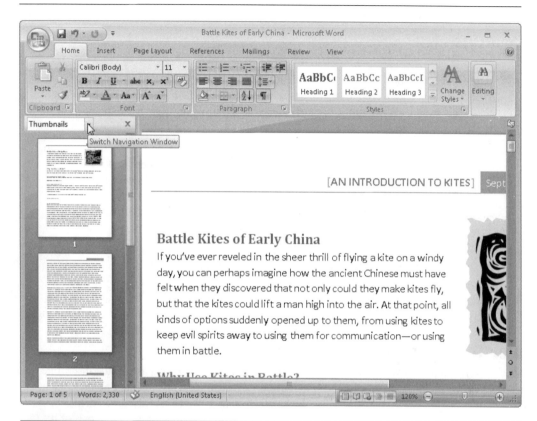

FIGURE 3-6   Use Thumbnails to navigate by the look of the pages. Click a thumbnail to display that page in the document pane.

Enter Text

Most documents need some text. You can enter it using the keyboard, by using copy and paste, by inserting an existing file, by using handwriting (if your PC has handwriting recognition capabilities), by using a scanner and optical character recognition, or via speech recognition. This section explores those options, starting with the keyboard.

Before entering any text, move the insertion point to the position where you want the text to appear. For example, if you want to add the text to the end of the document, move the insertion point there.

Enter Text Using the Keyboard

To enter text from the keyboard, simply type it in. Word inserts the characters you type.

As you type, Word monitors your text in several ways:

- **AutoCorrect** AutoCorrect watches the last few characters and replaces any AutoCorrect entry it detects with its replacement text—for example, replacing "aboutthe" with "about the." The section "Bring AutoCorrect Under Your Control" in Chapter 9 explains how to configure AutoCorrect.

- **AutoFormat As You Type** AutoFormat As You Type watches even more closely than AutoCorrect, trying to detect whether you're trying to type an element that it can replace for you—for example, replacing straight double quotation marks (") with smart quotes (" and "), applying an automatically numbered list, or inserting a parenthesis where you've forgotten it. The section "Tame AutoFormat As You Type" in Chapter 9 shows you how to tell AutoFormat As You Type what to format and what to leave alone.

- **Spell Checker** If you haven't turned it off, the spell checker monitors your text and puts a wavy red underline under any word that doesn't match an entry in its dictionaries. And if you've allowed the grammar checker to work as you type (as it's set to do by default), it puzzles over your grammar and puts a wavy green underline under any word or phrase it thinks might break a rule. Chapter 6 tells you how to turn off spelling and grammar checking.

Enter Text Using Copy and Paste

To enter text that already exists in another document, you can use copy and paste or the Insert File feature. Use copy and paste unless you need to insert either a complete document or all the contents of a bookmark that exists in the document—in which case, use Insert File (discussed next). A *bookmark* is an electronic marker that you can set in a document to mark a particular part of it.

To use copy and paste, follow these steps:

1. Open the document that contains the text you want.

2. Select the text and copy it, and then close the document. You can copy the text in any of these ways:

   - **Ribbon** Choose Home | Clipboard | Copy. Copy is the button that shows two small pages. (The word "Copy" appears if your Word window is wide enough.)

   - **Mouse** Right-click the selection, and then choose Copy.

   - **Keyboard** Press CTRL-C or CTRL-INSERT.

3. To close the document you copied from, click the Close button (the × button) or click the Office Button and then choose Close.

3

4. Position the insertion point where you want the text to appear in the other document, and paste it. You can paste the text in any of these ways:

- **Ribbon**   Choose Home | Clipboard | Paste. (Click the top part of the button, not the drop-down list.)
- **Mouse**   Right-click where you want the text, and then choose Paste.
- **Keyboard**   Press CTRL-V or SHIFT-INSERT.

5. If Word pastes the text using formatting you don't want, change the formatting by clicking the Paste Options button, and then clicking the option for the formatting you want:

- **Keep Source Formatting**   Maintains the formatting from the source document.
- **Match Destination Formatting**   Changes the formatting to that of the paragraph at which you pasted the text but maintains any direct formatting (for example, italics or boldface) applied to the text.
- **Keep Text Only**   Pastes the text with no formatting. The pasted text takes on the style from the paragraph where you pasted it and loses any direct formatting applied to the text.

How Word Decides Whether to Paste Formatting

Word uses complex criteria to decide whether to paste formatting. Here are the essentials:

- If you paste less than a paragraph (in other words, not including a paragraph mark), Word gives the pasted text the same style as the paragraph into which you paste it.
- If the pasted text contains one or more paragraph marks, and the pasted text has a different style than the paragraph at which you paste it, Word either leaves the existing style on the pasted text or applies the style that the destination has. How Word pastes the material depends on several settings, which you'll meet in the section "Configure Paste Options" in Chapter 9.

Insert a Document or Part of One

When you need to copy all the contents of an existing document into another document, you can use the Insert File command rather than copy and paste. Insert File saves you having to open and close the document that contains the material you want.

You can also use Insert File to copy only a part of the document rather than the whole document. To do so, mark that part of the text with a bookmark, an invisible electronic marker that you'll learn how to use in Chapter 12, and then tell Insert File to insert only that bookmark's contents.

To insert a document (or a bookmarked selection from a document), follow these steps:

1. Position the insertion point where you want the content from the document.

   ■ If you're inserting a whole document, place the insertion point at the beginning of a paragraph. You don't need to create a blank paragraph.

   ■ If you're inserting just the contents of a bookmark, position the insertion point wherever the text needs to fall.

2. Choose Insert | Text | Object | Text From File. Word displays the Insert File dialog box.

   ■ The Object button is the button that shows a cactus and the sun.

   ■ The word *Object* appears if the Word window is wide enough.

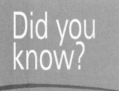

Why Insert File Can Be Better Than Copy and Paste

The Insert File command usually has the same effect as copy and paste but with two big advantages:

■ **Linking**   You can link what you insert to the source document, so that when the source document changes, you can update the content in the destination document.

■ **Keeping your tracked changes**   When you're using revision marks (discussed in the section "Track the Changes Made to a Document" in Chapter 10), Insert File lets you insert text in another document while maintaining the details of the tracked changes. If you use copy and paste instead, you can't keep the details of the tracked changes.

3. Select the document in the list.

   ■ If the drop-down list above the Insert button shows the wrong document type, open the list and choose the right type.

   ■ For example, to insert a .doc file, choose All Word Documents rather than Word Documents (*.docx).

4. If you want to insert only a bookmark's contents from the document, follow these steps:

   ■ Click the Range button. Word displays the Set Range dialog box, as shown here.

   ■ Type the bookmark's name in the Range text box. (If you're inserting cells from an Excel workbook, type the address or name of the range—hence the name.)

   ■ Click the OK button. Word closes the Set Range dialog box and returns you to the Insert File dialog box, where the name appears in the Range text box.

5. Choose how to insert the document.

   ■ To insert the document's or bookmark's content without linking, click the Insert button.

   ■ To insert and link the content, click the Insert button's drop-down arrow, and then choose Insert As Link.

6. Word inserts the content in the document. If you chose an entire document, it includes footnotes or endnotes but not any headers and footers.

Enter Text Using Handwriting

If your computer has a writing tablet (either one built into the screen, as on a Tablet PC, or a separate tablet), you can enter text via handwriting either into the input panel or directly into Word.

Enter Text Using a Scanner and OCR

If you have a scanner, you can use Office's built-in tools to scan a hard copy of a document into text that you can include in a Word document. Entering text via optical character recognition (OCR) should be faster than entering it manually—but you must proofread the text carefully after scanning it to root out any errors that creep in.

To scan a document and use OCR to turn it into text, connect your scanner if it's not already connected, and then follow these steps:

1. Choose Start | All Programs | Microsoft Office | Microsoft Office Tools | Microsoft Office Document Scanning. Windows displays the Scan New Document dialog box (see Figure 3-7). Choose Black And White if you're scanning a monochrome document. If you're scanning a color text document, choose Black And White From Color Page.

NOTE   *Administrators often configure Microsoft Office Document Scanning and Microsoft Office Document Imaging as components to be installed on first use—so if you haven't used these features yet, they may not be installed on your computer. If this is the case, the Windows Installer springs into action and installs them. As long as the installation files are stored on your computer (which is the default setting), you need do nothing but wait. But if the Windows Installer prompts you for the Office CD to install the features, insert the CD.*

FIGURE 3-7   In the Scan New Document dialog box, choose Black And White or Black And White From Color Page.

2. Choose settings for scanning, and then click the Scan button.

■ Select the Original Is Double Sided check box if the document is printed on both sides.

■ Select the Prompt For Additional Pages check box if the document has multiple pages.

■ Select the View File After Scanning check box to make Microsoft Office Document Scanning open automatically.

3. Click the Scan button. Microsoft Office Document Scanning scans the document, and then opens a Microsoft Office Document Imaging window displaying it.

4. Select the part of the document you want to recognize, and then choose Tools | Recognize Text Using OCR. Microsoft Office Document Imaging recognizes the text and then highlights it.

5. Choose Tools | Send Text To Word. Windows displays the Send Text To Word dialog box (see Figure 3-8).

6. In the upper part of the dialog box, specify which text to send to Word:

■ **Current Selection**   If you've selected part of the document, Microsoft Office Document Imaging normally selects this option button automatically. If there's no selection, this option button is unavailable.

■ **Selected Pages**   If you've selected one or more complete pages in the left pane, Microsoft Office Document Imaging normally selects this option button automatically. If you haven't selected pages, this option button is unavailable.

■ **All Pages**   Microsoft Office Document Imaging selects this option button automatically if you haven't selected a selection or pages. You can also select this option button even if one of the other option buttons is selected.

FIGURE 3-8   In the Send Text to Word dialog box, choose which parts of the text to export and decide whether to include any pictures the document contains.

7. If you want to include any pictures from the document, select the Maintain Pictures In Output check box. If you want only the document's text, clear this check box.

8. Click the OK button. Microsoft Office Document Imaging opens a new Word document, places the text in it, and displays the document so that you can start working in it.

In Word, run a spelling check on the new document and take care of any recognition errors. After that, proofread the text quickly against the original in case any whole words have been substituted during the recognition process. Any wrong words will be correctly spelled, so the spell checker will have no quarrel with them, but they will change the meaning of the text.

Enter Text Using Speech Recognition

In the 1990s, entering text via speech recognition seemed one of the most enticing attainable prospects for computing. But although speech recognition has matured enough to be usable, visions of entire offices filled with people talking clearly at their computers haven't yet materialized.

If you use your computer in a quiet place where your talking won't disturb others, Windows Vista's speech recognition is quite viable. Once you've set up your microphone by using the Speech Recognition applet in Control Panel, you can use dictation to enter text into a Word document (as shown here) or control Word via spoken commands.

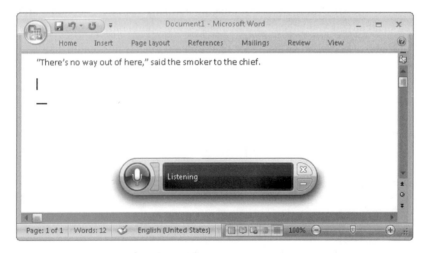

The Speech Recognition applet helps you dictate text into Word and control it via voice commands. To get good results with speech recognition, use a headset microphone rather than a desktop microphone or a microphone built into your laptop, and have the patience to follow through Windows' training program for speech recognition. The more you dictate—and in particular, the more mistakes that you correct—the more accurate the speech recognition becomes. Once you've trained speech recognition to recognize your full working vocabulary, it can be quite impressive.

When dictating via speech recognition, always read the dictated text closely as soon as possible after you dictate it. Speech recognition always enters whole words or phrases, but it may get entirely the wrong word (creating a "word-o" rather than a typo) or phrase (creating a "phrase-o"). Such errors can completely change the meaning of your text, but they're easy to miss if you don't reread your text closely enough.

Enter Symbols and Special Characters

When you need to insert a character that doesn't appear on your keyboard, use the Symbol panel and the Symbol dialog box.

The Symbol dialog box lets you browse through the available symbols. For symbols you need often, you can also use keyboard shortcuts or create AutoCorrect entries.

To insert a symbol or special character at the position of the insertion point, follow these steps.

1. Choose Insert | Symbols | Symbol. Word displays the Symbol panel, which contains 20 symbols, as shown here:

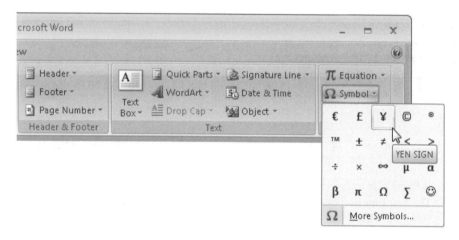

Word starts you off with frequently used symbols, and then replaces them with the symbols you use most frequently, so that as you continue to work, the Symbol panel contains the symbols you use the most.

2. If the symbol appears on the Symbol panel, click it, and Word inserts it. Skip the rest of the steps in this list. Otherwise, click the More Symbols item. Word displays the Symbol dialog box (see Figure 3-9). If the Subset drop-down list appears, you can use it to jump to a particular group of characters—such as Currency Symbols—but many of the names aren't helpful (for example, Arabic Extended or Latin Extended Additional).

3. Usually, the easiest place to start is on the Special Characters tab, which contains some common symbols including symbols that appear as blanks (for example, em spaces). If the symbol appears here, go to step 6.

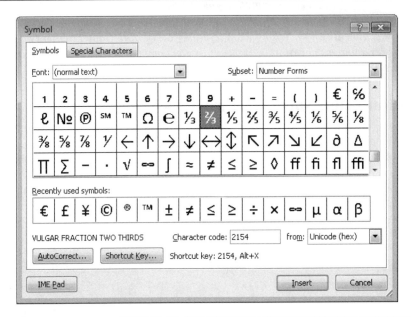

FIGURE 3-9 The Symbols tab in the Symbol dialog box lets you browse all available symbols on your computer.

4. If the symbol doesn't appear on the Special Characters tab, switch back to the Symbols tab, and look for the symbol in the list.

- If necessary, change the font in the Font drop-down list.

- The first time you open the Symbol dialog box in a Word session, Word selects the "(Normal Text)" item in the Font drop-down list. This means you're working with the font used where the insertion point is in the document.

- Use this font unless you find it doesn't contain the symbol you want. For example, if you need a graphical character rather than a textual character, you may need to use a font such as Symbol, Wingdings (or Wingdings 2 or 3), or Webdings.

- The next time the Symbol dialog box opens, the Font drop-down list shows the font that you last used in the dialog box.

5. Click the symbol or special character that you want.

6. Double-click the symbol to insert it in the document, then click the Close button.

- You can also click the symbol or special character, and then click the Insert button to insert it, but double-clicking is usually faster and easier.

- The Recently Used Symbols box at the bottom of the Symbols tab gives you quick access to the last 16 symbols you've inserted.

3

TIP
You can leave the Symbol dialog box open while you're working. This is handy when you need to insert multiple symbols with text in between them. To switch between the Symbol dialog box and the document, press CTRL-TAB, or simply click in one or the other.

Create a Shortcut Key for a Symbol or Special Character

Word comes with built-in keyboard shortcuts for many of the characters listed on the Special Characters tab and for a few of those on the Symbols tab. To save yourself time, create a shortcut key for each symbol or special character you'd like to be able to enter via a keyboard shortcut.

NOTE
Before you create shortcuts for any accented character, see the section "Type Accented Characters and Special Characters," later in this chapter.

To add a shortcut key for a symbol or special character, follow these steps:

1. Choose Insert | Symbols | Symbol. Word displays the Symbol dialog box.

2. Select the symbol or special character on the Symbols tab or the Special Characters tab.

3. Click the Shortcut Key button. Word displays the Customize Keyboard dialog box with the symbol or special character selected in the Commands list and the focus in the Press New Shortcut Key box.

4. Press the shortcut key you want to assign.

5. Make sure that the Currently Assigned To readout is either blank or shows only a keyboard shortcut that you're prepared to overwrite.

6. Choose the appropriate document or template in the Save Changes In drop-down list.

   ■ Normally, you'll want to save shortcut keys in Normal.dotm (the Normal template) so that they're always available when you're using Word.

Did you know?

What's the Difference Between a Symbol and a Special Character?

When using the Symbol panel and Symbol dialog box, you may find yourself wondering what the difference is between a symbol and a special character.

Don't waste time wondering, because there's not really a difference. Most of the characters that appear on the Special Characters tab are available on the Symbols tab as well, but the listing on the Special Characters tab, which includes each character's name, lets you find the characters easily and distinguish the blank characters from each other. For example, without the names, it would be hard to tell the No-Width Optional Break from the No-Width Non Break, as both of these "characters" appear as blanks in the squares.

■ Sometimes, however, you may want to save a shortcut key in a particular document or template so that it's available only for that document or for documents based on that template.

7. Click the Assign button. Word assigns the keyboard shortcut.

8. Click the Close button. Word closes the Customize Keyboard dialog box, returning you to the Symbol dialog box.

9. Click the Cancel button. Word closes the Symbol dialog box.

Create an AutoCorrect Entry for a Symbol or Special Character

Out of the box, Word includes AutoCorrect entries for entering common symbols (such as ® and ™) from the keyboard. You can add further AutoCorrect entries to enter symbols or special characters.

To add an AutoCorrect entry for a symbol, follow these steps:

1. Choose Insert | Symbols | Symbol. Word displays the Symbol dialog box.

2. Choose the symbol or special character for which you want to create an AutoCorrect entry.

3. Click the AutoCorrect button. Word displays the AutoCorrect dialog box with the symbol or special character entered in the With text box and the Formatted Text option button selected if this symbol or special character needs formatting. The AutoCorrect dialog box contains only the AutoCorrect tab and Math AutoCorrect tab, not the AutoFormat tab, the AutoFormat As You Type tab, and the Smart Tags tab.

4. Type the AutoCorrect term in the Replace box, and then click the OK button.

5. If the Formatted Text option button was selected when you closed the AutoCorrect dialog box, Word may prompt you to save changes to the Normal template when you close Word. The change is the addition of the formatted AutoCorrect entry, so click the Yes button. (If you've told Word not to prompt you about saving the Normal template, Word saves the changes without bothering you.)

Insert a Symbol by Typing Its Character Code

If you're feeling technologically hardcore, you can insert a symbol from the keyboard by typing its character code, the four-digit number that your computer uses to identify the character. The easiest way to learn a character's code is by looking at the Character Code text box on the Symbols tab of the Symbol dialog box. Make sure that ASCII (Decimal) is selected in the From drop-down list; if either ASCII (Hex) or Unicode (Hex) is selected, you'll see hexadecimal numbers (counting with the numerals 0 to 9 and the letters A to F).

The Shortcut Key readout below the Character Code text box shows the ALT-key combination you can use to enter the character code. If the character code has four digits, it's the same number; if the character code is shorter, the shortcut adds one or more leading zeros to make it four digits. For example, the decimal ASCII character code for a micro sign (μ) is 181, so the shortcut number is 0181.

How to ... Create AutoCorrect Entries for Words Containing Symbols

Entering a symbol or special character in a document via AutoCorrect works well only for a symbol or special character that you enter on its own rather than as part of a word: If you type the AutoCorrect entry with a letter after it, Word doesn't recognize it.

The workaround is to create an AutoCorrect entry for the word rather than for the symbol or special character.

1. Type the word in the document (inserting symbols as needed), and then select it.

2. Click the Office button, and then choose Word Options. Word displays the Word Options dialog box.

3. In the left pane, click the Proofing category.

4. Click the AutoCorrect Options button. Word displays the AutoCorrect Options dialog box with the word in the With text box and the Formatted Text option button selected if necessary.

5. In the Replace text box, type the AutoCorrect term.

6. Click the OK button. Word closes the AutoCorrect dialog box.

7. Click the OK button. Word closes the Word Options dialog box.

NOTE *If the Shortcut Key readout is blank, use the number shown in the Character Code text box, adding leading zeros as needed to make it four digits.*

To enter the shortcut key combination, make sure NUM LOCK is on, then hold down ALT while you type the number on the numeric keypad. Release the ALT key, and the character appears.

TIP *If you know the code for the character you want, you can type it in the Character Code text box to make Word select it in the symbols list. This can save you a lot of scrolling.*

Type Accented Characters and Special Characters

Word also allows you to enter accented characters and certain other special characters from the keyboard by using key combinations. Learning the key combinations for any such characters that you use often can save you time over using the Symbol dialog box. Table 3-2 lists these characters.

Character Description	Characters	Press This Key Combination	Example
Acute accent	Á á É é Í í Ó ó Ú ú	CTRL-', and then the letter	CTRL-', E (uppercase) produces É
Circumflex accent	Â â Ê ê Î î Ô ô Û û	CTRL-SHIFT-^, and then the letter	CTRL-SHIFT-^, I (lowercase) produces î
Dieresis	Ä ä Ë ë Ï ï Ö ö Ü ü	CTRL-SHIFT-:, and then the letter	CTRL-SHIFT-:, U produces Ü
Grave accent	À à È è Ì ì Ò ò Ù ù	CTRL-accent key, and then the letter	CTRL-accent, O (lowercase) produces ò
Cedilla	Ç ç	CTRL-, (comma), and then C (uppercase or lowercase)	CTRL-, (comma), C (uppercase) produces Ç
Diphthong	Æ æ Œ œ	CTRL-SHIFT-& (ampersand), and then the first letter	CTRL-SHIFT-& (ampersand), a produces æ
Enye	Ã ã Ñ ñ Õ õ	CTRL-SHIFT-~ (tilde), and then the letter	CTRL-SHIFT-~ (tilde), N (uppercase) produces Ñ
O-Slash	Ø ø	CTRL-/, and then O (uppercase or lowercase)	CTRL-/, O (uppercase) produces Ø
A with Ring	Å å	CTRL-SHIFT-@, and then A (uppercase or lowercase)	CTRL-SHIFT-@, A produces Å
S-zett (double S)	ß	CTRL-SHIFT-& (ampersand), and then s (lowercase)	CTRL-SHIFT-& (ampersand), s produces ß

TABLE 3-2   Key Combinations for Entering Accented Characters and Special Characters

Edit Text

Once you've entered some text in a document, you'll probably find you need to change it. Word processors excel at letting you change your documents quickly and easily, and Word offers a wide variety of editing features.

This section introduces you to the basic features for editing text: cut, copy, and paste; drag and drop; deleting text; and undo and redo. You'll meet the many other features later in this book. For example, Chapter 6 shows you how to check spelling and grammar, and Chapter 10 explains how to use revision marks to track the changes you make to a document.

Move or Copy Text

Often, you'll realize that some text actually needs to be moved to a different place in the document—or that you can get a jump-start on creating a new part of the document by copying an existing part. Word lets you move text by using either cut and paste or drag and drop, and copy text by using either copy and paste or drag and drop (with the CTRL key).

Use Cut and Paste or Copy and Paste

When you cut or copy text (or another object), Word puts it on the Office Clipboard, a storage area for cut and copied items in the Office programs. Word also puts the text on the Windows Clipboard, a storage area for sharing data among all Windows programs, so you can paste the text into a non-Office program if you want.

To work with the Office Clipboard, click the Home tab and use the buttons in the Clipboard group (shown here).

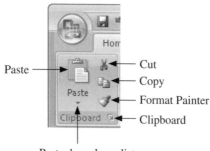

Paste — Cut
Copy
Format Painter
Clipboard
Paste drop-down list

To move text using cut and paste, or to copy text using copy and paste, follow these steps.

1. Select the text you want to cut or copy. (Use the selection techniques you learned earlier in this chapter.)

2. Issue a Cut command or a Copy command, making Word put the text on the Office Clipboard, a storage area for cut and copied items. Take one of the following actions:

   ■ **Cut** Click the Cut button, right-click and choose Cut from the context menu, or press CTRL-X. Word removes the text from the document.

   ■ **Copy** Click the Copy button, right-click and choose Copy from the context menu, or press CTRL-C.

3. Move the insertion point to where you want to place the text:

   ■ Move the mouse pointer to where you want the insertion point, and then click.

   ■ Alternatively, move the insertion point using the keyboard.

   ■ If you want what you're pasting in to replace some existing text, select that text.

4. Click the Paste button, right-click and choose Paste, or press CTRL-V. Word pastes in the text at the insertion point. The text remains on the Office Clipboard, so you can paste it in somewhere else if necessary.

Use Drag and Drop

Using the Clipboard is easy and methodical, but Word provides a quicker way of moving or copying text: drag and drop with the mouse. Follow these steps:

1. Select the text you want to move or copy. Drag and drop uses the mouse, so you'll probably want to make the selection using the mouse too. But you can use the keyboard instead—or the keyboard and mouse together—if you prefer.

2. Click anywhere in the selection, and then drag to the new location:

   ■ If you want to copy the text rather than move it, hold down CTRL as you drag.

   ■ As you drag, Word displays a shadow insertion point that shows where the text will land, together with a shadowy rectangle that indicates you're moving text.

   ■ If you're holding down CTRL to copy, Word displays a plus (+) sign on the shadowy rectangle.

3. Release the mouse button to move or copy the text. Release CTRL if you were holding it down.

Copy Several Items to the Clipboard

In Windows' early days, there was only one Clipboard: the Windows Clipboard, which could hold only one piece of information at a time. Each time you cut or copied another piece of information, it replaced the previous item.

People found this one-item limit restricting, so Microsoft added the Office Clipboard to the Office programs. The Office Clipboard can hold 24 pieces of information at once; cut or copy a 25th, and it knocks off the oldest piece of information. When you paste, the Office Clipboard always gives you the latest item you cut or copied, but you can also use the older items if you need.

To work with the Office Clipboard, choose Home | Clipboard | Clipboard. (The Clipboard button is the tiny button with the arrow pointing downward and to the right.) Word displays the Clipboard task pane (see Figure 3-10). You can then

■ Click an item to paste it.

■ Click the Paste All button to paste in all items in sequence.

■ Click the Clear All button to delete all the items from the Clipboard.

■ Hover the mouse over an item, click the button, and then choose Delete from the menu to delete the item.

If you want, you can set the Clipboard task pane to appear automatically. To configure the Clipboard's behavior, click the Options button at the bottom of the task pane and choose the options you want from the menu that appears (as shown here).

3

FIGURE 3-10   The Clipboard task pane shows the last 24 items you've cut or copied in the Office programs. Each item has a program icon to indicate where it came from.

- **Show Office Clipboard Automatically**   When you select this check box, the Clipboard task pane appears automatically when you cut or copy more than one item without pasting an item in between cuts or copies.

- **Show Office Clipboard When CTRL-C Pressed Twice**   When you select this check box, you can display the Clipboard by pressing CTRL-C twice in immediate succession. This shortcut can be easier than clicking the Clipboard button, especially if a tab other than the Home tab is displayed.

- **Collect Without Showing Office Clipboard**   When you select this check box, it prevents the Office Clipboard from appearing automatically, even if you've turned on either or both of the previous two settings.

- **Show Office Clipboard Icon On Taskbar**   When you select this check box, a clipboard icon appears in the system tray (or notification area) at the right or bottom end of the taskbar. You can double-click this icon to display the Clipboard task pane, or right-click it to access the same settings as the Options button menu offers.

- **Show Status Near Taskbar When Copying**   When you select this check box, Windows displays a Clipboard ScreenTip near the system tray when you cut or copy data to the Office Clipboard. The ScreenTip shows the ordinal number of the item you've collected— for example, "6 of 24 – Item Collected" for the sixth item you've cut or copied.

Perform Special Pasting

When you cut or copy text, you get its formatting as well; and when you paste text in, you paste in the formatting too. Sometimes this carryover works well, but other times you'll want just the text without the formatting.

Usually, the easiest way to proceed is to go ahead and paste. If pasting gives you a result you don't want, click the Paste Options Smart Tag that Word displays, and then choose the formatting option you want from the menu that appears, as shown here.

You can keep the source formatting, match the destination formatting, or keep only the text. The last item on the menu, Set Default Paste, opens the Word Options dialog box so that you can change the settings for pasting text (see the section "Configure Paste Options" in Chapter 9).

To control pasting before the text lands in your document, click the Home tab, go to the Clipboard group, click the Paste drop-down arrow, and choose Paste Special. The Paste Special dialog box opens (see Figure 3-11). Choose the item type you want to paste, and then click the OK button.

The Paste Special dialog box offers a confusing array of paste options that changes depending on which type of item is on the Clipboard. These choices are for a paragraph of text (which includes formatting). Normally, you'll want to choose either the Formatted Text (RTF) option to paste in the item with formatting or the Unformatted Text item to paste in the text without formatting.

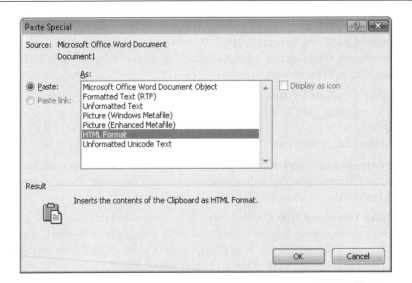

FIGURE 3-11 The Paste Special dialog box offers an array of paste options depending on which type of item is on the Clipboard.

3

Delete Text

To remove text from a document, delete it. You can use either the DELETE key or the BACKSPACE key, alone or in combination:

- **DELETE**   Press DELETE to delete selected text or objects or to delete the character to the right of the insertion point.
- **BACKSPACE**   Press BACKSPACE to delete the character to the left of the insertion point.
- **CTRL-DELETE**   Press CTRL-DELETE to delete from the insertion point to the start of the next word. When the insertion point is at the start of a word, pressing CTRL-DELETE deletes the word.
- **CTRL-BACKSPACE**   Press CTRL-BACKSPACE to delete from the insertion point to the start of the word. When the insertion point is at the start of a word, pressing CTRL-BACKSPACE deletes the previous word.

There's no easy way to delete text with the mouse, but you can use the Cut command to remove text from a document. The difference is that when you use Cut, Word places the cut material on the Clipboard so that you can paste it elsewhere. That makes Cut a poor way of disposing of items that you don't want to reuse.

You can also delete text by selecting it and typing over it. Usually, pressing DELETE is easier.

Use Undo and Redo

Sooner or later, you'll make a mistake—or you'll discover that you made a mistake a couple of minutes ago. You can use Word's Undo feature to undo one or more of the last changes you made.

To use Undo from the keyboard, press CTRL-Z once for each change you want to undo. Until you get the hang of what Word reckons is one change and what the next, press CTRL-Z once at a time and see which change is undone. If you undo too many changes and need to redo one, press CTRL-Y.

You can also undo and redo actions using the Undo button and Redo button on the Quick Access Toolbar:

- To undo one change with the mouse, click the Undo button. To see which change Word will undo, hover the mouse pointer over the Undo button so that Word displays a ScreenTip showing the change, as shown here.

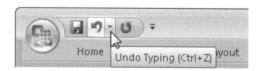

■ To undo multiple changes, choose the changes from the drop-down list, as shown here.

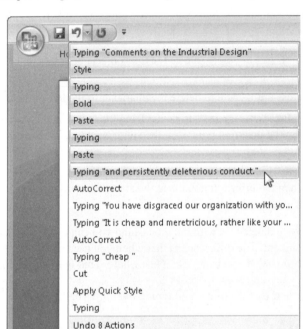

■ Click the Redo button to restore a change you've undone.

 *You can also press* CTRL-Y *or click the Redo button to repeat the last action you've taken. (When you haven't undone an action, the Redo button is called Repeat.)*

Use Find and Replace

When you're working in a long document, you'll often need to search for a particular word, phrase, or object.

Word's Find feature lets you quickly locate pretty much any part of a document, from a word or phrase to a special character (such as a paragraph mark), from direct formatting (such as bold) to style formatting, from text in a particular language to an object (such as a picture).

Find's sister feature, Replace, lets you replace text, formatting, or styles, either one instance at a time or all instances in a single sweep.

Find Text

What you'll probably want to search for first is text—for example, a word that you know occurs in the part of the document to which you want to turn your attention. Word lets you search for text on its own or text with formatting.

How to ... **Recover from an Undo Operation You Can't Undo**

Undo is a wonderful feature that can save your work on many occasions—but there are some changes that it can't undo. Here are a couple of examples—and ways you may be able to recover from them.

You save the document, close it, and then realize you've made a disastrous change. Word clears the Undo list for a document when you close it, so you can't recover by reopening the document and using Undo. But if you have set Word to create backup documents, you may be able to recover the document from a Word document backup.

1. Open a Windows Explorer window to the folder that contains the document you just wrecked.

2. Look for a file named "Backup of filename.wbk," where *filename* is the damaged file. For example, if the document is named July Orders.docx, the backup file is named Backup of July Orders.wbk.

3. Right-click the backup file, and then choose Open With. Windows displays the Open With dialog box.

4. Select Microsoft Office Word in the list box, and then click the OK button. The backup document opens in Word.

5. If the backup document is usable, click the Office Button, click Save As, and then use the Save As dialog box to save the document under a new name.

Or, say you realize you've made a terrible edit to the document—for instance, while looking at a paper document, you typed new text over a large chunk of text you had selected. You find that, for whatever reason, Undo doesn't get you back to before the edit. If you haven't saved the document since you made the edit, closing the document without saving changes may be your best bet. You'll lose any other changes you made since you last saved the document, but this loss may be better than the loss caused by your edit. Reopen the document and proceed with greater care.

To find text, follow these steps:

1. If the word or phrase appears in the part of the document you're using, select it, and then copy it.

   ■ By copying the word or phrase, and then pasting it into the Find dialog box, you can save time and avoid typing mistakes.

   ■ You might also copy the word or phrase from another source—for example, from an e-mail message or from a workbook.

2. Press CTRL-F or choose Home | Editing | Find. Word displays the Find And Replace dialog box with the Find tab foremost.

- The first time you open the Find And Replace dialog box in a Word session, you see the small version without the Search Options area. Click the More button to display the rest of the dialog box.

- The next time you open the dialog box, Word displays the full version (see Figure 3-12).

3. In the Find What text box, type or paste the search text. To paste, right-click and then choose Paste from the context menu, or press CTRL-V.

- For advanced searches, you can use *wildcards*—special characters that match a range of characters. See Table 3-4 later in this chapter for details.

- Word remembers the details of searches you've performed in this session. To retrieve an earlier search, click the drop-down arrow on the Find What text box and choose the search from the list. Word lists the searches in reverse order, so the latest search is first.

4. In the Search drop-down list, choose the search direction: All, Down, or Up.

- Word selects All at first, which makes Find search all of the document. Normally, you'll want to leave All selected.

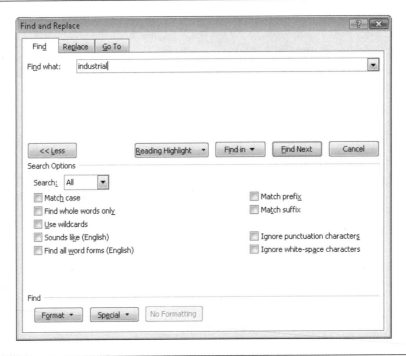

FIGURE 3-12   It's usually best to work with the full version of the Find And Replace dialog box so that you can see which search options are set.

■ If you want to search downward first, choose Down. When it reaches the end of the document, Word prompts you whether to continue searching at the beginning.

■ Similarly, you can search Up and have Word prompt you to continue when it reaches the start of the document. For example, you would search upward if you needed to find the previous instance of the search term.

5. Choose options for the search in the Search Options area. Word lists the options you've chosen under the Find What text box.

■ **Match Case**   Select this check box to make Word find only instances of the search text that have the same capitalization as you entered. For example, you might want to replace all instances of "Division" with "Department" but leave any instances of "division" (all lowercase) untouched.

■ **Find Whole Words Only**   Select this check box to make Word find the search text only when it's a whole word rather than part of another word. For example, you might want to find "other" but not "otherwise," "brother," or "another." Word makes this check box unavailable if the search text includes a space.

■ **Use Wildcards**   Select this check box if you want to use wildcards. See the section "Perform Advanced Searches with Wildcards and Pattern Matching," later in this chapter, for details.

■ **Match Prefix and Match Suffix**   Select the Match Prefix check box if you want to find the search text only at the beginning of a word. For example, you might want to find "fast" in "fastener" but not in "breakfast." Select the Match Suffix check box if you want to find it only at the end of a word—for example, to find "after" in "hereafter" but not in "afterward."

■ **Ignore Punctuation Characters**   Select this check box to make Word ignore any punctuation that occurs within the search string. For example, with this check box selected, searching for "oh mama" finds "Oh, Mama" and "Oh! Mama"; with the check box cleared, the search doesn't find these two examples.

■ **Ignore White-Space Characters**   Select this check box to have Word ignore spaces and tabs that appear in matches for the search string. If you clear this check box, any extra tabs or spaces prevent Word from finding instances that otherwise match the search string.

6. Start the search. For example, click the Find Next button.

■ **Find Next**   Click this button if you want to make Word locate and select the next instance of the search text. (If you choose Up in the Search drop-down list, Word finds the previous instance—the next one up in the document.) You can then edit that instance.

■ **Find In**   To find and select all instances of the search text, click the Find In drop-down button, and then choose which part of the document to search: Main Document, Headers and Footers, or Text Boxes in Main Document. This option lets you get an overview of how often, and where, the search text appears in the document (or in the headers and footers, or in the text boxes). Word maintains the selection when you close the Find And Replace dialog box, but as soon as you move the insertion point, the selection disappears.

■ **Reading Highlight** To make Word highlight all instances of the search text, click the Reading Highlight drop-down button, and then choose Highlight All. Word maintains the highlighting when you close the Find And Replace dialog box and move the insertion point, so this option lets you work through the found items at your leisure. To remove the highlighting, open the Find dialog box if you've closed it, and then choose Reading Highlight | Clear Highlighting.

7. When you've found what you were looking for, click the Close button to close the Find And Replace dialog box.

Instead of closing the Find And Replace dialog box, you can also work in the document while the dialog box is open: Click in the document, and edit as usual. Click in the dialog box to return to it. Alternatively, press CTRL-TAB to move the focus between the dialog box and the document.

Leaving the Find And Replace dialog box open can be handy, but you may find it gets in the way—and Word provides an easy way to continue the same search once you've closed the dialog box. When you perform the search, Word sets the Browse Object To Find, which turns the Previous and Next buttons at the foot of the vertical scroll bar into Previous Find/GoTo and Next Find/GoTo buttons. To search for the previous or next instance of the search term, click one of these buttons, or press the corresponding keyboard shortcuts, CTRL-PAGE UP and CTRL-PAGE DOWN.

Did you know?

The "Sounds Like" and "Find All Word Forms" Features Can Give Unexpected Results

Find and Replace includes two imaginative and powerful features that you should use with care: the Sounds Like feature and the Find All Word Forms feature. These features can be helpful, but you may find they give unpredictable results. Save your documents before using these features, especially if you use them with Replace rather than Find.

When you use either of these features, Word makes the Match Case check box and the Find Whole Words Only check box unavailable.

Select the Sounds Like check box if you want to find words that sound similar to the search string. You may get some surprises here. For example, searching for "there" with the Sounds Like feature on finds "their" but not "they're," which most people reckon sounds like "there."

Select the Find All Word Forms check box to find all forms of the search text. For example, if you enter "give" in the Find What box, Word finds "gives," "giving," "given," and "gave" as well. You can even use Find All Word Forms in Replace operations, although Word is smart enough to warn you that doing so may not be a good idea.

Find Characters You Can't Type

Sometimes you'll need to find a character that you can't type from your keyboard, such as a paragraph mark or a column break. To enter such a character into the Find What text box in the Find And Replace dialog box, you use Word's special characters.

You can enter the special characters by using the Special pop-up menu in the Find And Replace dialog box (as shown in Figure 3-13) or by typing the character codes (see Table 3-3). Even if you choose not to type the character codes, you'll probably find them useful to know, because you'll be able to read earlier searches in the Find What drop-down list and examples of advanced searches online. (If you see a different menu when you click the Special button, clear the Use Wildcards check box.)

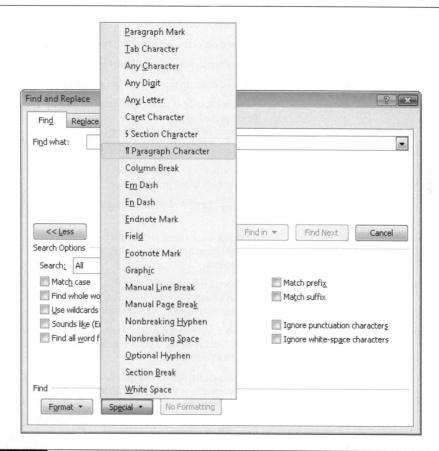

FIGURE 3-13   The Special pop-up menu provides an easy way to enter character codes in the Find And Replace dialog box.

To Find	Use This Character Code	Example or Explanation
Paragraph mark	^p	**^pThe** finds *The* at the beginning of a paragraph.
Tab	^t	**^t^t** finds two tabs in sequence.
Any character	^?	**tw^?^?** finds *twee*, *twin*, *TW07*, and other four-character strings beginning with *tw*.
Any digit	^#	**^#^#.^#^#** finds any two digits, a period, and two more digits—for example, *49.23*.
Any letter	^$	**b^$y** finds *bay*, *boy*, and *buy* but not *B2Y*.
Caret	^^	The caret denotes a character code, so the caret character needs its own code.
Column break	^n	A manual column break inserted from the Page Layout | Page Setup | Breaks panel.
Em dash	^+	An em dash is the longer of the two standard dashes.
En dash	^=	An en dash is the shorter of the two standard dashes.
Endnote mark	^e	Finds an endnote mark in the document's text.
Field	^d	Finds fields only if field codes rather than field results are displayed. (Press ALT-F9 to toggle all fields in a document between codes and results.)
Footnote mark	^f	Finds a footnote's mark in the document's text.
Graphic	^g	Finds only inline graphics (ones in the document's text), not graphics in the graphics layer.
Manual line break	^l	A manual line break is one you create by pressing SHIFT-ENTER.
Manual page break	^m	A manual page break is one you create by choosing Page Layout | Page Setup | Breaks | Page Break or pressing CTRL-ENTER.
Nonbreaking hyphen	^~	A nonbreaking hyphen is one that you insert from the Special Characters tab of the Symbol dialog box or by pressing CTRL-SHIFT-_ (underscore).
Nonbreaking space	^s	A nonbreaking space is one you insert from the Special Characters tab of the Symbol dialog box or by pressing CTRL-SHIFT-SPACEBAR.
Optional hyphen	^-	An optional hyphen is one you insert from the Special Characters tab of the Symbol dialog box or by pressing CTRL-- (hyphen).
Section break	^b	A section break is a break that you insert by choosing Page Layout | Page Setup | Breaks and selecting the type of break from the panel.
Section character	^%	A section character is §, the symbol used for "section."

TABLE 3-3   Special Character Codes for Searching (*Continued*)

To Find	Use This Character Code	Example or Explanation
White space	^w	White space is spaces, tabs, or any combination of the two.
ASCII character	^nnn	Replace nnn with the ASCII character code. For example, **^84** finds T (which is ASCII code 84). It also finds t (ASCII code 116) unless you select the Match Case check box.
ANSI character	^0nnn	Replace nnn with the ANSI character code; use leading zeros as needed to make a four-digit number. For example, **^0100** finds d (ANSI code 100). It also finds D (ANSI code 68) unless you select the Match Case check box.
Unicode character	^unnnn	Replace nnnn with the Unicode character code. For example, **^u230** finds æ, the a/e ligature. Note that the u is lowercase; a capital U gives an error.

TABLE 3-3   Special Character Codes for Searching

Perform Advanced Searches with Wildcards and Pattern Matching

Finding paragraphs, tabs, white space, and the like is helpful for many searches, but sometimes you'll need more power and flexibility in your searches. For example, you may need to find text that matches a certain pattern or text that excludes particular characters.

Word allows you to perform such searches by using *wildcard characters*—characters that specify a range of meanings. Table 3-4 explains the wildcards and what they mean, giving examples of how to use them.

To tell Word you're using wildcard characters, select the Use Wildcards check box in the Find and Replace dialog box. You can then enter the wildcards by using the Special pop-up menu and then typing the specific characters or by typing the wildcard characters and specific characters in the Find What box.

Replace Text

Rather than perform a Find operation and then deal with each instance of the search text manually, you may want to have Word replace some or all instances for you. The Replace feature lets you do so.

Once you've gotten the hang of finding text, replacing text is easy. Follow these steps:

1. Press CTRL-H or choose Home | Editing | Replace. Word displays the Find And Replace dialog box with the Replace tab foremost.

   ■ The first time you open the Find And Replace dialog box in a Word session, you see the small version. Click the More button to display the rest of the dialog box (see Figure 3-14).

Wildcard Characters	Use This to Find	Example
?	Any character	**dea?** finds *dead*, *dear*, and the first four letters of *death*.
*	Zero or more characters	**a?r*plane** finds both *airplane* and *aeroplane*.
[*characters*]	Any one of the characters entered between the brackets	**b[aiu]llet** finds *ballet*, *billet*, and *bullet*.
[*character1-character2*]	Any one character in the range between *character1* and *character2* (the characters must be entered in alphabetical order)	**P[Q-S]9** finds *PQ9*, *PR9*, and *PS9*.
[!*character1-character2*]	Any one character except the range specified by *character1* and *character2*	**Class [!B-D]** finds *Class A*, *Class E*, through to *Class Z*, but not *Class B*, *Class C*, or *Class D*.
character{*number*}	The *number* of occurrences of *character* or expression	**10{3}** finds *1000* (a 1 followed by three zeros).
character{*number1, number2*}	From *number1* to *number2* instances of *character* or expression	**1{3,5}** finds *111*, *1111*, and *11111*.
character@	One or more instances of *character* or expression	**10@m** finds *10m*, *100m*, and *1000m*, each of which contains a 1, one or more zeros, and an m.
<(*characters*)	*characters* (entered in parentheses) at the start of a word	**<(test)** finds *testing* and *tested* but not *protest*. It's usually easier to select the Match Prefix check box (which is new in Word 2007).
(*characters*)>	*characters* (entered in parentheses) at the end of a word	**(test)>** finds *contest* and *protest* but not *testing*. It's usually easier to select the Match Suffix check box (which is new in Word 2007).

TABLE 3-4   Wildcards for Advanced Searches

2. Type the search text in the Find What text box.

■ The Replace tab of the Find And Replace dialog box has the same controls as the Find tab but adds the Replace With text box for specifying the replacement text.

■ If you've already performed a search in this Word session, you can reuse a search term from the drop-down list on the Find What text box.

3. Choose Find options in the Search Options area:

■ Select any of the check boxes to apply an option to the search. For example, you might select the Match Case check box to restrict the search to the capitalization you use in the Find What text box.

■ The Options readout under the Find What text box summarizes the options you've applied.

3

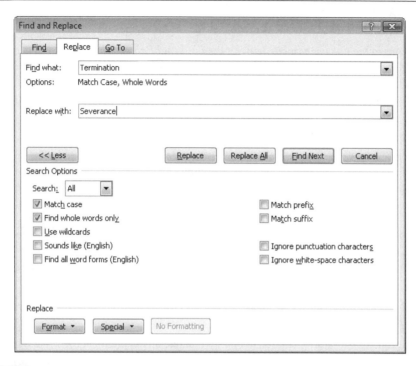

FIGURE 3-14   The Find And Replace dialog box offers a Replace All button for replacing all instances of the search text in the document without reviewing each change.

4. Type the replacement text in the Replace With text box. To reuse a replacement term, click the drop-down arrow on the Replace With text box, and then choose it from the drop-down list.

5. In the Search drop-down list, choose the search direction: All, Down, or Up.

6. Click the Find Next button, the Replace button, or the Replace All button, as appropriate:

■ Click the Find Next button to find the first instance of the search of the search term. (When you start the search, you can also click the Replace button to find the first instance.) Then click the Replace button to replace this instance alone and find the next instance, or click the Find Next button to leave this instance unchanged and find the next instance.

■ Click the Replace All button to replace all instances. If you chose All in the Search drop-down list, Word replaces all instances in the entire document. If you chose Down and started the search after the start of the document, Word prompts you to continue the search from the start; if you chose Up and started the search before the end of the document, Word prompts you to continue the search from the end.

7. After finishing the Replace operation, click the Close button. Word closes the Find And Replace dialog box.

To work in the document while leaving the Find And Replace dialog box open, click in the document or press CTRL-TAB. To return to the Find And Replace dialog box, click in it or press CTRL-TAB again.

Find and Replace Formatting or Styles

Find allows you to search not only for text but all kinds of formatting as well—either formatting applied to specific text or formatting on its own. For example, you may need to replace all instances of underlined text with italic or—better—with a character style that applies the italic. Or you may need to replace some instances of one style with another style.

To replace formatting, follow these steps:

1. Choose Home | Editing | Replace or press CTRL-H. Word displays the Find And Replace dialog box with the Replace tab foremost. If you see the small version of the dialog box, click the More button.

2. Enter your search text (if you're searching for any) in the Find What text box.

- If you want to replace particular text that has the formatting, type the text in the Find What text box.

- To replace formatting applied to any text, delete any contents in the Find What text box so that it is blank.

- When replacing one style with another style, you'll usually want to leave the Find What text box blank so that Word finds all the text that has the style.

3. Click the Format button; choose Font, Paragraph, Tabs, Language, Frame, Style, or Highlight from the pop-up menu; and then choose the formatting.

- For any formatting except highlight, Word displays the corresponding dialog box. (Highlight has no options, so Word simply turns it on.)

- Select the specifics of the formatting or choose the style, and then click the OK button.

4. Choose multiple types of formatting if necessary. For example, you might search for both paragraph and language formatting together.

5. To clear any existing formatting listed in the Format readout under the Find What text box, click the No Formatting button at the bottom of the dialog box.

6. Enter any replacement text in the Replace With text box.

- If you're searching for text that you want to replace, enter the replacement text.

- If you're just replacing formatting, leave the Replace With text box blank.

7. Click the Format button, and then use the techniques explained in step 3 to specify the replacement formatting.

8. Click the Find Next button, the Replace button, or the Replace All button, as appropriate. Word finds the text or formatting you specified and replaces it with the replacement text or formatting.

9. Click the Close button. Word closes the Find And Replace dialog box.

Replace Special Characters

Find's ability to search for special characters (such as paragraph marks and manual page breaks) is great for replace operations. For example, say you receive a document from someone who puts a useless tab at the beginning of each paragraph. By replacing **^p^t** with **^p**, you can replace each instance of a paragraph followed by a tab with a single paragraph.

Most of the special characters discussed in the section "Find Characters You Can't Type" (earlier in this chapter) work in the Replace With text box. For example, you can enter ^p in the Replace With text box to make Word insert a paragraph as the replacement text. Other special characters don't work, mostly for easily understandable reasons. For example, you can't use ^? (any character), ^# (any number), or ^$ (any letter) in the Replace With text box, because these codes don't say what the replacement character should be.

Word has two special codes that work in the Replace With text box but not in the Find What text box:

- **^c: Contents of the Clipboard**   This code is great for inserting a replacement item that you can't enter as an actual character—for example, a graphic or a text item with complex formatting. Select the graphic or text item in the document, and then press CTRL-C to copy it to the Clipboard. You can then use the ^c code to insert this item as the replacement for a search item.

- **^&: Contents of the Find What text box**   This code is useful for applying formatting to what you've found. For example, you might search using special characters and wildcards, and then use this code to apply emphasis formatting to each matching instance.

Chapter 4

Format Text Efficiently

How to…

- ■ Understand Word's main formatting methods
- ■ Apply fast font formatting
- ■ Apply fast paragraph formatting
- ■ Create bulleted and numbered lists
- ■ Understand and use language formatting
- ■ Format long documents efficiently
- ■ Use themes to apply complex formatting quickly

Apart from making it much easier to create and edit documents than typewriters do, word processors also make it easy to format documents—again, unlike typewriters. Word offers a wide variety of formatting that lets you make documents look pretty much exactly how you want them to: professional, casual, serious, fun, or anywhere in between. In fact, Word offers enough different formatting options to be confusing, as the effects of some options overlap with each other. This means that you can often produce the same look by using formatting in different ways.

Word starts off most new documents you create in its standard typeface, or *font*, which is called Calibri. Most people find Calibri much more appealing than typewriter-like fonts such as Courier, but you can change the font at any time if you don't like it or if you want to make your document look different or easier to read. You can also change the font size, font color, the alignment, the line spacing, and many more formatting options, most of which you'll meet in this chapter.

Word 2007 adds several new formatting options to those in earlier versions of Word. First, every document has a *theme*, a set of colors, fonts, and graphical objects that are designed to work together. Second, Word provides Quick Styles, suites of styles derived automatically from the fonts and colors in the theme. By applying Quick Styles (with a single click), you can give a document a consistent look. You can also use Word's long-standing regular styles to apply predefined sets of formatting to characters, paragraphs, lists, or tables. Styles give you precise control over formatting while helping you avoid reinventing the wheel every time you apply or change formatting.

Understand Word's Main Formatting Methods

Word puts the formatting you'll need most often within easy reach—on the new Mini Toolbar and on the Ribbon's Home tab. To apply less frequently used formatting, you usually need to open a dialog box. You can also use keyboard shortcuts to apply some formatting without reaching for the mouse. This section shows you these four ways of applying formatting.

Whichever formatting method you use, start by selecting the text you want to change. For example, drag through a sentence to select it, or use one of the selection maneuvers explained in Chapter 2.

TIP *An easy way to speed up your direct formatting is to apply it to multiple items at once rather than to one item at a time. To select multiple items, select the first item using either the mouse or the keyboard, and then hold down CTRL as you select the remaining items with the mouse. You can then apply formatting to all the selected items at the same time.*

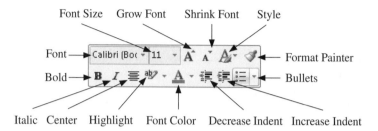

FIGURE 4-1 The most convenient way to apply formatting is to select some text with the mouse, and then use the Mini Toolbar that Word automatically pops up.

Format with the Mini Toolbar

When you select some text with the mouse (for example, by dragging or by double-clicking a word), Word pops up the Mini Toolbar (see Figure 4-1). From here, you can pick a different font or font size, make the text bold or italic, apply a different style, change the indentation or center the paragraph, or create a bulleted list. You'll learn all the possibilities later in this chapter.

TIP *If you select text using the keyboard, Word doesn't pop up the Mini Toolbar. To display the Mini Toolbar, right-click the selection. Word displays the shortcut menu at the same time.*

Format with the Ribbon's Home Tab

The second way you can apply formatting is to go to the Ribbon's Home tab (click the Home tab if another tab is displayed) and then use the options in the Font group, the Paragraph group, or the Styles group. For example, select some text, and then click the Underline button (the button with the U icon) to turn single underlining off or on for the text. Figure 4-2 shows the Home tab, these three groups, and the buttons you can click to get to the dialog boxes that contain more options. When you need to reach yet more options, click the tiny button in the lower-right corner of the group. For example, click the Font dialog button to open the Font dialog box.

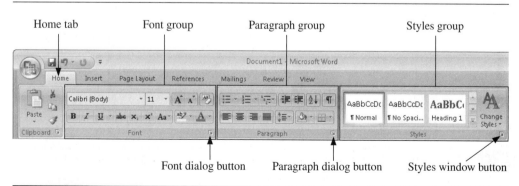

FIGURE 4-2 The Ribbon's Home tab is less handy than the Mini Toolbar, but it provides a fuller range of font, paragraph, and style formatting.

You'll learn how to use font formatting in the section "Apply Fast Font Formatting," later in this chapter; paragraph formatting in the section "Apply Fast Paragraph Formatting," later in this chapter; and styles in the section "Format Long Documents Efficiently," later in this chapter.

Format with Dialog Boxes

The Mini Toolbar and the Ribbon's Home tab keep everyday formatting close to hand. But when you need a specialized type of formatting that doesn't appear on the Mini Toolbar or the Home tab, you have to dig into a dialog box for it. For example, to get at the specialized font-formatting options, you open the Font dialog box (see Figure 4-3). The quickest way to open this dialog box is to press CTRL-D (not CTRL-F—that shortcut belongs to the Find feature). Similarly, you'll find the less frequently used paragraph-formatting options in the Paragraph dialog box. You'll meet these dialog boxes—and several others—in detail later in this chapter.

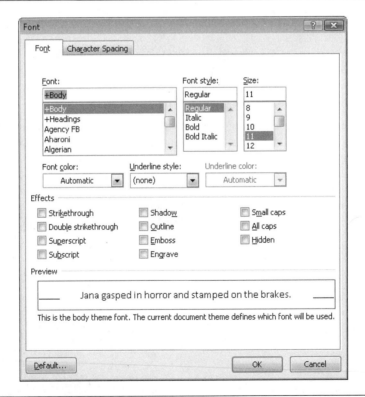

FIGURE 4-3   To reach the full range of font-formatting options Word offers, open the Font dialog box.

Format from the Keyboard

When your hands are on the keyboard, the quickest way to apply formatting is to press a key combination. For example, you can press CTRL-B to *toggle*, or turn, boldface on or off for the current word or whatever you've selected.

Word provides keyboard shortcuts for the most useful formatting options. You'll meet these keyboard shortcuts throughout the rest of this chapter.

Apply Fast Font Formatting

4

Changing the font or applying font formatting can make a huge difference in a document's look. For example, you may want to use a larger font for headings than for body text so that readers can easily distinguish them. Figure 4-4 shows a document before and after applying font formatting (and paragraph formatting—extra spacing between paragraphs).

FIGURE 4-4   If a document uses only one font and font size, it's hard to pick out the different elements (left). With font and paragraph formatting applied, it's much easier (right).

Word offers a wide variety of font formatting. You can change the font used, the font size, the character properties (such as bold, italic, or strikethrough), the horizontal spacing (or *kerning*), and the vertical spacing (creating superscript and subscript letters).

If you find yourself changing the font formatting for all the text in your documents, you should probably change the default font, the font in which Word starts most documents. See the sidebar "Change the Standard Font in Your Documents" in Chapter 2.

You can apply font formatting to as little as one character or as much as a whole document. And you can do it several ways.

To apply font formatting to a word, you don't need to select it—just click to place the insertion point in it. Word figures that you want to format the whole word. If you want to format just part of a word, select only that part, and then apply the formatting.

Apply Common Font Formats

When you start formatting your documents, you'll probably want to change font, change font size, and apply and remove bold, italic, and underline. This section shows you how to use these common font formats. The following section shows you how to use less common font formatting, from font color to special effects like engraving.

You can apply these common font formats from the Mini Toolbar, from the Ribbon's Home tab, or from the Font dialog box. To open the Font dialog box, use any of these methods:

- ■ **Ribbon** Choose Home | Font | Font Dialog. The Font dialog button is the tiny button at the right end of the bar that says Font. The button shows an arrow pointing down and to the right.
- ■ **Shortcut menu** Right-click in text, and then choose Font.
- ■ **Keyboard** Press CTRL-D.

Change the Font

Your first move in applying font formatting is to find a suitable font—or more than one. Most design gurus recommend that you use either one font for an entire document or one font for the body text and another for the headings. These recommendations are for business documents and other formal documents; if you're creating an informal document, such as an invitation to a children's party, you may choose to go wild.

Here's how you can change the font of selected text:

■ **Mini Toolbar or Font group**   Click the Font drop-down list, and then choose the font you want, as shown here. From the Font group, Word gives you a preview of the font; from the Mini Toolbar, Word doesn't give you a preview. To jump to a font in the list, type the first few letters of its name. For example, type **pl** to jump to the Plantagenet Cherokee font. If you don't like the effect when you've applied the font, go to the Quick Access Toolbar and click the Undo button.

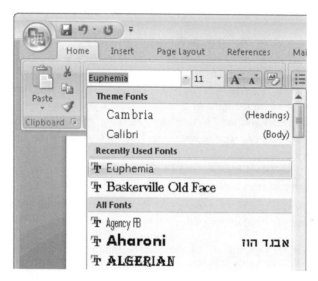

■ **Font dialog box**   In the Font list box, choose the font you want. Watch the Preview box at the bottom of the dialog box to see how the font looks.

Change the Font Size

Once you've chosen a font you like, choose the font size to use.

Font size is measured in points (a *point* is 1/72 inch). Body text is normally between 8 and 14 points, with larger sizes used for headings and other display text (for example, pull quotes). Word provides preset font size steps of 8, 9, 10, 11, 12, 14, 16, 18, 20, 22, 24, 26, 28, 36, 48, and 72 points. These steps give enough flexibility for most uses and help you choose font sizes consistently (for example, making it easy to choose 36 points rather than choosing 34 points by accident) by limiting your choices. But when you need to use a font size that doesn't appear on the list, you can.

You can set the font size in any of these ways:

■ **Mini Toolbar or Font group**   Click the Size drop-down list, and then choose the size you want. Alternatively, to move quickly from one font size step to another, click the Grow Font button or the Shrink Font button.

To Do This	Press This Keyboard Shortcut
Increase the font size by 1 point	CTRL-]
Increase the font size to the next larger size in the Size list	CTRL-SHIFT-. (period)
Decrease the font size by 1 point	CTRL-[
Decrease the font size to the next smaller size in the Size list	CTRL-SHIFT-, (comma)

TABLE 4-1   Keyboard Shortcuts for Changing the Font Size

- **Font dialog box**   In the Size box, pick the size you want.
- **Keyboard**   Press the keyboard shortcuts shown in Table 4-1.

TIP   *If you want to use a font size between one of the steps that the list shows, drag to select the number at the top of the list and then type the size you want. For example, if the 12-point step is too small and the 14-point step is too big, type **13** in the Size box and press ENTER to see if the 13-point size is just right. This trick works in the Font dialog box and in the Font group, but not in the Mini Toolbar.*

Apply Bold

Bold (also called *boldface*) is useful for making text jump out at the reader, as at the beginning of this paragraph. You can apply bold in any of these ways.

- **Mini Toolbar or Font group**   Click the Bold button once to turn bold on. Click again to turn it off.
- **Font dialog box**   In the Font Style list box, click the Bold item to turn bold on. To turn bold off, click Regular.
- **Keyboard**   Press CTRL-B once to turn bold on. Press again to turn bold off.

Apply Italic

Italic formatting (often called *italics*) is good for emphasizing a word or phrase—for example, a term that you're introducing and that you then explain. You can apply italic in any of these ways:

- **Mini Toolbar or Font group**   Click the Italic button once to turn italics on. Click again to turn italics off. Click the Bold Italic item if you want to apply both bold and italics.
- **Font dialog box**   In the Font Style list box, click the Italic item to turn italics on. To turn italics off, click Regular.
- **Keyboard**   Press CTRL-I once to turn italics on. Press again to turn italics off.

CAUTION   *Bold, italic, and underline can all be effective for drawing the reader's eye, but use them sparingly for best effect. If every other word has added emphasis, none will stand out.*

Apply Underlining

In the days of typewriters (which couldn't produce italics), <u>underlining</u> was the standard way of conveying emphasis. But now that word processors make italics easy, people tend to use italics instead. To make underlines more useful, Word lets you create not just basic (single) underlines but double underlines, "word-only" underlines (a line under words and punctuation but not under spaces), squiggly underlines, and other types.

You can apply underlines in any of these ways:

- **Font group**   Click the Underline button once to apply the last type of underline you used. At first in each Word session, this button gives you a standard underline, but you can click the drop-down arrow and choose a different type of underline from the panel. If you don't see the underline type you want, click the More Underlines item to open the Font dialog box. Click the Underline button again to turn the underline off. Use the Underline Color submenu to choose an underline color.

- **Font dialog box**   In the Underline Style drop-down list, choose the underline you want. To turn underlining off, choose the "(None)" option at the top of the list. In the Underline Color drop-down list, select the underline color you want.

- **Keyboard**   Press one of the following shortcuts to apply an underline. Press again to remove the underline.

Press These Keys	To Apply or Remove This Underline
CTRL-U	Single underline
CTRL-SHIFT-D	Double underline
CTRL-SHIFT-W	Word-only underline

Apply Less Common Font Formats

Fonts, font sizes, and bold, italic, and underline may be all the formatting you need for many documents. But when you need further formatting options, Word offers them—in plenty, from font colors to all caps, small caps, and superscripts. This section explains the other formatting options Word provides and shows you how to use them.

Change the Font Color

To make text look the way you want it, you can change its color. Use one of these methods:

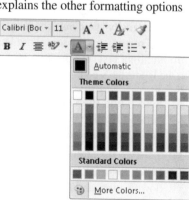

- **Mini Toolbar or Font group**   Click the drop-down arrow on the Font Color button and choose the color from the panel that appears, as shown here.

- **Font dialog box**   Open the Font Color drop-down list and choose the color from the panel that appears.

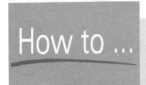 **Copy Formatting with the Format Painter**

Sometimes the easiest way to apply formatting to text is copy it from other text that already has the formatting. To do so, you use the Format Painter tool. Follow these steps:

1. Apply the formatting you want to one or more words, and then select the formatted text.

2. Turn on the Format Painter in one of these ways:

    ■ If you use the mouse to select the text, the Mini Toolbar appears automatically. Double-click the Format Painter button, the button with the paintbrush icon. The button takes on the pushed-in look to indicate that the Format Painter is on, and the mouse pointer gains a tiny paintbrush.

    ■ If you select the text using the keyboard, you can right-click the selection to display the Mini Toolbar. Alternatively, choose Home | Clipboard | Format Painter or press CTRL-SHIFT-C to turn on the Format Painter.

3. Drag over each word or text item you want to format. As you drag, Word applies the formatting to the text.

4. Press ESC, press CTRL-SHIFT-C again, or click the Format Painter button again to cancel the Format Painter.

 The Automatic option at the top of the Font color panel applies a color that contrasts with the background color. The Theme Colors section shows colors from the current theme, and the Standard Colors section shows standard colors (dark red, red, orange, yellow, and so on). You can apply a custom color by clicking More Colors and working in the Colors dialog box that opens.

Apply Highlighting

To make text really stand out, you can apply a highlight to it, just as you might highlight a sentence in a printed report—except that Word lets you instantly remove the highlight or change its color.

To highlight text, use the Text Highlight Color button and drop-down list on the Mini Toolbar or on the Home tab's Font group. You can work in two ways:

■ **Select, and then highlight**   Select some text, and then click the Text Highlight Color button to apply the highlight color shown on the button. To change color, click the drop-down button and choose the color you want.

■ **Turn on the highlighter, and then apply highlighting**   Click the Text Highlight Color button to turn on the highlighter in that color, or choose another color by clicking the drop-down button, and then clicking the color on the panel. Word adds a highlighter pen to the insertion point. Drag over each piece of text you want to highlight, and then press ESC to turn off the highlighter. You can also turn off the highlighter by clicking the Highlighter button again or by opening the Text Highlight Color panel and clicking Stop Highlighting.

To remove highlighting, select it, click the Text Highlight Color drop-down button, and then click No Color.

Use All Caps and Small Caps

If you want text to appear in all capital letters, you can press CAPS LOCK and type the letters as capitals. But often it's easier to apply all-caps formatting to existing text. You can also apply small-caps formatting to make text appear as small capital letters. Any letters that were capitals remain full-size capitals.

NOTE   *Applying all caps or small caps doesn't change the actual case of the letters—it just changes the way that Word displays the letters. When you remove all caps or small caps, the text appears with its previous capitalization.*

You can apply all caps or small caps in these ways:

- **Font dialog box**   In the Effects area, select the All Caps check box or the Small Caps check box.

- **Keyboard**   Press CTRL-SHIFT-A to turn all caps on or off. Press CTRL-SHIFT-K to turn small caps on or off.

Change the Case

Often, you'll need to change the case of text. For example, you might need to change a heading from all uppercase to Capitalize Each Word (with a capital letter at the beginning of each word).

Rather than type the changes manually, select the text, choose Home | Font | Change Case, and then choose the case you want from the list, as shown here.

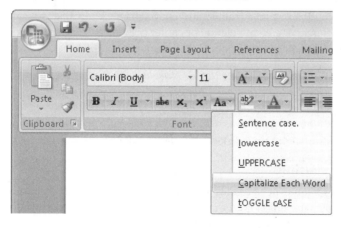

 *If you're following strict style guidelines, you'll need to lowercase the first letters of short conjunctions (and, but), prepositions (of, at), and articles (a, the) after applying Capitalize Each Word casing.*

Create Superscripts and Subscripts

In technical documents, you may need to use superscripts (raised and smaller characters, such as in "$y^2 = x^2 + z^2$") or subscripts (lowered and smaller characters, such as in "H_2O"). You can apply superscript and subscript in these ways:

- **Font group** Click the Superscript button or the Subscript button. Click the same button again if you want to remove the superscript or subscript.

- **Font dialog box** On the Font tab, select the Superscript check box or the Subscript check box in the Effects area. Clear the check box to remove the superscript or subscript.

- **Keyboard** Press CTRL-+ (in other words, CTRL-SHIFT-=) to apply superscript. Press CTRL-= to apply subscript. Press the same keyboard shortcut again to remove the superscript or subscript.

 *Word's AutoFormat As You Type feature automatically creates superscripts when you type ordinal numbers (numbers that give an item's position in a series). For example, when you type **1st** or **2nd**, Word gives you 1st or 2nd.*

Apply Strikethrough

For business documents, you may need to use *strikethrough*—text with a line drawn through it—to indicate formally that an item has been deleted. You can apply strikethrough in these ways:

- **Font group** Click the Strikethrough button once to apply strikethrough. Click it again to remove strikethrough.

- **Font dialog box** On the Font tab, select the Strikethrough check box in the Effects area. Here, you'll also find a Double Strikethrough check box that you can select to indicate a different degree of deletion or earlier deletion. Clear the appropriate check box to remove the strikethrough or double strikethrough.

 *Word also uses strikethrough and double strikethrough for Track Changes, its feature for marking revisions visibly. In Track Changes, strikethrough usually indicates a deletion and double strikethrough indicates text that has been moved to elsewhere in the document. If you find strikethrough or double strikethrough appearing unexpectedly in your documents, check if Track Changes is on. Chapter 10 shows you how to use Track Changes.*

Use Hidden Formatting

In some documents, you may need to hide some text so that it doesn't appear on screen or in printouts. For example, you might need to print a document without some sensitive paragraphs showing. Instead of cutting those paragraphs out, printing, and then pasting them back in, you can format them as hidden text. Word then hides the paragraphs until you turn on the display of hidden text (choose Home | Paragraph | Show/Hide ¶).

You probably won't need to use hidden text often. When you do, open the Font dialog box, and then select the Hidden check box in the Effects area. Word also uses hidden text for features such as cross-references.

CAUTION   *Avoid hidden text wherever possible, because if you forget about hidden parts of a document, they can cause you embarrassment when you distribute the document.*

4

Use Character Spacing to Create Typeset Text

When you're creating everyday documents (such as letters or reports), standard character spacing works fine: Word gives each character as much space as it needs and puts each character on the same *baseline*, the imaginary line on which the characters rest. (*Descenders*—the tails on characters such as *g*—go below the baseline.)

Sometimes, though, you may want to create documents with special typeset effects, such as characters raised above the baseline or compressed together. When you do, open the Font dialog box, click the Character Spacing tab and use these options:

- **Scale**   This drop-down list lets you stretch or squeeze the characters horizontally so that they occupy more or less space. Choose a preset value from the drop-down list or type a custom value (from 1 percent to 600 percent) in the box.

- **Spacing**   When you need to expand or condense the text by changing the amount of space between characters (rather than stretching or squeezing the characters themselves), choose Expanded or Condensed in the Spacing drop-down list and specify the distance in points in the By text box. To restore normal spacing, choose Normal.

- **Position**   To create raised or lowered characters (without making the characters smaller as superscript and subscript do), choose Raised or Lowered in the Position drop-down list, and then specify the distance in points in the By text box. The position of the characters is measured from the baseline, the imaginary line on which the letters rest.

- **Kerning for fonts**   To make Word adjust the *kerning* (the amount of space between letters), select the Kerning For Fonts check box and enter the minimum font size to kern in the Points And Above text box. Normally, you'd use kerning only for headings and other display text rather than for body text, so you would set a value such as 12 points in the Points And Above Text box.

Apply Other Special Formatting

To make text look more dramatic, use the Shadow, Outline, Emboss, or Engrave options in the Effects area of the Font tab of the Font dialog box. Some options are mutually exclusive: for example, selecting the Emboss check box clears the Engrave check box, and vice versa.

TIP   *If you want to make text look really dramatic, use WordArt (see the section "Add WordArt to Documents" in Chapter 7).*

 **Display Paragraph Marks So You Can See Where Paragraphs End**

When you're formatting paragraphs, it's often useful to see the paragraph marks, which are usually invisible (as are spaces, tabs, and other formatting marks).

To display the paragraph marks, follow these steps:

1. Click the Office button, and then click Word Options. Word displays the Word Options dialog box.

2. In the left pane, click the Display category.

3. In the Always Show These Formatting Marks On The Screen section, select the Paragraph Marks check box. Also select the check boxes for any other formatting marks you want to see. For example, you may want to view tabs.

4. Click the OK button. Word closes the Word Options dialog box.

You can also display all formatting marks by choosing Home | Paragraph | Show/Hide ¶. (The Show/Hide ¶ button is a toggle; click it again to hide all formatting marks apart from those whose check boxes you've turned on in the Word Options dialog box.)

Apply Fast Paragraph Formatting

Font formatting changes the look of the characters, but you'll often need to change the paragraph layout as well from the way that Word sets it automatically. To change the paragraph layout, you use paragraph formatting.

Paragraph formatting is slippery to grasp because Word provides a huge number of options that you can set. Some of these options are straightforward—for example, you can set alignment, indentation, and line spacing. But tabs and text flow (how Word decides to end one page and start the next) are also part of paragraph formatting.

The Mini Toolbar includes buttons for centering text and adjusting tabs, but most of the tools for formatting paragraphs are in the Paragraph group on the Home tab (see Figure 4-5) and the Paragraph dialog box. You can open the Paragraph dialog box in either of the following ways:

■ **Ribbon**   Choose Home | Paragraph | Paragraph Dialog. The Paragraph dialog button is the tiny button at the right end of the bar that says Paragraph. The button shows an arrow pointing down and to the right.

■ **Shortcut menu**   Right-click in text and choose Paragraph from the shortcut menu.

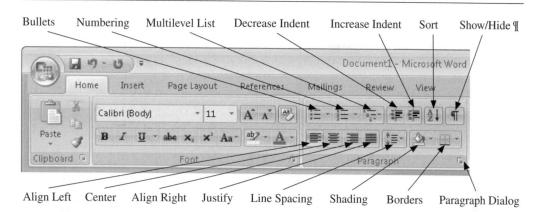

Bullets   Numbering   Multilevel List   Decrease Indent   Increase Indent   Sort   Show/Hide ¶

Align Left   Center   Align Right   Justify   Line Spacing   Shading   Borders   Paragraph Dialog

FIGURE 4-5   You can apply most of the paragraph formatting you need from the Home tab's Paragraph group.

Set Alignment

Like most word processors, Word offers left, right, centered, and justified alignment:

- **Left alignment**   The words line up along the left margin of the page. Left is the alignment Word comes set with. You'll probably want to stick with left alignment for most text.

- **Right alignment**   The words line up along the right margin of the page. Right alignment is useful for putting text up against the right margin. For example, you might create letterhead with the sender's address right-aligned.

- **Centering**   The words flow left and right from the center of the page. Centering is good for display text, such as headings and poetry.

- **Justified alignment**   This setting aligns the text with both the left margin and the right margin, except for the last line of the paragraph, which is allowed to fall short so that it doesn't require huge spaces between the words.

NOTE   *You may also need to align text vertically on the page—for example, so that a title is centered vertically. See the section "Align Text Vertically on a Page" in Chapter 5 for instructions.*

You can set alignment in any of these ways:

- **Mini Toolbar**   Click the Center button to center text. (Center is the only alignment the Mini Toolbar offers. Most paragraphs start out with left alignment, so you seldom need to apply it from the Mini Toolbar; and most people use centering more often than right alignment.)

■ **Paragraph group**   Click the Align Left button, the Center button, the Align Right button, or the Justify button.

■ **Paragraph dialog box**   On the Indents and Spacing tab (see Figure 4-6), go to the General area, and then, in the Alignment drop-down list, choose Left, Centered, Right, or Justified.

■ **Keyboard**   Use the following keyboard shortcuts:

Left-align	CTRL-L
Right-align	CTRL-R
Center	CTRL-E
Justify	CTRL-J

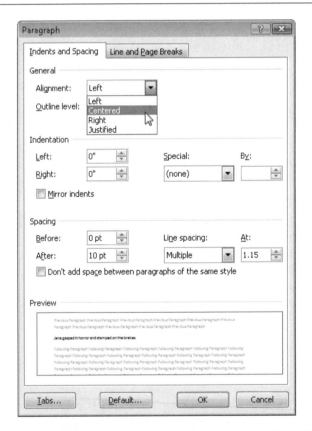

FIGURE 4-6   The Paragraph dialog box includes options for setting alignment and indentation, including options that don't appear on the Home tab.

Align Text Quickly Using Click And Type

Another way to set alignment is by using the Click And Type feature. Click And Type aligns only blank paragraphs (paragraphs with no content), not paragraphs that have contents, so it's useful only in certain circumstances—typically either when you're laying out a document that includes extra blank paragraphs or when you're working at the end of a document. (See the sidebar titled "It's Best to Avoid Blank Paragraphs in Your Documents" in Chapter 3 for details of why Word experts recommend avoiding having blank paragraphs in documents.)

Either in a blank paragraph or after the last paragraph in a document, double-click at the point where you want to place the insertion point. Word automatically changes the alignment of the paragraph to match where you double-clicked. For example, if you double-click at the right margin, Word applies right alignment. If you double-click after the end of the document, Word automatically adds as many blank paragraphs as it needs to reach that point, just as you might press ENTER a few times to move the insertion point farther down the document.

If Click And Type doesn't work, it's probably turned off. To turn it on, follow these steps:

1. Click the Office Button, and then click Word Options. Word displays the Word Options dialog box.
2. In the left panel, click the Advanced category.
3. In the Editing Options area at the top, select the Enable Click And Type check box.
4. In the Default Paragraph Style drop-down list below the Enable Click And Type check box, select the paragraph style to use for extra paragraphs that Click And Type inserts. Word uses Normal style to start with, but you might choose your standard style for body paragraphs (for example, Body Text) instead to avoid having Word insert paragraphs in the Normal style in your documents.
5. Click the OK button. Word closes the Word Options dialog box.

Use Indentation

Word normally aligns the left side of each paragraph with the left margin, but you may sometimes need to *indent* the text, setting it in from the margin. For example, you might use a first-line indent to emphasize where each paragraph starts. Or if a document needs a long quotation, you might follow the convention of indenting it from both the left and right margins to help the reader easily distinguish it from the main text.

Word lets you create five kinds of indents:

- **Left indent**   Word indents the left edge of the paragraph from the left margin. For example, you might indent a block quotation from both the left and right margins.
- **Right indent**   Word indents the right edge of the paragraph from the right margin.

■ **First-line indent**   Word indents the beginning of the first line of the paragraph, but not the other lines (unless you've also applied a left indent). You can create an indent by pressing TAB to insert a tab character, but applying an indent to the paragraph is easier, because Word automatically indents the first line of each subsequent paragraph you create.

■ **Hanging indent**   The first line of the paragraph hangs out to the left of the other lines. Numbered and bulleted lists usually use hanging indents to position the number or bullet to the left of the rest of the paragraph.

■ **Mirror indents**   For some document layouts, you may want to create facing pages that have mirror-image indents: The left (outside) indent on the left page matches the right (outside) indent on the right page, and the right (inside) indent on the left page matches the left (inside) indent on the right page. Mirror indents are new in Word 2007.

Word lets you set indents using the ruler, which provides the easiest way to make quick adjustments to indents; the Paragraph dialog box; and keyboard shortcuts.

Set Indents Using the Ruler

To set indents using the ruler, first display the ruler if it's hidden. Either pop the ruler up temporarily by hovering the mouse pointer at the bottom of the Ribbon for a moment, or display the ruler permanently by clicking the View Ruler button at the top of the vertical scroll bar.

With the ruler displayed, drag the appropriate indent marker to the spot where you want the indent to start. Figure 4-7 shows the ruler and the markers.

Drag the first-line indent marker to where you want the first line of the paragraph indented.

Drag the hanging indent marker to create a hanging indent or "outdent."

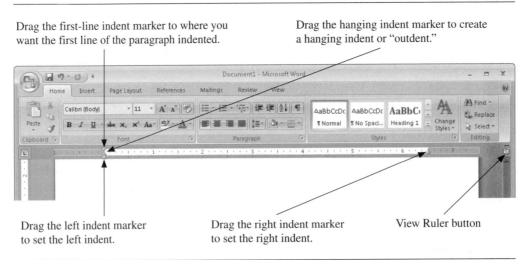

Drag the left indent marker to set the left indent.

Drag the right indent marker to set the right indent.

View Ruler button

FIGURE 4-7   The quickest way to set indents is to select the paragraphs you want to affect and then drag the indent markers on the ruler.

4

The ruler's inch marks and the tick marks between them let you get a rough idea of where you're placing indents. If you need to see an exact measurement of where an indent is, hold down ALT as you drag an indent marker to make the ruler display a readout in hundredths of an inch of the marker's position, as shown here.

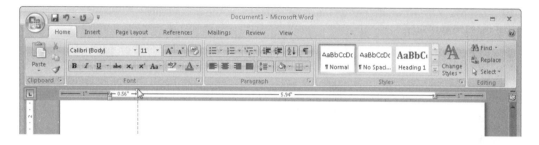

Set Indents Using the Paragraph Dialog Box

If you find it hard to position the indent markers on the ruler accurately, open the Paragraph dialog box and use its options to set indents. Watch the Preview box to see the effect of the indents as you set them.

- **Create a left indent**   In the Left box, set the distance from the left margin.
- **Create a right indent**   In the Right box, set the distance from the right margin.

Indents Start from the Margins

The indents you set are relative to the margins—so if you find you need to set indents frequently, you may need to adjust the margins. You may also need to adjust the page size.

Every page in a Word document has a page size. Word considers the page size to be part of the section formatting, so each section of the document can have a different page size if needed. Each new document has one section, so it has a single page size until you add new sections and change their page size. (Chapter 5 shows you how to work with sections.) Word starts you off with the page size set in the template on which you base the document (see Chapter 2 for more on templates). For most documents, the standard page size is 8.5 × 11 inches.

Within the page are the margins, which you can set to different sizes for each section if necessary. See the section "Change the Margins" in Chapter 5 for instructions on changing the margins.

- ■ **Create a first-line indent** In the Special drop-down list, choose First Line, and then set the distance in the By box.

- ■ **Create a hanging indent** In the Special drop-down list, choose Hanging, and then set the distance in the By box.

- ■ **Remove a first-line indent or hanging indent** In the Special drop-down list, choose the "(None)" item.

- ■ **Create mirror indents** Mirror indents are indents that are the same on pages that face each other, and can look good in book designs. To create mirror indents, select the Mirror Indents check box. Word changes the Left box to Inside and the Right box to Outside. Set the inside and outside measurements in these boxes.

When you've chosen your indentation, click the OK button. Word closes the Paragraph dialog box.

Adjust Indents Using the Keyboard

The ruler and the Paragraph dialog box give you fine control over the indents you set. But when you just want to adjust indents quickly, use the keyboard. Table 4-2 explains the keys to press. For each press, Word increases or decreases the indent set in the Tabs dialog box, in the Default Tab Stops list box (see the section "Use the Tabs Dialog Box to Place Tabs Precisely," later in this chapter).

How to ... Change Word's Measurement Units

Word lets you use inches, centimeters, millimeters, points, or picas as your measurement unit. A *pica* is 1/6 inch and a *point* is 1/72 inch (so there are 12 points to the pica). Picas and points are usually used for typesetting.

If Word is set to use the wrong units, follow these steps to change them:

1. Click the Office Button, and then click Word Options. Word displays the Word Options dialog box.

2. In the left panel, click the Advanced category, and then scroll down to the Display area (about halfway down the list).

3. In the Show Measurements In Units Of drop-down list, select Inches, Centimeters, Millimeters, Points, or Picas, as appropriate.

4. Click the OK button. Word closes the Word Options dialog box.

Action	Keyboard Shortcut
Increase the indent from the left	CTRL-M
Decrease or remove the indent from the left	CTRL-SHIFT-M
Create or increase a hanging indent	CTRL-T
Reduce or remove a hanging indent	CTRL-SHIFT-T

TABLE 4-2   Keystrokes for Changing Indentation

Change the Line Spacing and Paragraph Spacing

To make a document easy to read, you may want to increase or decrease the *line spacing*, the amount of vertical space between one line and the next. Word starts a typical paragraph with *single spacing*—each line has enough space to accommodate the tallest character, and a little more space so that that character doesn't touch the line above or the line below. Single spacing is based on the font size, so if you increase the font size, or put in a taller character, Word increases the line space so that the characters don't touch.

Word lets you move the lines of each paragraph farther apart or closer together as much as you want. For example, you can move the lines apart to make the text easier to read, to leave space for editing on paper, or simply to make a short document look longer.

You can choose from presets for single spacing (1.0 lines), 1.5 lines, double spacing (2.0 lines), 2.5 lines, and 3.0 lines. You can also set exact spacing by choosing the Exactly setting and specifying the number of points, minimum spacing by choosing the At Least setting and specifying the number of points, or a spacing that uses a different number of lines (for example, 1.05 or 3.5).

Instead of—or as well as—changing the spacing between lines, you can change the amount of space before or after a *paragraph*. By adding white space before and after each paragraph, you can separate paragraphs without typing a blank paragraph between them. For example, you might add extra space before each heading to make headings stand out on the page, as in this book.

Change the Line Spacing

You can apply line spacing in any of these ways:

- **Ribbon**   Choose Home | Paragraph | Line Spacing, and then choose the line spacing you want. If the setting you want doesn't appear, click the More item. Word displays the Paragraph dialog box.

- **Paragraph dialog box**   In the Line Spacing drop-down list, choose Single, 1.5 Lines, Double, At Least, Exactly, or Multiple. Watch the Preview box for a simulation of how the paragraph will look. For At Least, Exactly, and Multiple, Word enters the number of points in the At text box. You can increase or decrease this number to produce the spacing you want.

■ **Keyboard** Press the following keyboard shortcuts:

Line Spacing	Keyboard Shortcut
Single spacing	CTRL-1
1.5-line spacing	CTRL-5
Double spacing	CTRL-2

Change the Paragraph Spacing

You can change the paragraph spacing in these two ways:

■ **Ribbon** Choose Home | Paragraph | Line Spacing, and then choose Add Space Before Paragraph, Add Space After Paragraph, Remove Space Before Paragraph, or Remove Space After Paragraph, as appropriate.

NOTE *The Line Spacing drop-down list shows one "before" option and one "after" option: The Add Space Before Paragraph option appears if the paragraph has no space before it; the Remove Space Before Paragraph option appears if the paragraph does have space before it. Similarly, either the Add Space After Paragraph option or the Remove Space After Paragraph option appears. These settings let you quickly add space to or remove space from a paragraph.*

■ **Paragraph dialog box** On the Indents and Spacing tab, increase or decrease the numbers in the Before text box and After text box in the Spacing area. Word applies both these settings, so if you create a paragraph with 18 points after it and then a paragraph with 12 points before it, you get 30 points of space between the paragraphs. Select the Don't Add Space Between Paragraphs Of The Same Style check box if you want to prevent paragraphs that have the same style from receiving this extra space. For example, say you create a Quote style with 12 points before it and 12 points after to separate it from the paragraphs around it. By selecting this check box, you can prevent the extra space from appearing between two consecutive paragraphs in the Quote style.

Control the Flow of Text from Page to Page

When you've filled one page, Word automatically creates a new page for you and flows the text to it. You can just continue working and let Word handle the text flow and pagination for you.

Word comes set to prevent widows and orphans, two banes of typesetters and proofreaders:

■ **Widow** A single line of text at the top of a page, finishing a paragraph that starts on the previous page.

■ **Orphan** The first line of a paragraph appearing on its own at the bottom of a page, with the rest of the paragraph on the next page.

If you and your colleagues don't care about these kinds of widows and orphans, you can override this setting. You may also need to keep a particular paragraph with the paragraph after it, keep all the lines of a paragraph together, or ensure that a page break appears before a paragraph.

How to ... Get the Right Amount of Space Between Paragraphs

When you're adjusting the space between two paragraphs, you don't need to worry so much about whether the space is applied as "after" space for the first paragraph or "before" space for the second paragraph: As long as you get the right amount of total space, the paragraphs should look okay.

But when you're designing styles that will apply full sets of formatting to paragraphs, you'll need to balance one paragraph style's need for space after it against another paragraph style's need for space before it.

For example, when creating a heading style that will be followed by a body paragraph, subtract the space that the body paragraph needs before it from the total space you want between the paragraphs to establish how much space to apply after the heading style.

To control text flow, open the Paragraph dialog box and click the Line and Page Breaks tab to bring it to the front. In the Pagination area, turn the check boxes on or off to change these options:

- **Widow/Orphan Control**   Select this check box if you want Word to prevent widows and orphans from occurring. Widows and orphans tend to make your documents more difficult to read, so selecting this check box is a good idea.

- **Keep With Next**   Select this check box if you want to make Word keep this paragraph on the same page as the paragraph that follows it. This is the setting you're most likely to need to change. You'd use this setting in a heading style to make sure the heading doesn't get stuck as the last paragraph at the bottom of a page. Don't use it for body styles—if you do, Word has difficulty breaking the pages.

- **Keep Lines Together**   Select this check box if you need to prevent a paragraph from breaking from one page to the next page. Use this setting only for special paragraphs that must remain as one unit (for example, a note or the caption for an illustration) rather than for body text, or you may end up with very short pages.

- **Page Break Before**   Select this check box only for paragraphs that must appear at the start of a page. This behavior is useful for a chapter heading or a section heading.

NOTE   *On the Paragraph dialog box's Line and Page Breaks tab, you'll also find options for suppressing automatic line numbers (see the section "Add Line Numbers to Paragraphs" in Chapter 5) and automatic hyphenation (hyphens Word adds to enable it to create an even right margin), and for controlling wrapping in text boxes. Select the Suppress Line Numbers check box only when you're using line numbers in a document and you find you need to skip some paragraphs. Select the Don't Hyphenate check box when you need to prevent Word from hyphenating a particular paragraph. For example, you might select this check box for a paragraph that contained programming code that would become incorrect or confusing if hyphenated.*

Set Tabs for Positioning Text

Sometimes, instead of normal paragraphs with text all the way from margin to margin, you'll want to create columns or tables of data. For example, you may need to create a header that uses two or three different types of alignment, lay out a list of new hires with their departments and starting dates, or put together a letter-sized newsletter with three columns.

For these types of layouts, Word offers you the choice of using tab stops, tables, and newspaper-style columns:

- **Tab stops**   A tab stop is an electronic marker that you can set to align text at a particular point within a paragraph. (More details coming right up.) Tab stops are good for creating column layouts in which each paragraph has only one line. If any paragraph in the column layout has multiple lines, you'll need to break that paragraph into separate parts to get them aligned with tabs, flowing the text from line to line manually, which is labor-intensive. You can also use a tab to create a first-line indent in a paragraph, but it's better to use indentation as described earlier in this chapter.

- **Tables**   Word's tables are great for creating columns and rows of cells (boxes) separated by lines, but you can also create tables without lines when you need to lay out complex data. As a general rule, any time the contents of any entry in a column are more than one line long, a table is easier than tabs, because the table automatically wraps each line that won't fit into the cell. Chapter 11 explains how to use tables.

- **Newspaper-style columns**   These columns, in which text flows from the bottom of one column to the top of the next column on the same page, are easy to use because Word handles the text flow for you. Chapter 11 shows you how to create columns.

Figure 4-8 shows examples of an indented paragraph, a layout using tabs, and a table. For some layouts, you have the choice between using tabs and using a table—but as discussed in the preceding list, the choice between one and the other is usually pretty clear-cut.

If you start laying out tabular information with tabs and discover that you need to use a table instead, you can convert the tabbed layout to a table easily by using the Convert Text to Table command. See "Convert Existing Text to a Table" in Chapter 11 for details.

Understand How Tabs Work in Word

On a manual typewriter, a *tab stop* is a physical block that you set to specify the point at which you want the carriage to stop when you press the TAB key. The typewriter has a fixed number of tab stops that you position wherever you need them along the length of the line, between the left and right margins.

Word's implementation of a tab stop has the same general idea, but it's more flexible:

- A tab stop is an invisible (and nonprinting) electronic marker used for alignment. Pressing TAB inserts a tab character and moves the insertion point to the next tab stop (see the Note for exceptions). A "tab" usually refers to the nonprinting character that Word inserts when you press TAB, but many people use "tab" interchangeably with "tab stop."

A left-aligned paragraph with a centered tab and a right-aligned tab is an easy way to produce a header with three types of alignment.

Indentation is the tool to use for creating block quotes.

Use tabs to lay out columnar data that has only a single line in each paragraph.

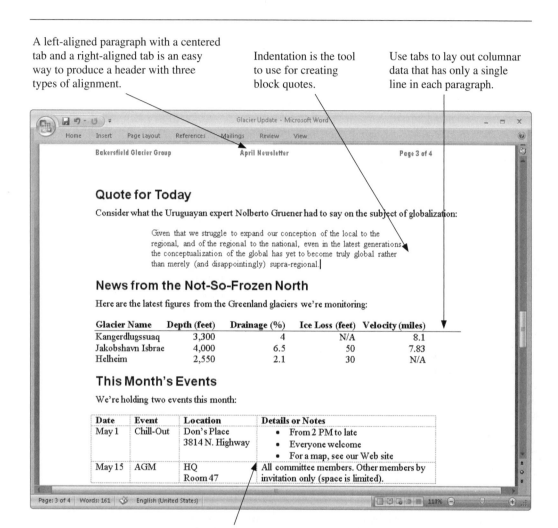

When some columns have multiple lines or multiple paragraphs, a table is much easier to use than tabs, because you don't have to leave partial blank lines padded with tabs. The gridlines appear on screen but don't print.

FIGURE 4-8   Use tabs to create headers that use several alignments or complex layouts in which each entry is one line. Tables let you put multiple lines or paragraphs in a single row.

NOTE   *Pressing TAB usually moves the insertion point to the next tab stop. But if the insertion point is in a table, pressing TAB selects the next cell (if there is one) or creates a new row (if the current cell is the last). To insert a tab in a table, press CTRL-TAB. If the document is a form that's locked, pressing TAB selects the next field. (Chapter 14 discusses forms and locking.)*

■ Word starts you off with tab stops set at half-inch intervals. Using these tab stops is almost always a mistake because they're too close together for most layout purposes. A minute spent customizing the tabs in a document (or better, the document's template) will save you many minutes down the road.

TIP *When you're working with tabs, you may find it helpful to see the tab characters. To view them quickly, display all formatting marks by choosing Home | Paragraph | Show/ Hide ¶. To display only tabs, click the Office Button, click Word Options, and then click the Display category. Select the Tab Characters check box in the Always Show These Formatting Marks On The Screen list, and then click the OK button.*

■ You can create tab stops with different alignments (left, right, and center), align decimal points on a tab stop, and even use *bar tab* stops to draw vertical lines. You can also specify a character to use as a *tab leader*, a character that Word repeats throughout the tab's width, like the dots used between a heading and the page number in the Table of Contents at the front of this book.

■ You can set as many tab stops as you want. Having many tab stops usually makes working in a paragraph unnecessarily complicated, but you may sometimes need many tab stops for complex layouts.

■ You can put tab stops outside the margins as well as within them. This trick is handy when you want to override the margins on a particular paragraph.

■ You can set different tab stops for each paragraph if you need to, but the most efficient way to set tab stops is via style formatting (style formatting is discussed later in this chapter). When the style includes the tab stops, each paragraph to which you apply that style receives the same tab stops, and you can adjust the tab stops in all those paragraphs at once by adjusting the tab stops in the style.

Grasp the Tab Types and Symbols

Word provides five kinds of tab stops that you can set freely:

■ **Left**   Word aligns the text left at the tab stop. Word uses left tab stops until you change the tab type.

■ **Right**   Word aligns the text right at the tab stop, so when you type at a right tab stop, the text moves backward to the left, across the space left by the tab. Right tab stops are useful for aligning text with the right margin, either in the body of a document or in a header or footer.

■ **Center**   Word centers the text at the position of the tab stop. Center tab stops are good for displaying information neatly in the middle of headers and footers.

■ **Decimal**   Word aligns the decimal point in the number at the tab stop. For example, if you type **123.45** at a decimal tab, 123 appears to the left of the tab stop and 45 to the right of the tab stop. Decimal tab stops are good for neatly aligning columns of numbers that include a decimal point.

■ **Bar**   Word displays a vertical bar at the tab position. The bar appears as soon as you set the tab stop: You don't have to type a tab to produce it. The bar extends to the paragraph above and below, forming a vertical line; this is the purpose of the bar tab stop. Word now includes better tools for drawing vertical lines, such as borders (see Chapter 7) and a line tool, so you'll seldom need to use bar tab stops. (Word includes bar tab stops for backward compatibility with earlier Word versions.)

The horizontal ruler displays the tab stops that are set for the current paragraph. (If you've selected multiple paragraphs that have different tab stops set, the ruler displays the tab stops grayed out so that they're barely visible.) Figure 4-9 shows the symbols that Word uses for the tab stops.

NOTE   *If the horizontal ruler isn't visible, go to the top of the vertical scroll bar and click the View Ruler button to display it. Alternatively, click the View tab, go to the Show/Hide group, and then select the Ruler check box. If you need the ruler only for a moment, hover the mouse pointer at the top edge of the document area (just below the lowermost docked toolbar or the menu bar) to make the ruler appear until you move the mouse away.*

To change the tab stops for a paragraph, you can use either the horizontal ruler or the Tabs dialog box. To change a single paragraph, position the insertion point anywhere in it; to change multiple paragraphs, select them.

TIP   *When setting tab stops for a multicolumn layout, you may find it helpful to enter some or all of the text first, separated by tab characters, so that you can see the effect of the tab stops as you place them. Alternatively, set preliminary tab stops, enter the text, and then adjust the tab stops as needed.*

Use the Horizontal Ruler to Position Tabs Quickly   The quickest way to set, adjust, and delete tabs for a paragraph is to use the horizontal ruler.

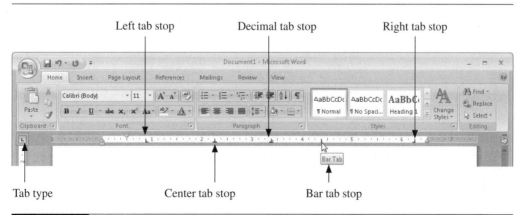

FIGURE 4-9   To see which tab stops the current paragraph contains, examine the tab stop symbols on the ruler.

Head to the left end of the horizontal ruler and click the Tab Type button to make the button display the symbol for the type of tab you want. (If you're not sure what a symbol represents, hover the mouse pointer over the Tab Type button to display a ScreenTip identifying the symbol.) Click the lower half of the ruler where you want the tab stop, as shown here. Word displays a vertical line down the document window to help you put the tab where you need it.

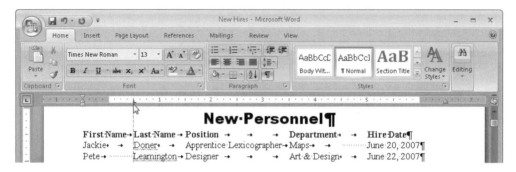

To see precise measurements, hold down ALT as you click or move a tab, as shown here.

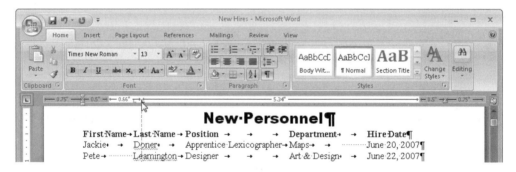

To adjust an existing tab stop, drag it along the ruler. To delete an existing tab stop, drag it upward or downward along the ruler.

Set your tab stops so that you need insert only one tab to move between one column and another. Avoid using double or triple tabs. Not only do they make document layout awkward, but they may exaggerate any changes in layout that happen when a document you've laid out opens on someone else's computer that has different fonts and Word settings.

Use the Tabs Dialog Box to Place Tabs Precisely If you find adjusting tab stops on the ruler difficult, or if you want to see the detail on each tab stop in an easier-to-grasp layout, use the Tabs dialog box instead. Choose Home | Paragraph | Paragraph to display the Paragraph dialog box, click the Tabs button to open the Tabs dialog box (see Figure 4-10), and then work as follows:

- **Examine the details for a tab stop** Click the tab stop in the Tab Stop Position list. Word selects the appropriate option buttons in the Alignment area and the Leader area to show the tab's alignment and leader (if it has one).

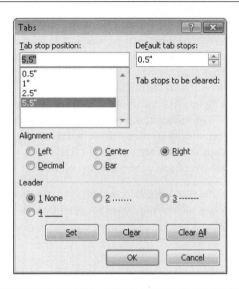

FIGURE 4-10 The Tabs dialog box lets you see the settings for the tab selected in the list box.

- **Set a tab stop** Type the position (for example, 4.5) in the Tab Stop Position text box, click the appropriate option button in the Alignment area, specify a tab leader if necessary, and then click the Set button.
- **Delete a tab stop** Select the tab stop in the Tab Stop Position list box, and then click the Clear button. To delete all tab stops, click the Clear All button.
- **Move a tab stop** Delete the existing tab stop, and then create a new tab stop.
- **Change the spacing of the standard tab stops** Use the spinners to adjust the value in the Default Tab Stops text box. Word's normal setting is 0.5 inches.

TIP

You can display the Tabs dialog box by double-clicking the lower half of the ruler. It's best to double-click an existing tab stop symbol, because otherwise the first click sets a tab stop of the type currently shown on the Tab Type button. Double-clicking the top half of the ruler doesn't set a tab, but it displays the Page Setup dialog box rather than the Tabs dialog box.

Create Bulleted and Numbered Lists

Many documents these days require lists of some type: numbered lists for giving a series of steps or instructions, or bulleted lists for making discrete points, or a combination of numbered and bulleted, or multilevel lists (for example, with numbering and subnumbering: section 1.a, section 1.a.i, section 1.a.ii, and so on).

You can create such lists manually if you choose, but Word offers powerful automated list features to save you time and effort. When you need to create a list quickly, you can use direct formatting, as discussed in this section. When you need to create a lot of lists, you can save time by using styles (see the section "Format Lists with List Styles," later in this chapter).

Whether you use direct formatting or styles, Word implements the bullets or numbering as formatting rather than actual characters in the document. So when you create a numbered list, the numbers that appear are not characters like those you type; you can't select the numbers and edit them, the way you can do with "real" characters. Once you've applied the list formatting, Word adds the numbers or bullets automatically to each new paragraph you create in the list. When you create a numbered list, Word keeps the numbering straight for you, so when you add or delete a paragraph within a numbered list, Word renumbers the rest of the list.

For legal documents and other formal documents, you may need to number each line. Word provides flexible line numbering either for complete documents or for sections. See the section "Add Line Numbers to Paragraphs" in Chapter 5.

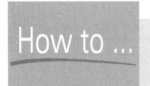

How to ... Create Lists with AutoFormat —or Turn It Off

With Word's normal settings, you can create standard numbered and bulleted lists by typing in a way that triggers the AutoFormat feature to apply list formatting. Here's how:

- At the beginning of a paragraph, type a number, a period or closing parenthesis, and then a space or tab. For example, type **1.** and then a space, or type **2)** and then press TAB. Word automatically changes the paragraph into part of a numbered list.

- At the beginning of a paragraph, type an asterisk (*) and a space or tab. Word automatically changes the asterisk to a bullet and applies a hanging indent to the paragraph. You can also type a hyphen (–) and a tab at the beginning of a paragraph to create a "bulleted" list that uses hyphens as the bullets (for example, for subpoints).

Creating lists automatically like this can be great when you use it intentionally, but all too many people run into this feature by accident—and it drives them nuts. If you're in this group, turn off AutoFormat creation of numbered and bulleted lists. Follow these steps:

1. Click the Office Button, and then click Word Options. Word displays the Word Options dialog box.

2. In the left pane, click the Proofing category, and then click the AutoCorrect Options button. Word displays the AutoCorrect dialog box.

3. Click the AutoFormat As You Type tab.

4. In the Apply As You Type area, clear the Automatic Bulleted Lists check box and the Automatic Numbered Lists check box.

5. Decide whether to clear the Border Lines check box, which creates lines automatically when you type a line of three or more of the following characters in a row:

   - **Hyphens** Thin line

   - **Underscores** Thick line

   - **Asterisks** Dotted line

   - **Equals signs** Double line

   - **Hash marks** Two thin lines with a thicker line between them

6. Decide whether to clear the Tables check box, which makes Word insert a table when you type a combination of plus signs and hyphens to denote the table format. Each plus sign represents a column border, and the groups of hyphens represent the relative width of the columns. For example, +--+--+--+--+--+ creates a table with five equal columns, and +--+--------+--+ creates a table with a narrow column, a wide column, and another narrow column.

7. Click the OK button. Word closes the AutoCorrect dialog box.

8. Click the OK button. Word closes the Word Options dialog box.

Create a Numbered List

The easiest way to create a numbered list is to apply direct formatting to an existing paragraph. By doing this, you maintain the paragraph's current style, its font formatting, and most of its paragraph formatting. All that you change is the numbering and indentation.

To create a numbered list using direct formatting, follow these steps.

1. Select the paragraphs you want to turn into the list. If you want to use only one paragraph, place the insertion point in it.

2. Choose Home | Paragraph | Numbering, and then choose the numbering format from the panel. Hover the mouse pointer over a format (without clicking) to make Word temporarily apply that format to the paragraphs, giving you a preview of how the format looks when applied.

   - To apply the last type of numbering you've used, click the main part of the Numbering button rather than the drop-down arrow.

   - If you want to apply one of the number formats you've used most recently in Word (not just in this document), choose it from the Recently Used Number Formats area at the top of the Numbering panel.

■ If you want one of the number formats you've used so far in this document or another open document, choose it from the Document Number Formats area at the bottom of the Numbering panel.

■ To create a different number format (for example, using the words "First," "Second," "Third," and so on), click the Define New Number Format item. Word displays the Define New Number Format dialog box, as shown here. Choose the number style, font, number format, and alignment, and then click the OK button.

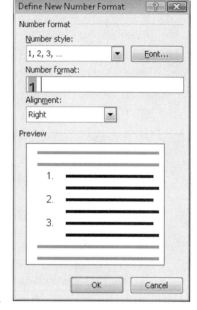

TIP *You can also access the Numbering panel by right-clicking a paragraph and choosing Numbering. You may find this easier than using the Numbering button because you don't have to display the Home tab of the Ribbon first.*

3. Continue typing the list as needed. Word automatically carries on the list numbering to the next paragraph when you press ENTER once.

4. To create a sublist (a list indented to a greater depth than the list that contains it):

   ■ Press TAB at the start of a paragraph.

   ■ Press ENTER at the end of a sublist paragraph to continue the sublist.

   ■ Press SHIFT-TAB at the start of a paragraph to move the paragraph up a level and restart the main list.

5. When you want to stop the numbered list, press ENTER twice.

NOTE *Sometimes you may need to convert a list that includes manually typed numbers to automatic numbering. For example, you might receive a manually numbered list in an e-mail message, and then paste it into a Word document. Good news here: When you apply numbering, Word automatically removes any existing manually typed numbers for you.*

Continue an Existing List or Change the Starting Number

Word starts each automatically numbered list at the number 1. This works well for normal lists, but you may sometimes need to continue a previous list after a break (rather than starting a new list at the number 1 again) or start a list at a different number than 1. You may also find that, when you apply numbering to a new list, Word decides you're continuing the previous list. When this happens, you'll need to restart numbering on the new list.

Here's how you can change the numbering on a list:

- **Restart the numbering at 1**   Right-click the first paragraph in the list and choose Restart At 1 from the context menu.

- **Continue the numbering from the previous list**   Right-click the first paragraph in the list and choose Continue Numbering from the context menu.

- **Change the starting number for the list**   Follow these steps:

    1. Right-click the first paragraph in the list and choose Set Numbering Value from the context menu. Word displays the Set Numbering Value dialog box, as shown here.

    2. Select the Start New List option button to start a new list. To continue the previous list, select the Continue From Previous List option button. When you continue the list, you have the option of selecting the Advance Value (Skip Numbers) check box. Selecting this check box makes Word insert hidden paragraphs for the skipped numbers, so that the numbering sequence in the list remains intact. To see the hidden paragraphs, choose Home | Paragraph | Show/Hide ¶ or press CTRL-SHIFT-8.

    3. Specify the value in the Set Value To text box.

    4. Click the OK button. Word closes the Set Numbering Value dialog box.

Change the Position of a List

If the list you've applied isn't positioned exactly where you want it, right-click it to open the shortcut menu.

- To make a quick adjustment, choose Decrease Indent or Increase Indent.

- To see all the options available to you, follow these steps:

    1. Choose Adjust List Indents. Word displays the Adjust List Indents dialog box, as shown here.

    2. Set the position of the number in the Number Position text box.

    3. Set the text indent (from the number) in the Text Indent text box.

    4. In the Follow Number With drop-down list, choose Tab Character, Space, or Nothing. If you choose Tab Character, you can add a custom tab stop after the number

by selecting the Add Tab Stop At check box, and then setting the distance you want between the number and the tab stop in the text box.

5. Click the OK button. Word closes the Adjust List Indents dialog box.

Create a Bulleted List

As with numbered lists, the easiest way to create a bulleted list is to apply direct formatting to an existing paragraph. By doing this, you maintain the paragraph's current style, its font formatting, and most of its paragraph formatting, but you add the bullets and change the indentation.

To create a bulleted list, follow these steps.

1. Select the paragraphs you want to turn into the list. If you want to use only one paragraph (for example, to start a list from it), place the insertion point in it.

2. Choose Home | Paragraph | Bullets to display the Bullets panel, as shown here.

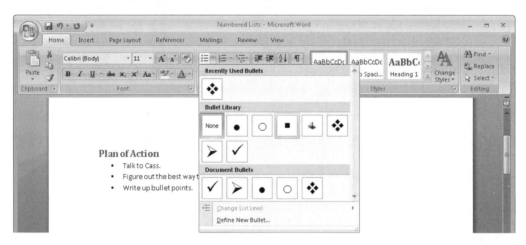

3. Choose a bullet by using one of these techniques:

■ Hover the mouse pointer over a format (without clicking) to make Word temporarily apply that format, giving you a preview.

■ To apply the last type of bullet you've used, click the main part of the Bullets button rather than the drop-down arrow.

■ To apply one of the bullet formats you've used most recently in Word (not just in this document), choose it from the Recently Used Bullets area at the top of the Bullets panel.

■ The Bullet Library area provides a choice of standard bullet types.

■ To use one of the bullet formats you've used so far in this document or another open document, choose it from the Document Bullets area at the bottom of the Bullets panel.

4. If necessary, create a custom bullet by following these steps:

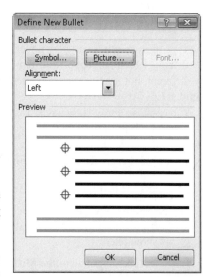

■ Click the Define New Bullet item on the Bullets panel. Word displays the Define New Bullet dialog box, as shown here.

■ To use a symbol for the bullet, click the Symbol button. Word displays the Symbol dialog box. Select the symbol as described in the section "Enter Symbols and Special Characters" in Chapter 3.

■ To use a picture for the bullet, click the Picture button. Word displays the Picture Bullet dialog box, with a wide variety of bullet pictures loaded. Either scroll down to find a bullet, or type a descriptive term (for example, **poetic** or **romanesque**) in the Search Text box, and then click the Go button. If your computer is connected to the Internet, you can make even more bullet pictures available for your search by selecting the Include Content From Office Online check box.

TIP *If you have extra bullet pictures of your own (for example, your company might have developed its own set), you can import them by clicking the Import button in the Picture Bullet dialog box, identifying the files in the Add Clips to Organizer dialog box, and then clicking the Add button.*

■ To change the font of the current bullet, click the Font button, choose the Font in the Font dialog box, and then click the OK button.

■ When you've chosen the bullet, click the OK button. Word closes the Picture Bullet dialog box.

5. To create a sublist (a list with a larger indent than the list that contains it):

■ Press TAB at the start of a paragraph.

■ Press ENTER at the end of a sublist paragraph to continue the sublist.

■ Press SHIFT-TAB at the start of a paragraph to move the paragraph up a level and restart the main list.

6. When you want to stop the bulleted list, press ENTER twice.

TIP *You can also access the Bullets panel by right-clicking a paragraph and choosing Bullets. This shortcut is handy when you don't have the Home tab of the Ribbon displayed.*

Understand and Use Language Formatting

One type of formatting you may never have considered is language formatting, which you apply to tell Word which language your text is in. Language formatting doesn't make your text look any different, but it helps the spell checker avoid querying foreign words in the belief that they're mangled English.

You can also apply "language" formatting that tells the spell checker not to check spelling on text. You might want to apply do-not-check language formatting for technical terms, programming code, and the like.

To apply language formatting, follow these steps:

1. Select the text you want to affect.

2. Choose Review | Proofing | Set Language. Word displays the Language dialog box, as shown here.

3. Select the language in the Mark Selected Text As list box.

4. If you need to prevent the spell checker from checking the text, select the Do Not Check Spelling Or Grammar check box.

5. Click the OK button. Word closes the Language dialog box and applies the language formatting.

Once you've told Word you're using a particular language, you can apply that language quickly to a word that the spell checker queries. Right-click the query, choose Language from the context menu, and then choose the language, as shown here.

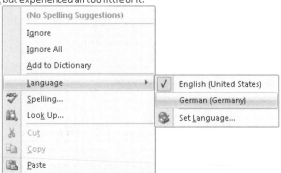

Language formatting is also useful when you need to search for foreign words in a document. For example, if you've formatted all the German words in a document with German language formatting, you can use Find to locate them all at once.

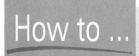 **Make the Detect Language Automatically Feature Work**

Word can automatically detect some languages—providing that you tell it to do so. Telling Word is easy but far from intuitive.

Languages Word can detect include English, Spanish, French, German, Italian, Portuguese, Swedish, Norwegian, Finnish, Danish, Dutch, Russian, Polish, Chinese (Simplified and Traditional), Japanese, Korean, Thai, Hebrew, Arabic, and Greek.

To set up automatic language detection, follow these steps:

1. Choose Start | All Programs | Microsoft Office | Microsoft Office Tools | Microsoft Office 2007 Language Settings. Windows displays the Microsoft Office 2007 Language Settings dialog box.

2. In the Available Editing Languages list box, select each language you want, and then click the Add button. Each language you selected appears in the Enabled Editing Languages list box. Remove any unwanted languages from this box by selecting them and clicking Remove.

3. Make sure that the Primary Editing Language drop-down list shows the language you want to use as the norm. For example, choose "English (U.S.)" if you want to use U.S. English.

4. Click the OK button. Windows closes the Microsoft Office 2007 Language Settings dialog box.

5. In Word, choose Review | Proofing | Set Language. Word displays the Language dialog box.

6. Select the Detect Language Automatically check box. This is where you toggle automatic detection on and off for the languages you've told Word to use.

7. Click the OK button. Word closes the Language dialog box.

4

TIP
You can also open the Language dialog box by right-clicking a spelling query and choosing Language | Set Language. This shortcut is handy when the spelling checker queries a word that's spelled correctly but in a different language.

Format Long Documents Efficiently

If you want to work as quickly and efficiently as possible, use styles whenever possible for formatting your documents. A *style* is a named collection of formatting that you can apply in a single click rather than applying several different types of formatting one after another.

For example, to make the main headings in a document stand out, you might give them a different font, a larger font size, an outdent, and some extra space before and after. Instead of applying the font, size, indentation, and spacing one at a time, you can create a style that includes them all, and then apply the style to each main heading.

Here are the five types of styles that Word lets you use, with examples of what the styles may contain:

- **Character style** A style that you can apply to characters within a paragraph or other element rather than to the paragraph or element. A character style can contain font, border, and language formatting, but not paragraph, tab, frame, or bullets and numbering formatting. For example, you can create a character style named Technical Term that applies a different font, a different color, and do-not-spell-check formatting. With the style, your technical terms not only stand out, but you can access them all at once.

- **Paragraph style** A style that you can apply to a paragraph of text at a time. A paragraph style can contain font, paragraph, tab, border, language, frame, and numbering formatting. For example, a Heading 1 style may use a different font than body text (for contrast), a large font size, extra white space before it and after it, and perhaps an outdent. (It might also have an automatic number.)

- **Linked paragraph and character style** A style that you can apply either to a whole paragraph or to one or more characters. Linked styles are new in Word 2007 and can save you a lot of time and effort instead of having to maintain separate character styles and paragraph styles (as in earlier versions of Word). A linked paragraph and character style effectively creates a character style and a paragraph style that share a name. If you select characters and apply the style, Word applies it as a character style; if you click in a paragraph, or select paragraphs, and then apply the style, Word applies it as a paragraph style.

- **List style** A style that you can apply to the paragraphs of a single-level or multilevel list. A list style can contain font and numbering formatting. For example, the top level of a list style may have a large, bold font and numbering in the *1*) style. The second level may use a smaller, regular font and numbering in the *a*) style, the third level that same regular font and numbering in the *i*) style, and so on for the lower levels of the list.

- **Table style** A style that you can apply to one or more cells or to an entire table. A table style can contain font, paragraph, and tabs formatting, but it can also contain table properties, borders and shading, and stripes (which control how the shading and patterns are applied in bands to the table). Chapter 10 explains how to use, create, and modify table styles.

Word provides seemingly endless options for styles, which provides great power when you must implement styles that perform exactly as you need them to. These options make styles appear daunting—but though styles do have a learning curve, you can get started with them quickly. This section shows you how to do so. Chapter 9 shows you how to create your own styles, modify existing styles, and use all the options Word offers for managing styles.

Understand the Essentials of Styles

In Word, just as every document must have a template attached to it (see the section "Create New Documents" in Chapter 2), every paragraph in a document must have a style applied to it. If you create a "blank" document without specifying which template to use, Word attaches the Normal template (*Normal.dotm*) to it. Similarly, Word gives the first paragraph in the Normal template the Normal style by default, so until you apply a different style manually, each paragraph receives the Normal style.

This automatically assigned style allows you to create documents in Word without understanding what styles are, how they work, and how to apply them, but it's a recipe for creating hard-to-manage documents: If every paragraph is in the Normal style, the only way to distinguish one paragraph from another is by looking at them or by identifying them by characteristics such as font and font size. By contrast, if you apply Heading 1 styles to your top-level headings, Heading 2 styles to the second-level headings, and Body Text style to the body paragraphs, you can distinguish the headings from the body text.

Once you've assigned styles to the paragraphs in your documents, you can change the formatting of the documents by changing the styles. For example, to make all the Body Text paragraphs in your documents larger, you simply change the font size in the Body Text style. That change automatically carries through to all the paragraphs that have the Body Text style applied.

To save you the effort of creating your own styles, Word comes with enough built-in styles for most conventional uses. You can adapt these styles as much as you need to make them look and work they way you want. And if you need further styles, you can create your own (see Chapter 9).

Learn Where Word Stores Styles

Word lets you store styles in templates and in documents. Most of the built-in styles that come with Word live in the Normal template. As Word keeps the Normal template loaded all the time you're using Word, these styles are available for use all the time. Other templates come with their own styles for specific elements. For example, the Fax Coversheet template has a Document Label style that the Normal template doesn't have. (The Fax Coversheet template uses the Document Label style for its "facsimile transmittal" line.) You can use such template-specific styles only when you're working on a document with the template attached (or when you have the template itself open for editing).

When you create your own styles, you can choose whether to store them in a template or in a document:

- **Styles stored in a template**   These styles are available to the template itself (if you open it for editing) and to each document attached to the template. Always store your styles in your templates unless you've got a very good reason to store them in the document (see next).

- **Styles stored in a document**   These styles are available only to the document that contains them. (You can transfer styles from one document to another, but doing so is clumsy and makes it hard to keep the styles synchronized.) Store styles in a document only when no other document will need them.

You'll have guessed the problem that can arise when you store the styles in the template: If you move the document or template relative to each other, the document may not be able to find its template. So even when you choose to store the styles in the template rather than the document itself, the document needs to contain information about the styles used in it.

(Otherwise, if someone sent you a document and you didn't have the template, the whole document would appear in your standard font, losing almost all its formatting.) This set of style information in the document itself can get out of sync with the master style information in the document's template, which can lead to formatting problems.

Apply Styles

The easiest way to get started with styles is to use Word's built-in styles. You can apply them in several ways.

Whichever way you use, start by selecting the characters or paragraphs to which you want to apply the style:

- ■ **Apply a style to some characters or words**   Select those characters or words.
- ■ **Apply a style to a paragraph**   Position the insertion point anywhere in that paragraph. You don't need to select the paragraph.
- ■ **Apply a style to multiple paragraphs**   Select those paragraphs (for example, drag through them).

Apply Styles Using the Mini Toolbar and Styles Group

One of the problems with styles in earlier versions of Word was that the main tool for applying them, the Styles drop-down list on the Formatting toolbar, didn't show the available styles very effectively. Word 2007 tackles this problem by putting a Styles panel on the Mini Toolbar (which appears when you select text) and a Styles group on the Home tab:

- ■ **Mini Toolbar**   Click the Styles button, and then click the style on the panel that appears.
- ■ **Styles group**   Click the drop-down arrow, and then click the style on the Quick Style Gallery that appears, as shown here. If the style you want appears in the row of styles in the Styles group, you can simply click it without opening the Quick Style Gallery. You can also use the scroll buttons to scroll through the rows of styles, but using the panel is usually faster.

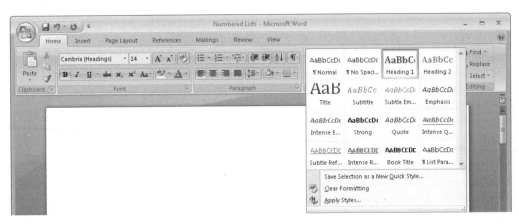

Use the Apply Styles Pane and the Styles Pane

Applying styles from the Mini Toolbar or the Home tab's Quick Styles Gallery is handy, but only some styles appear there. To get at the rest of the styles, you must use either the Apply Styles pane or the Styles pane.

Use the Apply Styles Pane   Of these two panes, the Apply Styles pane (shown next) should be your first choice for applying styles, as it's smaller than the Styles pane and faster to use. You can open the Apply Styles pane by pressing CTRL-SHIFT-S or choosing Home | Styles | Quick Styles Gallery | Apply Styles Pane.

To apply a style, open the Style Name drop-down list, and then click the style you want.

When the AutoComplete Style Names check box is selected, you can "type down" to the style you need. Click in the Style Name box, and then type the first few letters of the style name. Word automatically displays the first matching entry.

To close the Apply Styles pane, click the Close button (the × button) in its upper-right corner.

Use the Styles Pane   You can also apply styles from the Styles pane (see Figure 4-11). This method is useful when you have the Styles pane open already for managing styles. You can open the Styles pane by pressing CTRL-ALT-SHIFT-S, choosing Home | Styles | Styles (the tiny button at the right end of the Styles bar), or clicking the Styles button in the Apply Styles pane.

To close the Styles pane, click the Close button (the × button) in its upper-right corner.

Apply Styles via Keyboard Shortcuts

When you're typing, keyboard shortcuts are a great way to apply styles, because you can apply a style without moving either hand from the keyboard. Table 4-3 lists Word's built-in shortcuts for applying the most frequently used styles. You can create shortcuts for other styles by working from the Modify Style dialog box (see the section "Create Custom Styles" in Chapter 9).

> **TIP**   *To select all text or paragraphs that have a particular style, right-click that style in the Quick Style gallery or the Styles pane and choose Select All Instances. You can then apply a different style to the text or take another action with it—for example, you might copy the text.*

To Apply This Style	Press This Shortcut
Heading 1	CTRL-ALT-1
Heading 2	CTRL-ALT-2
Heading 3	CTRL-ALT-3
List Bullet	CTRL-SHIFT-l
Normal	CTRL-SHIFT-N or ALT-SHIFT-5 (numeric keypad with Num Lock off)

TABLE 4-3   Keyboard Shortcuts for Applying Styles

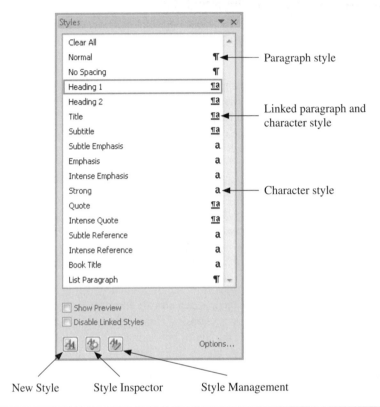

FIGURE 4-11 To apply styles from the Styles pane, scroll to the style you want, and then click it. The symbol to the right of each style name indicates the style type.

Know When to Use Each Type of Style

The key to formatting documents successfully with styles is to use the right style at the right time, so that you get the effect you want and don't need to waste time changing styles. Use paragraph and linked styles first to apply the broad strokes of formatting to each document, and then use character styles, table styles, and list styles to add further formatting only where required. When you use styles like this, you can often avoid using direct formatting at all, although sometimes you may need to apply direct formatting at the end of the formatting process to tweak individual elements in the document.

Apply Most Formatting with Paragraph Styles and Linked Styles

The bulk of most Word documents consists of paragraphs of text, so normally you use paragraph-type styles more than the other types of styles that Word offers. Apply a linked style or a paragraph style to each paragraph in each document you create:

- **Linked style** Use a linked (paragraph and character) style to apply formatting that you need to apply to both entire paragraphs and characters or words within paragraphs.

- **Paragraph style** Use a stand-alone (non-linked) paragraph style to apply formatting that you never need to apply to any unit of text smaller than a paragraph.

TIP

When you're working with Word's built-in styles, you usually needn't worry about the distinction between paragraph styles and linked styles. Some of Word's built-in styles are paragraph styles (for example, the Normal style and the Heading 1 through Heading 9 styles), while others are linked styles (for example, the Title style). Either a paragraph style or a linked style works fine for a paragraph.

4

Pick Out Text with Character Styles and Linked Styles

After you've applied a paragraph style or linked style to each paragraph, you may need to pick out individual phrases, words, or even characters within particular paragraphs. One possibility is to use direct formatting—for example, to select a word and click the Italic button on the floating toolbar to apply italics. But if you use character styles or linked styles instead, you can not only apply the required formatting quickly but also easily update all instances of the formatting (by changing the style) if needed.

- **Character style** Use a character style when applying formatting that contains only font formatting—for example, a style that consists of a different font, font size, and boldface.

- **Linked style** Use a linked style when applying formatting that you sometimes need to apply to entire paragraphs as well as to characters.

Format Lists with List Styles

If you need to use many numbered lists or bulleted lists in your documents, standardize them by using list styles rather than applying numbering or bullets as direct formatting.

To encourage you to use list styles, Word comes with plenty of built-in ones. You'll find the following list styles in the Normal template (the global template Word uses as the basis for "new blank" documents) and in other templates intended for standard documents (as opposed to, say, faxes, letters, or calendars). In each of these four types of styles, the indentation increases with the number, allowing you to create different levels of lists by using different styles of the same type. For example, the List Number style has minimal indentation, the List Number 2 style has a small indent, and so on up to the List Number 5 style, which has a large indent.

- **Hanging-indent list styles** Use the List through List 5 styles to create unnumbered and unbulleted lists that start with a hanging indent. This is an odd look that most people seldom use.

- **Numbered-list styles** Use the List Number through List Number 5 styles to create numbered lists. These styles are good for regular use.

- **Bulleted-list styles** Use the List Bullet through List Bullet 5 styles to create bulleted lists. These styles too are good for regular use.

■ **List-continuation styles** Use the List Continue through List Continue 5 styles to continue numbered or bulleted lists with unnumbered and unbulleted paragraphs. The indentation on these styles matches the corresponding List Number and List Bullet styles. For example, List Continue 3 has the same level of indent as List Number 3 and List Bullet 3.

If the built-in list styles don't meet your needs, create a custom list style that does. See the section "Create Custom Styles" in Chapter 9.

Update, Replace, or Remove Styles

Once you've applied styles to a document, you're ready to reap their benefits. These benefits include being able to quickly update all text or paragraphs to which a style is applied, replace one style with another style, or remove all instances of a style.

Update a Style

If you're lucky, Word's built-in styles will meet your needs. More likely, you'll need to change some styles so that they suit you.

When you change a style (see Chapter 9), Word automatically updates all the text in the document to which the style is applied.

Replace One Style with Another Style

You can replace all instances of one style with another style in either of two ways:

■ **Use the Select All Instances command** Right-click the style in the Quick Styles Gallery or the Styles pane, choose the Select All Instances command—for example, Select All 5 Instance(s)—and then click the style you want to apply. This method is great for quickly replacing one style with another style.

■ **Use the Replace feature** You can use Replace to replace one style with another style (see the section "Find and Replace Formatting or Styles" in Chapter 3). Use this method when you need to replace some instances of a style but not others.

Remove All Instances of a Style

Word also lets you "remove" all instances of a style. Removing the style doesn't delete the text or other objects to which the style is applied—it makes Word apply the Normal style instead. The Normal style tends to be the bane of properly formatted documents, so you may find "removing" a style useful only seldom (if ever). In most cases, you'll do better to replace the style with another style than Normal.

To remove a style from the text to which it is applied, right-click it in the Quick Style Gallery or the Styles pane, and then choose the Remove All Instances command—for example, Remove All 10 Instance(s).

Customize the Styles on the Quick Style Gallery

If you find the Quick Style Gallery a handy way of applying styles, you'll probably want to change its selection of styles so that it contains those styles you use the most. Here's how to change the styles:

- **Add an existing style** Right-click the style in the Styles pane and choose Add To Quick Style Gallery from the context menu.

- **Add a new style you create** When you create a style (see the section "Create Custom Styles" in Chapter 9), select the Add To Quick Style List check box. Word then adds the style to the Quick Style Gallery.

- **Remove a style** Right-click the style in the Quick Style Gallery and choose Remove From Quick Style Gallery from the context menu.

Let Word Pick Styles for You

If you and your colleagues apply styles as you create each document, you should never end up with a document that uses only the Normal style—but most people encounter such documents before too long.

To turn the document into a properly formatted document, you can apply styles to it manually. Or you can let Word's AutoFormat feature have a go at the job. If the document is laid out with extra blank paragraphs, tabs, and so on, AutoFormat can often do a good job of applying styles. And if it doesn't, you'll have wasted only a minute or two.

Choose AutoFormat Settings

Before you run AutoFormat, make sure that its settings are suitable.

1. Click the Office Button, and then click Word Options. Word displays the Word Options dialog box.

2. In the left panel, click the Proofing item, and then click the AutoCorrect Options button. Word displays the AutoCorrect dialog box.

3. Click the AutoFormat tab. Word displays its controls (see Figure 4-12).

4. Choose the settings you need:

   - **Apply area** To give Word the most room for maneuver, select all four check boxes: the Built-In Heading Styles check box, the List Styles check box, the Automatic Bulleted Lists check box, and the Other Paragraph Styles check box.

   - **Replace area** You'll probably want to select the first five check boxes (they may already be selected). Replacing straight quotes with smart (curly) quotes, ordinals with superscripts, typed fractions (such as 1/2) with fraction characters (such as ½), and two hyphens with em dashes (long dashes: —) is usually helpful, as is substituting boldface for items entered between asterisks ("You said *what*?") and italic for items entered between underscores ("_Mimetic_ means imitating the behavior of another person or group."). (These are two Internet-inspired formatting conventions for text-only documents.) Clear the Internet And Network Paths With Hyperlinks check box unless you actually want Word to change URLs and network paths into live hyperlinks in the formatted document. Live hyperlinks in Word documents are sometimes helpful, but many people prefer not to have documents automatically launch a browser.

■ **Preserve area** Select the Styles check box if you want Word to leave any existing styles in the document (other than Normal, which doesn't count).

■ **Always AutoFormat area** The Plain Text WordMail Documents check box doesn't apply to using AutoFormat on regular documents in the way this section describes. Instead, it's for when you're using Word as your e-mail editor for Outlook. Consult an Outlook book for coverage of this topic.

5. Click the OK button. Word closes the AutoCorrect dialog box.

6. Click the OK button. Word closes the Word Options dialog box.

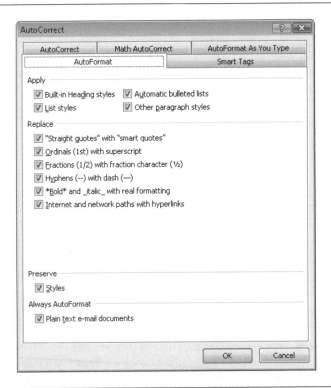

FIGURE 4-12   Word's AutoFormat feature can take the grunt work out of applying styles to a document that's formatted with blank paragraphs, spaces, and tabs rather than with styles.

Put the AutoFormat Command on the Quick Access Toolbar

To use the AutoFormat command, you must put it on the Quick Access Toolbar. Follow these steps:

1. Click the Customize Quick Access Toolbar button at the right end of the toolbar, and then choose More Commands from the drop-down menu. Word displays the Customize category in the Excel Options dialog box.

2. In the Customize Quick Access Toolbar drop-down list, select For All Documents item.

3. In the Choose Commands From drop-down list, select the Commands Not On The Ribbon item. The commands in the category appear in the list box.

4. In the left list box, select the AutoFormat command, and then click the Add button. Word adds the command to the right list box.

5. Click the OK button. Word closes the Word Options dialog box.

Run AutoFormat on a Document

Once you've chosen AutoFormat settings and put the AutoFormat button on the Quick Access Toolbar, open the document and run AutoFormat. Follow these steps:

1. Click the AutoFormat button on the Quick Access Toolbar. Word displays the AutoFormat dialog box, as shown here.

2. Select the AutoFormat Now option button unless you want to review each change in turn. Reviewing is slow work, but if you want to do it, select the AutoFormat And Review Each Change option button.

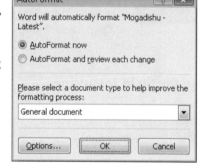

3. In the Please Select A Document Type To Help Improve The Formatting Process drop-down list, choose General Document unless the document is a letter (choose Letter) or an e-mail message (choose Email).

4. Click the OK button. Word runs AutoFormat on the document.

5. Examine the effect that AutoFormat has produced. If you don't want to keep the changes, click the Undo button or press CTRL-Z.

See Which Styles You've Applied

With all the different kinds of formatting that Word offers, you may sometimes find it hard to see exactly what formatting is applied to particular characters or a paragraph. Other times, you may be able to see *what* is applied but not *how* it is applied. For example, you can see that a paragraph is red, bold, centered, and in a large font size, but is it so because the style applied specifies that formatting, because direct formatting has been applied on top of a style that supplies some of the formatting, or because someone has gone wild with direct formatting without changing the style from Normal?

Word provides two tools to help you find out: the Style Inspector and the Reveal Formatting pane.

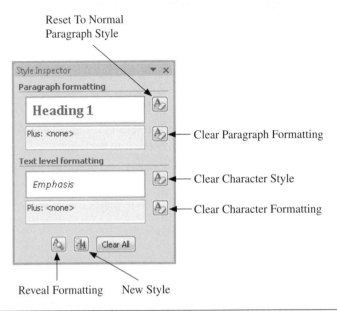

FIGURE 4-13 The Style Inspector pane shows you the paragraph style, any formatting added at the paragraph level, the text-level formatting, and any formatting added at the text level.

Use the Style Inspector

The Style Inspector (see Figure 4-13) is a pane that shows you the paragraph formatting separated from the text formatting. To open the Style Inspector, click the Style Inspector button in the Styles pane.

NOTE *"Default Paragraph Font" in the Text Level Formatting box means that no character style is applied. (There isn't a character style named "Default Paragraph Font.")*

What you'll often want to do in the Style Inspector is click the Clear Paragraph Formatting button or the Clear Character Formatting button:

- **Clear Paragraph Formatting** Click this button to remove any direct formatting that has been applied to the paragraph—in other words, to restore the paragraph to the formatting contained in its style. For example, if someone has changed the line spacing or tabs directly (rather than in the style), clicking this button restores them to the style's settings.

- **Clear Character Formatting** Click this button to remove any direct formatting applied on top of the character style. This has the effect of reapplying the character style. If the characters use Default Paragraph Font rather than another character style, clicking this button restores the font formatting in the paragraph style.

The Style Inspector also includes buttons for removing the character style, removing the paragraph style, and removing all formatting:

- **Remove Character Style**   Click this button to restore the Default Paragraph Font for the style. Removing any (or all) character styles like this is often useful.

- **Remove Paragraph Style**   Click this button to replace the paragraph's current style with the Normal style. (If the paragraph already uses Normal style, clicking this button has no effect.) Replacing the style with a style other than Normal is usually a better idea, because having paragraphs in Normal style is seldom helpful.

- **Clear All**   Click this button to remove all the formatting and reapply the Normal style. Clearing the character and paragraph formatting and then replacing the style with a style you want is usually a better idea.

Click the New Style button to open the larger Create New Style From Formatting dialog box (see the section "Create Custom Styles" in Chapter 9). Click the Reveal Formatting button to open the Reveal Formatting pane (see the next section).

Use the Reveal Formatting Pane

When you need to see more detail about formatting than the Style Inspector provides, click the Style Inspector's Reveal Formatting button to open the Reveal Formatting pane (see Figure 4-14).

FIGURE 4-14   Use the Reveal Formatting pane to see exactly text's formatting (left), to compare two selections (center), or to distinguish the different components of the formatting (right).

The Selected Text box shows the current selection, and the Formatting Of Selected Text box shows the details of the formatting applied to it. Click one of the underlined links (Font, Language, Alignment, Indentation, Margins, and so on) to open the right dialog box for changing that item. Click a plus (+) sign to expand a category. Click the resulting minus (–) sign to collapse the category again.

To compare two selections, choose the first, select the Compare To Another Selection check box, and then choose the second selection.

Select the Distinguish Style Source check box to split each category of formatting into the parts derived from the paragraph style, from the character style, and from direct formatting. This option isn't available when you're comparing two selections.

Use Themes to Apply Complex Formatting Quickly

The most sweeping type of formatting that the Office programs offer is themes, or Office Document Themes, to give them their full title. A *theme* is a suite of colors, fonts, and graphical effects that you can apply to an Office document either all at once or part by part. Themes let you change the overall look of a document all at once, giving it a coordinated look and color scheme. The Office programs share the themes, so you can use them in Excel and PowerPoint as well as Word.

NOTE   *Themes in Office 2007 are a new feature and are substantially different from themes in Word 2003.*

By using the same theme, you can give a whole suite of documents a similar look and feel. For example, you might want to use the same theme to emphasize that your web pages all belong together, even though you've derived some pages from Word documents, created another from an Excel spreadsheet, and exported a few from PowerPoint slides. Or, when creating a business proposal, you might use a theme on a presentation, spreadsheet, and Word document to establish a visual link among the three.

NOTE   *Themes rely on colors, so they're more effective for color documents than for black-and-white documents.*

Quick Styles, which are new in Word 2007, give you a way to apply themed formatting swiftly and easily to a document. Quick Styles draw on the theme fonts and theme colors to provide you with instant formatting choices that in theory always work together. Quick Styles can take much of the donkey work out of creating presentable-looking documents on your own and are good if you're using the templates that come with Word. But if you have professionally designed templates, you'll probably want to stick with them rather than using Quick Styles.

Understand What a Theme Is

Each theme consists of theme fonts, theme colors, and theme effects that work together pretty much no matter which combination of them you use.

Theme Fonts

Each theme has two "slots," or containers, for fonts: one for the headings and one for the body text. This means each theme can use either two fonts (one for headings, one for body text) or the same font for both headings and body text. Simplifying the fonts like this helps you avoid using too many fonts in a document, which at its worst can make your documents look like ransom notes. Theme fonts also help you avoid using fonts that clash with each other—although you may not like the font combinations that Microsoft's designers have chosen for the themes.

To tell which fonts you're currently using, choose Home | Font | Font, and then look at the Theme Fonts readout at the top. Cambria is Word 2007's standard heading font, and Calibri is the standard body font. Both these fonts are designed to be easy for reading onscreen.

Theme Colors

Each theme has twelve slots for color: four colors for text and backgrounds, six accent colors for items such as charts and graphs, and one color each for hyperlinks and followed hyperlinks.

Microsoft's designers set up the text and background colors so that light colors are legible against the dark colors and the dark colors legible against the light colors. Similarly, the designers chose accent colors that are always visible against the background colors. The net result is that you have a choice of colors for text and backgrounds that should always work in combination, even though you will need to experiment with different combinations of colors to produce a result that appeals to you.

The Theme Colors section in the color picker (which you can access from various parts of the Word interface, including the Font Color button) shows the colors available in the current theme. This selection of colors changes when you change the theme.

Theme Effects

The Office 2007 programs include a new graphics platform called OfficeArt 2.0, which can produce high-quality visual effects on pictures, shapes, diagrams, and charts. (In PowerPoint, you can apply visual effects to tables and text as well.) By using different combinations of line, fill, and shadow or 3D effects, OfficeArt creates theme effects that give graphical objects a particular feel—for example, a frosted-glass look or a metallic sheen.

If you create mostly text-based documents in Word, OfficeArt 2.0 probably won't be much of a boon for you. But if you use graphical objects in some of your documents, OfficeArt 2.0 should save you time and mouse-work by letting you easily create sets of graphical objects that have a similar feel and that work with the document's theme.

Learn Where to Find Your Themes

Office comes with a dozen or so built-in themes. You can download other themes from the Microsoft Office Online site (http://office.microsoft.com) or create your own themes (see the section "Create a New Theme," later in this chapter).

Themes are stored in theme files, which have the .thmx extension. Themes don't contain any content, just details of the colors and fonts to use and the types of graphical objects to create, so they're compact and quick to download.

You'll find your themes in the Document Themes folder inside the folder in which you installed Office 2007. For instance, if you installed Office in the Program Files\Microsoft Office folder, the themes are in the Program Files\Microsoft Office\Document Themes 12 folder. (The internal version number of Office 2007 is 12.)

The Document Themes 12 folder contains a Theme Colors folder, a Theme Effects folder, a Theme Fonts folder, and a Microsoft Office Theme file for each of the built-in themes. For example, the Technology theme is stored in the file Technology.thmx.

Get Started with Themes and Quick Styles

You don't need to add themes or Quick Styles to your documents, because Word does that for you. As soon as you create a document, you're using the theme that Word has applied to the template attached to the document. As soon as you start typing in the document, you're using Quick Styles. You can then apply other Quick Styles as needed, or switch to another theme.

Change the Theme or Parts of It

If you don't like the theme Word has applied automatically to a document you've created, change the theme. Choose Page Layout | Themes, and then click the theme you want on the Themes panel.

If none of the themes appeals to you, click the More Themes On Microsoft Office Online item to open a web browser window to the Microsoft Office Online web site, from which you can download extra themes.

To load any extra themes you have available (for example, themes your company has developed), click the Browse For Themes item, select the theme file or a document that has the theme applied, and then click the Open button.

Instead of changing the entire theme, you can change one or two of its three components: theme colors, theme fonts, and theme effects. To do so, click the Page Layout tab and go to the Themes group; click the Theme Colors button, the Theme Fonts button, or the Theme Effects button; and then choose the look you want from the resulting panel. As with the themes themselves, you can hover the mouse pointer over an item on each of these panels to make Word apply a preview to your document, which helps you find colors, fonts, and effects that suit your needs.

Create a New Theme

Office includes enough built-in themes to get you started, but if you use themes actively in your work, you may want to create your own themes to give your documents a unique look rather than the looks everyone else is using.

To create a theme, follow these steps:

1. Apply the built-in theme on which you want to base the new theme. You'll use this built-in theme as your starting point.

2. Define the colors for the theme:

■ Click the Theme Colors button, and then click the Create New Theme Colors item. Word displays the Create New Theme Colors dialog box, showing you the colors of the current theme.

■ The Create New Theme Colors dialog box provides a button for each color used in the theme. Click a button, and then choose from the resulting panel. To get the full range of colors, click More Colors, and then work on the Standard tab or the Custom tab of the Colors dialog box.

■ Type a name for the theme colors in the Name text box, and then click the Save button.

3. Define the fonts for the theme:

■ Click the Theme Fonts button, and then click the Create New Theme Fonts item. Word displays the Create New Theme Fonts dialog box.

■ Choose a heading font in the Heading Font drop-down list and a body font in the Body Font drop-down list.

■ Type the name for the theme fonts in the Name text box, and then click the Save button.

4. Click the Theme Effects button, and choose the built-in theme effects to use from the panel. You can't create your own theme effects at this writing.

5. In the Themes group, click the Themes button and choose Save Current Theme. Word displays the Save Current Theme dialog box. Assign a name and choose a folder, and then click the OK button.

NOTE *Word suggests saving each custom theme in the Document Themes folder. This is usually the best place unless you've set up another folder for themes. For example, your company might have a network folder for shared themes.*

Once you've saved your theme, you can apply it from the Custom section at the top of the Themes panel.

Restore a Template's Theme

If you decide you don't want to keep the changes you made to the document's theme, you can go back to the document's original look by restoring the theme in the document's template. To restore the theme, choose Page Layout | Themes | Themes | Reset To Theme From Template.

Work with Quick Styles

To apply a Quick Style, select the text you want to affect, and then choose the style either from the Style panel on the Mini Toolbar or from the Quick Style Gallery on the Home tab. You can get a preview of the formatting by hovering your mouse pointer over the style for a moment to make Word apply the formatting momentarily to the selected text.

To change the current set of Quick Styles, choose Home | Styles | Change Styles | Style Set, and then select the new set (see Figure 4-15). As usual, hover the mouse pointer over a set to get a preview in the document. If you don't like the effect your changes produce, you can return to the set of Quick Styles in the template by choosing Reset To Quick Styles From Template from this menu.

FIGURE 4-15 Use the Change Styles | Style Set submenu to switch to a different set of Quick Styles.

If you want to keep the changes you've made to the Quick Styles, you can save the Quick Styles as a set. Follow these steps:

1. Chose Home | Styles | Change Styles | Style Set | Save As Quick Style Set. Word displays the Save Quick Style Set dialog box.

2. Type a name for the set, choose the folder in which to store them, and then click the Save button.

NOTE *Word suggests saving the Quick Style set in the QuickStyles folder. This folder is located in the AppData\Roaming\Microsoft folder in your user profile folder and is a good place to store your Quick Style sets unless you need to share them with your colleagues (in which case, you'll probably want to use a network folder that your colleagues can access).*

If you really like the changes you've made to the Quick Styles, you may want to use them as your default Quick Styles, the ones that Word applies automatically for you. To make these Quick Styles your default ones, choose Home | Styles | Change Styles | Set As Default.

Chapter 5

Lay Out Pages and Use Headers and Footers

How to...

- ■ Break a document into sections
- ■ Change the margins
- ■ Set the page size and orientation
- ■ Add line numbers to paragraphs
- ■ Insert manual page breaks to control layout
- ■ Align text vertically on a page
- ■ Add headers and footers to your documents
- ■ Place text precisely with text boxes

In the previous chapter, you learned how to apply a wide range of formatting to your documents and give them a professional look. This chapter shows you how to set up pages so that they look the way you need them to and how to add headers and footers.

Word lets you change the page setup of a document at any point, but generally you'll do best to set up the page correctly when starting to create a document rather than change it midstream. That way, you'll be able to see roughly how your documents look from the start rather than getting unpleasant surprises about the page count or formatting when you change page setup after creating the document.

Word lets you change a document's paper size, paper orientation (portrait or landscape), and margins. When printing a document, you can also choose which printer tray the printer should take the paper from (for example, you might have a tray of letterhead for letters).

Depending on the types of documents you create, you may be able to choose page setup once and then forget about it until the next time you need to create a different type of document. However, you may also need to break a complex document up into sections so that you can apply different page formatting, or different headers and footers, to different sections.

Break a Document into Sections

In Word, a *section* is a subdivision of a document that allows you to apply different page formatting to different parts of the document. For example, say you need to create a business letter document that includes its own envelope text. By putting the letter in one section and the envelope in another, you can give each item the paper size and page layout it needs, rather than having one of them use the wrong type.

When you create a new document, it consists of a single section. Any changes you make to the document's page layout apply to the whole document.

You can add other sections when you need to apply different page formatting to different parts of the document. Once you've created sections, changes you make to page layout apply to the active section—the section in which the insertion point is currently positioned.

To affect multiple sections or the whole document, you can either select those sections or the document, or work in the Page Setup dialog box and choose the relevant part of the document (for example, choose Selected Sections, This Point Forward, or Whole Document in the Apply To drop-down list).

Understand Word's Four Types of Section Breaks

Word offers four types of section breaks:

- ■ **Next Page**   The new section starts on the next page. A next-page break is good for creating documents in which each part or chapter starts on a new page (as in this book) or for using a different paper size (for example, an envelope).

- ■ **Continuous**   The new section starts at the next paragraph on the same page. A next-page section is good for creating layouts that use different numbers of newspaper-style columns on the same page. Chapter 11 shows you how to create such columns.

- ■ **Even Page**   The new section starts on the next even page, even if that means adding a blank odd-numbered page after the current page. This is useful for some book layouts.

- ■ **Odd Page**   The new section starts on the next odd page, even if that means adding a blank even-numbered page after the current page. This is useful for other book layouts.

Insert Section Breaks

To insert a new section, follow these steps:

1. Position the insertion point at the beginning of the paragraph with which you want the new section to start.

2. Choose Page Layout | Page Setup | Breaks, and then click Next Page, Continuous, Even Page, or Odd Page on the panel. Word inserts the section break and rearranges the pages as necessary.

Like paragraph marks and spaces, section breaks are normally hidden. To see your section breaks, press CTRL-SHIFT-8 or choose Home | Paragraph | Show/Hide ¶. The next illustration shows a continuous section break and a next-page section break.

controls·on·the·Home·tab.·Most·controls·offer·a·choice·of·using·the·look·from·the·current·theme·or·
using·a·format·that·you·specify·directly.·⸻Section Break (Continuous)⸻

To·change·the·overall·look·of·your·document,·you·can·choose·new·Theme·elements·on·the·Page·Layout·
tab.⸻Section Break (Next Page)⸻

Once you've inserted one or more section breaks in a document, you may find it helpful to add the Section readout to the beginning of the status bar so that you can see which section the insertion point is currently in. To do so, right-click the status bar, select the Section check box on the Customize Status Bar menu, and then click anywhere in the document to hide the menu again.

There's a Hidden Section Break at the End of the Document

Each document has a hidden section break at the end, hidden in the last paragraph mark—the paragraph mark that appears when you create a new document and that you can't delete.

When the document contains only one section, this paragraph mark contains the page formatting for the entire document. When you create another section, this paragraph mark contains the page formatting for the final section only.

Delete a Section Break

To delete a section break, place the insertion point before it, and then press DELETE.

There's one complication: When you delete a section break, the section before the break becomes part of the section after the break. So if, for example, you delete the section break between Section 2 and Section 3 of your document, Section 2 becomes part of Section 3 and receives its formatting. Confusingly, though, because you've deleted Section 2, Section 3 now becomes Section 2.

Change the Margins

To make your documents look good, you'll often need to increase or decrease the top, bottom, left, and right margins.

 Some printers can print all the way up to the edges of a sheet of paper—but most printers can't. For example, most laser printers can print only up to 0.2 inches or 0.5 inches from the edges of the paper. Usually, it's a good idea to leave plenty of margin, both for the printer's needs and for those of a person holding the document. If you tell Word to print closer to the edge of a sheet of paper than your printer can handle, Word tells you that the margins are "set outside the printable area of the page." Word offers to let you continue, but normally you'll do better to change the margins so that they fall within the printable area before printing.

Change the Margins Quickly by Using a Preset Margin

The quick and easy way to set margins for a document is to choose Page Layout | Page Setup | Margins, and then choose one of the preset options on the Margins panel (see Figure 5-1). The choices are Normal, Narrow, Moderate, Wide, Mirrored (which creates mirrored margins for facing pages in a book), or Office 2003 Default (which uses the same measurements as Word 2003's default settings did).

5

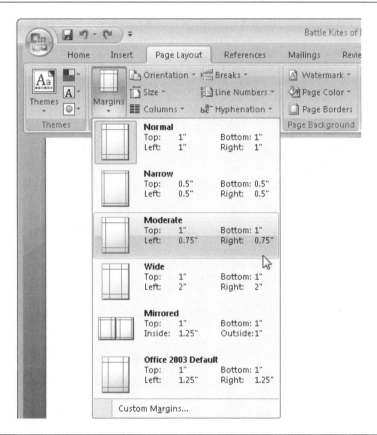

FIGURE 5-1   To change the margins quickly, choose a preset from the Margins panel.

Choose Custom Margins by Using the Page Setup Dialog Box

If none of the options on the Margins panel suits your document, click the Custom Margins icon. Word displays the Margins tab of the Page Setup dialog box (see Figure 5-2). You can then choose exactly the margins you want. Start by choosing the appropriate item in the Multiple Pages drop-down list, because this list controls which measurement boxes Word displays in the Margins area.

Most of the options are easy to grasp, but mirror margins and the gutter measurement are more complex:

■ **Mirror margins**   Facing pages have margins that "mirror" each other, so the left (outer) margin on the left page is the same width as the right (outer) margin on the right page. Similarly, the inner margins on the left and right pages are the same width as each other.

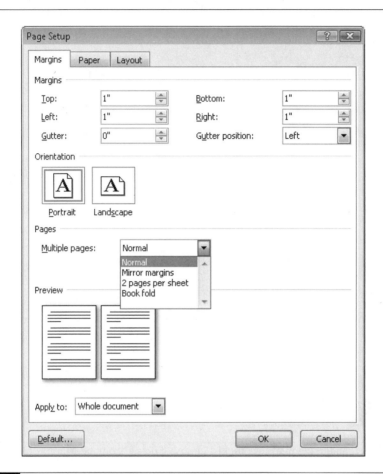

FIGURE 5-2   To set custom margins, use the controls on the Margins tab of the Page Setup
dialog box.

■ **Gutter**   The gutter is the amount of space to leave between two facing pages that will
be bound into a publication or book. (In this book, look at the space that's wasted through
being close to the book binding.) The gutter is separate from the margin setting and adds
to it. For regular pages, Word uses a zero-inch gutter—in other words, no gutter at all.
Word automatically handles the gutter position when you use mirror margins, multiple
pages per sheet, or a book fold. When you're printing regular pages, Word lets you
position the gutter at either the top or the left of the page.

Here are examples of margin settings you might choose:

- **Regular document**   Choose Normal in the Multiple Pages drop-down list, and then set margins in the Top text box, Bottom text box, Left text box, and Right text box. Use the Gutter text box to specify the gutter size (use 0" to have no gutter) and the Gutter Position text box to control the gutter placement (Left or Top).

- **Document with mirror margins**   Choose Mirror Margins in the Multiple Pages drop-down list, and then set margins in the Top text box, Bottom text box, Inside text box, and Outside text box. Use the Gutter text box to specify the gutter size. Word positions the gutter automatically on the left.

- **Document with two pages per sheet**   Choose 2 Pages Per Sheet in the Multiple Pages drop-down list, and then set margins in the Top text box, Bottom text box, Outside text box, and Inside text box. Use the Gutter text box to specify the gutter size. Word positions the gutter automatically on the inside.

5

TIP   *If you want to put more than two pages on a sheet of paper, you can do so by setting Word to print multiple pages on the same sheet. See the section "Print Multiple Pages on the Same Sheet of Paper" in Chapter 8 for details.*

- **Booklet**   Choose Book Fold in the Multiple Pages drop-down list, and then specify the number of sheets in the booklet in the Sheets Per Booklet drop-down list that appears below the Multiple Pages drop-down list. Set the margins in the Top text box, Bottom text box, Outside text box, and Inside text box. Use the Gutter text box to specify the gutter size. Word automatically positions the gutter on the inside.

Change the Margins to Suit the Contents of a Page

Usually, the easiest way to go is to set the margins before you create your document. That way, the document conforms to the margins you've chosen.

But what you may want to do at other times is change the margins to conform to your document—for example, when you need a document to take up a particular amount of space. In this case, it's easier to drag one (or more) of the margins than to use a preset margin setting or the Page Setup dialog box. Follow these steps:

1. If you're using any view except Print Layout or Print Preview, click the Print Layout button on the Status bar. Word displays the document in Print Layout view.

2. If the ruler is hidden, display it:

   - Normally, it's easiest to click the View Ruler button at the top of the vertical scroll bar to display the ruler permanently. (Click the button again when you want to hide the ruler.)

   - If you prefer, pop the ruler up temporarily by hovering the mouse pointer at the bottom of the Ribbon (to display the horizontal ruler) or the left edge of the window (to display the vertical ruler) for a moment.

3. Drag the appropriate margin marker on the horizontal ruler or vertical ruler to where you need it. Word displays a dotted line representing the margin as you drag. The next illustration shows an example of dragging the left margin marker on the horizontal ruler.

 *The margin marker is the border between the dark-shaded part of the ruler that represents the margin and the lighter-shaded part that represents the text area. If the First Line Indent marker and Hanging Indent Marker are positioned at the left margin, you may need to move one or the other before you can reach the Left Margin Marker.*

Set the Paper Size and Orientation

Word comes set to print on a standard size of paper (8.5 × 11 inches in the U.S.). You can use a different size of paper in either of these ways:

- Choose Page Layout | Page Setup | Size, and then choose the paper size from the panel. The list starts with the most widely used sizes, such as Letter (8.5 × 11 inches) and Tabloid (11 × 17 inches). Scroll down to find less-used sizes and a range of envelopes.

- To use a size that's not listed, open the Page Setup dialog box. Either choose Page Layout | Page Setup | Size | More Paper Sizes to go directly to the Paper tab (see Figure 5-3), or choose Page Layout | Page Setup | Page Setup (click the tiny button at the right end of the Page Setup bar), and then click the Paper tab.

To specify which paper tray Word uses to print the document, choose the appropriate trays in the First Page list box and the Other Pages list box. To print normally, choose the Default Tray (Automatically Select) item.

To change the orientation of the sheet, choose Page Layout | Page Setup | Orientation, and then choose Portrait or Landscape from the panel, as shown here.

If you're working in the Page Setup dialog box, you can also choose orientation in the Orientation area on the Margins tab.

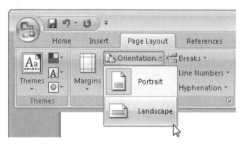

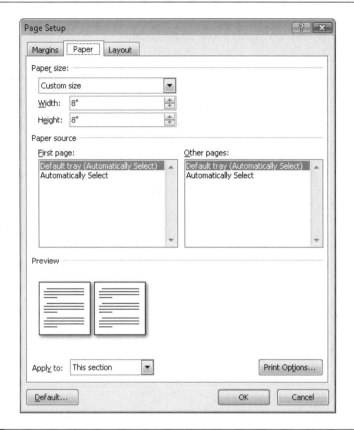

FIGURE 5-3 The Paper tab of the Page Setup dialog box lets you specify a custom size by choosing Custom Size in the Paper Size drop-down list and entering the measurements.

  To use a different paper size or orientation for part of a document, make that part into its own section. You can then click in that section and choose page setup options for it.

Add Line Numbers to Paragraphs

For legal documents and other formal documents, you may need to number each line. Word provides flexible line numbering either for complete documents or for sections.

Line numbering is part of section formatting, so normally you have to apply it to either an entire section or an entire document. However, Word offers a paragraph-formatting option that lets you suppress line numbering on any given paragraph.

To apply line numbering, follow these steps:

1. Choose the part of the document you want to number.

   ◼ If the document consists of only a single section, click anywhere in the document.

   ◼ If the document contains multiple sections, click in the section you want to affect.

   ◼ To work with multiple sections at once, select them.

   ◼ To work with the entire document, select it all by pressing CTRL-A or choosing Home | Editing | Select | Select All.

2. Choose Page Layout | Page Setup | Line Numbers, and then choose the appropriate command from the Line Numbers panel (shown here). This panel is a little confusing because some of the settings are mutually exclusive. The panel shows a check mark for each option that is currently applied.

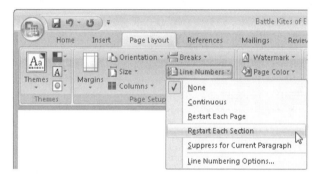

   ◼ **None**   Removes any existing line numbers. Cancels the Continuous setting, the Restart Each Page setting, or the Restart Each Section setting, if any of these are applied.

   ◼ **Continuous**   Applies line numbers. The line numbers are continuous, increasing from one page to the next rather than restarting at 1 at the top of each page.

   ◼ **Restart Each Page**   Applies line numbers. The line numbers restart at 1 at the top of each page, so any line reference must be accompanied by a page reference. If you select this setting, Word turns off the Restart Each Section setting (if it was on).

   ◼ **Restart Each Section**   Applies line numbering. The line numbers restart at 1 at the beginning of each section, so any line reference must be accompanied by a section reference. If you select this setting, Word turns off the Restart Each Page setting (if it was on).

   ◼ **Suppress for Current Paragraph**   Prevents line numbering from appearing on the current paragraph. If you've chosen continuous numbering, the numbering continues from the paragraph before the suppressed paragraph to the paragraph after the suppressed one.

3. If you need to change the starting number, adjust the distance between the line numbers to the text, or count in increments other than 1 (for example, you might want a line number to appear only on every fifth line), follow these steps:

- Click the Line Numbering Options item on the Line Numbers panel. Word displays the Layout tab of the Page Setup dialog box.

- In the Apply To drop-down list, choose which part of the document you want to affect: This Section, Selected Sections, Whole Document, Selected Text, or This Point Forward.

- Click the Line Numbers button. Word displays the Line Numbers dialog box, as shown here.

- Select the Add Line Numbering check box.

- In the Start At drop-down list, choose the number with which you want to start numbering (the default number is 1).

- In the From Text box, set the distance you want between the line numbers and the text. The default setting is Auto.

- In the Count By text box, set the increment (for example, 5). The default increment is 1.

- In the Numbering area, select the Restart Each Page option button, the Restart Each Section option button, or the Continuous option button, as needed. Word selects the option button for the current line numbering, so you may not need to change it.

- Click the OK button. Word closes the Line Numbers dialog box.

Insert Manual Page Breaks to Control Layout

Normally, Word breaks pages automatically for you, so you don't need to worry about it. Where a paragraph is too long to fit on the end of a page and must be broken, Word tries to place at least two lines on each page unless you've decided to allow widows and orphans (in the typesetting sense; see the section "Control the Flow of Text from Page to Page" in Chapter 4 for an explanation). If the paragraph is too short for this, Word moves the whole paragraph to the next page.

To control where page breaks fall, you can also insert page breaks manually as needed. To insert a page break, position the insertion point at the beginning of the paragraph with which you want the new page to start, and then press CTRL-ENTER or choose Page Layout | Page Setup | Breaks | Page.

Page breaks are normally hidden, but you can view them by pressing CTRL-SHIFT-8 or choosing Home | Paragraph | Show/Hide ¶ to turn on the display of formatting marks. The next illustration shows a page break.

They·set·a·meeting·for·November·15·in·Tupelo.¶

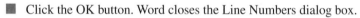

The·next·day,·Dana·awoke·with·a·splitting·headache—richly·deserved,·she·knew.¶

Align Text Vertically on a Page

Unlike horizontal alignment, which you can set for each paragraph (and for other objects, such as text boxes or pictures), vertical alignment does not normally need to be set: Word positions the text starting at the top of the page area and simply continues down the page, moving on to a new page as it becomes necessary.

Sometimes, however, you will need to set vertical alignment—for example, to create a visually impressive title page or other display item.

The rough-and-ready way to set vertical alignment is simply to use blank paragraphs or paragraph spacing (space before and space after) to position the text where you want it; and if your document is short and uncomplicated, you may find this an adequate solution. But there's a better way—to apply the appropriate vertical alignment to the document or to part of it.

To apply vertical alignment, follow these steps:

1. Choose the part of the document whose vertical alignment you want to change:

   ■ **Whole document**   Click anywhere in the document.

   ■ **An existing section**   Click anywhere in that section.

   ■ **Some paragraphs that aren't a separate section**   Select those paragraphs. Word creates a section from them for you when you apply the alignment.

   ■ **All of the document after a particular point**   Click at the cutoff point.

 Applying vertical alignment to less than a paragraph of text doesn't work well, because Word can't apply the alignment to less than a paragraph. For example, if you select a few words within a paragraph and tell Word to align Selected Text, Word creates a separate paragraph containing those words.

2. Choose Page Layout | Page Setup | Page Setup. (The Page Setup button is the tiny button at the right end of the Page Setup bar.) Word displays the Page Setup dialog box.

3. Click the Layout tab. Word displays its controls (see Figure 5-4).

4. Choose the alignment in the Vertical Alignment drop-down list:

   ■ **Top**   Starts the text at the top of the text area of the page. This is the default vertical alignment for most documents.

   ■ **Center**   Centers the text vertically within the text area of the page or section.

   ■ **Justified**   Justifies the text vertically within the text area of the page or section.

   ■ **Bottom**   Aligns the last line of the text with the bottom of the text area.

5. In the Apply To drop-down list, choose the appropriate part of the document. The choices depend on whether your document contains more than one section and whether you've selected some text or some sections. Here's the full range of choices:

   ■ **Whole Document**   Applies the vertical alignment to the whole document.

   ■ **Selected Text**   Creates a section from the selected text and applies the vertical alignment to this new section.

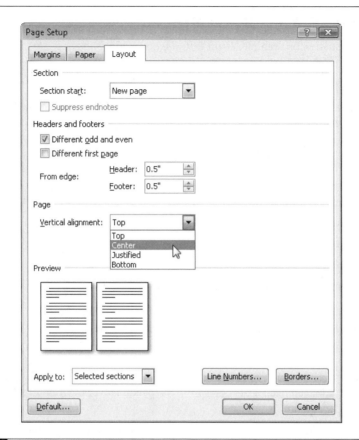

FIGURE 5-4 The Layout tab of the Page Setup dialog box allows you to align text vertically within a page or a section.

- **This Section**   Applies the vertical alignment to the current section.
- **Selected Sections**   Applies the vertical alignment to the selected sections.
- **This Point Forward**   Inserts a section break after the insertion point, creating a new section with the vertical alignment at the end of the document.

6. Click the OK button. Word closes the Page Setup dialog box and applies the vertical alignment.

Add Headers and Footers to Your Documents

Headers and footers make it easy to repeat identifying information on each page of a document:

- A *header* appears across the top of each page. You might include such information as the document's title and the author's name.

■ A *footer* appears across the bottom of each page. You might include such information as the date, the page number and total number of pages (such as *Page 4 of 25*), and the document's status (for example, *Draft* or *Company Confidential*).

Understand How Headers and Footers Work

Word allows you to repeat the same header and footer on each page of a document, or create different headers and footers on different pages as needed. For example, if you're producing a report that's broken up into several chapters, you might want to have the current chapter's title appear on each page.

Here's what you can do:

■ Insert a predefined header or footer from Word's gallery of canned headers or footers.

■ Suppress the header or footer on the first page of a document.

■ Use different headers and footers on odd and even pages.

■ Use different headers and footers in each section of a document if needed.

■ Combine some or all four of the preceding options.

Insert a Predefined Header or Footer

To insert a predefined header or footer, follow these steps:

1. Choose Insert | Header & Footer | Header or Insert | Header & Footer | Footer, and then choose the predefined header or footer from the panel. Hover the mouse pointer over a header to see a description.

2. Word inserts the header or footer, displays the header or footer area if the current view wasn't displaying it, adds the Header & Footer Tools section to the Ribbon, and displays the Design tab, as shown here.

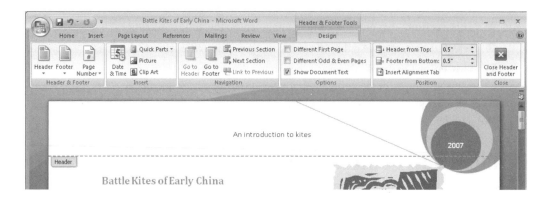

3. Complete any of the elements as needed. For example, you might need to type a text field. In this header, you can click the Year content control and use the date picker to change the date displayed, as shown here.

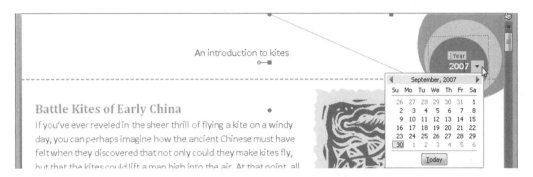

4. To remove a content control, right-click it, and then choose Remove Content Control from the context menu.

NOTE   *To move from the header area to the footer area, choose Design | Navigation | Go To Footer; choose Design | Navigation | Go To Header to go to the header. Alternatively, press ↓ from the last line of the header or ↑ from the first line of the footer.*

5. When you've finished changing the header or footer, choose Design | Close | Close Header And Footer or press either ESC or ALT-SHIFT-C. Word closes the header and footer area for editing, returning you to the main text of the document.

TIP   *You can also double-click in the main text to return to it from the header or footer. Likewise, if you can see the header or footer area, you can double-click in it to switch to it.*

Control Header and Footer Placement

To control where a header appears, change the value in the Header From Top text box in the Position group on the Design tab. To control where a footer appears, change the value in the Footer From Bottom text box.

CAUTION   *If you have a laser printer, allow some space at the ends of the page. Most laser printers cannot print at the very edges of the page, so if you position your header and footer right on the edge, you'll lose parts of them.*

To change the alignment of a header or footer item, follow these steps:

1. Select the item.

2. Choose Design | Position | Insert Alignment Tab. Word displays the Alignment Tab dialog box, as shown here.

3. In the Alignment area, select the Left option button, the Center option button, or the Right option button, as appropriate. In the Align Relative To drop-down list, choose Margin if you want the alignment to be relative to the margin; choose Indent if you want the alignment relative to the indent.

4. If you want a tab leader (for example, dots or underlines), select the appropriate option button in the Leader area. Tab leaders are sometimes useful, but normally you'll want to select the None option button.

5. Click the OK button. Word closes the Alignment Tab dialog box and applies your choices.

Headers and footers don't have to be confined to their normal areas at the top and bottom of pages. You can also use a header or footer to insert text or another object (for example, a picture) behind the main text of the documents. When you do so, you can clear the Show Document Text check box in the Options group on the Design tab to suppress the display of the text while you work on the header (rather than having the text be in the way as you work).

Use Different First-Page Headers and Footers

To create a different header or footer on the first page of your document, select the Different First Page check box in the Options group on the Design tab. Word marks the first page for different header and footer, naming the areas First Page Header and First Page Footer so that there's no confusion.

Click in the First Page Header area or First Page Footer area, and then create the header or footer you want for the first page. Move to the Header area or the Footer area on the second page, and then create the header or footer you want to use for the rest of the document.

Create Odd and Even Headers and Footers

To produce different headers on odd pages and even pages (as you might want in a book layout), select the Different Odd & Even Pages check box in the Options group on the Design tab. Word names the headers Odd Page Header and Even Page Header, and the footers correspondingly, so that you can easily see which is which.

Click in the Odd Page Header area or Odd Page Footer area, and then create the header or footer you want for odd-numbered (right-hand) pages. Move to the Even Page Header area or Even Page Footer area and create the header or footer for the even-numbered (left-hand) pages.

Many of Word's canned headers and footers come with odd and even page setups, so you may not need to create odd and even headers and footers of your own.

Create Different Headers and Footers in Different Sections

To create different headers and footers in different sections of the same document, divide the document into sections as described in the section "Break a Document into Sections," earlier in this chapter.

You can then create a different header or footer (or both) in each section. The easiest way to get all your headers into place is to go to the start of the document (for example, press CTRL-HOME), choose Insert | Header & Footer | Header, and then work through each section's headers in turn. Choose Design | Navigation | Next Section to move to the next section's header or Design | Navigation | Previous Section to move back to the previous section.

Word includes the section number in the header's tag, as shown here, so you can see where you are without having to look at the Section readout on the status bar.

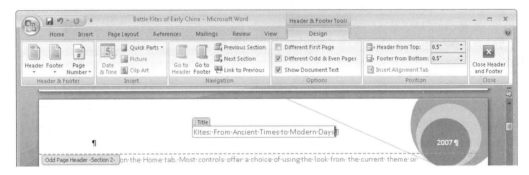

Word automatically links the header and footer in the second section and subsequent sections to the previous header and footer, giving you the same header and footer all the way through your document. For example, if you have a document with two sections and you create a header in the first section, Word automatically carries that header through to the second section.

To create separate headers and footers, choose Design | Navigation | Link To Previous to turn off this link. Issue the command again to establish a link to the previous section if needed.

Remove a Header or Footer

To remove a header, click in the section that contains the header, and then choose Insert | Header & Footer | Header | Remove Header. Similarly, to remove a footer, click in the appropriate section, and then choose Insert | Header & Footer | Footer | Remove Footer.

Add Page Numbers to Your Documents

Many documents need page numbers so that readers can tell easily which page they're on. The normal way to add page numbers in Word is to put them in a header or footer so that they repeat automatically on each page.

To add page numbers to a document, follow these steps:

1. Choose Insert | Header & Footer | Page Number, choose one of the placement categories on the menu, and then select the page number format from the panel. Word inserts the page number and displays the header area or footer area.

2. If necessary, change the page number formatting or the text that accompanies it. (For example, you might change "Page" to "Sheet" or another word.)

3. To change the format of the page number, choose Design | Header & Footer | Page Number | Format Page Numbers. Word displays the Page Number Format dialog box, as shown here.

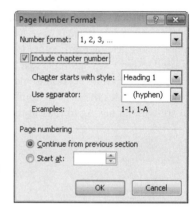

   ■ In the Number Format drop-down list, select the number formatting you want: 1, 2, 3; -1 -, - 2 -, - 3 -; a, b, c; A, B, C; i, ii, iii; or I, II, III.

   ■ If you want to include a chapter number, select the Include Chapter Number check box. In the Chapter Starts With Style drop-down list, choose the style that marks the start of each chapter (for example, Heading 1). In the Use Separator drop-down list, specify the separator to use between the chapter number and the page number: a hyphen, a period, a colon, an em dash (long), or an en dash (short).

4. To change the default numbering of the pages, select the Start At option button, and then set the starting number in the text box. To continue numbering from the previous section, select the Continue From Previous Section option button.

5. Click the OK button. Word closes the Page Number Format dialog box.

To remove page numbers, choose Insert | Header & Footer | Page Number | Remove Page Numbers. If you're already working in a header or footer, you can choose Design | Header & Footer | Page Number | Remove Page Numbers instead.

Add a Header or Footer to the Gallery So You Can Reuse It

If you create a header or footer that you want to reuse, add it to the Headers Gallery or Footers Gallery. Follow these steps:

1. Open the header or footer and select the parts you want to keep.

2. Choose Design | Header & Footer | Header | Save Selection To Header Gallery or Design | Header & Footer | Footer | Save Selection To Footer Gallery. Word displays the Create New Building Block dialog box.

3. Follow through the process described in the section "Create a Building Block of Your Own" in Chapter 9.

Place Text Precisely with Text Boxes

Normally, you'll want text to flow from page to page in your documents, but sometimes you may need to position some text exactly. To do so, you can use a text box.

You can either insert a text box of your own or use one of Word's preset text boxes. The presets have attractive designs and can enhance your documents. The only disadvantage is that millions of other Office users have them too, so they may look clichéd to your audience.

Insert a Preset Text Box

To insert a preset text box, choose Insert | Text | Text Box, and then choose the text box from the panel. Word adds the Text Box Tools section to the Ribbon and displays the Format tab, as shown here.

To change the size of the text box, either drag one of its handles, or use the Shape Height text box and Shape Width text box in the Size group on the Format tab.

Draw a Text Box of Your Own

To draw a text box of your own, choose Insert | Text | Text Box, and then choose Draw Text Box from the panel. Word changes the mouse pointer to a crosshair and switches the document to Print Layout view if it is in any other view.

Click in the document at the point where you want to place one of the text box's corners (it doesn't matter which one), and then drag diagonally to where you want the opposite corner to be.

Change the Formatting of a Text Box

The Format tab of the Text Box Styles section of the Ribbon lets you easily change the formatting of a text box. For example, you can apply a different style to the text box; change its outline, shadows, or 3-D effect; or even change its shape.

For coverage of these options, see the section "Format a Drawing Object" in Chapter 7.

Flow Text from One Text Box to Another

In some document layouts (for example, magazines), you may need to run a series of text boxes that contain a sequence of text. It's perfectly possible to cut the text up manually and paste the appropriate piece into each of the text boxes, but you don't need to do so, because Word lets you flow text from one text box to another: When the first text box is full, Word automatically moves to the next text box and fills it. If you add or delete text in a text box, Word adjusts the text in the subsequent text boxes accordingly.

To make text flow, you create a link between the text boxes. Follow these steps:

1. Insert the text boxes that you will link, and position them where you want them. Place all the content in the first text box. Most likely, only the first part of it will appear in the text box.

2. Right-click the frame of the first text box, and then choose Create Text Box Link from the context menu. Word changes the mouse pointer to a pouring jug, as shown here, and displays a prompt in the status bar telling you to click a text box.

3. Click the next text box. Word creates the link and flows the text from the first text box.

4. Right-click the second text box, and then repeat the linking process as needed.

Once you've linked text boxes, you can navigate from one to another by right-clicking the current text box and then choosing Next Text Box or Previous Text Box from the context menu.

To break a link, right-click a linked text box, and then choose Break Forward Link from the context menu.

Add a Text Box to the Text Box Gallery for Reuse

If you create a custom text box design that you want to reuse, add it to the Text Boxes Gallery. Follow these steps:

1. Click the text box's frame to select it.

2. Choose Insert | Text Box | Save Selection To Text Box Gallery. Word displays the Create New Building Block dialog box.

3. Follow through the process described in the section "Create a Building Block of Your Own" in Chapter 9.

Chapter 6

Spelling, Grammar, Research, and Translation

How to...

- Check spelling and grammar in your documents
- Research a word
- Translate words to and from other languages

Spelling and grammar are complex enough to trip up even the most fluent of writers—and Word is eager to help you with both. Word includes a powerful spell checker that can detect most spelling mistakes and save you any amount of grief. Word also includes a grammar checker that's complex enough to pick real or perceived nits out of almost any text—and, if allowed to operate uninhibitedly, cause you huge amounts of grief. You may well want to turn off the grammar checker or at least restrain its activities.

Automated checking of spelling can be a great boost—but even better, Word lets you research the meanings and definitions of words and even translate words, phrases, or whole documents into various major foreign languages.

Check Spelling and Grammar

By default, Word runs both the spell checker and the grammar checker on each document you create unless you tell it to stop. As you type text in a document, you'll notice the status bar shows a readout in which a pen skitters industriously across the pages of a book. When you pause your typing, the pen disappears and a green check mark or a red cross takes its place. If the red cross is there, one or more of the words in your document has gained a squiggly red line or green line under it. The red line indicates that the spell checker thinks that word is spelled wrongly. The green line means that the grammar checker has taken exception to a word, phrase, or sentence.

Decide Whether to Use the Spelling Checker

Checking spelling is one of the tasks that computers can do really well. Here's how spell checking works: The computer has a *dictionary file*, a list of approved words with which it compares each word in a document. If a word appears in the dictionary file, the computer lets it stand; if the word doesn't appear, the computer queries it. Each decision is easy, and you benefit from the computer's ability to automate the task. Most people benefit from using Word's spell checker, because it saves them effort and the potential embarrassment of making spelling mistakes. You'll probably want to accept Word's help here.

Spell checking in Word can be a bit more complicated than this, because you can create custom dictionary files containing words that you say are spelled correctly even if Word's built-in dictionary file says they're not. And you can have Word check your spelling either as you type or all at once when you're ready to concentrate on spelling. But the basic principle is pretty much as described.

Decide Whether to Use the Grammar Checker

By contrast with spelling, checking grammar is a task that computers can't yet do well. The English language does a great job at confusing humans with its flexible syntax, vast arrays of words (the official count is now over one million), and shades of meanings; and it's far more difficult for computers, which can do little more than identify some parts of speech (nouns, verbs, adjectives) with a modest hope of success and guess at their relationship to each other.

When you consider that *the grammar checker doesn't know what your document means*, you'll see that there's a strong argument for turning off grammar checking altogether (as discussed next). If your grammar's not up to scratch, you'll do better to have a colleague or a professional editor review your documents than to put your trust in Word's grammar-checking capabilities.

Is this being harsh on the grammar checker? Not at all. Take this example. You probably don't know Finnish, and it's an even tougher language than English to learn (although it has fewer words). Even if someone gave you the best books in the world on Finnish grammar and a list of set phrases to use for explaining grammatical problems, you'd struggle (to put it kindly) to detect problems with documents written in Finnish, wouldn't you?

6

> **TIP**   *Correct spelling and good grammar are an important part of professional-quality documents, but they're only a start. Your documents must also use suitable words to convey the meaning you intend, develop your theme or argument, and engage the reader. These also are issues that your colleagues or an editor can help you with, but Word cannot.*

Set Spelling and Grammar Options

Before you start checking spelling or grammar, tell Word how much (or how little) help you want in these areas:

- If you find it distracting to have red and green underlines pop out under your text while you work, turn off spelling and grammar checking as you work.

- If you're confident of your grammar or leery of the grammar checker's suggestions, turn off grammar checking altogether.

- If you decide to continue using the grammar checker, configure its settings so that it checks only those grammatical items you want it to.

To set spelling and grammar options, follow these steps:

1. Click the Office button, and then click the Word Options button. Word displays the Word Options dialog box.

2. In the left panel, click the Proofing category. Word displays the Proofing options (see Figure 6-1). These options control four different areas of spell checking and grammar checking. You can set spelling options for all Office programs, options for correcting spelling and grammar in all Word documents, and even hide spelling or grammar errors in the current document.

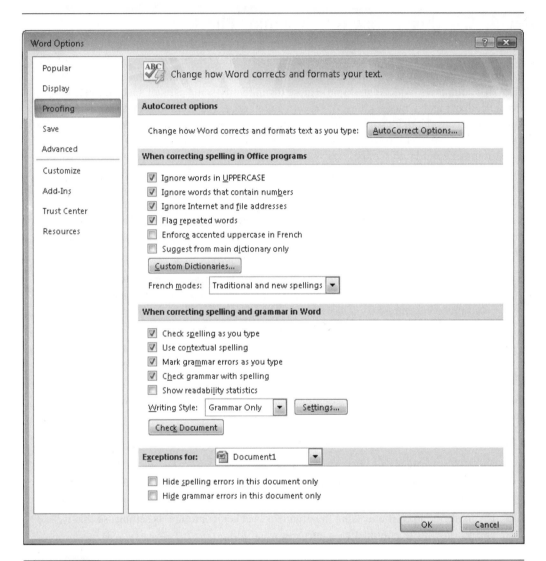

FIGURE 6-1   Give yourself a few minutes to come to grips with the Word Options dialog box's Proofing category.

3. In the When Correcting Spelling in Office Programs area, choose how the spell checker works across all Office programs: Word, Excel, PowerPoint, Outlook, Access, Publisher, and any others.

■ **Ignore Words In UPPERCASE**   Select this check box if you want to make the spell checker ignore words that you type in all capital letters or assign All Caps formatting.

(The spell checker still checks words with Small Caps formatting.) This setting is useful for excluding acronyms and capitalized technical terms from spelling checks.

- **Ignore Words That Contain Numbers**   Select this check box if you want the spell checker to skip any word that includes one or more digits. Names and technical terms such as Portuguese4U or BootLoader2 are the usual offenders. Even if your documents contain few such words, ignoring them is usually helpful.

- **Ignore Internet And File Addresses**   Select this check box to make the spell checker ignore Internet paths (URLs) such as http://www.mcgraw-hill.com and file paths such as \\lysistrata\shared\dox\Great_Firewall_of_China.docx. Clear this check box only if you actually need to spell-check URLs and file paths. For example, when creating a vital document that needed total accuracy, you could put all the permissible URLs and file paths in a custom dictionary. You could then use this feature to check that no URL or file path contained a typo.

- **Flag Repeated Words**   This feature makes Word query any word you repeat. You'll normally want to select this check box to avoid finding "the the" and other easy-to-miss repetitions in your otherwise immaculate final documents. You may occasionally need to tell the spell and grammar checker to ignore a word that you've repeated intentionally, but this is easy to do.

- **Enforce Accented Uppercase In French**   Select this check box if you're using a dialect (for example, Canadian French) that puts accents on uppercase words rather than suppressing the accent (as standard French does). Otherwise, clear this check box.

- **Suggest From Main Dictionary Only**   Select this check box if you want Word to use only the main dictionary file, not any of the custom dictionaries. Normally, you'll want to clear this check box so that Word uses your custom dictionaries—after all, that's what the custom dictionaries are for. If you normally work with custom dictionaries that contain technical terms, you may need to select this check box to exclude the custom dictionaries while you work on a document that must *not* contain those technical terms.

- **French Modes**   In this drop-down list, choose which type of spelling you want to use: Traditional And New Spellings, Traditional Spelling, or New Spelling.

4. In the When Correcting Spelling And Grammar In Word area, choose whether to check spelling as you type and whether to use contextual spelling.

- **Check Spelling As You Type**   Select this check box if you want the spell checker to check spelling on the fly as you create documents. Select this check box if you prefer to correct errors as you make them; clear this box if you prefer to work undisturbed. You may find your preferred setting depends on what you're doing: For instance, you may choose to compose documents with on-the-fly spell checking turned off, but edit with it on. On-the-fly spelling checking slows your computer down a little, so try clearing this check box if your computer is running too slowly.

6

Understand the Use Contextual Spelling Option

Word 2007's new Use Contextual Spelling feature tries to help you eliminate *contextual errors*—errors caused by using the wrong word for the meaning rather than entering a word spelled incorrectly. This feature works impressively, but only some of the time.

For example, if you type "the write thing to do" or "the rite thing to do," the spell checker flags "write" or "rite" and suggests "right" as the replacement, because neither "write" nor "rite" usually makes sense in the context. (Both work for puns or poems.) This checking can help you avoid word usage mistakes, especially with words that sound alike (for example, "Billie went their" instead of "Billie went there").

Given the complexity of the English language, it's no surprise that Word's contextual spelling check doesn't work all the time. For example, if you write "They performed a strange right involving chalk," the spell checker doesn't query "right," even though "right" is wrong here.

- **Use Contextual Spelling** Select this check box if you want Word to check for contextual errors—using the wrong word for the meaning—as well as spelling errors. See the sidebar for details.

- **Mark Grammar Errors As You Type** Select this check box if you want the grammar checker to put a squiggly underline under the words it's querying as you type. Clear this check box if you prefer to check grammar manually or not at all (see the next item).

- **Check Grammar With Spelling** Clear this check box if you want to turn off the grammar checker so that it never runs (not even when you run a spelling check).

- **Show Readability Statistics** Select this check box if you want Word to display the Readability Statistics dialog box at the end of a spelling check. The readability statistics include counts of words, characters, paragraphs, and sentences; averages of sentences per paragraph, words per sentence, and characters per word; and readouts of the percentage of passive verbs, the Flesch Reading Ease measurement (a computed statistic), and the Flesch-Kincaid Grade Level measurement (likewise). These statistics can be entertaining but provide no worthwhile measurement of the readability (or otherwise) of your document.

- **Writing Style** If you choose to use the grammar checker, tell the checker what you want it to do. In the Writing Style drop-down list, choose Grammar & Style if you want the checker to query style issues (such as the use of clichés or passive verbs) as well as grammar issues, or choose Grammar Only if you prefer to exclude style issues. Then click the Settings button. The Grammar Settings dialog box opens. Choose settings as explained in the sidebar "Choose Settings for Checking Grammar," and then click the OK button.

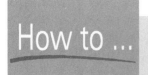

Choose Settings for Checking Grammar

If you choose to use the grammar checker rather than turn it off completely, tell it which grammar items you want it to check and which you don't. To do so, follow these steps:

1. Click the Settings button. Word displays the Grammar Settings dialog box, as shown here. The illustration on the left shows the Require area and part of the Grammar area at the top of the dialog box's scrolling section. The illustration on the right shows part of the Style area, further down the scrolling section.

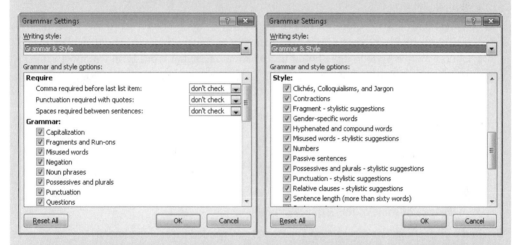

2. In the Writing Style drop-down list, select the Grammar item if you want the checker to check only grammar items; Word clears all the check boxes in the Style area. Select the Grammar & Style item if you want the checker to check both grammar and style issues; Word selects all the check boxes in the Style area. (This drop-down list shows the choice you made in the Writing Style drop-down list in the Proofing category of the Word Options dialog box.)

3. Choose options in the Require area:

- **Comma Required Before Last List Item** This drop-down list lets you choose whether to check for a serial comma ("x, y, and z" rather than "x, y and z"). Choose Always if you want to use the serial comma, Never if you don't, and Don't Check if either is okay.

■ **Punctuation Required With Quotes**   This drop-down list lets you choose whether to check the placement of punctuation with quotes. Choose Inside (for example, *"John," said Meg*), Outside (for example, *"John", said Meg*), or Don't Check. U.S. English normally places punctuation inside quotes.

■ **Space Required Between Sentences**   To make the checker enforce a standard number of spaces after a period and before the next character, select the 1 item or the 2 item in this drop-down list. Otherwise, select the Don't Check item.

4. In the Grammar area, select the check box for each grammar option you want to use. Clear all the other options. (To see a brief explanation of each item, press F1, and then click the Choose Which Grammar Errors Should Be Detected link in the Word Help window.)

5. In the Style area, select the check box for each style option you want to use. Clear all the other options. (To see a brief explanation of each item, press F1, and then click the Choose Which Style Errors Should Be Detected link in the Word Help window.)

6. Click the OK button. Word closes the Grammar Settings dialog box, retuning you to the Word Options dialog box.

■ **Check Document**   Click this button to force Word to check the document's grammar again. You may want to recheck a document for which you've told the grammar checker to ignore certain issues, but you've now realized that you should take care of some of these issues after all.

5. In the Exceptions For area, set up any exceptions needed for the document:

■ **Exceptions For**   In this drop-down list, select the document you want to affect. Word selects the current document when you open the Word Options dialog box, so you probably won't need to change the setting. Your alternatives are any other open document (select the document by name) or All New Documents.

■ **Hide Spelling Errors In This Document Only**   Select this check box if you want to hide spelling errors in this document. Word still checks the spelling in your other open documents.

■ **Hide Grammar Errors In This Document Only**   Select this check box if you want to hide grammar errors in this document. Word still checks grammar in your other open documents.

6. Click the Advanced category in the left pane, scroll down to the Grammar area, and then either turn the grammar checker off altogether or configure it to query only those issues you want to fix.

Check Spelling and Grammar

Once you've told the spell and grammar checker what you want it to do, you're ready to check spelling—and grammar as well (if you chose to check it).

Check Spelling as You Work

Word checks spelling as you work unless you tell it to desist. (See the section "Set Spelling and Grammar Options," earlier in this chapter.) When you enter a word that doesn't have a match in Word's dictionary file or any other dictionary file that you have loaded, Word puts a red squiggly underline under it to indicate that it's querying that word. The Proofing readout in the status bar then displays a red cross instead of the green check mark on the open book.

To deal with a spelling query, right-click it. You then have the following choices:

- Change the word to one of the spell checker's suggestions. Click the word you want on the list of suggestions. You'd want to do this when the word is wrong and the spell checker has come up with a suitable suggestion.

- Prevent the spell checker from querying the word again in this document. Click the Ignore All item. Do this when you know the word is correct, but you don't want to add it to your custom dictionary.

- Add the word to your custom dictionary so that Word doesn't query it again in the future. Click the Add To Dictionary item. Do this if the word is correct and you expect to use it again.

- Change the word and create an AutoCorrect entry to fix the typo automatically. Click the AutoCorrect item to open the AutoCorrect submenu, and then choose the correct word from it (see Figure 6-2). Adding AutoCorrect entries while checking spelling like this is a great way to help reduce spelling mistakes in your documents in future.

- Tell the Spell Checker that the word is in another language (and to stop checking it). Click Language to open the Language submenu, and then click the language the word is in. If the language doesn't appear on the Language submenu, click Set Language to open the Language dialog box, choose the language in it, and then click the OK button. When you do this, the spell checker knows that the word isn't English and stops querying it.

TIP   *Press ALT-F7 to jump to the next spelling or grammar query and open the context menu of options for it in a single step.*

Check Grammar as You Work

On-the-fly grammar checking works in a similar way to on-the-fly spell checking. As you enter text, the spelling and grammar checker tries to figure out which part of speech each word is, what its relationship to other words in the sentence is, and whether any of what the checker decides is going on contravenes any of the rules that the checker is using. The checker puts a green squiggly underline under any word or phrase that raises a query.

6

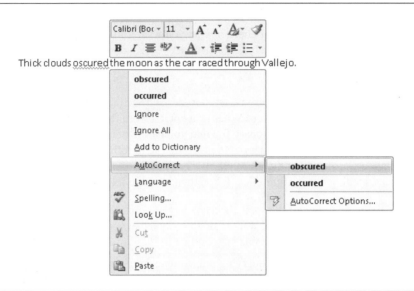

FIGURE 6-2   The AutoCorrect submenu shows the same suggestions as the main spelling menu but lets you create an AutoCorrect entry to automatically fix the typo in future.

To resolve a grammar query, right-click it. The menu (see Figure 6-3) then offers you these options:

- **Accept one of the suggestions**   Click the suggestion you want.
- **Ignore the problem this time**   Click the Ignore Once item to tell Word to ignore this instance of the rule.
- **Open the Grammar dialog box so that you can ignore the rule**   Click the Grammar item to open the Grammar dialog box. You can then click the Explain button to pop up an explanation of the rule the grammar checker is applying, but what you'll often want to do is click the Ignore Rule button to tell the checker to stop using this rule on your documents.
- **View an explanation of the problem the checker thinks it has found**   Click the About This Sentence item to open a Help window that explains the problem and usually gives examples of what's wrong and what would be better. Armed with this information, you'll be better equipped to decide whether to accept one of the grammar checker's suggested fixes.

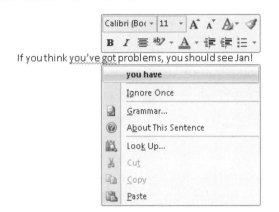

FIGURE 6-3 The grammar checker can sometimes help you avoid mistakes, but you run the risk of being driven up the wall by its style suggestions.

TIP *Grammar decisions are much more complex than spelling decisions, so checking grammar requires much more effort on your computer's part. If your computer is old or underpowered, turning off on-the-fly grammar checking usually improves Word's performance.*

Check the Spelling and Grammar in an Entire Document

If you've turned off on-the-fly spell checking and grammar checking (or if you've left them on and are content to let the squiggly underlines stack up in your document), you can check the spelling and grammar in an entire document at once. You may find creating documents easier if you separate the checking from the composition and editing like this.

To check spelling and grammar, follow these steps:

1. Place the insertion point where you want to start the check:

- If you want to check the whole document starting from the beginning, place the insertion point at the beginning (press CTRL-HOME, or scroll and then click).

- Otherwise, place the insertion point where you want to start checking. For example, click at the beginning of the paragraph at which you want to start. When it reaches the end of the document, the spelling and grammar checker goes back to the beginning and continues from there to where you started. You can stop the spelling check at this point, leaving the first part of the document unchecked (for example, because you know it needs further work before it's worth checking).

- If you want to check only part of the document, select it.

2. Click the Proofing icon in the status bar, press F7, or choose Review | Proofing | Spelling & Grammar. The Spelling and Grammar dialog box opens and displays the first query in the document:

  ■ The next illustration shows you an example of a spelling query.

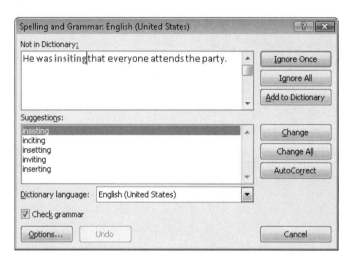

  ■ The next illustration shows you an example of a grammar query.

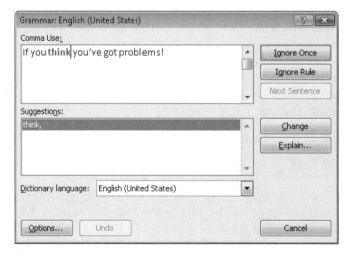

  ■ If the spell checker and grammar checker find nothing to query in the document, Word displays a message box telling you that the spelling and grammar check is complete. If you've told Word to display readability statistics, the Readability Statistics dialog box appears instead.

3. Deal with each query the spelling and grammar checker raises:

- To tell the spell checker to ignore the word this time, click the Ignore Once button. To ignore every instance in this document, click the Ignore All button.

- To tell the grammar checker to ignore the issue this time, so that you can see whether the issue occurs again, click the Ignore Once button. To ignore every instance in this document, click the Ignore Rule button. To move on to the next sentence that contains a query, skipping this issue and any other issues with this sentence, click the Next Sentence button. Do this when you feel the sentence is fine as it stands and you don't want to deal with any more grammatical queries the grammar checker may think it contains.

- To accept one of the suggestions, click it in the Suggestions box and click the Change button. For a spelling query, you can also change every instance in this document by clicking the suggestion and then clicking the Change All button. For a grammar query, you can click the Explain button to open a Help window showing an explanation of the issue the spelling and grammar checker thinks you need to resolve.

- For a spelling query, you can also create an AutoCorrect entry that will automatically correct the mistake in future when you type it. Click the suggestion in the Suggestions box, and then click the AutoCorrect button. Creating an AutoCorrect entry is almost always a good idea, because it helps you avoid having to correct the same mistake again.

- If you need to edit the document directly to make the change, click in the document, and then make the edit. Working in the document itself is useful both when the document needs a change other than those the checker has suggested and when you notice a problem unrelated to spelling or grammar in the document that needs fixing. When you've finished editing, click in the Spelling and Grammar dialog box again. Instead of clicking, you can press CTRL-TAB to move the focus from the dialog box to the document and back. Click the Resume button to start the spell and grammar check again.

- Once you've dealt with the query, the spelling and grammar checker displays the next query.

- You can select or clear the Check Grammar check box to control whether Word checks grammar along with spelling. (This check box has the same effect as the Check Grammar With Spelling check box in the Proofing category of the Word Options dialog box.)

- If you realize you just clicked the wrong button, click the Undo button to undo the change.

4. Continue until you've dealt with all the queries, and then end the check.

- If you checked the whole document, the spelling and grammar checker displays a message box to tell you that the check is complete.

- If you checked part of the document, Word prompts you to check the rest of it. You'll probably want to click the No button, given that you chose not to check the whole of the document in the first place.

■ You can end the check at any time by clicking the Close button in the Spelling And Grammar dialog box. For example, you might reach a part of the document that's incomplete and so isn't worth checking.

5. After checking, you'll often want to save your document to avoid losing any changes you've made.

Create, Maintain, and Manage Custom Dictionaries

To get good results from a spelling check, you need the spell checker to be using as complete a list of words as possible. The spell checker's main list of words comes from Office's dictionary file, but you can supplement this file with custom dictionaries.

When you install Office, the installation includes a dictionary file for the language you're using in Windows (for example, U.S. English) and any other languages you've installed—for example, Spanish (United States). The Office programs use this dictionary file for checking spelling. The file is pretty comprehensive: While it doesn't contain anything like the full list of words generally recognized as belonging to the English language, nor even all those in the size of dictionary you might use to prop open a door, it contains most of those used in "normal" writing—which is what you need.

Sooner or later (probably sooner), you'll find that the spell checker queries a word that you've entered. You know the word is correct (perhaps you looked it up in the dictionary and let the door swing gently closed), but it's not in the Office dictionary file.

The Office programs don't let you modify the dictionary file—in fact, the programs don't get to modify it themselves. But they do let you create two kinds of auxiliary dictionary files:

■ **Custom dictionary file**   A custom dictionary is a file that contains words that you claim are correctly spelled—specialist words, technical terms, slang, or even words you've invented. You can create as many custom dictionary files as you want, although most people find that having more than a handful is more trouble than it's worth. This is because you can add words to only one dictionary at a time, and the mechanism for switching the dictionary to which you're adding words is cumbersome.

■ **Exclusion dictionary file**   An exclusion dictionary is a file that contains words that are in Office's main dictionary file but that you want to force the spelling and grammar checker to query every time you use them. Candidates include sensitive words (for example, racial, medical, or bodily terms), obscenities, or your manager's pet hates ("decentralize," "impacting," and others you can add). Office lets you create only one exclusion file for each language you use.

Add Words to a Custom Dictionary

When you install Office, the installation automatically creates a custom dictionary called Custom.dic and sets the Office programs to add words to it. To add a word, click the Add To Dictionary item on the spelling context menu or the Add To Dictionary button in the Spelling And Grammar dialog box.

Open the Custom Dictionaries Dialog Box

To work with custom dictionaries, open the Custom Dictionaries dialog box. Follow these steps:

1. Click the Office Button, and then click Word Options. Word displays the Word Options dialog box.

2. In the left pane, click the Proofing category. Word displays the Proofing options.

3. Click the Custom Dictionaries button. Word displays the Custom Dictionaries dialog box, as shown here.

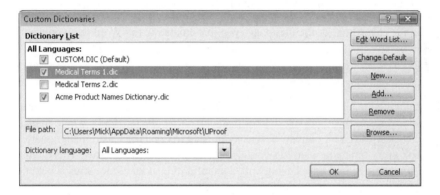

Create a Custom Dictionary

Storing all your approved words in a single custom dictionary file can be handy, especially if you need to have the words available all the time. But what you may need to do is have certain words available only when you're working on certain types of documents. For example, when editing your company's product manuals, you may want the spell checker to accept various technical terms related to your company's products. But when you're writing business correspondence or catching up on your business class, you don't want to use those technical terms—in fact, you *want* the spell checker to query them.

To create separate lists of terms like this, you need two or more custom dictionaries. To create a new custom dictionary, follow these steps:

1. Open the Custom Dictionaries dialog box.

2. Click the New button. Word displays the Create Custom Dictionary dialog box. This is a Save As dialog box with a different name.

3. Type the dictionary's name, change the folder if necessary, and then click the Save button. Word creates the dictionary file and adds it to the Dictionary List box in the Custom Dictionaries dialog box.

   ■ You can give the dictionary any name you want except Custom.dic (the name of your default custom dictionary). If you plan to create several custom dictionaries for different vocabulary topics, use descriptive names so that you can easily identify each dictionary by file name.

■ Word stores custom dictionaries in the %userprofile%\AppData\Roaming\Microsoft\ UProof folder. That %userprofile% is a Windows shortcut called an *environment variable* that stores the path to your user profile folder, the folder that contains your personal Windows settings (for example, C:\Users\Mick).

4. If you want to make the spell checker use the dictionary only for words formatted as being in a particular language, choose the language in the Dictionary Language drop-down list.

NOTE   *If you don't specify a language, the spell checker uses the dictionary for all languages. Normally, using the dictionary for all languages is what you need, but you may sometimes need to restrict a custom dictionary to a particular language.*

5. Select the check box for the dictionary you just created to tell Word that you want to use the dictionary.

6. Click the Change Default button if you want to make Word add words to this dictionary when you give the Add To Dictionary command.

■ Clicking the Change Default button makes Word (and the other Office programs) add words to this dictionary rather than any of the others. Here's where managing dictionaries is a bit clumsy, because you need to open the Custom Dictionaries dialog box every time you want to switch from one dictionary to another. This clumsiness is the main reason why having only a handful of custom dictionaries is better than having many custom dictionaries: You'll spend less time and effort switching from one dictionary to another.

■ Instead of adding words to your custom dictionary when checking spelling, you can add words to the dictionary file directly. The section "Edit a Custom Dictionary to Add or Remove Words," later in this chapter, explains how to add and remove words.

7. Click the OK button. Word closes the Custom Dictionaries dialog box.

8. Click the OK button. Word closes the Word Options dialog box.

Your custom dictionary is now ready for use.

Add an Existing Dictionary to Your List of Custom Dictionaries

Instead of creating a custom dictionary, you may receive one from a colleague or friend. To add such a new custom dictionary to the list of dictionaries the spell checker uses, follow these steps:

1. Open the Custom Dictionaries dialog box.

2. Click the Add button. Word displays the Add Custom Dictionary dialog box. This dialog box is a renamed version of the standard Open dialog box.

3. Navigate to the folder that contains the dictionary file, select the file, and then click the Open button. Word adds the dictionary to the Dictionary List in the Custom Dictionaries dialog box.

4. Select the check box for the dictionary.

Taking these steps makes Word use the existing dictionary for checking spelling but doesn't make Word start adding words to the dictionary. If you want to add words to this dictionary, click the dictionary's name in the Custom Dictionaries dialog box, and then click the Change Default button.

Edit a Custom Dictionary to Add or Delete Words

Trudging through a spell check tends to be mind-numbing rather than mind-expanding, and it's all too easy to click the Add To Dictionary button once too often when you're teaching Word a list of technical terms that its dictionary file doesn't recognize. If you catch your mistake immediately, you can click Undo to remove the term from your default custom dictionary, but it's all too easy to end up with bogus words in your custom dictionary. Word (and the other Office programs) then treat the bogus words as genuine, so you need to remove them.

To remove a word from your custom dictionary, or to add a slew of terms to the dictionary all at once rather than one-by-one during a spell check, follow these steps:

1. Open the Custom Dictionaries dialog box.

2. In the Dictionary List box, click the dictionary in the Dictionary List box, and then click the Edit Word List button. Word displays a dialog box that shows the list of words in the custom dictionary. The dialog box's title bar shows the name of the custom dictionary, as shown here.

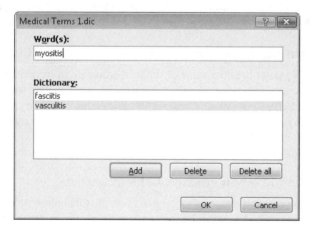

3. Add or delete words as needed.

- To add a word, type it in the Word(s) box, and then press ENTER or click the Add button.

- To delete a word, select it in the Dictionary box, and then click the Delete button.

- To scroll the list of words, use the scroll bar or click in the list and then press the letter to which you want to jump.

■ To clear the dictionary, click Delete All, and then click the OK button in the confirmation message box.

4. Click the OK button. Word closes the dialog box.

Word saves the dictionary for you automatically, so you don't need to save it manually.

Remove or Delete a Custom Dictionary

When you don't need to use a custom dictionary for a while, but you will need to use it again before too long, you can leave it in place but dormant by unchecking the box next to its name in the Custom Dictionaries dialog box.

If you probably won't need the dictionary file for a while, but you don't want to get rid of it, remove it from the Custom Dictionaries dialog box so that it doesn't clutter up the list. To remove the dictionary, click it in the list, and then click the Remove button. The dictionary file remains in its current folder, but Word stops listing the dictionary in the Custom Dictionaries dialog box. (You can add it again by clicking the Add button.)

If you're certain you'll never need a particular custom dictionary file again, remove the dictionary from Word as described in the previous paragraph, and then delete the dictionary file from your computer by using Windows Explorer (or another file-management program). Don't skip the step of removing the dictionary from Word before you delete it. Otherwise, when Word discovers that it can't find the dictionary, it creates a replacement dictionary with that name. Word doesn't tell you that it has created the replacement, so you may get the impression that the dictionary is digging itself out of the Recycle Bin on its own.

Create an Exclusion Dictionary to Tell Word Not to Allow Certain Words

When you need to tell Word not to allow some of the words that are in its main dictionary in your documents, create an *exclusion dictionary*—a file that lists correctly spelled words you want the spell checker to query when you use them. Office 2007 creates this dictionary for you, but you have to add words to it manually using a text editor rather than working through the Custom Dictionaries dialog box.

To set up an exclusion dictionary, follow these steps:

1. Press WINDOWS KEY-R. Windows displays the Run dialog box.

2. Type **%userprofile%** and then press ENTER or click the OK button. Windows opens a Windows Explorer window showing the contents of your user profile folder.

3. If you don't see a folder named AppData, Windows is set to keep hidden files and folders out of view (as it does by default). Follow these steps to display them:

■ Choose Organize | Folder And Search Options. Windows displays the Folder Options dialog box.

■ Click the View tab.

■ Select the Show Hidden Files And Folders option button.

■ Click the OK button.

4. Double-click the AppData folder, double-click the Roaming folder, double-click the Microsoft folder, and then double-click the UProof folder.

5. Right-click the file named ExcludeDictionaryEN0409 (if you've set Windows to display file extensions, the file appears as ExcludeDictionaryEN0409.lex), and then highlight Open With on the context menu.

6. If Notepad appears on the Open With submenu, select it and go to step 7. Otherwise, follow these steps:

  ■ Click the Choose Default Program item. Windows displays a dialog box telling you it cannot open the file.

  ■ Choose the Select A Program From A List Of Installed Programs option button, and then click the OK button. Windows displays the Open With dialog box.

  ■ Click the Browse button. Windows displays another Open With dialog box. This one is a regular Open dialog box that's customized to open program files.

  ■ Navigate to your Windows folder, select the notepad.exe file, and then click the Open button. Windows returns you to the first Open With dialog box and adds a Notepad item to it.

  ■ Select the Notepad item, make sure the Always Use The Selected Program To Open This Kind Of File check box is selected, and then click the OK button. Windows opens the exclusion dictionary file in Notepad.

7. Type the words you want to exclude from the dictionary, entering each in lowercase and putting one to a line, as shown here.

8. When you've finished adding terms, choose File | Save to save changes to the file, and then choose File | Exit to close Notepad.

9. If you want to be able to open the exclusion dictionary easily so that you can add further terms to it, create a shortcut to it: Right-click the ExcludeDictionaryEN0409 file, and then choose Create Shortcut from the context menu. Drag the shortcut to a convenient folder (for example, your Documents folder) or to your Desktop. You can then open the exclusion dictionary by double-clicking the shortcut.

10. If you turned on the display of hidden files and folders in step 2, turn them off again: Follow the same procedure, but this time select the Do Not Show Hidden Files And Folders option button on the View tab of the Folder Options dialog box.

Your exclusion dictionary is now ready for use. Test it as follows:

1. Save any unsaved work, and then exit Word and restart it. You must restart Word to force it to read the exclusion dictionary.

2. In the new document that Word creates when it starts, type one of the words you entered in the exclusion dictionary. Verify that the spell checker queries the word you've typed.

Turn Off Spell Checking Temporarily

Spell checking can save you plenty of effort and embarrassment, but sometimes you may want to turn it off temporarily, so that you can work uninterrupted or your computer can run Word faster. You may also want to prevent Word from checking certain paragraphs that contain code or technical terms that you don't want to add to a dictionary.

To turn off spell checking and grammar checking permanently, see the section "Set Spelling and Grammar Options," earlier in this chapter.

Turn Off Spell-Checking and Grammar-Checking for an Entire Document

To turn off spell-checking and grammar checking for an entire document, follow these steps:

1. Open the document. If the document is already open, activate it by clicking in it or by clicking its button on the Taskbar.

2. Click the Office Button, and then click Word Options. Word displays the Word Options dialog box.

3. In the left panel, click the Proofing category. Word displays the Proofing options. The Proofing options appear.

4. Select the Hide Spelling Errors In This Document Only check box and the Hide Grammar Errors In This Document Only check box.

5. Click the OK button. Word closes the Word Options dialog box.

Turn Off Spelling and Grammar Checking for Specific Words or Paragraphs

If you create technical documents, you may need to tell the spelling and grammar checker to leave certain words and paragraphs alone—for example, so that the checker doesn't query every other word of programming code. You do this by changing the language formatting of the text. You then don't need to add those words to a custom dictionary to prevent the spelling and grammar checker from querying them.

You can change the language formatting by using direct formatting, but in most cases you'll save time and effort by using either a character style or a paragraph style.

Turn Off Spelling and Grammar Checking Using Direct Formatting   To turn off spelling and grammar checking using direct formatting, follow these steps:

1. Select the word or phrase. To affect only a single word, click in it. You don't need to select the word.

2. Open the Language dialog box:

   ■ If the spelling and grammar checker has queried the word in the document, right-click the word and choose Language | Set Language from the context menu.

   ■ Otherwise, choose Review | Proofing | Set Language.

3. Select the Do Not Check Spelling Or Grammar check box.

4. Click the OK button. Word applies the do-not-check formatting to the text and removes any query underline from it.

Turn Off Spelling and Grammar Checking Using a Style   The better way to turn off spelling and grammar checking is to create a linked paragraph and character style that you can apply to text that doesn't need checking. The advantage to using a style is that you can apply it more quickly than other formatting—and you can change it if you need to.

> **TIP**   *If you need to turn off checking only for a few words within paragraphs rather than for entire paragraphs, create a character style rather than a linked paragraph and character style.*

6

To create a do-not-check style, follow these steps:

1. Choose some suitable text as the basis for the style.

    ■ Create (or find) a paragraph with the style on which you want to base your new style.

    ■ You can save a step by selecting a word to which you've already applied do-not-check direct formatting.

2. Right-click the selection or paragraph and choose Styles | Save Selection As A New Quick Style from the context menu. Word displays the small Create New Style From Formatting dialog box.

3. In the Name box, type a name for the style—for example, "Body Without Checking" or "Technical No Checking."

4. Click the Modify button. Word displays the larger version of the Create New Style From Formatting dialog box.

5. In the Style Type drop-down list, select Linked (Paragraph And Character) if you want to create a linked style. If you want to create only a character style, choose Character in the Style Type drop-down list, and then select Default Paragraph Font in the Style Based On drop-down list.

6. Select the All Documents Based On The Template option button to make Word add the style to the template rather than creating it only in the active document. (Having the style in the template makes the style available to all documents based on that template.)

7. Select the Add To Quick Style List check box if you want the style to appear in the Quick Style list so that you can access it easily using the mouse.

8. Click the Format button, and then choose Language from the shortcut menu. Word displays the Language dialog box.

9. Check the Do Not Check Spelling Or Grammar check box.

10. Click the OK button. Word closes the Language dialog box.

11. Click the OK button. Word closes the Create New Style From Formatting dialog box.

You can now apply your new style from the Style group on the Home tab of the Ribbon or from the Styles pane.

If you need to exempt only a few often-used words from spelling and grammar checking, creating a style may be overkill. Instead, consider creating a formatted AutoCorrect entry for each of the words: Enter the word, select it, apply do-not-check formatting to it, and then create an AutoCorrect entry to enter it easily. Alternatively, add the words to a custom dictionary, as discussed earlier in this chapter.

Research a Word

When you don't know the meaning of a word, or you want to check the nuances of a word that might provoke your colleagues, use Word's built-in research feature. Word implements this through the Research pane, which lets you access large amounts of online reference materials via your Internet connection.

The easiest way to open the Research pane is to look up a word in a document: Either ALT-click the word, or right-click it and then choose Look Up from the context menu. The Research pane (see Figure 6-4) opens and enters the word you clicked in the Search For text box.

If the word you want to look up doesn't appear in your document, choose Review | Proofing | Research to open the Research pane manually. Type your term in the Search For text box, choose the reference type in the drop-down list, and then press ENTER or click the green arrow button.

Configure Research Options

Office can connect you to a variety of reference books, research sites, business and financial sites, and other services. The Research feature starts off with a fair selection of these, but you may want to include or exclude particular ones so that you receive only the results you want.

To choose which books, sites, and services the Research tool uses, open the Research pane and follow these steps:

1. At the bottom of the Research pane, click the Research Options link. Word displays the Research Options dialog box.

2. Select the check box for each book, site, or service you want to use. Clear all the other check boxes. Scroll the Services list to reach the Research Sites category, the Businesses And Financial Sites category, and the Other Services category.

3. To add a service, follow these steps:

   ▪ Click the Add Services button. Word displays the Add Services dialog box.

   ▪ Choose the service in the list box, or type the URL in the Address box.

   ▪ Click the Add button. Word closes the Add Services dialog box and adds the service to the Research Options dialog box.

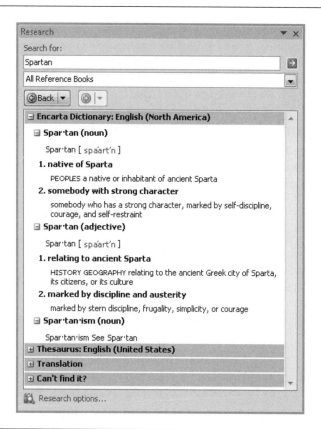

FIGURE 6-4   You can expand and collapse the results in the Research pane by clicking the +
and – buttons.

4. To update a service or remove a service, follow these steps:

■ Click the Update/Remove button. Word displays the Update Or Remove Services
dialog box.

■ Select the service you want to affect, and then click the Update button or the Remove
button, as appropriate.

■ When you've finished, click the Close button. Word closes the Update Or Remove
Services dialog box.

5. Click the OK button. Word closes the Research Options dialog box.

NOTE   *If you want to find out more about a service, click it in the list, and then click the Properties button. Word opens the Service Properties dialog box. Here you can find a description of the service, links to web sites with more information about the service and its terms of use, and details of the service's provider, web site, and content type (for example, "Business and Financial Sites" or "Research Sites." Use this information to decide whether you want to use the service, and then click the Close button.*

Use Parental Control to Filter Out Offensive Content

To help you deal with the Internet's notorious morasses of vice and depravity, the Research tool includes filtering that can block offensive content. To turn on parental control and filter content, open the Research pane and follow these steps:

1. Open the Research pane, and then click the Research Options link. Word displays the Research Options dialog box.

2. Click the Parental Control button. Word displays the Parental Control dialog box.

   ■ If you've already enabled parental control and assigned a password, the Password dialog box opens to make sure that you're allowed to use parental control. Type your password to establish your authority, and then the Parental Control dialog box opens.

3. Select the Turn On Content Filtering To Make Services Block Offensive Results check box.

4. If you want to prevent users from using any search that cannot block offensive content, select the Allow Users To Search Only The Services That Can Block Offensive Content check box. Selecting this check box helps prevent offensive content from reaching your computer, but it greatly limits the services that the Research tool searches.

5. Type a new parental control password in the Specify A Password For The Parental Control Settings text box.

6. Click the OK button. Word displays the Confirm Password dialog box.

7. Type the password again, and then click the OK button. The Research Options dialog box displays a banner across the top to indicate that Parental Control is switched on and that some services may not be available as a result.

The password is case sensitive, and there's no official way to recover it. (You may be able to find password-cracking tools on the Internet that can recover it for you. So may your children.)

Translate Words

Word can work in more languages than most people can recognize—but it realizes that you may not have sufficient knowledge of all the languages you need to use and provides a Translate tool for translating between English and major languages including Spanish, Portuguese, Chinese (People's Republic and Taiwan), French, German, Italian, Greek, Japanese, and Korean. Translate is part of the Research pane. You can access Translate by choosing Review | Proofing | Translate.

You can translate either a single word at a time or a phrase or more (up to a whole document).

■ **Translate a single word**   When you translate a single word (as shown here), Translate looks up the word in a dictionary and shows you the results. If the word can be two or more parts of speech (for example, "need" is a noun and a verb, and "good" is a noun, adjective, and informal adverb), you can choose which part you want.

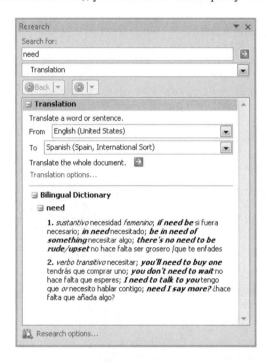

6

TIP *To translate a single word in a document, right-click the word and open the Translate submenu on the shortcut menu. If the language into which you want to translate the word appears on the submenu, click it to translate the word. If not, click Translate on the submenu, and then choose the language in the Research task pane as usual.*

■ **Translate a phrase or more**   When you translate a phrase or more, Translate sends the document to WorldLingo.com, a translation site for machine (automated) translation. Translate asks your permission to send the text in unencrypted format; click the Yes button if you want to proceed. The problem with sending the text unencrypted is that anyone who intercepts the text can read it—so click the No button if your text is private or sensitive.

Machine translation usually ranges in accuracy from the understandable through the amusing to the terrifying. If you can read one of the languages, you can get some idea of the translation's accuracy by translating a document into (or from) a language you know. If you can't read any of the languages, you can try translating a document from English to the target language, copying the result, and then translating it back, and seeing what the twice-translated version is within easy commuting distance of the original. Bear in mind that the result of a double translation like this is likely to be clumsier than a single translation—any errors that occur in the first translation may be amplified by the second translation.

Word's standard settings for translation work well enough for most people, but if you use translation extensively, you may want to remove some of the language pairs so that the From and To drop-down lists in the Translation pane are more compact. For example, if you don't need Swedish, Korean, Arabic, Greek, or Russian, you could remove all the language pairs that contain them. To do so, follow these steps:

1. Open the Research pane. (For example, choose Review | Proofing | Research.)

2. In the middle of the Research pane, click the Translation Options link. Word displays the Translation Options dialog box. Here you can choose which language pairs (for example, English to French and English to Spanish) are available in the bilingual dictionary and for machine translation. Depending on the language, you may also be able to choose a different language service for machine translation.

3. If you want to use the online dictionary to supplement your installed dictionaries, select the Use Online Dictionary check box. You can then select the Use Only When The Installed Dictionary Is Unavailable check box if you want to use the online dictionary only when the installed dictionary can't provide a translation.

4. In the upper Available Language Pairs list box, select the check box for each language pair you want to have available. Clear all the other check boxes.

5. If you want to use online machine translation, select the Use Online Machine Translation check box. In the lower Available Language Pairs list box, select the check box for each language pair you want to have available, and choose the provider in the drop-down list.

6. Click the OK button. Word closes the Translation Options dialog box.

When you use a foreign word or term in a document, the spell checker queries it unless it appears in the Office dictionary file for English—for example, *Doppelganger* or *déjà vu*. (Word includes an AutoCorrect entry to put the accents on *déjà vu* for you. Perhaps you've seen this already.)

If you need to use the word frequently in your documents, you can add it to your custom dictionary to prevent the spell checker from querying it in the future. If you need to use the word only seldom, apply language formatting to it to tell the spell checker to leave it alone. Right-click the queried word, choose Language | Set Language to open the Language dialog box, choose the language in the Mark Selected Text As list box, and then click the OK button.

Chapter 7

Add Graphics, Diagrams, and Borders to Your Documents

How to...

- Understand how Word handles graphical objects
- Insert clip art, photos, movies, and sounds
- Work with shapes, AutoShapes, and WordArt
- Add graphics to documents
- Format, position, and layer drawing objects
- Add borders and shading
- Insert equations

To give your documents more visual impact, or simply to make them more comprehensible, you'll often need to add pictures, shapes, diagrams, or other graphical objects. In this chapter, you'll learn about the wide variety of features that Word offers for adding graphical objects—everything from a modest shape or textual note to a slick and professional organization chart—to your documents.

Understand How Word Handles Graphical Objects

Although Word documents appear to be flat, Word actually treats them as consisting of several different layers. The main layers are the text layer (where the body text of a document appears), the header and footer layer, and the drawing layer. When you open a document, you work in the text layer until you specifically go to work with an object that resides in a different layer—for example, a graphical object in the drawing layer.

The layers are transparent unless they contain an object, so when you look at a document, you see the contents of all the layers together, making up the entire appearance of the document. You can change the order in which the layers appear, so you can change the way the objects appear to be superimposed on each other. For example, you can position a graphic so that it appears behind the text in a document, inline with the text (usually with the text wrapped around the graphic), or in front of the text, blocking the view to the text that's directly behind it.

The drawing layer consists of as many sublayers as you need. You can create multiple objects in the drawing layer, either keeping them separate from each other or arranging them into groups that you can keep together and manipulate with a single command. You can arrange objects in the drawing layer so that they overlap each other, and you can alter the order in which they appear by moving the objects forward (up the stack of sublayers toward the top) or backward (down the stack of sublayers toward the bottom).

When you start working with an object in the drawing layer, Word automatically adds to the Ribbon an extra section of tabs containing tools for working with that type of object. For example:

- When you insert or select a SmartArt item, the Ribbon displays the SmartArt Tools tab set, which includes a Design tab and a Format tab (see Figure 7-1).
- When you insert or select a picture, the Ribbon displays the Picture Tools set, which has just a Format tab.

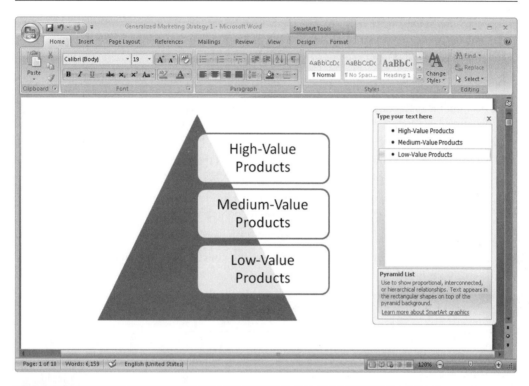

FIGURE 7-1   The Ribbon automatically displays extra tabs when you start working with a graphical object.

■ When you insert a chart, the Ribbon displays the Chart Tools set, which has a Design tab, a Layout tab, and a Format tab.

The controls on the Format tab change to suit the type of graphical object you're working with.

Insert Clip Art, Photographs, Movies, and Sounds in Documents

Clip art is generally understood to mean pictures, but Office's Clip Art feature lets you easily access a wide selection of graphics, photographs, movie clips, and sounds that you can use freely in your documents, and insert them easily. When using these items, exercise discretion and restraint—a unique picture may still be worth the thousand words of the cliché, but a tired clip-art graphic may detract from a document rather than enhance it.

Graphics and photos work well in both printed documents and online documents. Movie clips and sounds work less well even in online documents, as you must double-click a movie clip or sound to play it—and then it plays in a different program (for example, Windows Media Player) rather than in Word.

To insert one of Office's included "clip art" items, follow these steps:

1. Position the insertion point at the beginning of the paragraph where you want to position the upper-left corner of the item. It's best to use an empty paragraph. You can move the item later as needed.

2. Choose Insert | Illustrations | Clip Art. Word displays the Clip Art task pane. Figure 7-2 shows the Clip Art task pane after a successful search.

3. Use the Search For box, the Search In drop-down list, and the Results Should Be drop-down list to specify which types of files you're looking for:

   ■ In the Search For box, specify one or more keywords.

   ■ In the Search In drop-down list, choose which collections to search (or choose Everywhere).

   ■ In the Results Should Be drop-down list, choose the media types you're interested in: All Media File Types, Clip Art, Photographs, Movies, or Sounds.

FIGURE 7-2   The Clip Art task pane makes it easy to find clip art, photos, movies, and sounds to insert in your worksheets.

4. Click the Go button. Word searches for matching media types and displays them in the pane.

NOTE *The first time you search, a Microsoft Clip Organizer dialog box may prompt you to decide whether to include extra clip art images and photos from Microsoft Office Online in your searches. If you have a fast Internet connection, searching Microsoft Office Online is usually a good idea, as you'll find a wider range of images.*

Once you find a clip that matches your needs, you can insert it in your document by clicking its thumbnail. You can also move the mouse pointer over the thumbnail, click the drop-down button that appears, and choose one of the following actions from the menu (shown here):

7

- **Insert** Inserts the clip, just as if you had clicked the thumbnail. (Normally, it's easier to click.)

- **Copy** Copies the clip so you can paste it elsewhere.

- **Delete From Clip Organizer** Deletes the clip from all collections in the Clip Organizer. Office makes you confirm the deletion in case you clicked by accident. This option is available only for clips you add, not for clips that come with Office.

- **Make Available Offline** Displays the Make Available Online dialog box so you can download this clip from its online source to one of your collections. This option is available only for online clips.

- **Copy To Collection** Displays the Copy To Collection dialog box so you can add a copy of the clip to another collection—for example, your Favorites. This option is useful for making a collection of clips you use often. This option is available only for clips stored on local drives.

- **Move To Collection** Displays the Move To Collection dialog box so you can move the clip to another collection. This option is useful for relocating clips in your collections. You can move only clips you add to the collection, not the clips included with Office.

- **Edit Keywords** Displays the Keywords dialog box (see Figure 7-3), in which you can add, modify, or delete the keywords associated with the clip. You can't change the keywords for the clips included with Office, but only for those clips you add.

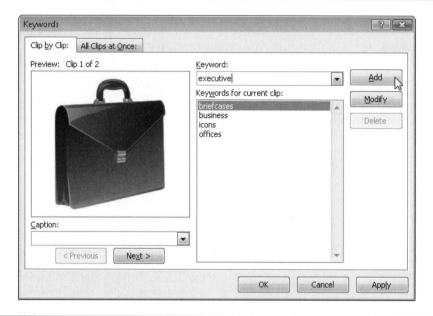

FIGURE 7-3 You can associate keywords with clips you add to the collection, which helps you search for them in the future.

- **Find Similar Style** Searches for clips that have a similar style to the clip that is currently selected when you issue this command. This option is useful when you need multiple clips in the same style to convey a certain impression in a document. The clips returned by a style search can span an interesting range of subjects and keywords.

- **Preview/Properties** Displays the Preview/Properties dialog box, in which you can view the image and its details. The Paths section of this dialog box shows the full path for the image's file and the catalog that contains the image.

To organize your clips, click the Organize Clips link at the foot of the Clip Art task pane. Word opens the Microsoft Clip Organizer applet (see Figure 7-4).

These are the key commands for working with Microsoft Clip Organizer:

- To navigate your collections, click the Collection List button, and then work in the Collection List task pane.

- To search for clips, click the Search button, and then use the Search task pane.

- To add clips, choose File | Add Clips To Organizer, and then choose Automatically, On My Own, or From Scanner Or Camera from the submenu.

- To edit the keywords for a selected clip, choose Edit | Keywords. Alternatively, click the clip's button, and then choose Edit Keywords from the drop-down menu.

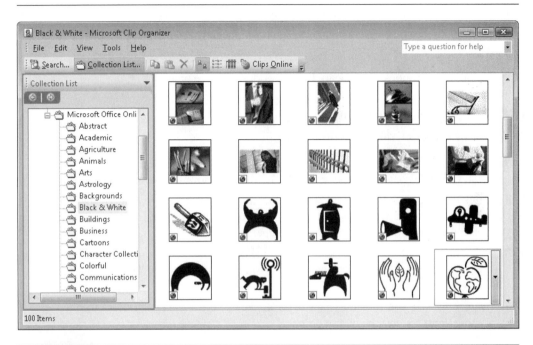

7

FIGURE 7-4   Microsoft Clip Organizer enables you to add, browse, collate, and search clips.

■ To compact your clips collection so that it takes up as little space as possible, choose Tools | Compact. Compacting doesn't degrade the image quality of the clips, so it's a good idea if you're short of disk space.

NOTE   *After inserting a picture, you can use the controls on the Format tab of the Picture Tools section of the Ribbon to configure the picture. You'll learn how to use these controls later in this chapter. They are similar to the tools on the other Format tabs of the Ribbon—for example, the Format tab on the SmartArt Tools section.*

Work with Shapes, WordArt, and Charts

Word provides four types of tools for creating drawing objects:

■ *Shapes* range from basic shapes (such as squares and circles) to more complex shapes with some built-in intelligence—for example, a callout that continues to point to the same spot in the document even when you move it.

■ *WordArt* items are pictures made by applying effects to text.

■ *Charts* are charts and graphs inserted using Excel's charting features.

■ *SmartArt* items are diagrams, such as organization charts and hierarchy diagrams, with built-in intelligence.

In the following sections, you'll learn how to work with these objects.

Add Shapes to Documents

To add a shape to a document, follow these steps:

1. Choose Insert | Illustrations | Shapes. Word displays the Shapes panel, which provides a wide variety of shapes, from lines and basic shapes to flowchart shapes and callouts.

2. Click the shape you want. Word changes the mouse pointer to a crosshair. If the document is in Draft view or Outline view, Word switches to Print Layout view so that you can see how you're positioning the shape.

3. Click (and hold down the mouse button) in the document to position one corner of the shape. It doesn't matter which corner you position, so position whichever corner is most convenient.

4. Drag to the size you want the shape to be, as shown here. When you release the mouse button, Word restores the mouse pointer.

You can also center the shape, constrain it, or create multiple shapes of the same type:

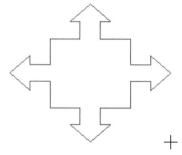

■ To create the shape centered on the point where you click and start dragging, instead of having one corner of the shape (or the rectangular frame that surrounds a nonrectangular shape) appear there, hold down CTRL as you click and drag.

■ To constrain a rectangle to a square, or to constrain an ellipse to a circle, hold down SHIFT as you click and drag.

■ Hold down CTRL-SHIFT to apply both the centering and the constraint.

■ To create multiple shapes of the same type (for example, several rectangles), right-click the tool, and then choose Lock Drawing Mode from the shortcut menu. Then, when you release the mouse button after creating a shape, the tool remains active, so that you can create another shape of the same type. Press ESC to toggle the tool off when you've finished creating all the shapes of that type. (Alternatively, click another tool to start using that tool.)

Add Text to a Shape

You can add text inside just about any shape that has enough space inside—that is, most of them except for those shapes in the Lines category and a few of the others. To add text, follow these steps:

1. Right-click the shape, and then choose Add Text from the shortcut menu. Word displays an insertion point in the shape. (If the shape already contains text, choose Edit Text from the context menu.)

> **NOTE** *If the Add Text command doesn't appear on the shortcut menu, you can't add text to the shape. Instead, place a text box or one of the shapes from the Callouts category next to the line. Then format the line color for the text box or Callout with the No Line option, and set the Fill color to No Fill (as discussed later in this chapter).*

2. Type the text in the AutoShape, as shown here.

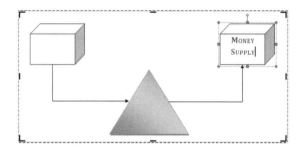

3. If you want to change the formatting, select the text, and then apply formatting as discussed in Chapter 4.

4. Click elsewhere to select another object.

Add WordArt Objects to Documents

Another element you can add to documents is a WordArt object. WordArt is an Office applet for creating text-based designs, such as logos or decorations.

> **NOTE** *Like all means of making text more difficult to read, WordArt is best used only when necessary and, even then, only in moderation.*

To insert a WordArt object in a drawing, follow these steps:

1. Place the insertion point at the beginning of the paragraph where you want the WordArt item to appear. It's best to use a blank paragraph. You can move the WordArt item later if you need to.

7

2. Choose Insert | Text | WordArt. Word displays the WordArt panel, as shown here.

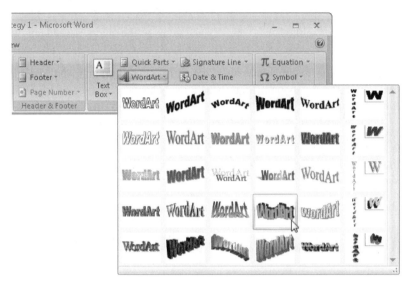

3. Click the style of WordArt item you want. Word displays the Edit WordArt Text dialog box, as shown here. (The "Your Text Here" text is sample text that Word provides so that you can see the current font in use.)

4. Over the sample text, type the text you want the WordArt to have.

5. In the Font drop-down list, choose the font you want to use.

6. In the Size drop-down list, choose the font size for the WordArt.

7. If you want, click the Bold button to apply boldface or the Italic button to apply italics.

8. Click the OK button. Word closes the Edit WordArt Text dialog box, and inserts the WordArt item in your document, as shown here. Word also displays the WordArt Tools section of the Ribbon, which contains a Format tab (also shown here).

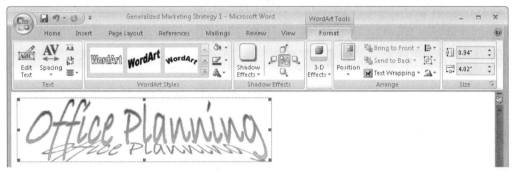

9. If necessary, change the WordArt's size:

- To resize the WordArt item proportionally, drag one of the corner handles.

- To resize the WordArt item only horizontally or vertically, drag one of the handles in the middle of the sides or the top or bottom.

10. If Word has placed the WordArt item in line with text, you cannot rotate it. If you need to rotate it, choose Format | Arrange | Position, and then choose one of the options in the With Text Wrapping area of the Position panel. You can then rotate the item by moving the mouse pointer over the green rotation handle attached to the WordArt object, and then dragging left to rotate it counterclockwise or right to rotate it clockwise, as shown here.

11. To change the spacing of the text, choose Format | Text | Spacing, and then choose the spacing from the panel, as shown here:

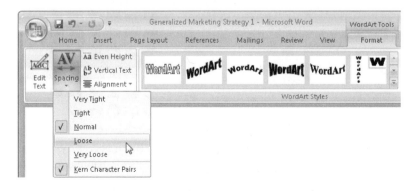

7

- ■ Your choices are Very Tight (with very little spacing), Tight, Normal, Loose, or Very Loose (with plenty of spacing).

- ■ The Spacing panel also contains the Kern Character Pairs option, which is turned on by default. This option makes Word reduce the space between pairs of characters that would otherwise have too much space between them—for example, capital A and V. If you want to change the spacing, try turning this option off.

12. To make all the letters in the WordArt item the same height, choose Format | Text | Even Height. Standardizing the height can sometimes look good, even though it makes some letters harder to read. Click the Even Height button again if you want to restore the letters to their normal heights.

13. To switch the text to vertical orientation, choose Format | Text | Vertical Text. Click the Vertical Text button again if you want to make the text horizontal once more.

14. To change the alignment of the text, choose Format | Text | Align Text, and then choose the alignment from the Align Text panel. Your choices are Left Align, Center, Right Align, Word Justify, Letter Justify, and Stretch Justify.

15. To change the style of the WordArt item (as you may need to after making other changes), choose Format | WordArt Styles | Styles, and then choose the new style from the Styles panel. You can preview a style by hovering the mouse pointer over it without clicking.

16. To change the shape of the WordArt item, choose Format | WordArt Styles | Change Shape, and then select a shape from the Change Shape panel, shown here.

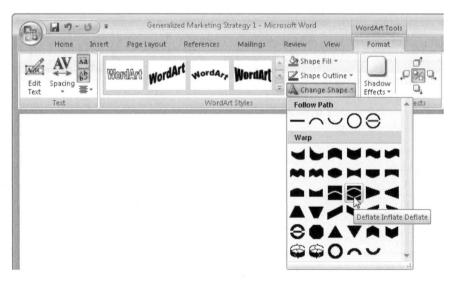

By now, your WordArt item should be looking pretty good. But if necessary, you can adjust it further by changing its fill or outline, working with shadow effects, or manipulating 3-D effects. You'll learn about these features later in this chapter.

You may also need to change the size or position of the WordArt item. You'll learn about these commands too, later in this chapter.

Add Charts to Documents

Shapes are good for illustrating key points, and WordArt can add dramatic impact to text, but to present statistical information graphically, you'll often need a chart. Word borrows Excel's charting capabilities, which gives you plenty of power to create attractive and convincing charts.

To add a chart to the active document, follow these steps:

1. Place the insertion point at the beginning of the paragraph where you want the chart to appear. It's best to use a blank paragraph. You can move the chart later if you need to.

2. Choose Insert | Illustrations | Chart. Word displays the Insert Chart dialog box, shown here.

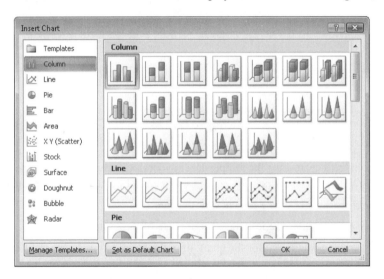

3. Choose the chart type you want:

- The right pane in the Insert Chart dialog box contains a scrolling list showing all the chart subtypes broken up by chart type. The list starts with the Column section, showing the column chart subtypes; continues with the Line section, showing the line chart subtypes; and so on down to the Radar section, which shows the few types of radar charts.

- If you know which chart type you want, click it in the left pane to display that section of the list.

- Otherwise, scroll the list until you find the chart type you want.

- To see the name of a chart subtype, hover the mouse pointer over it for a moment so that Word displays a ScreenTip.

4. Click the OK button. Two things now happen:

■ Word launches Excel, which creates a workbook named Chart In Microsoft Office Word. This workbook consists of a single worksheet containing sample categories, series, and data, as in the example shown here.

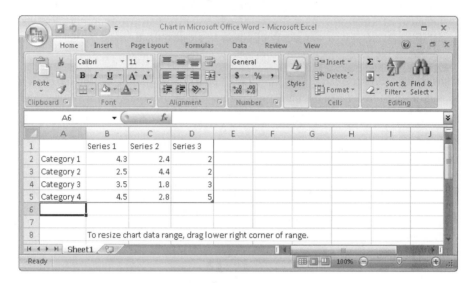

■ Word inserts a chart using the sample data in your document and displays the Chart Tools section of the Ribbon, which contains a Design tab, a Layout tab, and a Format tab.

5. In the Excel workbook, create the data for the chart:

■ Type your categories, series, and data in place of the sample data.

■ To change the data range for the chart, drag the handle in its lower-right corner, as shown here. You may not need to change the data range manually, as Excel automatically extends it for you when you enter data in cells outside but adjoining the data range.

	A	B	C	D	E	F	G
1		2006	2007	2008			
2	Richmond	8	12	11			
3	Sacramento	3	3	7			
4	Elko	1	1	1			
5	Jackson	9	11	14			
6	Flagstaff	1	4	16			
7							
8		To resize chart data range, drag lower right corner of range.					

■ As you work, Excel changes the chart in the Word document.

6. When you've finished changing the chart, click the Close button (the × button) on the Excel window. Excel closes, returning you to the Word window.

You can then change the chart's type and appearance by using the controls on the three tabs of the Chart Tools section of the Ribbon. Here are examples of the types of changes you can make. For more detail, see Chapter 13 in *How to Do Everything with Microsoft Office Excel 2007*.

- **Resize the chart**   On the box around the chart, drag one of the corner handles (to resize the chart proportionally) or one of the side handles (to resize the chart in one dimension only). Alternatively, use the Format | Size | Shape Height or Format | Size | Shape Width commands. There's one more option—choose Format | Size | Size, and then work on the Size tab of the Size dialog box—but this has no advantage.

- **Change the chart type**   Choose Design | Type | Change Chart Type. Word displays the Change Chart Type dialog box, which is the Insert Chart dialog box by a different name. Select the chart type, and then click the OK button.

- **Change the chart layout**   Choose Design | Chart Layouts | Chart Layout, and then select the layout from the panel.

- **Change the chart style**   Choose Design | Chart Styles | Chart Style, and then select the style from the panel.

- **Add a chart title**   Choose Layout | Chart Labels | Chart Title, and then choose Centered Overlay Title or Above Chart. To remove the chart's existing title, choose Layout | Chart Labels | Chart Title | None.

- **Add axis titles**   Choose Layout | Chart Labels | Axis Titles, and then use the options on the panel to add a horizontal axis title or a vertical axis title.

- **Add data labels**   To add data labels, identifying the value of each data point, choose Layout | Chart Labels | Data Labels, and then choose Center, Inside End, Inside Base, or Outside End. To remove data labels, choose Layout | Chart Labels | Data Labels | None.

- **Format a chart element**   Click the element you want to format, or choose Format | Current Selection | Chart Elements. (Chart Elements is the drop-down list at the top of the Current Selection group.) Choose Format | Current Selection | Format Selection, and then work in the Format dialog box for the element you chose.

7

Add SmartArt Diagrams to Documents

Individual shapes and pictures can make a huge difference to your documents, but you'll often need to create more complex diagrams. You can combine shapes as needed to create diagrams, but first you should try Word's SmartArt feature, which makes inserting various types of diagrams in your documents a snap.

This section uses an organization chart as an example, as this is one of the most widely used forms of diagrams. The other SmartArt items work in similar ways.

NOTE   *SmartArt is a huge improvement on the Diagram applet and Organization Chart applet in Word 2003 and earlier versions.*

Insert a SmartArt Graphic

To insert a SmartArt graphic, follow these steps:

1. Click at the beginning of the paragraph in which you want to place the upper-left corner of the SmartArt graphic. It's best to use an empty paragraph. You can move the SmartArt graphic later if needed.

2. Choose Insert | Illustrations | SmartArt. Word displays the Choose A SmartArt Graphic dialog box (see Figure 7-5). This dialog box breaks the diagrams up into List, Process, Cycle, Hierarchy, Relationship, Matrix, and Pyramid categories. The Hierarchy category offers various designs of organization charts.

3. In the left panel, select the category of SmartArt you want. For example, if you want to create an organization chart, select the Hierarchy category. Word displays the available diagrams in the main box.

4. Click the diagram you want, and then use the sample picture and description to verify that it's suitable.

5. Click the OK button. Word closes the Choose A SmartArt Graphic dialog box, inserts the diagram in the document, and displays the SmartArt Tools section of the Ribbon (see Figure 7-6), which contains a Design tab and a Format tab. The Text pane contains paragraphs that map to the shapes in the SmartArt and lets you work on the text separately from the layout.

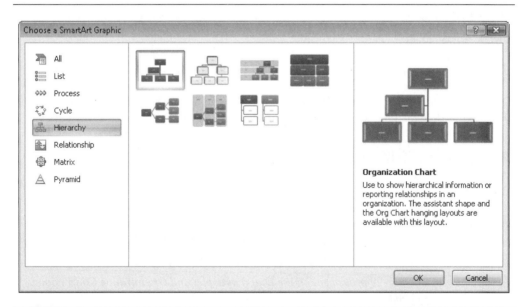

FIGURE 7-5　The Choose A SmartArt Graphic dialog box provides several different types of diagrams.

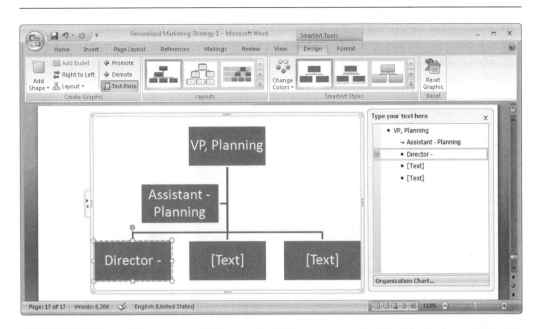

FIGURE 7-6 When you've selected a SmartArt item, the Ribbon displays the SmartArt Tools section.

NOTE *If Word doesn't display the Text pane, click the button with two sideways arrows on the left side of the SmartArt graphic's frame.*

6. Enter text by clicking a paragraph in the Text pane and then typing the text. You can also click in a box in the SmartArt graphic, but in most cases, using the text pane is easier.

7. To add a shape to the diagram, click the paragraph or shape to which the new item will be related, click the Add Shape button in the Create Graphic group, and then choose a command from the menu. For example, the Hierarchy diagrams offer the Add Shape After, Add Shape Before, Add Shape Above, Add Shape Below, and Add Assistant commands, as shown here.

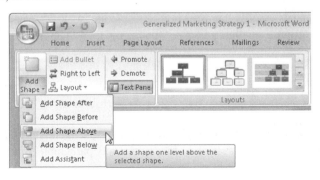

8. If you need to change the layout of the diagram, select the new layout in the Layouts panel. SmartArt lets you change from one kind of a diagram to another without losing the data you've entered, although you may need to rearrange the data to suit the new layout you've chosen.

Format a SmartArt Diagram

Once you've entered the text for your SmartArt diagram, you can format it so that it looks attractive and polished. Follow these steps:

1. Click the Format tab on the SmartArt Tools section of the Ribbon to display the formatting tools, shown here:

2. To change the shape used for an individual shape in the diagram, click the shape, choose Format | Shapes | Change Shape, and then choose the shape from the Change Shape panel.

3. To change the size of an individual shape, click the shape, and then choose Format | Shapes | Larger or Format | Shapes | Smaller.

4. To change the style of the shape, choose Format | Shape Styles | Shape Style, and then choose a graphical style for the SmartArt from the Shape Styles panel.

5. If necessary, use the Shape Fill panel, the Shape Outline panel, or the Shape Effects panel (all in the Shape Styles group) to adjust the shape style you chose.

6. If you want to apply a WordArt style to the text in the SmartArt shapes, use the controls in the WordArt Styles group. Make sure the result is readable.

7. To change the size of your SmartArt diagram, either drag a sizing handle, or choose Format | Size | Height or Format | Size | Width.

Add Pictures to Documents

To enhance your documents, you'll often need to insert a picture, such as a custom illustration, photograph, or screen capture, and then adjust it—for example, by changing its contrast or cropping it.

Insert a Picture

To insert a picture, follow these steps:

1. Place the insertion point at the beginning of the paragraph where you want the upper-left corner of the picture to appear. It's best to use an empty paragraph. You can move the picture later if you need to.

 **Control How Word Inserts Pictures in Your Documents**

When you insert a picture, Word may position it inline in the text layer or in one of the sublayers of the graphics layer. To control where Word positions pictures, follow these steps:

1. Click the Office Button, and then click Word Options. Word displays the Word Options dialog box.

2. In the left pane, click the Advanced category. Word displays the Advanced options.

3. In the Cut, Copy, And Paste section, open the Insert/Paste Pictures As drop-down list and choose the position you want: In Line With Text, Square, Tight, Behind Text, In Front Of Text, Through, or Top And Bottom.

4. Click the OK button. Word closes the Word Options dialog box.

2. Choose Insert | Illustrations | Picture. Word displays the Insert Picture dialog box, which is a common Open dialog box.

3. Navigate to the picture you want to add, and then select it.

4. Click the Insert button. Word closes the Insert Picture dialog box and inserts the picture.

Crop a Picture

If you don't want to show the whole of a picture, you can *crop* it, cutting off the parts you don't want to keep. To crop a picture, follow these steps:

1. Click the picture to select it. Word displays the Picture Tools section of the Ribbon, which contains the Format tab, shown here.

2. Choose Format | Size | Crop. Word displays crop handles at each corner and at the midpoint of each side.

3. Drag a crop handle to crop the picture:

   ▪ SHIFT-drag a corner crop handle to crop proportionally.

   ▪ CTRL-drag a crop handle to crop from both sides simultaneously.

   ▪ CTRL-SHIFT-drag to crop proportionally and from both sides.

For more precise cropping, choose Format | Size | Size (click the tiny button at the right end of the Size bar), and then use the Crop From controls on the Size tab of the Size And Properties dialog box.

Format a Picture

The Format tab of the Picture Tools section of the Ribbon lets you quickly and easily make sweeping changes to a picture.

Change a Picture's Brightness, Contrast, or Color

Start by making any needed changes to the picture's brightness, contrast, and colors by using the Brightness panel, the Contrast panel, and the Recolor panel in the Adjust group. These tools are easy to use but can make a dramatic difference to how a picture looks.

If you produce an effect you don't like, choose Format | Adjust | Reset Picture to restore the picture to its former state.

If you decide that a different picture would look better, choose Format | Adjust | Change Picture, and then choose the picture in the Insert Picture dialog box.

NOTE *When you use the Format | Adjust | Change Picture command to replace one picture with another, Word retains the picture's position, size, and formatting. By contrast, if you delete the picture and insert another picture, you have to start again from scratch. (Sometimes starting again from scratch may be the better option, but it's good to have the choice of continuing with your current settings.)*

Compress the Pictures in a Document

If you use large pictures in a document, its file size increases rapidly. You can reduce this problem by telling Word to compress the pictures. Follow these steps:

1. If you want to compress only some pictures, select them. Otherwise, click one picture so that Word makes the Picture Tools section of the Ribbon available.

2. Choose Format | Adjust | Compress Pictures button. Word displays the Compress Pictures dialog box, shown here.

3. If you want to compress only the picture or pictures you chose in step 1, select the Apply To Selected Pictures Only check box. To compress all the pictures, leave this check box cleared.

4. Click the Options button. Word displays the Compression Settings dialog box, shown here:

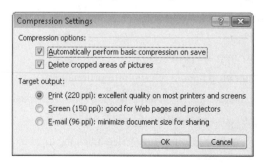

5. Choose settings in the Compression Options area:

- ■ **Automatically Perform Basic Compression On Save**   Select this check box if you want Word to use its normal compression whenever you save the document. This compression retains high quality but minimizes bloat.

- ■ **Delete Cropped Areas Of Pictures**   Select this check box if you want Word to get rid of any parts you crop off pictures. If you clear this check box, Word merely hides the "cropped" parts. This hiding is good if you want to be able to restore the cropped parts, but it's bad for file size, and it may also have security implications (for example, a customer may be able to restore a part of a graphic that you had intended to crop off a document).

6. In the Target Output area, select the Print (220 ppi) option button, the Screen (150 ppi) option button, or the E-mail (96 ppi) option button to tell Word what picture quality you need (*ppi* is pixels per inch, and a higher number indicates higher quality). If you're not sure, use the Print setting—you can always reduce it later, but you can't restore information if you choose a lower setting.

7. Click the OK button. Word closes the Compression Settings dialog box and displays the Compress Pictures dialog box.

8. Click the OK button. Word compresses the pictures in the document.

Format, Position, and Layer Drawing Objects

Once you've inserted one of the objects discussed so far in this chapter (such as pictures, shapes, WordArt items, or diagrams), you can format it and position it so that it appears the way you want it. You may also need to layer drawing objects so that one object appears in front of another object. The following sections show you how to format, position, and layer drawing objects.

Format a Drawing Object

You can format a selected drawing object by using the controls on the Format tab of the Drawing Tools section of the Ribbon or by using the Format dialog box for the shape. The capabilities of the two overlap, but generally speaking the Format tab is better for making sweeping changes to a shape's look, while the Format dialog box is better for finer adjustments.

To display the Format dialog box, right-click the drawing object and issue the Format command from the shortcut menu. The name of the command and the dialog box depend on the object you're formatting—for example, Format Picture for a picture, Format Shape for a shape, or Format Text Box for a text box.

Apply a Style and Graphical Effects to a Drawing Object

The best way to start formatting a drawing object is to give it a suitable style and then adjust the fill, outline, and effects as necessary. Follow these steps:

1. Select the drawing object. Word adds the Drawing Tools section to the Ribbon and displays the Format tab. (If Word doesn't select the Format tab, click it.)

2. Choose Format | Shape Styles | Shape Style, and then choose the style from the Shape Styles panel.

3. To change the fill of the shape, choose Format | Shape Styles | Shape Fill, and then choose a fill from the Shape Fill panel.

4. To change the outline of the shape, choose Format | Shape Styles | Shape Outline, and then choose an outline color, weight, or style from the Shape Outline panel. You may need to use the Shape Outline panel twice or more if you need to change more than one attribute. Use the Arrow subpanel to choose the ends for an arrow.

5. To apply a new shadow effect to the shape, choose Format | Shadow Effects | Shadow Effects, and then select the effect you want from the Shadow Effects panel.

Resize a Drawing Object

You can resize a drawing object in the following ways:

- Drag a sizing handle on the object with the mouse.

- Select the object, and then use the Height control and Width control in the Size group on the Format tab.

- Choose Format | Size | Size (click the tiny button at the right end of the Size bar), and then work on the Size tab of the Format dialog box for the object. Figure 7-7 shows the

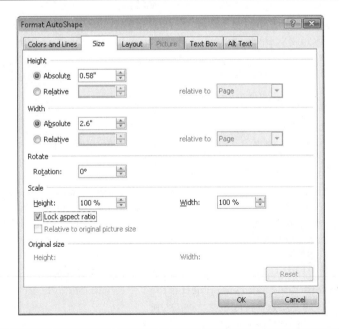

FIGURE 7-7   Use the options on the Size tab of the Format dialog box to resize or rotate an object.

Size tab of the Format AutoShape dialog box. The key setting here is the Lock Aspect Ratio check box. If this check box is selected, Word maintains the object's aspect ratio, so if you change the height, the width changes correspondingly.

NOTE   *The Reset button on the Size tab of the Format dialog box works only for objects such as pictures.*

Choose Whether an Object Moves with Text and Whether It Prints

When you insert an object in a document, Word needs to track the object's position. Depending on where the object is, Word tracks it in one of two ways:

- ■ **Inline**   When the object is inline, Word treats it as a character and tracks it by character position.

- ■ **Not inline**   When the object is not inline, Word secures it with an *object anchor*, a small symbol (shaped like an anchor) that represents the point in the document to which the object is attached. Object anchors are normally invisible, but you can make Word display the anchor for a selected object by choosing Home | Paragraph | Show/Hide ¶ (or pressing CTRL-SHIFT-8). The next illustration shows an object and its anchor.

7

THE·DEAD·SEA¶

A·thrilling·tale·set·of·the·shores·of·the·famous·body·of·water.¶

TIP   *If you want to display object anchors permanently, click the Office Button, and then click Word Options. In the Word Options dialog box, click the Display category, select the Object Anchors check box, and then click the OK button.*

Normally, when you move the paragraph or other object to which an object anchor is attached, Word moves the anchored object correspondingly. In many cases, this behavior is helpful, but you may sometimes want to prevent Word from moving an object.

To tell Word not to move an object, follow these steps:

1. Right-click the object, and then choose the Format command from the context menu. Word displays the Format dialog box for the object.

2. Click the Layout tab to bring it to the front.

3. Click the Advanced button. Word displays the Advanced Layout dialog box (see Figure 7-8).

4. In the Options area, clear the Move Object With Text check box.

5. If you want to lock the anchor in place so that you can't move it accidentally, select the Lock Anchor text box.

6. Click the OK button. Word closes the Advanced Layout dialog box.

7. Click the OK button. Word closes the Format dialog box.

Specify Alternative Text for an Object

On the Alt Text tab of the Size And Properties dialog box for an object, you can specify alternative text to be displayed while a web browser is loading the picture, when the picture isn't

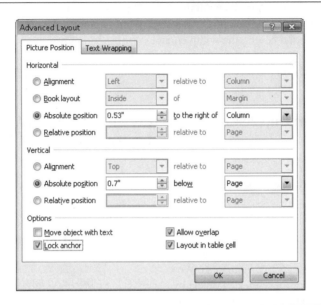

FIGURE 7-8 To prevent an object from moving with text, clear the Move Object With Text check box on the Picture Position tab of the Advanced Layout dialog box. To lock the anchor in place, select the Lock Anchor check box.

available, or when the user has chosen not to display pictures. For example, you might supply a text description of the picture so that the user knows what they're missing.

Position Drawing Objects

You can position drawing objects in various ways. You can drag objects roughly into position, nudge them precisely into position, align one object according to another, and create groups of objects that you can format and move together. You can also adjust the granularity of Word's hidden drawing grid and choose whether objects snap to the grid or not.

Drag and Nudge Objects

To position an object roughly where you want it, drag the object. To constrain the movement to either horizontal or vertical, SHIFT-drag the object.

To move an object a shorter distance, *nudge* it. Select the object and press the appropriate arrow key ($\uparrow$, $\downarrow$, $\leftarrow$, or $\rightarrow$) to move the object one square up, down, left, or right on the underlying grid that Word uses for positioning objects.

Snap an Object to the Grid or to a Shape

By default, Word makes objects *snap* (jump) to an underlying grid laid across the document. If you drag an object, such as a shape, you'll notice that it moves in little jerks rather than smoothly. This is because of the grid—but because the grid is normally invisible, it's not obvious.

To configure the grid, or to turn off snapping, follow these steps:

1. Select a shape. Word adds the Drawing Tools section to the Ribbon.

2. Choose Format | Arrange | Align | View Gridlines if you want to turn on the display of the grid.

3. Choose Format | Arrange | Align | Grid Settings. Word displays the Drawing Grid dialog box (see Figure 7-9).

4. Select the Snap Objects To Other Objects check box if you want Word to make an object you're dragging snap to another nearby object. This feature lets you create multiobject drawings more quickly and is usually helpful.

5. In the Grid Settings area, you can use the Horizontal Spacing text box and the Vertical Spacing text box to change the size of the grid's rectangles. The rectangles start off as squares, but you don't have to keep them that way.

6. In the Grid Origin area, select the Use Margins check box if you want the grid to start at the document's margins. If you need to position objects in the margins, clear the Use Margins check box, and then set the horizontal starting position for the grid in the Horizontal Origin text box and the vertical starting position in the Vertical Origin text box.

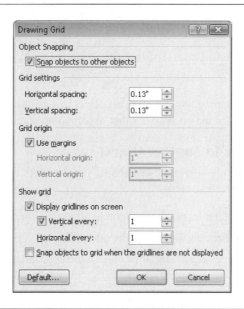

FIGURE 7-9   Use the options in the Drawing Grid dialog box to configure the underlying grid that Word uses to position objects in your documents.

7. Choose settings in the Show Grid area:

■ **Display Gridlines On Screen**   Select this check box if you want to see gridlines onscreen. Seeing them can be helpful for positioning objects, but they tend to make working with text hard.

■ **Vertical Every**   Select this check box if you want to see vertical gridlines. In the text box, specify the number of vertical grid intervals between displayed lines. For example, to see one line for each five vertical units, enter **5** in the text box.

■ **Horizontal Every**   In this text box, specify the number of horizontal grid intervals between displayed lines.

■ **Snap Objects To Grid When The Gridlines Are Not Displayed**   Select this check box if you want Word to snap objects to the grid even when you can't see the gridlines.

8. If you want to make these grid settings the default for the current template, click the Default button, and then click the Yes button in the confirmation dialog box. The example dialog box shown here is for a document based on the Normal template.

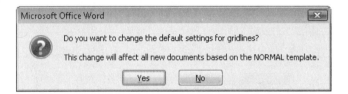

9. Click the OK button. Word closes the Drawing Grid dialog box and applies your choices.

Once you've turned on snapping, you can drag an object to a gridline or to another object and have Word snap the object to the gridline or other object automatically.

Align an Object Relative to Another Object

Instead of positioning an object by a gridline or a shape, you can align an object relative to another object. To do so, follow these steps:

1. Select the object according to which you want to align the other object or objects.

2. Hold down SHIFT, and then click to select the other objects.

3. Choose Format | Arrange | Align, and then choose the appropriate command from the menu (shown next). Most of the options are self-explanatory, but the following options merit explanation:

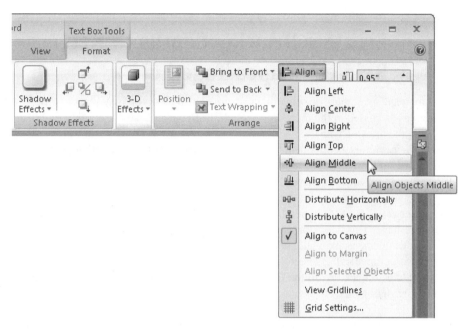

- The Align Center option applies horizontal centering, while the Align Middle option applies vertical centering.

- The Distribute Horizontally option and the Distribute Vertically option place the objects evenly across the area. These commands are available only when you have three or more objects selected.

- The Align To Canvas option aligns the object with the drawing canvas it is on. (This option is available only when you're using a drawing canvas—which is explained in the sidebar titled "Create a Drawing Canvas to Keep Related Shapes Together.")

Group and Ungroup Objects

When you've selected multiple objects by SHIFT-clicking or CTRL-clicking, you can treat them as an informal group—for example, you can drag an object to move all the objects, or apply shared formatting to all the objects at once.

To apply formal grouping so that you can quickly work with these objects as a unit in future, choose the Format | Arrange | Group command, or right-click one of the objects and choose Grouping | Group from the context menu. Word puts a single box around the objects instead of a separate box around each object.

To ungroup grouped objects, choose Format | Arrange | Ungroup, or right-click a grouped object, and then choose Grouping | Ungroup from the context menu. To regroup objects, choose Format | Arrange | Regroup, or right-click an object, and then choose Grouping | Regroup from the context menu.

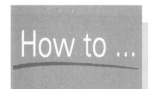

How to ... Create a Drawing Canvas to Keep Related Shapes Together

If you need to create a complex drawing that uses several shapes, you may want to group them together, as discussed in the preceding section. But you can also use another tool that Word provides, the drawing canvas.

The *drawing canvas* is a container shape that you insert in your document to give you a canvas on which to place drawing objects. By creating a drawing canvas, you can give yourself a cordoned-off area for shapes and other objects, which often makes working with them easier.

Some earlier versions of Word automatically inserted a drawing canvas whenever you went to insert a shape. This behavior tended to confuse and annoy people, so Word 2007 lets you insert a drawing canvas manually when you want one. (If you want to have Word insert a drawing canvas automatically, select the Automatically Create Drawing Canvas When Inserting AutoShapes check box in the Editing Options section of the Advanced category in the Word Options dialog box.)

To insert a drawing canvas, choose Insert | Illustrations | Shapes | New Drawing Canvas. Word inserts a dotted rectangle (as shown here) with black side handles and corner handles that you can drag to resize the canvas.

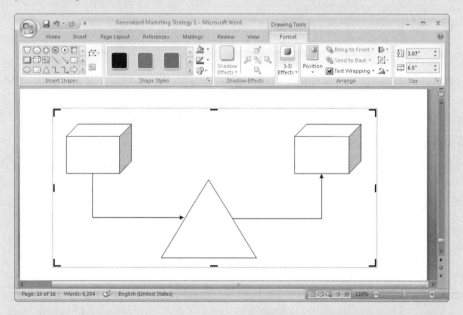

You can then arrange shapes on the canvas as needed. You can format the canvas to give a background to the shapes, or simply format each shape as needed.

Layer Drawing Objects

To adjust the layer order in which drawing objects appear, follow these steps:

1. Click the object you want to affect.

2. Use the commands in the Arrange group on the Format tab to move the object:

   - To bring the object all the way to the topmost layer, choose Format | Arrange | Bring To Front. (Click the Bring To Front button.)

   - To bring the object up the stack by one layer, choose Format | Arrange | Bring To Front | Bring Forward. (Click the Bring To Front drop-down button, and then choose Bring Forward.)

   - To bring the object in front of text, choose Format | Arrange | Bring To Front | Bring In Front Of Text. (Click the Bring To Front drop-down list, and then choose Bring In Front Of Text.)

   - To send the object all the way to the lowest layer, choose Format | Arrange | Send To Back. (Click the Send To Back button.)

   - To place the object one layer farther down the stack, choose Format | Arrange | Send To Back | Send Backward. (Click the Send To Back drop-down button, and then choose Send Backward.)

   - To place the object behind the text, choose Format | Arrange | Send To Back | Send Behind Text. (Click the Send To Back drop-down button, and then choose Send Behind Text.)

> NOTE *You can also right-click an object, choose Order, and then choose one of the commands from the submenu: Bring To Front, Send To Back, Bring Forward, Send Backward, Bring In Front Of Text, or Send Behind Text.*

7

Add Borders and Shading to Provide Emphasis

To provide emphasis or to give a document a particular look, you can add borders and shading to it.

Some documents benefit greatly from borders and shading, but many don't. For example, a color flyer for a party invitation may look great with a page border or with shading behind some text. By contrast, a letter to the IRS explaining discrepancies in your tax return will probably suffer from borders or shading.

Add a Border to Text or a Paragraph

To add a border to text or a paragraph, select it, choose Home | Paragraph | All Borders (click the All Borders drop-down button), and then choose the border from the All Borders panel, shown here.

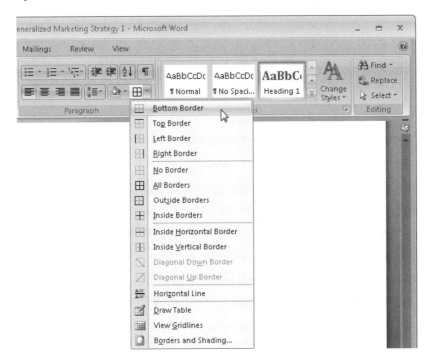

TIP *The All Borders button lets you quickly apply the last type of border you used without clicking the drop-down button and using the panel.*

To apply a more complex type of border, follow these steps:

1. Choose Home | Paragraph | All Borders | Borders And Shading. Word displays the Borders tab of the Borders And Shading dialog box (see Figure 7-10).

2. In the Apply To drop-down list, make sure that Paragraph is selected if you want to apply the border to paragraphs. If you want to apply the border to selected text, choose Text.

3. Create the border you want:

   ■ In the Setting area, click the Box item, the Shadow button, or the 3-D button if you want to apply one of these preset options. Click the None item if you need to remove an existing border.

   ■ Otherwise, click the Custom item in the Setting area, and then click the sides of the Preview diagram to indicate where to place borders.

   ■ Use the Style list, Color drop-down list, and Width drop-down list to create the type of border you want.

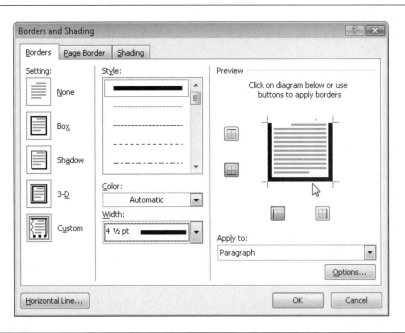

FIGURE 7-10   Use the controls on the Borders tab of the Borders And Shading dialog box to create custom borders.

4. If you need to adjust the distance from the border to the text, click the Options button, use the controls in the smaller Border And Shading Options dialog box (shown here), and then click the OK button.

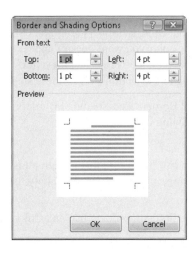

5. Click the OK button. Word closes the Borders And Shading dialog box and applies your border choices.

Add a Border to a Page

To add a border to a page, follow these steps:

1. Choose Page Layout | Page Background | Page Borders. Word displays the Page Border tab of the Borders And Shading dialog box.

2. In the Apply To drop-down list, choose the part of the document to which you want to apply the border: Whole Document, This Section, This Section – First Page Only, or This Section – All Except First Page.

3. Create the border you want:

   ■ In the Setting area, click the Box item, the Shadow button, or the 3-D button if you want to apply one of these preset options. Click the None item if you need to remove an existing border.

   ■ Otherwise, click the Custom item in the Setting area, and then click the sides of the Preview diagram to indicate where to place borders.

   ■ Use the Style list, Color drop-down list, and Width text box to create the type of border you want.

   ■ If you want to create the border from graphics rather than lines, choose the graphic in the Art drop-down list.

4. If you need to adjust the positioning of the border, click the Options button, use the controls in the larger Border And Shading Options dialog box (shown in Figure 7-11), and then click the OK button.

5. Click the OK button. Word closes the Borders And Shading dialog box and applies the page borders.

Apply Shading

To apply color shading to a selection, choose Home | Paragraph | Shading, and then choose a color from the Shading panel. If the color you want doesn't appear on the panel, click the More Colors item, and then use the Colors dialog box to select the color.

To apply more complex shading to a selection, follow these steps:

1. Choose Home | Paragraph | Borders And Shading | Borders And Shading. Word displays the Borders And Shading dialog box.

2. Click the Shading tab.

3. In the Apply To drop-down list, make sure that Paragraph is selected if you want to apply the shading to complete paragraphs. If you want to apply the shading to selected text, choose Text.

4. Use the Fill drop-down list, Style drop-down list, and Color drop-down list to set up the shading you want.

5. Click the OK button. Word closes the Borders And Shading dialog box and applies the shading.

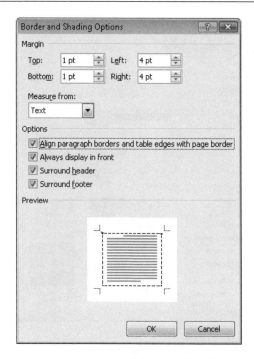

FIGURE 7-11   The larger Border And Shading Options dialog box lets you position a page border precisely where you want it.

Apply a Background to a Page

To apply a background color to a page, choose Page Layout | Page Background | Page Color, and then choose the color from the Page Color panel. If the color you want doesn't appear on the panel, click the More Colors item, and then use the Colors dialog box to select the color.

To apply a gradient, texture, pattern, or picture to a page, follow these steps:

1. Choose Page Layout | Page Background | Page Color | Fill Effects. Word displays the Fill Effects dialog box.

2. Choose the type of background you want:

   ■ **Gradient**   On the Gradient tab (see Figure 7-12), choose which colors to use, whether to have a degree of transparency, and which shading style to use.

   ■ **Texture**   On the Texture tab, select one of the built-in textures, or click the Other Texture button, use the Select Texture dialog box to select the file that contains the texture, and then click the OK button.

   ■ **Pattern**   On the Pattern tab, choose a pattern in the Pattern list box, and then select the foreground and background colors to use.

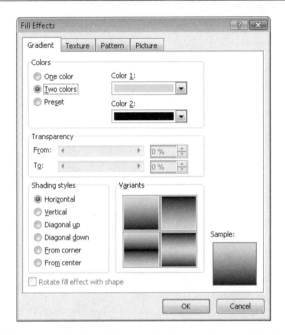

FIGURE 7-12 The Gradient tab of the Fill Effects dialog box lets you create a custom fill for a page background.

- **Picture** On the Picture tab, click the Select Picture button, use the Select Picture dialog box to select the picture file, and then click the Insert button.

3. Click the OK button. Word closes the Fill Effects dialog box and applies the background.

Position Background Text on Every Page

To position background text on every page, you apply a watermark. A watermark is technically part of a document's header or footer, because Word uses the header and footer areas to define the items that appear on each page rather than flowing from page to page—but Word makes the process of inserting a watermark so simple that you hardly need worry about this.

To insert a watermark, choose Page Layout | Page Background | Watermark. From the panel, you can choose one of Word's built-in watermarks (such as "Urgent" or "Confidential"), or choose the Custom Watermark item, and then work in the Printed Watermark dialog box, shown here with a picture chosen.

TIP *If you need to use two or more watermarks in different parts of your document, divide the document into sections. You can then use a different watermark in each section.*

Create a Picture Watermark

To create a watermark from a picture, follow these steps:

1. Click the Select Picture button in the Printed Watermark dialog box. Word displays the Insert Picture dialog box.

2. Navigate to the folder that contains the picture, select the picture, and then click the Insert button. Word closes the Insert Picture dialog box and adds the picture's name to the Printed Watermark dialog box.

3. In the Scale drop-down list, select Auto if you want Word to scale the picture automatically to what Word considers a suitable size. Otherwise, select the scaling percentage you want: 50%, 100%, 150%, 200%, 500%, or a custom percentage that you type into the Scale box.

4. Select the Washout check box if you want Word to wash the picture out to give a more subtle effect. If the picture is already subtle enough, clear this check box.

5. Click the Apply button. Word applies the watermark to the document so you can see how it looks. Make any adjustments needed. For example, you may need to choose a different value in the Scale drop-down list.

6. Click the OK button. Word closes the Printed Watermark dialog box and inserts the picture.

Create a Text Watermark

To create a text watermark, follow these steps:

1. Select the Text Watermark option button in the Printed Watermark dialog box.

2. In the Language drop-down list, change the language if necessary. (Normally, you won't need to change it.)

3. In the Text drop-down list, either type the text you want or select one of Word's built-in phrases (such as Top Secret or Urgent).

4. Use the Font drop-down list, Size drop-down list, and Color drop-down list to specify the font, font size, and font color you want.

5. Select the Semitransparent check box if you want the watermark to be partly transparent (so that it doesn't mask the document's text).

6. In the Layout area, select the Diagonal option button or the Horizontal option button to control how the watermark appears.

7. Click the Apply button. Word applies the watermark to the document so you can see how it looks. Make any adjustments needed. For example, you may need to change the font size.

8. Click the OK button. Word closes the Printed Watermark dialog box and inserts the picture.

7

Remove a Watermark

To remove a watermark, choose Page Layout | Page Background | Remove Watermark.

Insert Equations

If your work involves math or science, you may need to insert equations in your documents. Word includes prebuilt equations for common operations, such as calculating the area of a circle or the expansion of a sum; you can also create custom equations as needed.

To insert an equation, follow these steps:

1. Position the insertion point where you want the equation to appear.

2. Choose Insert | Symbols | Equation, and then either choose a prebuilt equation from the Equation panel or choose Insert New Equation to insert a blank equation.

3. Word inserts the prebuilt equation or blank equation in Display mode (as a separate object), adds the Equation Tools section to the Ribbon, and displays the Design tab, shown here.

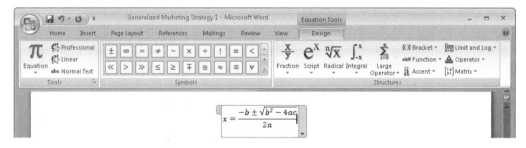

4. Use the tools on the Design tab to create or customize the equation.

To change an equation from Display mode to Inline mode, right-click the equation and choose Change To Inline from the context menu. To change back to Display mode, right-click the equation and choose Change To Display from the context menu.

Chapter 8

Print and Fax Documents

How to...

- Choose suitable printing options
- Use Print Preview
- Print a document
- Print directly from the Desktop or a Windows Explorer window
- Fax a document

For at least 15 years, futurists have been predicting that computers will wean us off paper documents—but that's still nearly as far from happening as it's ever been. Every home with a computer has at least one printer, and most offices have many printers, all busy churning out many pages a minute and many documents an hour.

So you'll probably need to print some—perhaps many—of your Word documents. This chapter shows you how to do so. The best place to start is by making sure that you have suitable printing options set. You'll then be ready to preview a document, print a document the conventional way, print directly from the Desktop or from a Windows Explorer window, or fax a document (if your version of Windows provides faxing).

Choose Printing Options

Before you print at all, it's a good idea to verify that Word's printing options are set to print the document elements you need to print. The default settings work well for many people, but you may need to change some of them.

To set printing options, follow these steps:

1. Click the Office Button, and then click Word Options. Word displays the Word Options dialog box.

2. In the left pane, click the Display category. Word shows the Display items.

3. In the Printing Options area, choose options for all the documents you print:

   - **Print Drawings Created In Word**   Select this check box to include text boxes, shapes, and graphics you've created in Word in the printout. Normally, you'll want to include them. Clear this check box if you want to print the document with only placeholder boxes (for example, to save ink on a draft).

   - **Print Background Colors And Images**   Select this check box to include any background colors or images in the printout. Printing these items lets you see the full document on paper, but it both uses more ink and can make busy documents harder to read.

   - **Print Document Properties**   Select this check box to print out the document's property information (such as its subject, title, and author) on a separate sheet of paper. If you use document properties to make your documents more complete and searchable, you may find this option useful on occasion.

■ **Print Hidden Text**   Select this check box if you want to print out all the hidden text in the document along with the rest of the document. Word prints the hidden text as normal text rather than giving it the dotted underline the hidden text uses on screen. Normally, you'll want to print hidden text only when reviewing a document that contains sections that may be hidden. For example, a contract may contain hidden boilerplate text for different eventualities.

> **TIP**   *Use the Document Inspector to remove hidden text from a document before distributing it (see the section "Remove Sensitive or Personal Information from a Document" in Chapter 18).*

■ **Update Fields Before Printing**   Select this check box if you want Word to update all the fields in a document automatically when you issue a Print command. Such updating is normally a good idea. (Chapter 15 explains what fields are and how to work with them.)

■ **Update Linked Data Before Printing**   Select this check box if you want Word to update any linked information from other documents before printing. Such updating ensures that your document is up-to-date and is a good idea unless the linked documents may not be available to your computer when you print. (For example, if you take a document home from the office, any linked documents on the office network may not be available.)

4. In the left pane, click the Advanced category. Word displays the Advanced options.

5. Scroll down to the Print area, about halfway down the dialog box, and then choose options for all the documents you print:

■ **Use Draft Quality**   Select this check box if you want to try "draft-quality" printing, which omits much font formatting and most graphics so as to print faster and use less ink. Only some printers support draft-quality printing. Normally, the easiest way to find out if your printer supports it is to select this check box, print a test document, and see what happens.

■ **Print In Background**   Select this check box to tell Word to use *background printing*, in which Word lets you continue working while it sends the print job to the printer. If you find Word is unresponsive while the document is printing, clear this check box and simply leave Word alone until it has finished sending the print job.

■ **Print Pages In Reverse Order**   Select this check box to make Word print the last page first and the first page last. This setting can be helpful when you're printing a document for a photocopier that reverses the order of pages.

■ **Print XML Tags**   Select this check box if you want to include XML tags in a printout.

■ **Print Field Codes Instead Of Their Values**   Select this check box if you need your printout to contain field codes (such as date codes and page-number codes) instead of their values (the dates and the page numbers).

■ **Print On Front Of The Sheet For Duplex Printing**   See the section "Print on the Back and Front of Paper," later in this chapter.

- **Print On Back Of The Sheet For Duplex Printing** See the section "Print on the Back and Front of Paper," later in this chapter.

- **Scale Content For A4 Or 8.5 × 11" Paper Sizes** Select this check box to make Word adjust an 8.5 × 11" document to A4 size, or vice versa, when Word finds that the document has one of these sizes and the printer's paper tray has the other. Word doesn't change the document's formatting, just the printout.

- **Default Tray** In this drop-down list, either choose Use Printer Settings to use the paper tray the printer is set to use, or choose a particular tray from the list.

6. In the When Printing This Document drop-down list, you can set two options for any document you have open. Select the document in the drop-down list (Word selects the active document for you), and then choose settings:

- **Print PostScript Over Text** Select this check box to print PostScript codes in places where the document contains PRINT fields. (PostScript is a formatting language for printing.) You'll seldom need to do this.

- **Print Only The Data From A Form** Select this check box if you want to print only the data (the fields that the user has filled in) in an online form rather than all the form's text (including the static text). This feature is useful for printing the contents of an online form onto an already partly printed paper-based form.

7. Click the OK button. Word closes the Word Options dialog box and applies your choices.

Use Print Preview

Before you print a document, use Print Preview (see Figure 8-1) to make sure that the document looks the way you want it to and (if appropriate) that it fits on the paper size you've chosen.

Open Print Preview

You can display the active document in Print Preview in either of these ways:

- Click the Office Button, highlight the Print item or click the arrow next to it to display the Preview And Print The Document submenu, and then click Print Preview. Word displays only the Print Preview tab of the Ribbon, suppressing all the other tabs.

- Press CTRL-ALT-I. This shortcut is handy for keyboard enthusiasts.

Preview the Document

Click the Next Page button or the Previous Page button to navigate to the previews next page or previous page. (These buttons have no effect if there is no next page or previous page.) You can also scroll or press PAGE DOWN or PAGE UP.

Use the controls in the Zoom group and the Preview group of the Print Preview tab of the Ribbon to preview your document.

Select the Show Ruler check box in the Preview group to display the ruler. (You can also click the Show Ruler button at the top of the vertical scroll bar.)

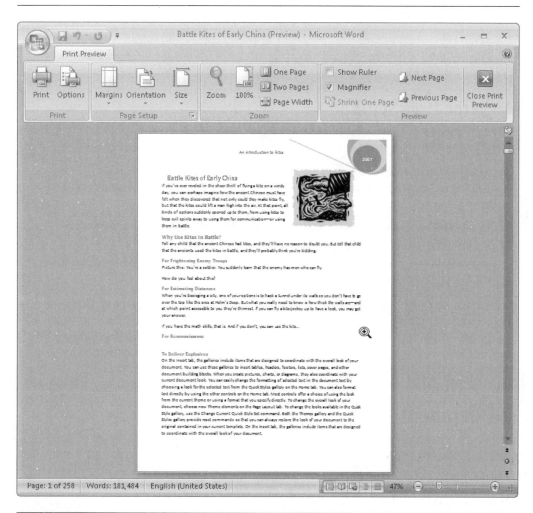

FIGURE 8-1   Use Print Preview to check the print layout before you commit a document to paper.

When you switch to Print Preview, Word automatically displays the document in Magnifier mode. The mouse pointer appears as a magnifying glass containing either a plus (+) sign or a minus (−) sign. Click with the plus sign to zoom in quickly. Word changes the mouse pointer to the minus sign, and you can then click to zoom back out.

For more precise zooming, use the controls in the Zoom group:

- **Zoom**   Click this button to display the Zoom dialog box, in which you can choose a full range of zoom percentages and options.

- **100%**   Click this button to zoom to actual size.

- **One Page** Click this button to zoom so that the window shows one full page.
- **Two Pages** Click this button to zoom so that the window shows two full pages.
- **Page Width** Click this button to zoom the document so that the window shows the page's full width.

Change the Page Setup

If your document doesn't look the way you planned, use the controls in the Page Setup group on the Print Preview tab:

- **Margins** Click this button, and then choose a preset margin from the panel. Alternatively, choose Custom Margins from the panel to display the Margins tab of the Page Setup dialog box.
- **Orientation** Click this button, and then choose Portrait or Landscape, as needed.
- **Size** Click this button, and then choose a preset size from the panel. For more choices or a custom size, click the More Paper Sizes item, and then work on the Paper tab of the Page Setup dialog box.

To shrink a multipage document by one page, click the Shrink One Page button. This option works best when the document has only a small amount of text on the last page, so that Word can reduce the page count by one page by making small adjustments to the line spacing, paragraph spacing, or font size. If you find that clicking this button produces changes too great to be acceptable, click the Undo button on the Quick Access Toolbar to undo the changes.

Print a Document

When a document is ready to print, you can print it with any necessary options by using the Print dialog box. If you often need to print the whole document, you can put the Quick Print button on the Quick Access Toolbar, and then click that button to print instantly. (See the sidebar "Put the Quick Print Button on the Quick Access Toolbar for Instant Printing," later in this chapter, for instructions on how to do this.)

Choose options as discussed in the following sections, and then click the OK button. Word closes the Print dialog box and prints the document using the settings you chose.

Control Printing Using the Print Dialog Box

For normal printing, when you need to control what you print and how you print it, click the Office Button, and then click Print. Word displays the Print dialog box (see Figure 8-2).

 *You can also display the Print dialog box by pressing CTRL-P or, from Print Preview, choosing Print Preview | Print | Print.*

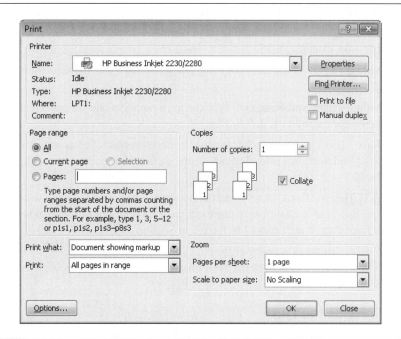

FIGURE 8-2 Use the Print dialog box to choose what to print, which printer to use, and whether to print multiple copies.

Choose Which Printer to Use

The Name drop-down list shows the printer that Word will use unless you change the printer. To choose a different printer, open the drop-down list, and then click the printer.

If your computer is running Windows Vista Business Edition or Windows XP Professional and is part of a Windows Server network, you can click the Find Printer button and use the Find Printers dialog box to locate available printers. You can't use the Find Printer button on home networks.

Choose Which Pages to Print

In the Print Range group box, choose which pages to print:

■ **All**   Select this option button to print all the pages in the document. This is often convenient, and Word selects this option button by default.

■ **Current Page**   Select this option button to print the page on which the insertion point is currently positioned.

■ **Selection**   Select this option button to print the selection you made in the document before you displayed the Print dialog box. If you didn't make a selection in the document, this option button is unavailable.

- **Pages**   Select this option button to print the range of pages you specify in the text box.
  - **Range of Pages**   Type the starting page number, a hyphen, and the ending page number—for example, **8-16**.
  - **Individual Pages**   Type each page number separated by a comma—for example, **1, 3, 6, 8**.
  - **Individual Pages and Ranges**   Type the page numbers and ranges separated by commas—for example, **1, 3, 5-8, 18**.
  - **Sections**   Use *s* and the number to represent each section. For example, **s1, s3** prints Section 1 and Section 3; **s1, s3-s5, s8** prints Section 1, Sections 3 through 5, and Section 8.
  - **Pages Within Sections**   Use *p* and the number to represent the page within the section, and *s* and the number to represent each section. For example, **p3s4-p5s7** prints from Page 3 in Section 4 to Page 5 in Section 7.

If you need to print just the odd pages of the page range you've specified, or just the even pages, select Odd Pages or Even Pages in the Print drop-down list. Otherwise, leave All Pages In Range selected, as it is by default.

Choose Which Items to Print

In the Print What drop-down list, choose which item or items to print:

- **Document**   Select this item to print the document itself. This is the item you'll want most often. Word selects Document by default unless the document contains markup, in which case Word selects Document Showing Markup.
- **Document Properties**   Select this item to print a list of the document's properties, such as the title, subject, and author name.
- **Document Showing Markup**   Select this item to print the document showing all tracked changes, comments, and other markup. Word selects this item by default if the document contains markup. Word prints the markup using the formatting you've selected in the Track Changes Options dialog box (discussed in Chapter 10).
- **List Of Markup**   Select this item to print only the markup from the document—tracked changes, comments, and other markup. (This is essentially a printout of the Reviewing pane.)
- **Styles**   Select this item to print a list of the styles used in the document.
- **Building Blocks Entries**   Select this item to print a list of the building blocks in the document's template.

If the document has the Normal template attached, printing out Building Blocks Entries prints out all the entries in the Normal template, which is many pages' worth. You will seldom benefit from doing this, even at your employer's expense.

- **Key Assignments**   Select this item to print a list of the custom key assignments in the document.

Choose the Number of Copies and How to Collate Them

Set the number of copies to print in the Number Of Copies box. The default is one copy.

If you print multiple copies, select the Collate check box to print the full set of each copy at once (followed by the next copy), or clear the Collate check box to print all of the copies of each page together (followed by all of the copies of the next page).

Print Multiple Pages on the Same Sheet of Paper

When creating some kinds of documents, you may need to print multiple pages of the document on the same physical sheet of paper. To do so, choose the number in the Pages Per Sheet drop-down list: 1 Page, 2 Pages, 4 Pages, 6 Pages, 8 Pages, or 16 Pages.

Print a Document on a Different Paper Size

To print the document on a different paper size than that used in its page setup, choose the paper size in the Scale To Paper Size drop-down list. This list offers a wide range of choices, from Post Card up to Legal. To print a document normally, make sure the No Scaling item is selected. (Word selects No Scaling by default.)

8

NOTE
As long as you've selected the Scale Content For A4 Or 8.5 × 11" Paper Sizes check box in the Advanced category in the Word Options dialog box, you don't need to specify scaling for A4 documents you're printing on letter paper (or vice versa).

Print to a File

Sometimes, you may need to print a document to a print file rather than print it to paper. The print file is a file that describes how the printout should look—a file that contains a printed version of the Word document. You can then send or take the print file to another computer for printing. For example, you might use a specialist print shop for high-quality printouts.

To print to a file, select the Print To File check box. When you click the OK button in the Print dialog box, Word displays the Print To File dialog box. Type or paste the path and filename for the print file in the File Name text box, and then click the OK button.

Choose Further Options in the Printer Properties Dialog Box

You can choose further options by clicking the Properties button in the Print dialog box and working in the Properties dialog box for the printer. The contents of the Properties dialog box vary greatly depending on the printer (Figure 8-3 shows an example), but you'll often find options such as these:

- Printing in back-to-front order instead of the default front-to-back order. (Back-to-front order is sometimes useful for photocopying tasks.)
- Printing multiple pages on the same sheet of paper.
- Using different paper trays. For example, you might need to print invoices on letterhead loaded into a different paper tray than plain paper.

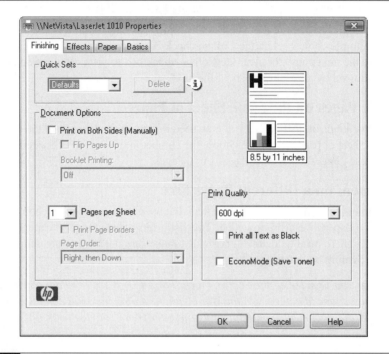

FIGURE 8-3 The settings in the Properties dialog box for a printer depend on the printer's capabilities.

- Using different print quality—for example, 300 dpi (dots per inch) instead of 600 dpi.

After choosing options, click the OK button. Word closes the Properties dialog box.

NOTE *You can also display the Properties dialog box for the printer by clicking the Options button on any of the tabs in the Page Setup dialog box.*

Print on the Back and Front of Paper

If you need to produce documents printed on both sides, but you don't have a printer capable of duplexing (printing on both sides), you can use Word's Manual Duplex option. Follow these steps:

1. In the Print dialog box, select the Manual Duplex check box.

2. Check that you have suitable duplex options set:

- Click the Options button. Word displays the Word Options dialog box.
- Click the Advanced category. Word displays the Advanced options.

■ In the Print area, select the Print On Front Of The Sheet For Duplex Printing check box. Make sure the Print On Back Of The Sheet For Duplex Printing check box is cleared.

3. Click the Print button. Word prints the odd-numbered pages in reverse order and then displays the dialog box shown here.

4. Take the printout from the printer, and then put the sheets in the printer's paper tray so that the side that wasn't printed will be printed this time. Most printers have an icon near the paper tray indicating which side of the paper the printer prints on—for example, an arrow pointing up or pointing down.

5. Click the OK button. Word prints the even-numbered pages of the printout on the backs of the pages you reinserted.

NOTE   *If you forget to select the Print On Front Of The Sheet For Duplex Printing check box before printing with the Manual Duplex check box selected, you'll need to reverse the order of the printouts when you put the printout back in the paper tray in step 4.*

8

Put the Quick Print Button on the Quick Access Toolbar for Instant Printing

If you often need to print a whole document, going through the Print dialog box is a waste of time. Instead, you can put the Quick Print button on the Quick Access Toolbar for one-click printing. To do so, click the Customize Quick Access Toolbar button (the drop-down button at the right end of the Quick Access Toolbar), and then choose Quick Print from the drop-down menu, selecting the check box next to the Quick Print item.

You can then print instantly by clicking the Quick Print button on the Quick Access toolbar. Word prints the active document with the existing print settings without displaying the Print dialog box.

Print Directly from the Desktop or a Windows Explorer Window

If you typically print a Word document after you've finished creating or editing it, printing from Word tends to be most convenient. But if you need to quickly print a completed document, you can do so directly from your Desktop (if the file is stored there) or from a Windows Explorer window.

To print a document to your default printer, right-click the document file on your Desktop or in the Windows Explorer window, and then choose Print from the context menu. Windows opens the document in Word, prints it, and then closes it automatically.

You can use a similar technique to print to different printers by creating Desktop shortcuts to the printers you want to use. To create Desktop shortcuts to printers, follow these steps:

1. Open the Printers window (on Windows Vista) or the Printers And Faxes window (on Windows XP):

   ■ On Windows Vista, choose Start | Printers. If no Printers item appears on the Start menu, choose Start | Control Panel, click the Classic View item in the left pane if it's not already selected, and then double-click the Printers item.

   ■ On Windows XP, choose Start | Printers And Faxes. If no Printers And Faxes item appears on the Start menu, choose Start | Control Panel, click the Switch To Classic View item in the Control Panel task pane if Control Panel is in Category view, and then double-click the Printers And Faxes item.

2. Right-click the desired printer, and then choose Create Shortcut from the context menu.

   ■ Windows Vista automatically creates the shortcut on the Desktop.

   ■ Windows XP tells you it cannot create a shortcut in the Printers And Faxes folder and asks if you want to create it on the Desktop instead. Click the Yes button.

3. Repeat step 2 for each printer for which you need a shortcut.

4. Click the Close button (the × button). Windows closes the Printers window or the Printers And Faxes window.

You can now print by dragging a document from a Windows Explorer window (or the Desktop) to the printer shortcut on the Desktop.

 *If you prefer not to create printer shortcuts on your Desktop, you can simply open the Printers window (on Windows Vista) or the Printers And Faxes window (on Windows XP), and then drag documents to the printer entries in that window to print.*

Fax a Document

If you have Windows Vista Business Edition, Windows Vista Ultimate Edition, or Windows Vista Enterprise Edition, you can fax documents directly from your PC.

To fax a document, follow these steps:

1. Complete the document you want to fax. For example, you might use one of Word's fax templates as the basis for the fax.

2. Press CTRL-P or click the Office Button and then click Print. Word displays the Print dialog box.

3. In the Name drop-down list, select the Fax item.

4. Choose any other options needed. For example, specify the range of pages to include in the fax.

5. Click the OK button. Word closes the Print dialog box and displays the New Fax window, shown here.

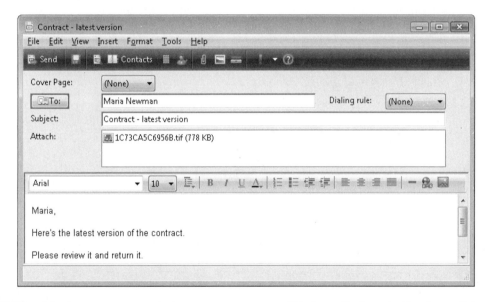

8

NOTE *The first time you use faxing on your computer, Windows displays the Fax Setup dialog box. Click the Connect To A Fax Modem button to use a fax modem attached to your computer, or click the Connect To A Fax Server On My Network button to connect to a fax server on your network. Follow through the process of setting up the fax modem or fax server for your computer.*

6. In the Cover Page drop-down list, choose whether to include a cover page for the fax.

NOTE *The first time you use a cover page, Windows walks you through the process of entering information about yourself—your name, fax number, title, company, and so on—that Windows stores for use in future faxes. Windows calls this data "sender information."*

7. Enter the recipient's name in the To text box. You can click the To button and then use the Select Recipients dialog box to choose recipients from your Windows address book, or simply type the phone number in the text box.

8. In the Dialing Rule drop-down list, choose any drop-down list that you need to use for dialing the fax call. For example, you might use a rule that dials 9 to get an outside line.

9. Type a subject in the Subject text box.

10. Type any message required in the main text box at the bottom of the window.

11. Click the Send button. Windows sends the fax, and then returns you to the Word document.

Chapter 9

Make Word Easier to Use

How to...

- Configure essential editing options
- Make the most of AutoCorrect entries and exceptions
- Create a new template
- Create custom styles
- Work with building blocks
- Customize the Quick Access Toolbar
- Customize the status bar
- Customize keyboard shortcuts
- Install add-ins

As you've seen from the major changes to the interface, Microsoft has made huge efforts to make Word 2007 as easy to use as possible. In particular, the Ribbon brings to the fore some commands that used to be hard to find, while removing various little-used and more advanced commands from immediate view.

Needless to say, these changes don't suit everyone. This chapter shows you how to make Word easier to use, starting with configuring essential editing options and then moving along to using the powerful AutoCorrect feature to the full. After that, you'll learn how to create templates and custom styles, and how to use building blocks to assemble documents more quickly. Finally, the chapter shows you how to customize the Quick Access Toolbar with the buttons you need most, make the status bar show only the information you want, assign shortcuts to commands you want to run from the keyboard, and install add-ins to increase Word's functionality.

Configure Essential Editing Options

Word comes set to watch as you enter and edit text and automatically make changes based on what it thinks you're trying to do. Members of Microsoft's focus groups presumably found this behavior desirable—but most people in the real world object to some or all of Word's interventions.

Many people grit their teeth, let Word have its head, and then use Undo to remove the change or formatting Word has applied. But it's much better—and less frustrating—to configure Word's editing options so that they suit you.

The main culprits are AutoCorrect, AutoFormat As You Type, and Smart Cut and Paste. This section shows you how to configure these potentially disruptive features so that they help you rather than drive you crazy with their interference.

Bring AutoCorrect Under Your Control

AutoCorrect automatically replaces designated terms with their replacement terms as you type. An AutoCorrect entry consists of a text term and the replacement item for it. The replacement item can be text only (so that it takes on whatever formatting the text currently has) or formatted text (so that AutoCorrect inserts text with particular formatting). An entry can also include graphics, tables, and other Word elements. For example, you could create an AutoCorrect entry that replaced a term with your company's name, address, and logo.

Word comes with several hundred built-in AutoCorrect entries that fix common typing errors (for example, Word changes "abbout" to "about") and grammatical errors (for example, changing "should of had" to "should have had"), and make it easier to enter common symbols (for example, changing "(r)" to "®"). You can create as many of your own AutoCorrect entries as you like.

When you type a character that might indicate the end of a word, AutoCorrect compares the last group of characters with its list of entries. If there's a match, AutoCorrect replaces the term with its replacement text.

AutoCorrect's text-replacement feature, which is called Replace Text As You Type, is widely popular and useful, although some people choose to delete some of its built-in terms because they trigger them inadvertently. (You'll learn how to add and delete AutoCorrect entries later in this chapter.)

AutoCorrect's other features, which include capitalizing the first letter of any table cell and of any word that AutoCorrect thinks is the first in a sentence, tend to be less useful. If you want to adjust AutoCorrect settings, follow these steps:

1. Click the Office Button, and then click Word Options. Word displays the Word Options dialog box.

2. In the left panel, click the Proofing category, and then click the AutoCorrect Options button. Word displays the AutoCorrect dialog box (see Figure 9-1).

3. Clear the check box for any AutoCorrect feature you don't want to use. Here are recommendations:

- **Correct TWo INitial CApitals**   Select this check box, as this feature is usually helpful. You can define exceptions for words you need to use that have two initial capitals (for example, IDs).

- **Correct Accidental Usage Of cAPS LOCK Key**   Select this check box, because this feature works well. If Word thinks you've got Caps Lock on unintentionally (for example, if you've typed *tODAY*), it turns Caps Lock off and reverses the case of the letters you typed.

- **Capitalize Names Of Days**   Select this check box unless you need to enter the names of days starting with a lowercase letter.

- **Capitalize First Letter Of Sentences**   If you type your work in full sentences, this feature works pretty well. But if you jot down partial sentences, each starting in a new paragraph, the unwanted capitalization can drive you mad. If you find that AutoCorrect thinks that an abbreviation you type indicates the end of a sentence, create an AutoCorrect exception for the abbreviation. See the section "Create AutoCorrect Exceptions," later in this chapter.

9

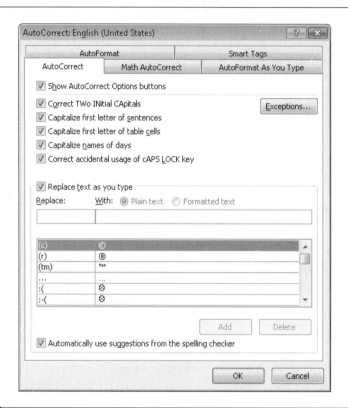

FIGURE 9-1   In the AutoCorrect Options dialog box you can adjust AutoCorrect and Math AutoCorrect settings plus AutoFormat As You Type, AutoFormat, and Smart Tags.

- ■ **Replace Text As You Type**   Select this check box so that you can use AutoCorrect's most helpful feature. If you find you trigger some of Word's existing AutoCorrect entries unintentionally, delete them. (See the section "Delete an AutoCorrect Entry," later in this chapter).

4. If you want Word to display an AutoCorrect Options button after each change it makes, select the Show AutoCorrect Options Buttons check box. The button appears as a small blue underline (as shown on the left here) until you move the mouse pointer over it to produce a button, which you then click to display a menu that lets you undo the correction or stop AutoCorrect from making the correction again (as shown on the right here).

NOTE *You'll find the AutoCorrect options buttons useful if you haven't customized your AutoCorrect list, because the buttons let you instantly delete any AutoCorrect entries that you stumble upon and decide you don't want to keep. Once you've deleted any AutoCorrect entries that bug you, you'll probably want to suppress the AutoCorrect options buttons, because having buttons popping out whenever you move the mouse pointer around the Word window tends to be distracting.*

5. Select the Automatically Use Suggestions From The Spelling Checker check box if you want AutoCorrect to use suggestions from the spell checker to augment its built-in entries. This behavior is usually helpful.

Leave the AutoCorrect dialog box open so that you can work through the next section.

Set Up Math AutoCorrect If You Need It

If your documents include math symbols or expressions, click the Math AutoCorrect tab of the AutoCorrect dialog box and make sure it's set up for your needs:

- **Use Math AutoCorrect Rules Outside Of Math Regions**   Select this check box if you want to be able to use Math AutoCorrect entries in regular document areas as well as in math regions (such as equations you insert by choosing Insert | Symbols | Equation). For example, if you need to describe the effect of an equation in a text paragraph, selecting this check box will be helpful. Otherwise, clear this check box.

- **Replace Text As You Type**   Select this check box so that you can use Math AutoCorrect.

- **Recognized Functions**   To verify or change the list of math-related functions that Math AutoCorrect recognizes and doesn't italicize, click this button, and then work in the Recognized Math Functions dialog box, shown here. Normally, you'll want to add extra functions to this list, but you can remove functions from Word's built-in list if you need to.

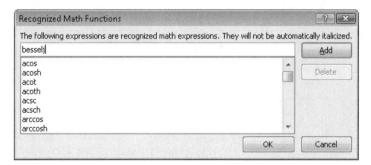

Leave the AutoCorrect dialog box open so that you can work through the next section.

Tame AutoFormat As You Type

If you value your sanity, take a few minutes to configure the AutoFormat As You Type feature, because Word's standard settings cause this feature to make changes frequently as you type in your documents.

To configure AutoFormat As You Type, follow these steps:

1. In the AutoCorrect dialog box, click the AutoFormat As You Type tab to bring it to the front (see Figure 9-2).

2. Choose which Replace As You Type options to use. These options are like AutoCorrect entries but a little more sophisticated:

   ■ **"Straight Quotes" With "Smart Quotes"** Select this check box to have Word replace straight single (') and double (") quotation marks with *smart quotes*, quotes that curl in the correct directions for typeset quotes. This feature is usually helpful, but you may need to turn it off if you're typing measurements with feet and inch marks (for example, 6'4") or working with HTML or another programming language.

   ■ **Ordinals (1st) With Superscript** Select this check box to have Word replace ordinal numbers (1st, 2nd, and so on) you type using regular characters with superscript characters, as in this sentence. This feature is usually helpful.

   ■ **Fractions (1/2) With Fraction Character (½)** Select this check box to have Word replace common fractions you type (using a number, a forward slash, and another number) with real fraction characters. This feature is usually helpful.

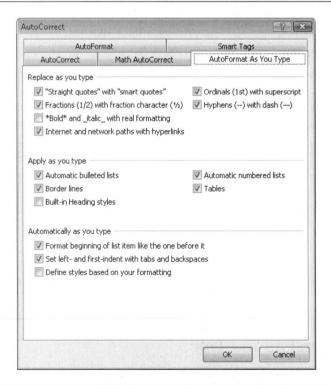

FIGURE 9-2 AutoFormat As You Type mixes helpful features with meddling features.

■ **Hyphens (--) With Dash (—)**   Select this check box to have Word replace two hyphens between words with an em dash. This feature gives you an easy way to enter em dashes without using the Symbol gallery.

■ ***Bold* And _Italic_ With Real Formatting**   Select this check box to have Word substitute boldface for a word entered with an asterisk before and after it ("*Where*?") and italic for a word entered between underscores ("_Cerveza_ means beer."). These are two Internet-inspired formatting conventions for text-only documents. If you deal with such documents, this feature may be useful. Otherwise, you can apply boldface and italic more easily via keyboard shortcuts (see Chapter 4).

■ **Internet And Network Paths With Hyperlinks**   Select this check box to make Word change URLs (for example, http://www.mcgraw-hill.com) and network paths (for example, \\server\drive) into live hyperlinks in the formatted document. Live hyperlinks in Word documents can be helpful if you need to launch a browser or Explorer window from a document, but they get in the way if you're creating conventional documents.

3. In the Apply As You Type area, choose whether to let AutoFormat apply styles as you type. Most people experience these options as Word unexpectedly changing text they've typed and so prefer to turn these options off. But if you know what triggers these features, you may be able to turn them to your advantage.

■ **Automatic Bulleted Lists**   At the beginning of a paragraph, type an asterisk, a hyphen, or a greater-than sign followed by a space or tab.

■ **Automatic Numbered Lists**   At the beginning of a paragraph, type a number or letter followed by a period or closing parenthesis, and then either a space or a tab.

■ **Border Lines**   At the beginning of a paragraph, type three or more hyphens (for a thin line), underscores (for a thick line), asterisks (for a dotted line), tildes (for a zigzag line), equal signs (for a double line), or hash marks (for two thin lines with a thick line between them), and then press ENTER.

■ **Tables**   At the beginning of a paragraph, type plus signs and hyphens in the code for the type of table you want. A plus sign indicates a column, and the number of hyphens between the plus signs indicates the relative width of the columns. For example, typing +---+---+----------+ and pressing ENTER produces a three-column table with the first two columns narrow and the third column wider.

■ **Built-In Heading Styles**   AutoFormat applies the built-in Heading styles when you type an extra blank paragraph before and after a short paragraph. (Chapter 4 explains styles.) For Heading 1 style, press ENTER twice, type a short paragraph, and press ENTER twice more. For Heading 2 style, press ENTER twice, type a tab and a short paragraph, and press ENTER twice more. For Heading 3 style, do the same, but type two tabs; for Heading 4, type three tabs, and so on. Word removes the tabs and the extra paragraph after the heading paragraph when it applies the style. A problem is that the extra paragraph before the heading paragraph remains.

9

4. In the Automatically As You Type area, choose whether to let AutoFormat automatically format other items as you type them. Unless you find that one of these features is really useful to you, it's best to turn them all off.

■ **Format Beginning Of List Item Like The One Before It**   Select this check box to make Word apply formatting to the beginning of a list item so that it matches the previous list item. For example, say you create a bulleted list, and then apply bold to the first few words. With this feature on, when you create a new paragraph in the list, Word automatically switches bold on at the beginning of the paragraph. (You'll need to switch bold off after typing the first few words—assuming you want bold at all.)

■ **Set Left- And First-Indent With Tabs And Backspaces**   Select this check box to make Word move the left indent and first-line indent to the left when you press Backspace when the insertion point is at the beginning of a blank paragraph. Similarly, you can move the indents to the right by pressing Tab. This feature seems to work only intermittently. Normally, it's easier to set indents manually.

■ **Define Styles Based On Your Formatting**   Select this check box to have Word automatically apply a style when it thinks you should have applied one. For example, if you create a short paragraph, apply boldface and a larger font, and add space before and after, Word may decide you're trying to create a heading. Word then applies a Heading style without consulting you. With ingenuity, you can turn this feature to your advantage, but applying styles manually (see Chapter 4) is not only easier and faster but also gives you better control. You'll probably want to clear this check box.

5. Click the OK button. Word closes the AutoCorrect Options dialog box.

6. Click the OK button. Word closes the Word Options dialog box.

The AutoFormat As You Type features take effect immediately. So if you chose to leave some of the features turned on, try them out, and make sure they work to your satisfaction.

Configure Paste Options

When you paste formatted text into a document, Word has to decide whether to apply the formatting the text originally had (when you cut or copied it) or the formatting the destination has. Frequently, Word makes the wrong choice, and you need to use the Paste Options Smart Tag to change the formatting.

If you find yourself making these changes all the time, configure the paste options so that Word uses your preferred form of pasting. You'll still need to change it now and then, but less frequently overall.

To configure paste options, follow these steps:

1. Click the Office Button, and then click Word Options. Word displays the Word Options dialog box.

2. In the left panel, click the Advanced category. Word displays the Advanced options. Scroll down a little so that you can see all of the Cut, Copy, And Paste options.

3. In the first four drop-down lists, select your preferred pasting options.

- **Pasting Within The Same Document**   In this drop-down list, you can choose Keep Source Formatting to keep the text's original formatting, Match Destination Formatting to make the pasted text take on the formatting of the paragraph into which you paste it, or Keep Text Only to paste only the text with no formatting or other objects.

- **Pasting Between Documents**   In this drop-down list, you can choose Keep Source Formatting to keep the text's original formatting, Use Destination Styles to use the style definitions in the destination document, Match Destination Formatting to make the pasted text take on the formatting of the paragraph into which you paste it, or Keep Text Only to paste only the text with no formatting or other objects.

- **Pasting Between Documents When Style Definitions Conflict**   In this drop-down list, choose what should happen when what you're pasting has a style that appears in both the source document and the destination document but has a different look in each. Choose Keep Source Formatting to keep the text's original formatting, Use Destination Styles to keep the style's name but change the formatting to that of the style in the destination document (often a good choice), Match Destination Formatting to make the pasted text take on the formatting of the paragraph into which you paste it, or Keep Text Only to paste only the text with no formatting or other objects.

- **Pasting From Other Programs**   In this drop-down list, you can choose Keep Source Formatting to keep the text's original formatting, Match Destination Formatting to make the pasted text take on the formatting of the paragraph into which you paste it, or Keep Text Only to paste only the text with no formatting or other objects.

4. Select the Keep Bullets And Numbers When Pasting With Keep Text Only check box if you want Word to retain bullets or numbers when you paste text using Keep Text Only. If you paste numbered lists from e-mail or text-only notes, this setting can be useful.

5. Select the Use Smart Cut And Paste check box, and then click the Settings button next to it. Word displays the Settings dialog box, shown here. The following are the most important settings:

- **Adjust Sentence And Word Spacing Automatically**   Select this check box if you want Word to add and remove spaces automatically when you paste in text. For example, if you paste a sentence just after a period, Word adds a space between the period and the start of the sentence. This setting is usually helpful.

- **Adjust Paragraph Spacing On Paste**   Select this check box if you want Word to adjust the space before and after paragraphs when you paste text. You'll usually get better results by applying a style (see Chapter 4) to the pasted text.

■ **Merge Pasted Lists With Surrounding Lists**   Select this check box if you want Word to integrate any pasted list paragraph into the list in which you paste it. This setting is useful if you typically work with one-level lists. But if you need to be able to paste bulleted sublists into numbered lists, clear this check box.

6. Click the OK button. Word closes the Settings dialog box.

7. Click the OK button. Word closes the Word Options dialog box.

Before you forget, try some copy and paste operations to make sure that the settings you've chosen suit your working style. If not, try changing the settings.

Save Time and Keystrokes with AutoCorrect Entries and Exceptions

Would you like to be able to type faster and more accurately? If so, be sure to use AutoCorrect to the full.

Most people think of AutoCorrect as a tool for correcting errors. Given that AutoCorrect's name suggests just that, and that a typical Word user's experience of AutoCorrect is it jumping in to correct an error, that's not surprising. But AutoCorrect's Replace Text As You Type feature is a great way to enter standard text without typing it in full.

Understand What AutoCorrect Is and How It Works

AutoCorrect is a mechanism that watches as you type and replaces any predefined group of characters with its designated "correction." Each time you press a key that might mark the end of a word, AutoCorrect checks to see if the previous group of characters matches one of its entries. If so, it replaces the characters.

NOTE   *That bit about "key that might mark the end of a word" seems vague. That's because AutoCorrect checks for an entry when you press SPACEBAR, TAB, CTRL-ENTER (creating a page break), SHIFT-ENTER (creating a line break), or type a punctuation mark (including question marks, exclamation points, and quotes as well as commas, periods, semicolons, and colons), or even a parenthesis or a vertical bar (or "pipe character": |).*

Word uses two types of AutoCorrect entries:

■ **Plain Text Entries**   A plain text entry consists of only text and can be up to 255 characters long. Word shares these entries with the other Office applications (for example, Excel and PowerPoint). The applications store these entries in a text file (see the upcoming sidebar "Where AutoCorrect Entries Are Stored" for details).

■ **Formatted Entries**   A formatted entry consists of text and formatting, other objects (for example, shapes), or a combination of them. Formatted entries can be as long as you like. Word stores these entries in the Normal template.

The name of an AutoCorrect entry can be up to 31 characters long, either a single word or multiple words.

Create AutoCorrect Entries

To create an AutoCorrect entry, follow these steps:

1. If the replacement text (or other element—for example, a graphic) for the AutoCorrect entry is in a Word document, select it. If the replacement text is in another program, select it, and then copy it to the Clipboard (for example, press CTRL-C).

2. Click the Office Button, and then click Word Options. Word displays the Word Options dialog box.

3. In the left panel, click the Proofing category, and then click the AutoCorrect Options button. Word displays the AutoCorrect dialog box (see Figure 9-3).

■ If you made a selection in step 1, it appears in the With text box.

■ If the selection contains formatting, Word selects the Formatted Text option button automatically.

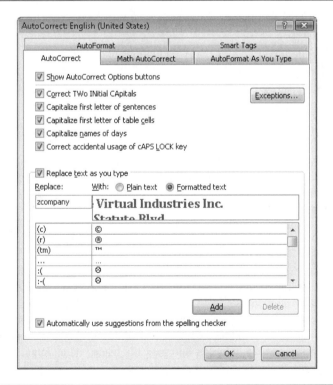

FIGURE 9-3   Create AutoCorrect entries to help you enter text more quickly and accurately.

TIP

Having to go through the Word Options dialog box to access the AutoCorrect dialog box is awkward and slow—especially as you must close the Word Options dialog box after you close the AutoCorrect dialog box. If you create many AutoCorrect entries (as you should), put the AutoCorrect Options command on the Quick Access Toolbar (see the section "Put Any Command on the Quick Access Toolbar or Rearrange Items," later in this chapter) or assign it to a convenient keyboard shortcut (see the section "Customize Keyboard Shortcuts," later in this chapter) so that you can open it instantly.

4. In the Replace text box, type the name you want to give the AutoCorrect entry. This name must be 31 characters or fewer and normally shouldn't be a real word you'll ever type.

5. In the With text box, type or paste (press CTRL-V) the replacement text. (If you made a selection in step 1, skip this step.)

6. Click the Add button. Word adds the AutoCorrect entry.

NOTE

If there's already an AutoCorrect entry with the name you use, Word changes the Add button to a Replace button. When you click this button, Word prompts you to decide whether to replace the existing AutoCorrect entry.

7. Click the OK button. Word closes the AutoCorrect dialog box, returning you to the Word Options dialog box.

8. Click the OK button. Word closes the Word Options dialog box.

Delete an AutoCorrect Entry

To delete an AutoCorrect entry, follow these steps:

1. Open the AutoCorrect dialog box as discussed in the previous section.

2. Select the entry you want to delete. The easiest way to reach the entry is to type the first few letters of its name in the Replace text box, but you can also simply scroll down the list box of entries and then click the entry.

3. Click the Delete button. Word deletes the entry.

Create AutoCorrect Exceptions

To prevent AutoCorrect's Capitalize First Letter Of Sentences feature from capitalizing the first letter of the word after an abbreviation, Word includes a list of abbreviations and other terms ending with a period that AutoCorrect should ignore. These are called *AutoCorrect exceptions*.

You can add your own exceptions, or delete existing ones, as necessary. Word also keeps a list of initial-caps exceptions, terms that the Correct TWo INitial CApitals feature shouldn't fix, and a list of other corrections, which it builds automatically when you undo a correction that AutoCorrect has made.

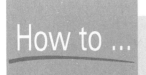

Choose Effective Names for AutoCorrect Entries

When choosing the name for an AutoCorrect entry, avoid using any real word that you need to type in your documents. Otherwise, each time you type that word, AutoCorrect will change it. The exception to this rule is if you want to prevent yourself from using a word; in that case, AutoCorrect can help you. For example, if your company's style guide frowns on the phrase "prior to," you might create an AutoCorrect entry that changes "prior to" to "before."

Usually it's best to create AutoCorrect terms that are abbreviations of the words or phrases that replace them: *ind* for *industry*, *inds* for *industries*, *indl* for *industrial*, and so on. You might also choose to start each AutoCorrect term with a particular character and use a mnemonic term unabbreviated. For example, the term *zcompany* might expand to your full company name (and perhaps address), *zboss* to your boss's name (and maybe title), and the like.

However carefully you name your AutoCorrect entries, you may still trigger them unintentionally at times—for example, when you're working in tables, where AutoCorrect fires when you move the insertion point from one cell to another using the keyboard. (It doesn't matter whether you press TAB, SHIFT-TAB, or an arrow key to move the keyboard from cell to cell: Any of these triggers an AutoCorrect check.) If the table includes an abbreviation or other text that doesn't usually appear in your documents, and that abbreviation or text matches an AutoCorrect term, Word substitutes the replacement text. The only workaround is to move the insertion point using the mouse rather than the keyboard.

9

To see your current lists of AutoCorrect exceptions, click the Exceptions button on the AutoCorrect tab of the AutoCorrect dialog box, and then click the appropriate tab in the AutoCorrect Exceptions dialog box (shown here).

Where AutoCorrect Entries Are Stored

Word and the other Office programs manage AutoCorrect entries automatically for you, so you don't usually need to worry about where AutoCorrect entries are stored. But if you create many AutoCorrect entries, it's a good idea to back them up so that you can restore them if your computer suffers a disaster or copy them to other computers that you use.

The Office programs store unformatted (text-only) AutoCorrect entries in a file named MS*ONNNN*.acl, where *NNNN* is the four-digit locale ID (LCID) that identifies the language locale you're using. The LCID for U.S. English is 1033, so the AutoCorrect file for U.S. English entries is named MSO1033.acl. The LCID for Canadian English is 4105; for U.K. English, 2057; and for Australian English, 3081. If you use multiple languages with the Office programs, you'll have an ACL file for each language in which you create AutoCorrect entries.

The ACL files are stored in the *%userprofile%*\AppData\Roaming\Microsoft\Office folder, where *%userprofile%* is the Windows environment variable that stores the path of the folder that contains your user profile. (Windows uses environment variables to store information that varies from one computer to another but needs to be kept easily accessible.)

To access this folder, press WINDOWS KEY-R, type *%userprofile%*\AppData\Roaming\ Microsoft\Office (or use Windows' type-down feature to select each folder after you type the first part of its name), and then press ENTER.

Word stores formatted AutoCorrect entries in your Normal template, *Normal.dotm*. Word loads *Normal.dotm* automatically at start-up, so your AutoCorrect entries are always available. Word stores *Normal.dotm* in the *%userprofile%*\AppData\Roaming\Microsoft\ Templates folder. It's a good idea to back up *Normal.dotm* as well.

To delete an existing entry, click it in the list, and then click the Delete button. To add an entry, type it in the Don't Capitalize After text box (on the First Letter tab) or the Don't Correct text box (on the INitial CAps tab or the Other Corrections tab), and then click the Add button.

Each tab in the AutoCorrect Exceptions dialog box includes an Automatically Add Words To List check box that is selected by default. This means that Word creates AutoCorrect exceptions automatically when you undo a correction that AutoCorrect has made. You can undo a correction either immediately by clicking the Undo button, pressing CTRL-Z, or by clicking the AutoCorrect Options button for the correction and choosing the Stop Automatically Correcting item from the pop-up menu.

Create a New Template

The easiest way to save time and effort in Word is to use a suitable template for each new document you create. A template is a document that you use to create other documents. The template contains all the common features of the type of document you're creating.

For example, a customer service letter template may contain your company's name and address, a formatted area for the recipient's name and address, a subject line, a partial salutation ("Dear _____,"), the standard format for the information to be imparted, and a closing and sender's name. By filling in the recipient's name and address, the salutation, and other details, you can quickly create a finished letter without any unnecessary typing.

To create a new template, follow these steps:

1. Click the Office Button, and then click New. Word displays the New Document dialog box.

2. Take one of the following actions:

- In the Templates list on the left, select the Installed Templates item. In the Installed Templates list in the middle of the dialog box, choose the template on which you want to base the new template. Select the Template option button in the Create New area in the lower-right corner, and then click the Create button.

- In the Templates list on the left, select the My Templates item. Word displays the New dialog box. Choose the template on which you want to base the new template, select the Template option button in the Create New area in the lower-right corner, and then click the OK button.

3. In the new template that Word creates, enter the text and objects that the template needs, and apply any required formatting.

4. Click the Office Button, and then click Save. Word displays the Save As dialog box, which it switches automatically to your Templates folder to make sure that you save the template in the right place for use.

5. Type the name for the template. If the template is visually distinctive, and you want to create a thumbnail picture to help you or others identify it in the New dialog box, select the Save Thumbnail check box.

6. Verify that Word Template is selected in the Save As Type drop-down list.

7. Click the Save button. Word saves the template.

8. Click the Office Button, and then click Close.

You can now base a new document on your template.

9

 **Turn a Document into a Template**

You may sometimes find that you've created a document that you want to turn into a template. At the file level, the differences between a document and a template are small. But usually, if you're using one file as the basis for another file, it's neater to use a template than a document—even though Word 2007 makes it easy to base a new document on an existing document.

Templates have two main advantages:

■ Word helps you organize the templates you've created into your user templates folder. From here, you can easily back up all your templates.

■ Word displays all your templates in the New dialog box, so you can easily see which templates you have available.

To turn a document into a template, click the Office Button, and then click Save As. In the Save As Type drop-down list, select the Word Template item. You'll need to switch manually to your user templates folder—otherwise, Word saves the template in your current folder.

Create Custom Styles

As you saw in Chapter 4, a style is a collection of formatting—for example, a paragraph style typically contains all the formatting required for a paragraph in a particular style (say, Heading 1 or Body Text). In your templates, you can use the many and varied styles that Word provides, but you may also want to create custom styles of your own so that you have exactly the styles you want. (Alternatively, you can adapt Word's built-in styles to your needs.)

You can create a style either manually, setting all the formatting one step at a time, or by using the formatting on existing text.

Create a Style Manually

To create a style manually, follow these steps:

1. Choose Home | Styles | Styles (click the tiny button with the arrow at the right end of the Styles bar) or press CTRL-ALT-SHIFT-S. Word displays the Styles pane.

2. Click the style on which you want to base the new style, and then click the New Style button in the lower-left corner. Word displays the larger version of the Create New Style From Formatting dialog box (see Figure 9-4).

3. In the Style Type drop-down list, choose Paragraph, Character, Linked (Paragraph And Character), Table, or List, as appropriate. (See the section "Format Long Documents Efficiently" in Chapter 4 for an explanation of the five style types.)

FIGURE 9-4   Use the larger version of the Create New Style From Formatting dialog box to create a style by example.

4. The Style Based On drop-down list shows the existing style that you chose in step 2. Normally, you won't need to change this choice.

5. In the Style For Following Paragraph drop-down list, select the style you want Word to use for the following paragraph. (This setting applies only to Paragraph styles and Linked styles.)

6. Use the controls in the Formatting section to change the formatting of the style. For example:

- Use the top line of controls to choose the font and font size, attributes (bold, italic, and underline), and color.

- Use the second line of controls to apply alignment, line spacing and paragraph spacing, and indentation.

- For other types of formatting, click the Format button; choose Font, Paragraph, Tabs, Border, Language, Frame, Numbering, or Shortcut Key from the drop-down menu; and then work in the resulting dialog box.

NOTE *The Frame item on the Format drop-down menu opens the Frame dialog box, which you can use to create a frame, a text box–like object for positioning text out of the main document flow. The Shortcut Key item opens the Customize Keyboard dialog box so that you can assign a keyboard shortcut to the style. See the section "Customize Keyboard Shortcuts," later in this chapter, for instructions on using this dialog box.*

7. At the bottom of the dialog box, select the New Documents Based On This Template option button if you want to save the new style in the document's template rather than in the document (as the Only In This Document option button does). By saving the style in the template, you make it available for any open document that has this template attached.

8. Verify that the Automatically Update check box is cleared.

9. Select the Add To Quick Style List check box if you want to add the style to your Quick Style list. Doing so is usually helpful.

10. Click the OK button. Word closes the Create New Style From Formatting dialog box and creates the style.

11. Click the Save button on the Quick Access Toolbar. Word saves any unsaved changes to the document and prompts you to save changes to the template.

12. Click the Yes button. Word saves the changes.

Create a Style by Example

Word also lets you create a style *by example*—in other words, by setting up some text with the formatting you want the style to have, and then creating a style from that formatting. You may find this to be a convenient way of creating a style, especially if you're designing a document or template on the fly.

To create a style by example, follow these steps:

1. Create some text and apply to it exactly the formatting you want the style to have. For example:

■ For a character style, choose a font and the font size, weight, and color.

■ For a paragraph style or linked style, choose the font attributes, and also adjust the line spacing, the amount of space before and after the paragraph, and text-flow options (such as whether Word should keep the paragraph with the next paragraph or keep paragraphs together). You may also need to apply language formatting, border formatting, or shading.

2. Select the formatted text, right-click the selection, and then choose Styles | Save Selection As A New Quick Style from the context menu. Word displays the smaller version of the Create New Style From Formatting dialog box, as shown here.

3. In the Name text box, type the name you want to give the style.

TIP *At this point, you can simply click the OK button to create the style in the current document, but normally it's best to continue and save the style in the template.*

4. Click the Modify button. Word displays the larger version of the Create New Style From Formatting dialog box. From here on, the process is the same as explained in step 3 onward in the previous section.

Work with Building Blocks

By creating templates as described in the previous section, you can give yourself a variety of partially or mostly complete document types that you can quickly turn into complete documents. But sometimes you'll need to reuse smaller sections of boilerplate text (or other boilerplate objects). Word provides two features for doing so: building blocks (discussed in this section) and AutoCorrect (discussed previously in this chapter).

A *building block* is simply a chunk of text or an object saved for future use. Word comes with a useful number of building blocks, which you can use or adapt; you can also create your own building blocks when you need to.

NOTE *If you've used AutoText in an earlier version of Word, you'll most likely welcome the new features that building blocks bring to the principle of reusing blocks of text. Building blocks are like AutoText—expanded to cover a wider variety of needs and contents.*

Insert a Building Block

To insert a building block in your document, follow these steps:

1. Position the insertion point where you want the building block to appear in your document.

2. Choose Insert | Text | Quick Parts | Building Blocks Organizer. Word displays the Building Blocks Organizer dialog box.

3. In the Building Blocks list box, select the item you want:

- ■ You can sort the building blocks by any column heading—Name, Gallery, Category, Template, Behavior, or Description—by clicking that column heading.

- ■ For most purposes, sorting by the Gallery column is the easiest way to find the building blocks you need.

4. Click the Insert button. Word closes the Building Blocks Organizer dialog box and inserts the building block at the position of the insertion point.

TIP *If you know the name of the building block you want to insert, you can insert it directly in the document without opening the Building Blocks Organizer dialog box. Position the insertion point where you want the block, type enough of the name to identify the building block uniquely, and then press F3. Word inserts the building block.*

Create a Building Block of Your Own

Word's preset building blocks are useful, but to get the most use out of the feature, you'll probably want to create building blocks of your own. To do so, follow these steps:

1. In a document, create the text or other object that you want to turn into a building block. Include all the formatting that the building block will need.

NOTE *If you're well organized, perhaps you'll plan your building blocks ahead of time. But what many people find is that, while creating a particular document, they build a block that they realize they can use again later. Either way, you can easily create a building block. Or, if you find yourself opening an old document so that you can reuse part of it in a new document, you should consider creating a building block from that part.*

2. Select the material for the building block.

3. Choose Insert | Text | Quick Parts | Save Selection To Quick Part Gallery. Word displays the Create New Building Block dialog box, shown here with choices made.

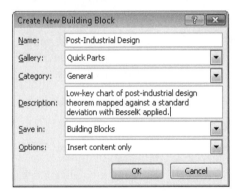

4. In the Name text box, type the descriptive name that you want to assign to the building block.

5. In the Gallery drop-down list, select the building-blocks gallery to which you want to assign this building block.

   ■ The galleries range from AutoText, Bibliographies, and Cover Pages through various kinds of page numbers to Quick Parts, Table Of Contents, Tables, Text Boxes, and Watermarks.

   ■ There are also five Custom galleries (numbered Custom 1 through Custom 5), plus a Custom version of each built-in gallery: Custom AutoText, Custom Bibliographies, and so on.

   ■ If you're not sure which gallery to use, choose the Quick Parts gallery.

6. In the Category drop-down list, select the category to which you want to assign the new building block. The category is a subdivision of the gallery, so your choices here depend on which gallery you chose in step 5. You can create a new category by clicking the drop-down list, choosing New Category, typing the name in the Create New Category dialog box that appears, and then clicking the OK button.

7. In the Description text box, type a description of the building block. This description is optional, but since it can help you and your colleagues choose the correct building block, it's normally worth filling in.

8. In the Save In drop-down list, choose the template in which to save the building block.

    ■ Word saves building blocks in the Building Blocks template by default. Usually, this is a handy place to keep your building blocks.

    ■ You can also save building blocks in the Normal template, but usually it's best not to fill this important template with unnecessary content.

9. In the Options drop-down list, choose how you want to insert the building block:

    ■ **Insert Content Only**   Select this item if you want to be able to insert the building block anywhere in a document.

    ■ **Insert Content In Its Own Paragraph**   Select this item if you want to insert the building block always as its own paragraph (rather than as part of another paragraph).

    ■ **Insert Content In Its Own Page**   Select this item if the building block is a complete page.

10. Click the OK button. Word closes the Create New Building Block dialog box and adds the building block to the template you specified.

Customize the Quick Access Toolbar

If you've worked with earlier versions of Word, you may have been reluctant to customize the interface because of the drastic nature of the changes you could make. For example, Word 2003 makes it trivially easy to remove one or more of the main menus—but you can end up making Word almost impossible to use.

With the Ribbon, Word 2007 makes customization faster and simpler but greatly reduces your options. You can change the position of the Quick Access Toolbar, and you can add controls to it and remove them from it. You can decide which items to display on the status bar. And that's about it. While there *is* a way of changing the Ribbon—for example, you can add a new tab to it containing custom commands, or suppress some or all of the built-in tabs—it's highly complex and suitable for developers only.

Change the Position of the Quick Access Toolbar

At first, the Quick Access Toolbar appears in its upper position, to the right of the Microsoft Office Button and taking up part of the title bar, as shown here.

When the Quick Access Toolbar has only a few buttons on it, as it does to start with, this is the best position for it, as it takes up a minimal amount of space. But if you add many controls to the Quick Access Toolbar (as described next), it starts taking up too much of the title bar for comfort. When this happens, click anywhere on the Ribbon, and then choose Show Quick Access Toolbar Below The Ribbon from the context menu, as shown here.

 *To customize the Quick Access Toolbar, you can also click the Customize Quick Access Toolbar button at the right end of the toolbar, and then choose Show Below The Ribbon from the drop-down menu.*

Word moves the Quick Access Toolbar to its lower position, below the Ribbon, as shown here.

 *You can also move the Quick Access Toolbar from one position to another by selecting or clearing the Show Quick Access Toolbar Below The Ribbon check box in the Customize category in the Word Options dialog box—but using the drop-down menu is faster and more convenient.*

To move the Quick Access Toolbar back to its position in the title bar, right-click the Ribbon, and then choose Show Quick Access Toolbar Above The Ribbon from the context menu. Alternatively, click the Customize Quick Access Toolbar button at the right end of the toolbar, and then choose Show Above The Ribbon from the drop-down menu.

Customize the Items on the Quick Access Toolbar

Word lets you add pretty much any command or interface item to the Quick Access Toolbar, so you can put on the Quick Access Toolbar all the commands and groups you use most frequently.

Add a Popular Button to the Quick Access Toolbar

Although the Quick Access Toolbar normally displays only three buttons at first, you can quickly display other buttons from the Quick Access Toolbar's existing set. Click the Customize Quick Access Toolbar button at the right end of the Quick Access Toolbar, and then click the item on the Customize Quick Access Toolbar menu to select its check box, as shown here.

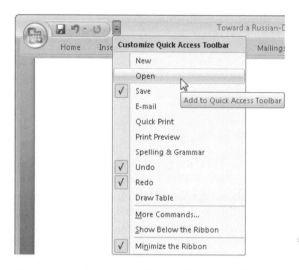

To remove an item that's currently displayed, open the Customize Quick Access Toolbar menu, and then click the item to clear its check box.

TIP   *Each time you add a button to the Quick Access Toolbar, Word puts it in the last position. To reshuffle the buttons into your preferred order, remove all the existing buttons, and then add them one by one in the order you want. Alternatively, use the Customize category in the Word Options dialog box, as described in the section after next.*

Quickly Put a Ribbon Item on the Quick Access Toolbar

To add an item that appears on the Ribbon to the Quick Access Toolbar, right-click the item, and then choose Add To Quick Access Toolbar from the drop-down menu.

NOTE   *When you add an item to the Quick Access Toolbar by right-clicking the item and then choosing Add To Quick Access Toolbar, Word makes the change in the Normal template, so it applies to all documents. You can't customize only one document using this technique. Instead, use the next technique.*

When you add a single control to the Quick Access Toolbar, it appears as a button. When you add a group, it appears as a panel that pops out when you click it, as shown here.

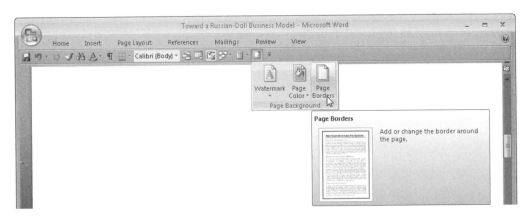

If you add so many controls that the Quick Access Toolbar is too long to fit in either the upper position or the lower position, Word displays a More Controls button at the right end of the Quick Access Toolbar. Click this button to display a panel containing the remaining controls. This arrangement works, but it's awkward to use, so it's better to keep down the number of buttons on the Quick Access Toolbar so that all are visible.

Put Any Command on the Quick Access Toolbar or Rearrange Items

To put any command on the Quick Access Toolbar, or to rearrange the items on the Quick Access Toolbar, follow these steps:

1. Right-click anywhere in the Quick Access Toolbar or in the Ribbon, and then choose Customize Quick Access Toolbar from the context menu. Alternatively, click the Customize Quick Access Toolbar button at the right end of the toolbar, and then choose More Commands from the drop-down menu. Word displays the Customize category in the Word Options dialog box (see Figure 9-5).

2. In the Customize Quick Access Toolbar drop-down list, select For All Documents if you want to apply the changes to Word itself, so that the commands are available for any document that you open. If you want to apply the changes to only an open document, select it in the drop-down list.

3. In the Choose Commands From drop-down list, select the category of command. The commands in the category appear in the list box.

   ■ The File category contains the commands on the Microsoft Office Button menu.

   ■ The Home Tab, Insert Tab, Page Layout Tab, and other categories include the commands from those tabs in the Ribbon.

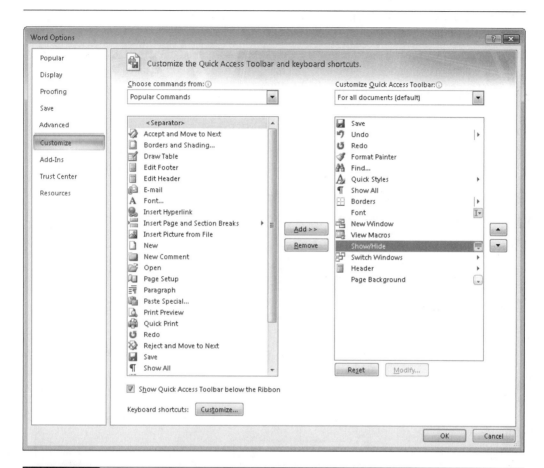

FIGURE 9-5 The Customize category in the Word Options dialog box lets you add any command to either Word itself or to just an open document.

- You'll also find Macros (custom commands you create), Commands Not In The Ribbon (which are mostly specialized commands), and All Commands. The All Commands list is extremely long, but if you know the name of the command you want, it can be a handy way of finding a command.

4. In the left list box, select the command you want to add.

5. In the right list box, select the command after which you want to add the new command. (You can rearrange the commands later, but you might as well place the command where you want it when adding it.)

6. Click the Add button. Word adds the command to the right list box.

7. If you need to remove an item from the Quick Access Toolbar, click it in the right list box, and then click the Remove button.

8. To rearrange the items on the Quick Access Toolbar, click an item in the list box, and then click the Up button or the Down button.

9. When you've finished customizing the Quick Access Toolbar, click the OK button. Word closes the Word Options dialog box, and the Quick Access Toolbar takes on the items you added.

Remove an Item from the Quick Access Toolbar

To remove an item from the Quick Access Toolbar, right-click the item on the Quick Access Toolbar, and then choose Remove From Quick Access Toolbar from the context menu.

Reset the Quick Access Toolbar to Its Original State

To reset the Quick Access Toolbar to its original selection of items, follow these steps:

1. Right-click anywhere on the Ribbon or the Quick Access Toolbar, and then choose Customize Quick Access Toolbar from the context menu. Word displays the Customization category of the Word Options dialog box.

2. In the Customize Quick Access Toolbar drop-down list, choose For All Documents if you want to affect all documents. Otherwise, choose the name of the open document you want to affect.

3. Click the Reset button. Word displays the Reset Customizations dialog box, as shown here:

4. Click the Yes button. Word resets the customizations.

5. Click the OK button. Word closes the Word Options dialog box.

Customize the Status Bar

Word 2007's streamlined status bar at first displays a minimum of information—the page readout (for example, "Page 1 of 2"), the word count, and the language (for example, "English (United States)").

As needed, the status bar displays further information or controls. For example, when Word has recovered a document, the status bar displays "Recovered." And once you've recorded a macro, the status bar displays the Macro Recording button so that you can easily record another macro.

If you want other items on the status bar, you can customize it. Follow these steps:

1. Right-click anywhere in the status bar. Word displays the Customize Status Bar menu, as shown here.

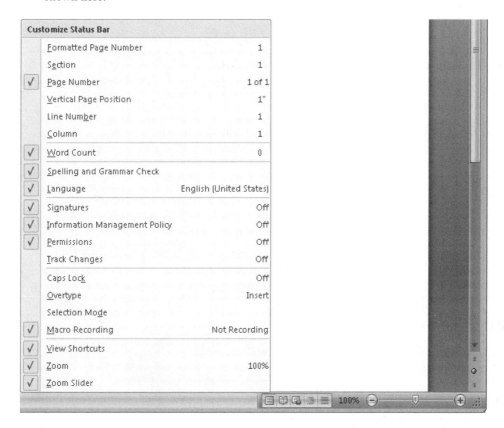

NOTE *Status-bar customizations apply to all documents.*

2. The check marks indicate which items will appear, either permanently or when they're active. Click an item to toggle its check mark on or off. Table 9-1 explains what the items are.

3. Click the status bar or click anywhere in your worksheet. Word closes the Customize Status Bar menu.

Status Bar Item	What It Displays When Turned On
Formatted Page Number	The page number using the current format (for example, "Page 2")
Section	The number of the document section the insertion point is in
Page Number	The page number in "Page 3 of 48" format
Vertical Page Position	The vertical position from the top of the page—for example, "At 4.5""
Line Number	The number of the line on the current page—for example, "15" means the 15th line from the beginning of the page
Column	The "column" number of the current character—for example, "Column: 35" indicates that the current character is the 35th from the beginning of the line
Word Count	A count of the document's total number of words (for example, "Words: 18,149") or of the selected number of words out of the total (for example, "Words: 115/18,149")
Spelling And Grammar Check	The proofing status—a book icon with a green check on it (indicating no proofing errors) or a red cross (indicating that proofing errors were found)
Language	The current text language—for example, "English (United States)"
Signatures	A seal-like indicator to show that the document has a digital signature applied; no indicator appears if there's no signature
Information Management Policy	An indicator near the left end of the status bar showing that the document has an information management policy applied to it (for example, to meet auditing or retention requirements).
Permissions	An indicator near the left end of the status bar showing that the document has permission restrictions applied (for example, to prevent unauthorized distribution).
Track Changes	A "Track Changes: On" or "Track Changes: Off" indicator
Caps Lock	A "Caps Lock" readout when the Caps Lock key on the keyboard is switched on
Overtype	An "Insert" readout when the document is in Insert mode (the normal mode for adding text); an "Overtype" readout when the document is in Overtype mode
Selection Mode	An "Extend Selection" readout when Extend mode is on
Macro Recording	A button that you can click to start recording a macro
View Shortcuts	The five View buttons—Print Layout, Full Screen Reading, Web Layout, Outline, and Draft
Zoom	The Zoom Level readout
Zoom Slider	The Zoom slider and its control buttons

TABLE 9-1 Customize Status Bar Menu Items

Customize Keyboard Shortcuts

If you're comfortable with the keyboard, the fastest way to issue commands in Word is by using keyboard shortcuts. Word comes with various keyboard shortcuts built in (see the Appendix for a list), but you can also create custom keyboard shortcuts so that you can issue the commands you need. Keyboard shortcuts are especially useful if you find the Ribbon an awkward way to control Word.

To customize keyboard shortcuts, follow these steps:

1. Right-click the Ribbon, and then choose Customize Quick Access Toolbar from the context menu. Word displays the Customize category in the Word Options dialog box.

2. Click the Customize button in the Keyboard Shortcuts area near the bottom of the dialog box. Word displays the Customize Keyboard dialog box (shown in Figure 9-6 with customization under way).

3. In the Save Changes In drop-down list, choose the document or template in which you want to save the keyboard shortcuts:

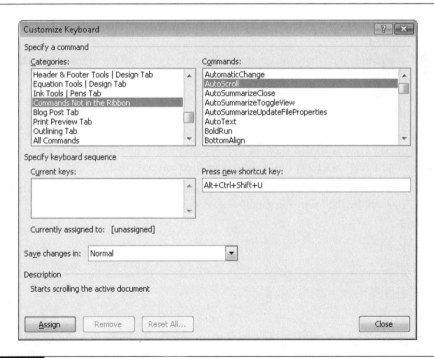

FIGURE 9-6 The Customize Keyboard dialog box lets you set up Word for control from the keyboard.

■ **Normal**   Select this item to store the keyboard shortcuts in your Normal template, the background template that Word loads when you start the application. The keyboard shortcuts are then available no matter which document you're working in, unless that document or its template has the same keyboard shortcut defined for a different command.

■ **Template attached to the active document**   The template's name appears in the list and isn't marked as being a template, which can be confusing. If the active document uses the Normal template, no other template appears in the list. When you store the keyboard shortcut in the template, the keyboard shortcut is available whenever the template is open or a document to which the template is attached is open—unless that document has the same keyboard shortcut defined for a different command.

■ **Active document**   The document's name appears in the list. When you store the keyboard shortcut in the document, the keyboard shortcut is available only when the document is open.

4. In the Categories list box, select the category of command:

■ If you know which Ribbon tab the command is on, select that tab. Word displays the tab's commands in the Commands list box.

■ If the command doesn't appear on the Ribbon, try the Commands Not In The Ribbon category.

■ If you're not sure where the command appears, try the All Commands list. This list is comprehensive, which makes it very long.

■ At the bottom of the Categories list, you'll find categories for Macros, Fonts, AutoText, Styles, and Common Symbols.

5. In the Commands list box, select the command you want to assign a keyboard shortcut. Word displays any keyboard shortcut already assigned in the Current Keys list box. Some commands have two or more keyboard shortcuts assigned.

6. Click in the Press New Shortcut Key text box, and then press the keyboard shortcut you want. You can use the following modifier keys or combinations:

■ CTRL

■ CTRL-ALT

■ CTRL-ALT-SHIFT

■ CTRL-SHIFT

■ ALT-SHIFT

TIP   *You can also create a two-stage keyboard shortcut by pressing the first part of the shortcut, followed by the second. For example, you might press CTRL-SHIFT-S and then press D. Two-stage shortcuts sound awkward, but they're useful when you want to create many shortcuts—for example, to apply a wide variety of styles or to run many different macros.*

7. Look at the Currently Assigned To readout under the Current Keys list box. If the keyboard shortcut you just pressed is marked "[unassigned]," you're in the clear. If the readout shows the name of a command, decide whether to overwrite that keyboard shortcut. If not, delete the contents of the Press New Shortcut Key text box, and then press another keyboard shortcut.

8. Click the Assign button to assign the keyboard shortcut to the command.

9. Assign other keyboard shortcuts as needed, and then click the Close button. Word closes the Customize Keyboard dialog box.

10. Click the OK button. Word closes the Word Options dialog box.

To keep your keyboard customizations, you must save them in the document or template:

- If you created the keyboard shortcuts in the document or template, click the Save button. If the changes are to the template, Word prompts you to save them. Click the Yes button.

- If you created the keyboard shortcuts in the Normal template, Word either saves them automatically when you quit Word or prompts you to do so. (This depends on whether you have selected the Prompt Before Saving Normal Template check box in the Advanced category in the Word Options dialog box.) If Word prompts you to save changes to Normal, click the Yes button.

Install Add-Ins

Word provides a huge range of functionality—but not enough for everyone. Your company may provide extra (and perhaps company-specific) functionality via *add-ins*, components that work together with Word. You can also buy add-ins from developers—for example, for using Word for special purposes such as indexing or publishing.

Some add-ins come with custom installation routines, but often you'll need to install an add-in manually. To do so, follow the instructions in the following section (for a Word add-in, such as a template) or in the next section but one (for a COM add-in, one built using a programming tool and the Component Object Model programming structure).

Install a Word Add-In

To install a Word add-in, follow these steps:

1. Click the Office Button, and then click Word Options. Word displays the Word Options dialog box.

2. In the left panel, click the Add-Ins item. Word displays the Add-Ins category, which lists the add-ins currently installed.

3. In the Manage drop-down list, select the Word Add-Ins item, and then click the Go button. Word displays the Templates And Add-Ins dialog box.

4. Click the Add button. Word displays the Add Template dialog box, which is a standard Open dialog box with a different name.

5. If you want to add an add-in rather than a template, select Word Add-Ins in the drop-down list above the Cancel button.

6. Navigate to the template or add-in, select it, and then click the OK button. (This button is named Open until you select a file.) Word closes the Add Template dialog box and returns you to the Templates And Add-Ins dialog box, where the template or add-in appears in the Global Templates And Add-Ins list box.

7. Click the OK button, Word closes the Templates And Add-Ins dialog box.

The add-in appears on the Add-Ins tab of the Ribbon. (Word displays the Add-Ins tab only when you have loaded an add-in.) The following illustration shows an example of an add-in.

To remove an add-in, open the Templates And Add-Ins dialog box (by following steps 1 through 3 of the preceding list), select the add-in in the Global Templates And Add-Ins list box, and then click the Remove button. To leave an add-in available but not loaded, clear its check box in the Global Templates And Add-Ins list box.

Install a COM Add-In

To install a COM add-in, follow these steps:

1. Click the Office Button, and then click Word Options. Word displays the Word Options dialog box.

2. In the left panel, click the Add-Ins item. Word displays the Add-Ins category, which lists the add-ins currently installed.

3. In the Manage drop-down list, select the COM Add-Ins item (it's normally selected by default), and then click the Go button. Word displays the COM Add-Ins dialog box.

4. If the add-in appears in the Add-Ins Available list box, select it. If not, click the Add button, use the Add Add-In dialog box to select the add-in, and then click the OK button. Then select the add-in in the Add-Ins Available list box.

5. Click the OK button. Word closes the COM Add-Ins dialog box and makes the add-in available.

Chapter 10

Share, Edit, and Revise Documents

How to...

- Track the changes made to a document
- Use comments in documents
- Print comments and other markup
- Share documents with your colleagues via a network
- Send documents via e-mail

No man is an island, entire of himself... everyone is a piece of the company, a part of the main organization. Working solo is normal for a document such as a personal letter or a blog post, but for many business documents, you'll need to collaborate with your colleagues.

This chapter shows you how to make the most of Word's features for sharing, editing, and revising documents. You can track all the edits made to a document and integrate edits made by different people into a single document. You can simply use comments to flag issues with a document. You can share documents with your colleagues via a network. And you can send documents easily via e-mail by using commands built into Word.

Track the Changes Made to a Document

Perhaps the most widely used of Word's collaborative editing tools is Track Changes, which allows you to track the revisions made to a document. By turning on Track Changes, you can see which colleague inserted which text, deleted which other text, or applied which formatting.

NOTE   *Word 2007 improves Track Changes over earlier versions by including tracking for changes to table cells that are inserted, deleted, merged, or split. Even so, Word 2007 still doesn't track some changes, such as changes of capitalization using the Change Case command (for example, choosing Home | Font | Change Case or pressing SHIFT-F3), so it's good to be clear that not every change you (or others) make will be tracked.*

Verify Your User Name and Initials

The only thing more irritating than finding that one of your colleagues' changes are being logged as "Authorized User" is finding that *your* changes are. So before you start using Track Changes, make sure that your user name and initials are correct. Follow these steps:

1. Click the Office Button, and then click Word Options. Word displays the Word Options dialog box with the Popular category selected.

2. Verify your name in the User Name text box and your initials in the Initials text box. Change them if necessary.

3. Click the OK button. Word closes the Word Options dialog box.

Configure Options for Track Changes

After verifying your name and initials, it's a good idea to check Word's Track Changes settings to make sure you have suitable markup options set. Follow these steps:

1. Choose Review | Tracking | Track Changes (click the lower part of the Track Changes button to produce the drop-down menu), and then choose Change Tracking Options. Word displays the Track Changes Options dialog box (see Figure 10-1).

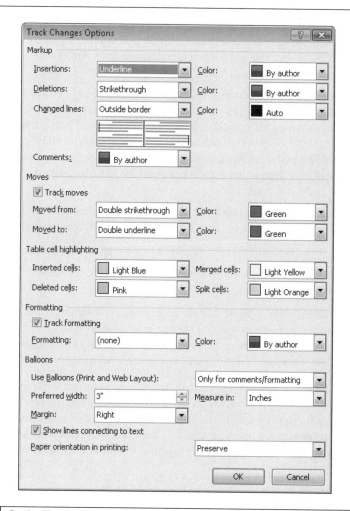

FIGURE 10-1 In the Track Changes Options dialog box, tell Word how to mark each type of change and whether to track moved text and changed formatting.

2. In the Markup area, choose how to mark tracked changes:

- ■ **Insertions**   In this drop-down list, choose how to format inserted text: "(none)," Color Only, Bold, Italic, Underline, Double Underline, or Strikethrough. The Color Only, Underline, and Double Underline settings tend to be most useful. In the top Color drop-down list, select By Author if you want each user (identified by their user name) to receive a separate color automatically. Otherwise, select the color that you want all insertions to have.

- ■ **Deletions**   In this drop-down list, choose how to format deleted text: "(none)," Color Only, Bold, Italic, Underline, Double Underline, Strikethrough, Hidden, ^ (a single caret appears to indicate deleted text), # (a single pound sign appears), or Double Strikethrough. In the second Color drop-down list, select By Author if you want each user to receive a separate color automatically. Otherwise, select the color that you want all deletions to have.

- ■ **Changed Lines**   In this drop-down list, choose the type of vertical line you want Word to display in the margin to indicate that a line of text has changed. The "(none)" choice uses no vertical line. The Left Border item puts a line in the left margin, the Right Border item puts a line in the right margin, and the Outside Border item puts a line in the left margin on left pages and the right margin on right pages. In the third Color drop-down list, choose Auto for Word's standard color, or pick the particular color you want.

- ■ **Comments**   In this drop-down list, choose By Author to have each user's comments appear in a different color, or choose the color you want to use for all comments.

3. In the Moves area, choose how you want Word to track text you move:

- ■ **Track Moves**   Select this check box to turn on tracking of text moves. Normally, tracking moves is helpful.

NOTE   *In some earlier versions of Word, a move appeared as a deletion (of the text in its original position) and an insertion (of the text in its new position). Such marking is logical enough but tends to be confusing in practice—so Word 2007's ability to mark moved text differently from deletions and insertions is normally helpful.*

- ■ **Moved From**   In this drop-down list, choose how to format the original version of text that has moved (in other words, the text that is no longer there). Your choices are the same as for deletions, but usually it's helpful to use different formatting so that you can tell moves and deletions apart. In the Color drop-down list level with the Moved From drop-down list, choose the color to use, or choose By Author to have color-coded moves.

- ■ **Moved To**   In this drop-down list, choose how to format the new version of text that has moved. Your choices are the same as for insertions, but usually it's helpful to use different formatting so that you can distinguish moves from insertions. In the Color drop-down list level with the Moved To drop-down list, choose the color to use, or choose By Author to have Word apply color coding.

4. In the Table Cell Highlighting area, choose how Word should format table cells you change:

   - **Inserted Cells** In this drop-down list, choose By Author for color-coded formatting, or choose the color you want for cells that users insert.

   - **Deleted Cells** In this drop-down list, choose By Author or a particular color for cells that users delete. (The deleted cells still appear in the table.)

   - **Merged Cells** In this drop-down list, choose By Author or a particular color for cells that users merge. (Merging turns two or more selected cells into a single cell.)

   - **Split Cells** In this drop-down list, choose By Author or a particular color for cells that users divide.

5. In the Formatting area, choose whether to track formatting and, if so, how to mark the formatting changes:

   - **Track Formatting** Select this check box to track formatting changes. Tracking such changes is helpful on some documents, but on heavily edited documents it can produce so many tracked changes that they are hard to follow.

   - **Formatting** In this drop-down list, choose the type of formatting Word uses to indicate a change of formatting: "(none)," Color Only, Bold, Italic, Underline, Double Underline, Strikethrough, or Double Strikethrough. In the Color drop-down list level with the Formatting drop-down list, select By Author, Auto, or a particular color.

6. In the Balloons area, choose whether to use balloons to show tracked changes in Print Layout view and Web Layout view. (You'll see examples of balloons in a moment.)

   - **Use Balloons (Print And Web Layout)** In this drop-down list, choose Always to use balloons for all changes, Only For Comments/Formatting to use balloons only for comments and formatting, or Never to not use balloons.

   - **Preferred Width** In this text box, choose the width of the balloons—for example, 3" or 35%. Use the Measure In drop-down list to switch between your current measurement unit (for example, Inches) and Percent.

   - **Margin** In this drop-down list, choose which margin to display the balloons in—Right (the default) or Left.

   - **Show Lines Connecting To Text** Select this check box to display a line from each balloon to the text referenced. These lines are usually helpful.

   - **Paper Orientation In Printing** In this drop-down list, select Preserve to keep the paper's normal orientation, Auto to use the default orientation, or Force Landscape to print all pages landscape (even if they're set up as portrait). Force Landscape can be useful when a document is packed with comment balloons.

7. Click the OK button. Word closes the Track Changes Options dialog box and applies your choices.

10

Work with Track Changes

Once you've chosen how to display tracked changes, you're ready to track changes to a document. Start by turning Track Changes on in any of the following ways:

- ■ **Ribbon** Choose Review | Tracking | Track Changes. (Click the top part of the Track Changes button, as shown next. You can also click the drop-down part of the button and then choose Track Changes from the drop-down menu, but doing so takes more effort.)

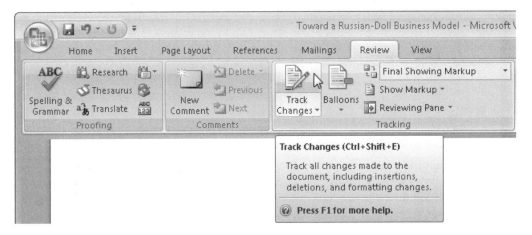

- ■ **Keyboard** Press CTRL-SHIFT-E.

- ■ **Status Bar** If you've displayed the Track Changes indicator on the status bar, click it to toggle Track Changes on or off, as shown next. To display the Track Changes indicator, right-click the status bar, click the Track Changes item on the Customize Status Bar menu, and then click anywhere in the document.

With Track Changes on, Word starts tracking the changes you make to a document. Here are some quick examples:

- ■ When you delete a word and replace it with other text, or select a word and then type over it, Word marks the deletion and the insertion. The next illustration shows the deletion with strikethrough, the insertion with underline, and the changed line with a vertical bar to its left.

> Here's an example of the kind of ~~commitment~~ <u>enthusiasm and drive</u> that we need from YOU and from each of our Sales Associates:

■ In Draft view and Outline view, Word displays all the changes inline. You can hover the mouse pointer over a change to pop up a ScreenTip showing who made the change and when, as in this example.

> **Michaela Pell, 1/16/2007 1:11:00 PM**
> **inserted:**
> enthusiasm and drive

Here's an example of the kind of ~~commitment~~ enthusiasm and drive that we need from YOU and from each of our Sales Associates:

■ In Print Layout view, Web Layout view, and Full Screen Reading view, Word displays the changes in balloons with a line connecting each change to its text (depending on the settings you chose). Here is an example.

When an industry **dedines** at this rate, the weaker get going and the strong get better job opportunities

> **Formatted:** Font: Bold
> **Deleted:** going gets tough
> **Deleted:** and the weaker get going

■ Where one line has several changes, it can be difficult to tell which is which. However, you can click a balloon to display a heavier line to its source, as shown here, or you can hover the mouse pointer over a change to display a ScreenTip showing its details.

When an industry **dedines** at this rate, the weaker get going and the strong get better job opportunities

> **Formatted:** Font: Bold
> **Deleted:** going gets tough
> **Deleted:** and the weaker get going

10

TIP   *Balloons can be great for seeing the details of the changes, but they tend to get in the way when you're editing the document yourself. You can switch balloons on and off easily by choosing Review | Tracking | Balloons, and then choosing Show Revisions In Balloons, Show All Revisions Inline, or Show Only Comments And Formatting In Balloons from the drop-down menu.*

Review Tracked Changes in a Document

When you've created a document and sent it out to your colleagues for editing, you'll probably need to review the tracked changes and decide which to keep and which to jettison.

Change the Version of the Document Displayed

To control which version of the document Word displays, choose Review | Tracking | Display For Review, and then choose the version from the menu:

■ **Final Showing Markup**   The final version of the document, with all the tracked markup displayed (depending on the markup settings you've chosen).

■ **Final**   The final version of the document, with changes shown but no markup.

- **Original Showing Markup**   The original version of the document, with all the tracked markup displayed (again, depending on the markup settings you've chosen).
- **Original**   The original version of the document, with no changes (and no markup).

See Only Some Types of Changes

By default, Word shows you all the changes to the document—as you'd expect. To focus on a particular type of change, choose Review | Tracking | Show Markup, and then clear each check box for changes you don't want to see. For example, you might want to see only formatting changes, as in the illustration here.

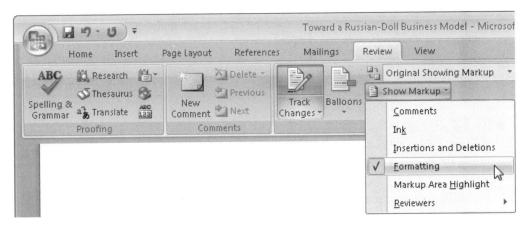

See Changes from Only Some Reviewers

If you need to see only the changes made by one or more particular reviewers, choose Review | Tracking | Show Markup | Reviewers. On the Reviewers submenu (shown here), clear the check box for any reviewer whose changes you do not want to see.

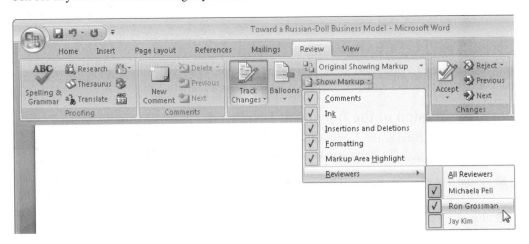

Use the Reviewing Pane

If a document has many changes, a muddle of balloons can become hard to decipher. Instead, you can use the Reviewing pane, a separate section of the Word window that lists each change in turn.

To display the Reviewing pane, choose Review | Tracking | Reviewing Pane | Reviewing Pane Vertical or Review | Tracking | Reviewing Pane | Reviewing Pane Horizontal, depending on whether you want the pane to be vertical or horizontal. Figure 10-2 shows the Reviewing pane in its horizontal orientation.

These are the main actions you can take in the Reviewing pane:

- ■ Double-click a change in the pane to display the related text in the main document area.

- ■ Right-click a change, and then choose the Accept command (for example, Accept Deletion) or the Reject command (for example, Reject Deletion) from the context menu.

- ■ Click the Show/Hide Detailed Summary button to toggle the display of the Summary bar at the top of the pane.

- ■ Click the Update Revision Count button to refresh the Summary bar's count of revisions.

To close the Reviewing pane, choose Review | Tracking | Reviewing Pane (click the button, not the drop-down button), click the pane's Close button (the × button), press ALT-SHIFT-C, or double-click the bar that separates the pane from the main document window.

Accept or Reject Changes

10

To accept or reject changes, use the controls in the Changes group on the Review tab:

- ■ **Accept And Move To Next**   Click the top part of the Accept button to accept the current change and move on to the next. Word integrates the change in the document and removes the revision marking from it.

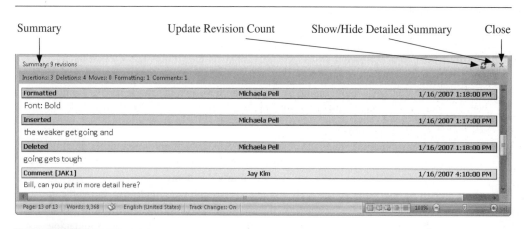

Summary   Update Revision Count   Show/Hide Detailed Summary   Close

Summary: 9 revisions		
Insertions: 3 Deletions: 4 Moves: 0 Formatting: 1 Comments: 1		
Formatted	Michaela Pell	1/16/2007 1:18:00 PM
Font: Bold		
Inserted	Michaela Pell	1/16/2007 1:17:00 PM
the weaker get going and		
Deleted	Michaela Pell	1/16/2007 1:18:00 PM
going gets tough		
Comment [JAK1]	Jay Kim	1/16/2007 4:10:00 PM
Bill, can you put in more detail here?		

Page: 13 of 13   Words: 9,368   English (United States)   Track Changes: On   100%

FIGURE 10-2   Use the Reviewing pane to see an easy-to-distinguish list of the changes to a document.

■ **Reject And Move To Next**   Click the Reject button (not the drop-down button) to reject the current change and move on to the next change. Word changes the document back to how it was before the change was applied.

■ **Previous**   Click this button to move back to the previous change, leaving the current change unaltered.

■ **Next**   Click this button to move on to the next change, leaving the current change unaltered.

■ **Accept drop-down list**   Click the drop-down button to reach other choices, including Accept All Changes In Document, as shown here.

■ **Reject drop-down list**   Click the drop-down button to reach other choices, including Reject All Changes In Document.

Compare or Combine Two Documents

Having all your reviewers mark up the same copy of a document works well but isn't always practical. When your colleagues need to review a document in parallel rather than in series, you'll end up with multiple versions of the document. To integrate the changes into a single document, use Word's Compare tool or its Combine tool:

■ **Compare**   Compare creates a new document that shows all the changes that have been made to both documents. Compare assigns all the changes to a single author rather than marking each change as being made by the person who actually made it. Use Compare when you need to focus on the difference between two documents rather than see who made each change.

■ **Combine**   Combine integrates the changes from one document into another document, maintaining the details of each change made. For example, say you've given Bill and Joy each a copy of a document to review. By combining the changes from Joy's copy with those in Bill's copy, you can see both sets of changes and who made which. (You can then combine someone else's copy with the combined copy as needed.) If both Bill and Joy have changed the same text, you'll see both their changes and will need to decide which to keep.

To compare or combine two copies of the same document, follow these steps:

1.   With neither of the documents open, choose Review | Compare | Compare | Compare or Review | Compare | Compare | Combine. Word displays the Compare Documents dialog box (shown here with two documents selected) or the Combine Documents dialog box, which is the same dialog box with a different name.

2.   In the Original Document text box, enter the name of the original document with which you want to compare or combine the revised document.

▪   The drop-down list contains the documents on the Recent Documents list on the Office Button menu.

▪   To choose another document, click the Browse For Original button (the Open button), use the resulting Open dialog box to select the document, and then click the Open button.

▪   In the left Label Changes With text box, Word enters the name of the last reviewer who has used revision marks in the document. You may need to change the name. If the document contains no revisions, this box is blank and unavailable.

3.   In the Revised Document text box, enter the revised document's name.

▪   Either select a recent document from the drop-down list, or click the Browse For Revised button, use the resulting Open dialog box to select the document, and then click the Open button.

▪   In the right Label Changes With text box, Word enters the name of the last reviewer who has used revision marks in the document. You may need to change the name— for example, if two or more people have reviewed the document.

4.   To reach the full range of comparison choices, click the More button. Word displays the remainder of the Compare Documents dialog box (see Figure 10-3) or Combine Documents dialog box.

5.   In the Comparison Settings area, select the check box for each item you want to compare or combine.

▪   Normally, you'll want to compare or combine all these items, but sometimes it's useful to switch off those for which you're not interested in seeing your colleagues' changes.

▪   For example, you might want to ignore your colleagues' artistic header and footer contributions.

10

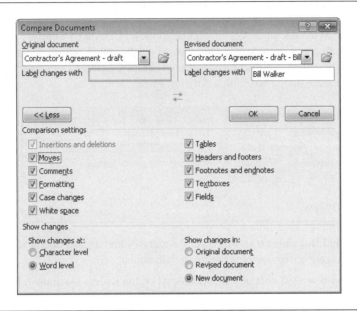

FIGURE 10-3 The Comparison Settings area of the Compare Documents dialog box (shown here) or Combine Documents dialog box lets you choose which items to compare or combine.

6. In the Show Changes area, choose the level of changes and the document in which to show them:

   ■ **Show Changes At**   Select the Character Level option button if you want Word to analyze the changes to each character. Usually, it's better to select the Word Level option button to make Word analyze the changes word by word, as this produces fewer changes.

   ■ **Show Changes In**   Select the New Document option button if you want Word to put the changes in a new document. Otherwise, select the Original Document option button or the Revised Document option button as appropriate.

7. Click the OK button. Word analyzes the changes and then displays the document you specified (a new document, the revised document, or the original document) with the changes integrated.

   ■ If either of the documents contains tracked changes, Word displays the following dialog box, telling you that it will consider the changes to have been accepted for the purposes of the comparison. Click the Yes button to proceed with the comparison.

You can use the Review | Compare | Show Source Documents drop-down menu to control which of the merged documents Word displays. Your choices are Hide Source Documents, Show Original, Show Revised, or Show Both. Figure 10-4 shows a new document (named "Compared Document"), the original document and revised document from which it was created, and the Reviewing pane.

Move Tracked Changes from One Document to Another

Sometimes, you may need to move tracked changes from one document to another *without* using the Compare command or the Combine command. This is the sort of situation that in theory should never occur but in practice often does.

You could paste each part containing tracked changes into the destination document—except that when you do so, you lose the tracked changes. If you have Track Changes turned on, Word pastes the material as an insertion, losing any nuances of tracked changes it contains; if you have Track Changes turned off, Word pastes the material without any tracking of changes.

To solve this problem, proceed as follows:

1. In the document that contains the tracked changes, create a bookmark for each part (for example, a paragraph) that you want to copy:

    ■ Select the part or paragraph.

    ■ Choose Insert | Links | Bookmark. Word displays the Bookmark dialog box.

    ■ In the Bookmark Name text box, type the name for the bookmark.

    ■ Click the Add button. Word adds the bookmark and closes the Bookmark dialog box.

2. After creating all the bookmarks, save the document. For example, click the Save button on the Quick Access Toolbar.

3. In the destination document, position the insertion point where you want to insert the first paragraph, and then follow these steps:

    ■ Choose Insert | Text | Object | Text From File. Word displays the Insert File dialog box.

    ■ Select the source document.

    ■ Click the Range button. Word displays the Set Range dialog box.

    ■ Type the name of the bookmark for the content you want to insert.

    ■ Click the OK button. Word closes the Set Range dialog box and returns you to the Insert File dialog box.

    ■ Click the Insert button. Word inserts the text including the changes.

4. Repeat step 3 as necessary for each of the parts that contain tracked changes.

10

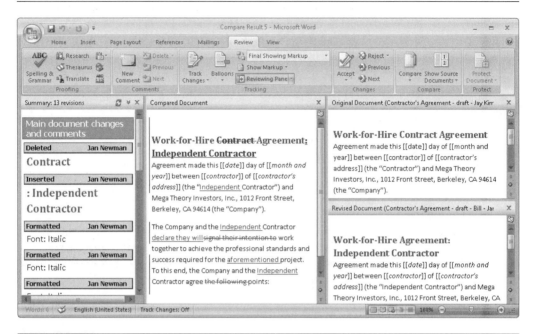

FIGURE 10-4 Word's Compare feature lets you merge the revisions from a "revised" document into the original document.

Use Comments in Documents

In addition to using Track Changes to apply revision marks to the changes made to a document, you can insert comments attached to particular pieces of text. Comments appear in balloons by default, which makes them easy to locate unless the document is peppered with them. You can also use the Reviewing pane to go through the comments in a document.

 *You can protect a document so that reviewers can only add comments rather than edit the document. See Chapter 18 for details.*

Insert a Comment

To insert a comment, follow these steps:

1. Select the text to which you want to attach the comment.

2. Choose Review | Comments | New Comment. Word places colored parentheses around the selected text or around the word in which you placed the insertion point and starts a comment with your initials and the comment's number in the series of comments you've created. For example, if your initials are JPC, Word marks your first comment JPC1, the second comment JPC2, and so on.

NOTE *In Full Screen Reading view, insert a comment by clicking the Tools button and then choosing New Comment.*

3. Type the text of the comment:

■ If the document is in Print Layout view, Web Layout view, or Full Screen Reading view, Word displays a comment balloon in the revisions area at the side of the page (normally on the right), as shown here. Type the text in the balloon.

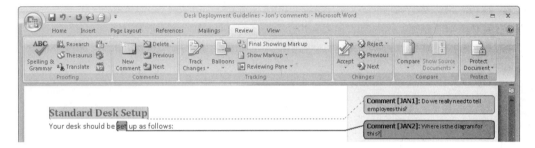

■ If the document is in Draft view or Outline view, or if you've turned off balloons, Word displays the Reviewing pane. Type the text of the comment. The comment initials and number appear in brackets after the commented word, as shown here.

Standard Desk Setup[JAN1]

Your desk should be set[JAN2] up as follows:

10

TIP *Comments are normally text, but you can paste other items, such as graphics and tables, into them if necessary.*

Edit a Comment

To edit a comment, either click in its balloon or in its text in the Reviewing pane, or right-click the comment marker and choose Edit Comment from the context menu.

View Comments

If you're viewing comments inline rather than with balloons or the Reviewing pane, you can display a comment's ScreenTip by hovering the mouse pointer over the commented text or the comment number, as shown here.

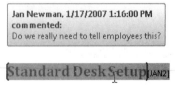

Jan Newman, 1/17/2007 1:16:00 PM commented:
Do we really need to tell employees this?

Standard Desk Setup[JAN2]

Your desk should be set up as follows:

Navigate from Comment to Comment

You can move from comment to comment easily enough by using the comment balloons or the Reviewing pane. From the Ribbon, you can choose Review | Comments | Previous or Review | Comments | Next.

Delete a Comment or All Comments

You can delete a comment in any of these ways:

- Right-click the comment in the text, and then choose Delete Comment from the context menu.

- Right-click the comment in the Reviewing pane, and then choose Delete Comment from the context menu.

- Right-click the comment's balloon, and then choose Delete Comment from the context menu.

- Click the comment, and then choose Review | Comments | Delete. (Click the main part of the Delete button rather than the drop-down button—or click the drop-down button and then choose Delete.)

To remove all the comments from the active document, choose Review | Comments | Delete | Delete All Comments In Document.

Print Comments and Other Markup

When printing a document that contains comments and markup, bear these two considerations in mind:

- **Choose whether to print markup** To print the comments and markup in a document, choose the Document Showing Markup item in the Print What drop-down list in the Print dialog box. To print the document without markup, select the Document item in the Print What drop-down list.

- **Choose the paper orientation** Make sure you've chosen the right paper orientation in the Paper Orientation In Printing drop-down list in the Track Changes Options dialog box, as discussed earlier in this chapter.

Share Documents with Your Colleagues via a Network

Unless you work entirely on your own, you're likely to need to share the documents you develop and use with your colleagues. You can share documents by using a shared folder on a network, as discussed in this section, or by using e-mail (discussed in the next section).

In an office, the simplest way to share a Word document with your colleagues is to save the document in a shared folder on your network. Each of your colleagues who's permitted to access that folder can then open the document file, make changes to it, and save them.

However, only one user can open the document file at a time for editing—a limitation that may cause problems. If you try to open the document file while another user has it open, Word displays the File In Use dialog box to warn you of the problem:

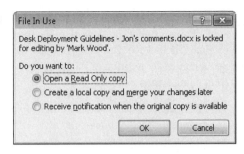

NOTE *The user name that Word displays in the File In Use dialog box comes from the User Name text box in the Popular category in the Word Options dialog box (click the Office Button, and then click Word Options). So if Word announces that a file is locked for editing by "Authorized User" or something equally unhelpful, you may have to tour the office to find out which of your colleagues actually has the file open. But if you see the user identified as "another user" (in lowercase like that), it usually means that another user is just opening the file and that Word hasn't yet transferred the details of who they are. Click the Cancel button, wait a second or two, and then try opening the file again. This time, Word should be able to tell you the user's name.*

When you run into the File In Use dialog box, you have four choices:

- Cancel opening the document.
- Open a read-only copy of the document.
- Create a new copy of the document, and then merge your changes into the original document when it becomes available.
- Tell Word to notify you when the document becomes available.

The following sections discuss these choices in detail.

Cancel Opening a Document That's in Use

When the document you need is in use, the easiest course of action is to click the Cancel button to give up on opening the document for the time being. You can then try again later to open the document.

Open a Read-Only Copy of the Document

Canceling opening the document doesn't get you far. Often, you'll need to make some progress with the document right now—even if that progress comes at a cost.

Your first option for making progress is to open the document in what Windows calls a "read-only" state. To do so, select the Open A Read Only Copy option button in the File In Use dialog box, and then click the OK button. Word displays "(Read-Only)" after the document's name in the title bar to remind you that the document is read-only.

Read-only doesn't actually mean you can't make changes to the document; you just can't save any changes under the document's current path and name (because the other user has the original file locked). But you can click the Office Button, and then click Save As to save the document under a different name in the same location or under either the same name or a different name with a different path.

The problem with creating a new document containing your changes is that you'll probably need to integrate them with the original version of the document later. But in a pinch (for example, if you need to print out a changed version of a document by the deadline for an imminent meeting), saving changes to a new file may be your best choice.

Create a Local Copy and Merge Your Changes Later

Your second option for making progress is to create a local copy of the document and then merge the changes you make in it with the original document after the current user closes it.

To do so, select the Create A Local Copy And Merge Your Changes Later option button in the File In Use dialog box, and then click the OK button. Confusingly, Word displays "(Read Only)" after the document's name in the title bar, so this option seems to have the same effect as the Open A Read Only Copy option button.

However, there are two main differences. First, when you try to save changes to your new copy of the document, Word checks to see if the original document is available. If it's not, Word displays this message box telling you that you need to save your document to a different location.

Click the OK button. Word displays the Save As dialog box, suggesting the document's original name with "– for merge" added to the end. Change the name if needed, and then click the Save button.

The second difference is that, when your colleague closes the document, Word lets you know the document is available for editing, and offers to merge your changes into the original document, as shown here.

Click the Merge button. If there are changes (as usually there will be), Word merges the changes into the original document and displays it. Work your way through the changes, accepting or rejecting them as needed, and then save the document.

If you're lucky, neither your colleague who had the document open nor you will have made changes. In this case, Word tells you that it found no differences between the documents, as shown here.

Tell Word to Notify You When the File Becomes Available

Your third option for making progress is to open the existing document in read-only mode and tell Word to notify you when the original document becomes available. To do this, select the Receive Notification When The Original Copy Is Available option button in the File In Use dialog box, and then click the OK button. Word opens a read-only copy of the document and displays the Server Document bar below the Ribbon, telling you that a newer version of the document is available, as shown here.

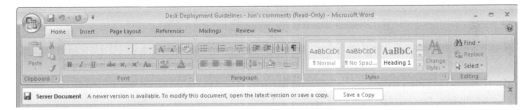

You can't make changes to the document unless you click the Save A Copy button on the Server Document bar (or click the Office Button, and then click Save As) and use the Save As dialog box to save a copy of the document.

When Word discovers that your colleague has closed the file, or has just shared it, Word displays the File Now Available dialog box (as shown here), and you can click the Read-Write button to open the file for editing.

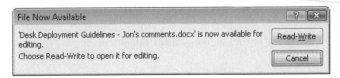

If you're still viewing the read-only copy of the document at this point, Word simply closes the read-only copy and opens the original document. You can then edit the document as you normally would.

If you've saved a copy of the document that was read-only, Word leaves this document open when it opens the original document. You can then use the Compare command or the Combine command to integrate your changes with the original.

 *Word doesn't keep a waiting list of notifications requested for a file. If two or more people ask to be notified when the same file is available, Word notifies them both (or all) when it discovers the file is available. So if you're competing with your colleagues for a document, act quickly when Word displays the File Now Available dialog box.*

Send Documents via E-mail

Depending on the type of company or organization you work for, you may need to send documents to your colleagues via e-mail. Word makes it easy to send a Word document via e-mail as an attachment to an Outlook message.

Send a Document as an E-mail Attachment

To send a document as an e-mail attachment, follow these steps:

1. Open the document and make sure it's ready for distribution.

2. Click the Office button, and then choose Send | E-mail. Word activates Outlook (if it's running) or launches it (if it isn't running), creates a new message, enters the document's name in the Subject field, and attaches the document to the message.

3. Enter the names of the recipient or recipients and any cc recipients.

4. Adjust the Subject line if necessary (often, the document's name on its own isn't very informative).

5. Enter any further information required in the body of the document. For example, you might tell the recipient what the document contains, why you're sending it, and what action you're expecting them to take with it.

6. Choose any further options for the message, as you would for any other message. For example, you might choose Options | Tracking | Request A Read Receipt so that you receive a notice when the recipient opens the message.

7. Click the Send button. Outlook sends the message with the document as an attachment.

Receive a Document Sent as an Attachment

When you receive a document sent as an attachment, simply save it to the appropriate folder. You can then work with it as you would with any other document.

Chapter 11

Create Tables and Columns

How to...

- Create simple and complex tables
- Sort table data and perform calculations
- Create columns of text

As you saw in Chapter 4, you can use tabs to lay out tabular data—but tabs work well only when each paragraph in the table consists of a single line. For more complex data, you should use one of Word's tables.

In Word, a table consists of rows of cells divided up into columns. You can create both simple and complex tables as needed: a table can consist of a single cell, but normally has multiple cells and columns. Word provides various predefined table styles for common items such as calendars, tabular lists, and tables that have subheads.

Word also lets you create "newspaper-style" text columns—columns in which the text flows all the way down the first column, then to the top of the second, down that column, then to the top of the next column, and so on. You'll normally use such columns only for documents such as newsletters. These columns are easy to create, but each part of the document that has a different number of columns must be placed in a separate section.

Work with Tables

This section shows you how to work with tables—everything from creating a table to performing table calculations or sorting a table.

Create a Table

Word lets you create a table in four ways:

- Convert existing text to a table
- Create a new table from scratch
- Insert one of Word's predefined Quick Tables
- Draw a table manually by placing the lines where you need them

Create a New Standard Table

To create a new standard table, choose Insert | Tables | Table, and then choose the table size from the Table panel. The readout at the top of the Table panel displays the size of table you've chosen, as shown here.

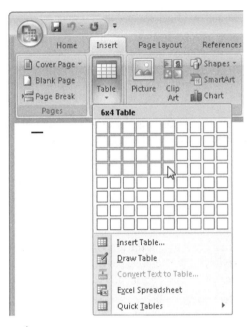

Word inserts the table, adds the Table Tools section to the Ribbon, and displays the Design tab on that section, as shown here.

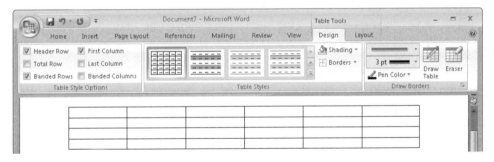

If you need to insert a table that has more columns or rows (or both) than appear on the Table panel, or if you want to choose further options for your table, follow these steps:

1. Position the insertion point where you want the table to appear.

2. Choose Insert | Tables | Table | Insert Table. Word displays the Insert Table dialog box, shown here.

3. In the Number Of Columns text box, specify the number of columns.

4. In the Number Of Rows text box, specify the number of rows.

You can easily add more rows to the end of a table, so you don't need to get the number of rows right when inserting the table. By contrast, adding further columns involves greater changes in layout, so it's more important to get the number of columns right from the start.

5. In the AutoFit Behavior area, decide whether to use a fixed column width or have Word automatically fit the table to its contents or the Word window:

■ **Fixed Column Width** Select this option button if you want each column in the table to have a fixed width. In the text box, choose Auto if you want Word to share out the available space equally among the columns. Alternatively, specify the standard width you want to use for each column.

■ **AutoFit To Contents** Select this option button if you want Word to adjust the column width automatically to suit the amount of text (or other objects) each column contains. This behavior can be helpful, but it may mean that Word constantly adjusts column width while you're creating the first few rows in the table.

■ **AutoFit To Window** Select this option button if you want Word to adjust the column width to fit the width of the Word window. This option can be handy for making sure that the full width of the table is visible.

6. Select the Remember Dimensions For New Tables check box if you want Word to use the configuration you've just set as the default for new tables.

7. Click the OK button. Word closes the Insert Table dialog box and inserts the table in the document. Word also adds the Table Tools section to the Ribbon and displays the Design tab on that section.

Convert Existing Text to a Table

Often, you'll need to turn existing text into a table. For example, you may start laying out tabular data using tabs, and then realize that a table would be better.

To convert existing text to a table, follow these steps:

1. If the text is divided into columns using tabs, commas, or another character, make sure that each paragraph contains the same number of columns. To see tab characters, choose Home | Paragraph | Show/ Hide ¶.

2. Select the text you want to turn into the table. Include the paragraph mark at the end of the last paragraph.

3. Choose Insert | Tables | Table | Convert Text To Table. Word displays the Convert Text To Table dialog box, shown here.

4. In the Table Size area, make sure that the Number Of Columns text box is showing the number of columns you expect. If the number seems wrong, look at the Separate Text At area, and verify that the correct option button is selected:

- ■ **Paragraphs**   Select this option button to turn each paragraph into a cell in the table. You may need to adjust the Number Of Columns setting manually, as Word normally sets it to 1.

- ■ **Commas**   Select this option button to turn each section that's cordoned off with commas into a cell in the table. Normally, you'll use this setting when dealing with a Comma Separated Values (CSV) file—for example, when you've exported spreadsheet or database data in CSV format.

- ■ **Tabs**   Select this option button to divide the text at each tab. This setting is widely useful.

- ■ **Other**   To divide the text at another character, select this option button and type the character in the text box. For example, you might need to divide the text at a character such as a brace ({) or an exclamation point (!). You can use only one character.

5. In the AutoFit Behavior area, choose the automatic-fitting option you want. See step 5 in the previous list for details.

6. Click the OK button. Word closes the Convert Text To Table dialog box and applies the table to the selected text. Word also adds the Table Tools section to the Ribbon and displays the Design tab on that section.

Make sure that Word has divided your text as needed. If there's a problem, click the Undo button on the Quick Access Toolbar to remove the table. Fix the problem with the divisor character (for example, add a missing tab, or delete a surplus tab), and then convert the text to a table again.

Create a New Quick Table

To create a new table based on one of Word's Quick Table designs, follow these steps:

1. Position the insertion point where you want the table to appear.

2. Choose Insert | Tables | Table | Quick Tables, and then choose the design from the Quick Tables panel. Word inserts the table, adds the Table Tools section to the Ribbon, and displays the Design tab on that section. The following illustration shows an example of a Quick Table.

ITEM	NEEDED
Books	1
Magazines	3
Notebooks	1
Paper pads	1
Pens	3
Pencils	2
Highlighter	2 colors
Scissors	1 pair

3. Change the sample data in the Quick Table to the data you want the table to have.

Create a Custom Quick Table from One of Your Tables

If you like a table you've created, you can save it as a Quick Table for future use. Follow these steps:

1. Position the insertion point in the table from which you want to create a Quick Table.

2. Choose Layout | Table | Select | Select Table.

3. Choose Insert | Tables | Table | Quick Tables | Save Selection To Quick Tables Gallery. Word displays the Create New Building Block dialog box.

4. In the Name text box, type the name you want to give the Quick Table style. Word suggests a name based on the text in the first cell in the table, so you'll often want to change it.

5. In the Description text box, type a description for the Quick Table. This description appears in the ScreenTip in the Quick Tables panel.

6. Choose other building-block options as discussed in the section "Create Your Own Building Blocks" in Chapter 9.

7. Click the OK button. Word closes the Create New Building Block dialog box and creates the building block.

Draw a Table

If you need a complex table rather than a simple one, you can draw it yourself. To draw a table, follow these steps:

1. Choose Insert | Tables | Table | Draw Table. Word changes the mouse pointer to a pen. If the window is in Draft view, Word switches it to Print Layout view.

2. Click in the document where you want one corner of the table to appear, and then drag diagonally to the opposite corner, as shown here. You can drag diagonally in any direction. After you create the first part of the table, Word adds the Table Tools section to the Ribbon and displays the Design tab.

3. Click and drag to draw other lines as needed to create the table layout you need.

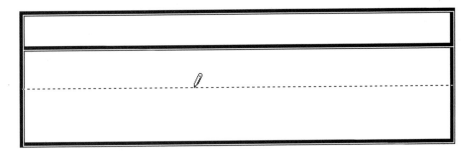

- To change the line style, choose Design | Draw Borders | Line Style, and then choose the style from the Line Style panel.

- To change the line weight, choose Design | Draw Borders | Line Weight, and then choose the weight from the Line Weight panel.

- To change the pen color, choose Design | Draw Borders | Pen Color, and then choose the pen color from the Pen Color panel.

- To erase an existing line, choose Design | Draw Borders | Eraser, and then click each line you want to erase with the eraser mouse pointer. To cancel the eraser, press ESC or choose Design | Draw Borders | Eraser again.

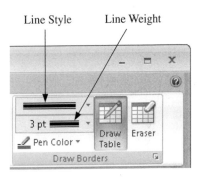

Line Style   Line Weight

Enter Text, Navigate, and Edit in Tables

To enter text in a table cell, click in the cell, and then type the text.

You can also enter other items in table cells. For example, to insert a picture, choose Insert | Illustrations | Picture, select the picture in the Insert Picture dialog box, and then click the Insert button.

To enter a tab in a table cell, press CTRL-TAB.

Navigate from Cell to Cell

You can navigate easily from one cell to another by using the mouse. Alternatively:

- Press TAB to move to the next cell and select any contents it has (but not the end-of-cell marker). Press ← to collapse the selection to the beginning of the cell or → to collapse the selection to the end of the cell.

- Press SHIFT-TAB to move to the previous cell and select its contents. Press ← to collapse the selection to the beginning of the cell or → to collapse the selection to the end of the cell.

- Press ← or → to move through the contents of a cell one character at a time.

- From the beginning of a cell, press ← to move to the previous cell.
- From the end of a cell, press → to move to the next cell.
- Press ↑ to move to the previous line or paragraph in the cell. From the first line or paragraph of the cell, press ↑ to move to the row above.
- Press ↓ to move to the next line or paragraph in the cell. From the last line or paragraph of the cell, press ↓ to move to the row below.

Select Parts of a Table

You can select parts of a table by dragging with the mouse, but Word also provides these tools for selecting quickly:

- A vertical cell-selection bar at the left edge of each cell. When you move the mouse pointer over the cell-selection bar, the mouse pointer changes to a thick black arrow pointing up and to the right, as shown here:

- A table-selection bar to the left of the table's leftmost column. When you move the mouse pointer over the table-selection bar, the mouse pointer changes to an arrow pointing up and to the right, as shown here:

- A column-selection bar just above any column. When you move the mouse pointer over the column-selection bar, the mouse pointer changes to a thick black arrow pointing straight down, as shown here:

- A table button that appears at the upper-left corner of the table when the mouse pointer is over the table, as shown here:

To Select This	Do This	Or Choose
A cell	Click in the cell-selection bar.	Layout | Table | Select | Select Cell
A column	Click in the column-selection bar. Drag left or right to select multiple columns.	Layout | Table | Select | Select Column
A row	Click in the table-selection bar beside the row. Drag up or down to select multiple rows.	Layout | Table | Select | Select Row
The entire table	Click the table button.	Layout | Table | Select | Select Table

Insert and Delete Cells, Rows, and Columns

You can delete cells, rows, and columns from a table as needed. But before you do, you should know that Word lets you delete the contents of a cell, row, column, or table without deleting the item itself.

Understand the End-of-Cell Markers and End-of-Row Markers

If you make Word display formatting marks (choose Home | Paragraph | Show/Hide ¶ or press CTRL-SHIFT-8), you'll see a mark like a letter *o* with corners at the end of each cell and each row, as shown here.

Company¤	Department¤	¤
Acme·Baking¤	Manufacturing¶ Engineering¶ Logistics¤	¤
Acme·Fitness¤	Personnel¤	¤
¤	¤	¤

The marks at the end of the cells are the end-of-cell markers and store any formatting applied to the cell. The marks at the end of the rows are the end-of-row markers and store any formatting applied to the row.

When you select an entire cell, you select the end-of-cell marker as well, even if it is hidden. If you copy that cell and paste it into another location, the formatting comes too.

- To delete the contents of part of the table, select that part of the table, and then press DELETE. Word leaves the table structure in place. For example, if you select a row, and then press DELETE, Word deletes the row's contents but leaves the row where it was.

- To delete part of a table as well as its contents, select it, and then press BACKSPACE.

Similarly, you can add cells, rows, and columns to a table.

Delete Cells

To delete individual cells and their contents, follow these steps:

1. Select the cells.

2. Choose Layout | Rows & Columns | Delete | Delete Cells. Word displays the Delete Cells dialog box, shown here.

3. Choose how to handle the deletion:

- **Shift Cells Left**   Select this option button if you want Word to move the cells in the table to the left to fill in the space left by the deleted cells.

- **Shift Cells Up**   Select this option button if you want Word to move the cells in the table up to fill in the space left by the deleted cells.

- **Delete Entire Row**   Select this option button if you want to delete each entire row in which you've selected a cell. Usually, it's easiest to use the Layout | Rows & Columns | Delete | Delete Row command.

- **Delete Entire Column**   Select this option button if you want to delete each entire column in which you've selected a cell. Usually, it's easiest to use the Layout | Rows & Columns | Delete | Delete Column command, discussed next.

4. Click the OK button. Word closes the Delete Cells dialog box, deletes the cells (or rows, or columns), and moves the remainder of the table as specified.

Delete an Entire Row, Column, or Table

To delete an entire row, column, or table, click in a cell in it, and then:

- **Row**   Choose Layout | Rows & Columns | Delete | Delete Rows.
- **Column**   Choose Layout | Rows & Columns | Delete | Delete Columns.
- **Table**   Choose Layout | Rows & Columns | Delete | Delete Table.

Add Cells

To add cells to a table, follow these steps:

1. Select the cells above, below, to the left of, or to the right of which you want to insert the new cells.

2. Choose the appropriate command, and Word inserts the cells:

- To insert cells above, choose Layout | Rows & Columns | Insert Above.
- To insert cells below, choose Layout | Rows & Columns | Insert Below.
- To insert cells to the left, choose Layout | Rows & Columns | Insert Left.
- To insert cells to the right, choose Layout | Rows & Columns | Insert Right.

Add Entire Rows or Columns

Word lets you insert entire rows or columns in two ways:

- Select the rows above or below which you want to insert a row, or the columns to the left or right of which you want to insert a column. Then choose Layout | Rows & Columns | Insert Above or Layout | Rows & Columns | Insert Below to insert a row. Choose Layout | Rows & Columns | Insert Left or Layout | Rows & Columns | Insert Right to insert a column.

TIP   *To insert two or more rows or columns at once, select the corresponding number of existing rows or columns before issuing the Insert command. For example, to insert three new rows, select three existing rows, and then issue the Insert command.*

■ Select a cell in the row above which you want to insert a row, or the column to the left of which you want to insert a column. Choose Layout | Rows & Columns | Table Insert Cells (click the tiny button at the right end of the Rows & Columns bar). Word displays the Insert Cells dialog box, shown here. Select the Insert Entire Row option button or the Insert Entire Column option button, and then click the OK button.

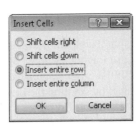

TIP *Word also provides the Insert commands on the context menu for tables (right-click, choose Insert, and then choose the command), together with the Delete Cells command and the Split Cells command.*

Move Cells, Rows, and Columns

Within a table, you can move cells, rows, and columns by using drag and drop or by cutting and pasting:

■ When you move a cell, its contents replace any contents in the destination cell.

■ When you move a row or column, Word moves it from its current position and inserts it in the new position, so the other rows or columns remain unchanged.

Merge and Split Cells

When you need to create a larger cell or a spanner heading (a heading going across two or more columns), you can merge two or more cells together into a single cell.

To merge cells, select the cells, and then choose Layout | Merge | Merge Cells. Word merges the cells together. Word separates the contents of the previous cells with paragraphs in the merged cell.

Similarly, you can split an existing cell into two or more cells. Follow these steps:

1. Click in the cell you want to split. Alternatively, select multiple cells.

2. Choose Layout | Merge | Split Cells. Word displays the Split Cells dialog box, shown here.

3. In the Number Of Columns text box, specify how many columns Word should create.

4. In the Number Of Rows text box, specify how many rows Word should create.

5. Select the Merge Cells Before Split check box if you've selected multiple cells in step 1 and you want Word to apply the changes across the cells. If you want Word to apply changes on a per-cell basis, clear this check box. (If you've selected only one cell, this setting makes no difference.)

6. Click the OK button. Word closes the Split Cells dialog box and divides the cells as you specified.

Split a Table

To split a table into two parts, click in the row above which you want to break the table, and then choose Layout | Merge | Split Table. Alternatively, press CTRL-SHIFT-ENTER.

If the original table has a table style applied to it, Word applies the style to each of the tables created by splitting the original table.

You can also use the Layout | Merge | Split Table command or the CTRL-SHIFT-ENTER keystroke when you've created an inline table at the very beginning of a document and you need to place the insertion point before the table to create a paragraph at the beginning of the document.

Create a Nested Table

As you've seen, you can create a nonstandard table by merging or splitting cells within a standard table. But Word also lets you create a *nested* table—a table that's placed inside a cell in another table, as in the next illustration. Nested tables can be very useful for displaying complex information.

Governors	Faculty	Students			

To create a nested table, click in the cell in which you want to place the new table, and then insert a table as normal—for example, choose Insert | Tables | Table, and then choose the table from the grid, or choose Insert | Tables | Table | Insert Table, and then use the Insert Table dialog box to specify the details of the nested table.

You can also draw a nested table within a table cell, or paste an existing table within a table cell (right-click within the destination cell, and then choose Paste As Nested Table from the context menu).

Apply a Design to a Table

To make a table look good, you can apply a table style to it—and then adjust the style as needed. Or, if you prefer, you can apply borders and shading to a table manually.

Apply a Table Style

To apply a table style, click in the table, choose Design | Table Styles | Table Styles, and then select the style from the Table Styles panel.

Once you've applied the style, you can adjust parts of the table style by using the six check boxes in the Table Style Options group on the Design tab, shown here. These check boxes let you turn off formatting for the header row, total row (the last row), the first column, and the last column. You can also choose whether to have color-banded columns or color-banded rows—columns or rows with bands of different shading. (You can apply banding to both columns and rows, but in most cases, tables look best from having only one or the other banded, not both.)

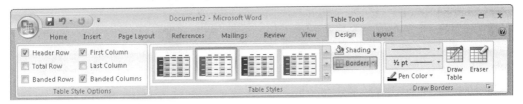

To remove a table style from a table, choose Design | Table Styles | Table Styles | Clear.

Apply Borders and Shading

If you decide to apply borders and shading to a table manually, work as follows:

- To apply shading quickly, select the cells you want to affect, choose Design | Table Styles | Shading, and then choose the color from the Shading panel.

- To apply a border quickly, select the cells you want to affect, choose Design | Table Styles | Borders, and then choose the border from the Borders panel.

- To apply custom borders to a cell or an entire table, click in the cell or table, choose Design | Table Styles | Borders | Borders And Shading, and then work on the Borders tab of the Borders And Shading dialog box. In the Apply To drop-down list, select Cell if you want to affect the cell, or select Table if you want to affect the entire table.

Set Up the Rows, Columns, and Cells in a Table

As you saw earlier in this chapter, you can either let Word set column width for you automatically or specify your preferred column width when you create a table. You can change this setting at any time by clicking in the table and choosing Layout | Cell Size | AutoFit, and then choosing AutoFit Contents, AutoFit Window, or Fixed Column Width from the AutoFit panel, as shown here. You can also change column width manually.

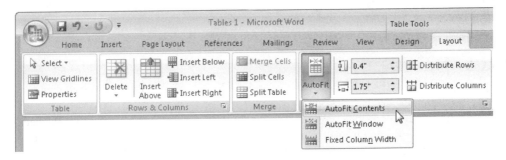

Similarly, Word handles row height automatically, but you can change height manually as needed. And you can change cell margins and alignment if you want.

Create a Custom Table Style

If none of Word's built-in table styles appeals to you, you can create a custom table style. Follow these steps:

1. Choose Design | Table Styles | Table Styles | New Table Style. Word displays the Create New Style From Formatting dialog box.

2. Type the name for the table style in the Name text box. (This is the name you'll use to identify the style, so make it descriptive.)

3. Make sure that Table is selected in the Style Type drop-down list.

4. In the Style Based On drop-down list, select the existing style on which you want to base your custom style. Word applies that style's formatting to the sample table in the Formatting area.

5. Use the controls in the Formatting area to set up the formatting for the table style. Follow these general steps, repeating as often as necessary:

   ■ In the Apply Formatting To drop-down list, select the item you want to affect: Whole Table, Header Row, Total Row, First Column, Last Column, Odd Banded Rows, Even Banded Rows, Odd Banded Columns, Even Banded Columns, Top Left Cell, Top Right Cell, Bottom Left Cell, or Bottom Right Cell.

   ■ Use the two rows of controls to define the formatting. For example, you can apply font formatting or change the borders or shading.

   ■ To make other changes to the table's formatting, properties, or banding, click the Format button, click the item you want to change, and then work in the dialog box. For example, to change banding settings, choose Format | Banding, and then work in the Banding dialog box.

6. To make the table style available to all documents that use this document's template, select the New Documents Based On This Template option button. To confine the table style to this document, select the Only In This Document option button.

7. Click the OK button. Word closes the Create New Style From Formatting dialog box and creates the table style.

After creating the table style, you can apply it from the Custom area at the top of the Table Styles panel.

Adjust Column Width

The quickest way to change column width is to position the mouse pointer over the right border of a column, so that the insertion point changes into a two-headed arrow, as shown here. Then drag the column border to where you want it to appear.

Department		Company
Manufacturing Engineering Logistics		Acme Baking

TIP   *If you have the ruler displayed, you can also drag the column-division mark, which looks like a tiny table within the ruler, instead of the column border.*

If there's a column after the border you drag, Word resizes that column to accommodate the change you make. For example, if you widen the second column in a three-column table, Word makes the third column correspondingly narrower. You can tell Word not to change the next column's width by holding down SHIFT when you're dragging the border.

To make Word share the space evenly among the columns, choose Layout | Cell Size | Distribute Columns.

You can set an exact width for a column in either of these ways:

- Click in the column, and then choose Layout | Cell Size | Table Column Width (enter the width in the Table Column Width text box).

- Click in the column, choose Layout | Cell Size | Table Properties (click the Table Properties button, the tiny button at the right end of the Cell Size bar), and then work on the Column tab of the Table Properties dialog box. Click the Previous Column button to move to the previous column so that you can set its width, or click the Next Column button to move to the next column.

Adjust Row Height

The quickest way to change row height in Print Layout view or Web Layout view is to drag the row's bottom horizontal border up or down. Alternatively, if you have the vertical ruler displayed, you can drag the row-break mark that appears on it.

To make Word make each row the same height, choose Layout | Cell Size | Distribute Rows.

To set an exact height for a row, click in the row, and then choose Layout | Cell Size | Table Row Height (enter the height in the Table Row Height text box). Alternatively, follow these steps:

1. Click in the row you want to affect.

2. Choose Layout | Cell Size | Table Properties (click the Table Properties button, the tiny button at the right end of the Cell Size bar). Word displays the Table Properties dialog box.

3. Click the Row tab. Word displays its contents. The top part of the Row tab is shown here.

4. To set the height for the row, select the Specify Height check box, and then set the height in the text box. In the Row Height Is drop-down list, choose Exactly if you want the row to remain this height, or choose At Least if you want the row to be able to grow from this minimum height.

5. Select the Allow Row To Break Across Pages check box if you want to let Word put part of this row on one page and part on the next page. Normally, you'll want to select this check box only for rows that contain many lines or paragraphs of information. You will normally not want to select this check box for heading rows.

6. Select the Repeat As Header Row At The Top Of Each Page check box if you want this row to be a header row. (Usually, it's easier to use the Layout | Data | Repeat Header Rows command to define any header rows.)

7. Click the Previous Row button if you want to work with the next row, or click the Next Row button to work with the next row.

8. When you've finished changing row height, click the OK button. Word closes the Table Properties dialog box and applies your choices.

Set a Table's Size, Alignment, and Indentation

When you insert a table, Word automatically places it inline with the document's text and applies left alignment. To change the table's size, alignment, indentation, or wrapping, follow these steps:

1. Click in the table.

2. Choose Layout | Table | Properties. Word displays the Table tab of the Table Properties dialog box (see Figure 11-1).

3. To specify the table's size, select the Preferred Width check box, and then set the width in the text box. In the Measure In drop-down list, choose Inches to measure the table in inches or Percent to measure it as a percentage of the line length. For example, you could specify 75% to make the table's width three-quarters of the line length.

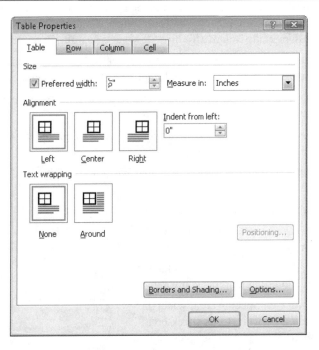

FIGURE 11-1 The Table tab of the Table Properties dialog box lets you specify the table's size, change its alignment or indentation, or change the text wrapping.

4. In the Alignment area, click the Left button, the Center button, or the Right button to set the table's alignment relative to the page's margins. (This alignment is separate from the text alignment within the individual cells.) If you choose Left alignment, you can set the indent distance from the left margin in the Indent From Left text box.

5. In the Text Wrapping area, click the None button if you don't want text to wrap around the table. If you do want wrapping, click the Around button, and then follow these steps:

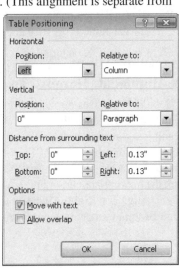

   ▪ Click the Positioning button. Word displays the Table Positioning dialog box, shown here.

   ▪ In the Horizontal area, select the position in the Position drop-down list (Left, Right, Center, Inside, or Outside), and then choose the item in the Relative To drop-down list: Margin, Page, or Column.

■ In the Vertical area, select the position in the Position drop-down list (either a measurement—for example, 0"—or Top, Bottom, Center, Inside, or Outside), then choose the item in the Relative To drop-down list: Margin, Page, or Paragraph.

■ In the Distance From Surrounding Text area, set the amount of space you want between the top, bottom, left side, and right side of the table and the surrounding text.

■ Select the Move With Text check box if you want the table to move with text (as you edit the text) rather than being fixed in place on the page.

■ Select the Allow Overlap check box if you want text to be able to overlap the table. This is useful occasionally for special effects.

■ Click the OK button. Word closes the Table Positioning dialog box, returning you to the Table Properties dialog box.

6. To choose default cell margins and spacing, follow these steps:

■ Click the Options button. Word displays the Table Options dialog box, shown here.

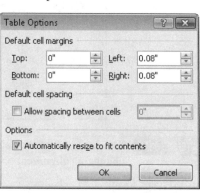

■ In the Default Cell Margins area, set the top, bottom, left, and right margins you want.

■ In the Default Cell Spacing area, select the Allow Spacing Between Cells check box if you want to have spacing between cells. (Normally, cells are flush with one another.) In the text box, enter the measurement.

■ Select the Automatically Resize To Fit Contents check box if you want Word to automatically resize the table to accommodate its contents.

■ Click the OK button. Word closes the Table Options dialog box and returns you to the Table Properties dialog box.

7. Click the OK button. Word closes the Table Properties dialog box and applies your changes.

Set Alignment, Margins, and Text Direction for Cells

By default, Word uses the same alignment and margins for all cells in the table. (You can change the default cell margins for a table as discussed in step 6 in the previous list.) Word also uses the default text direction in the cells—for example, horizontal from left to right when the language is set to U.S. English.

To change the alignment for one or more cells, click in the cell or select the cells, and then click the appropriate button in the Alignment group on the Layout tab: Align Top Left, Align Top Center, Align Top Right, Align Center Left, Align Center, Align Center Right, Align Bottom Left, Align Bottom Center, or Align Bottom Right.

To change the margins for one or more cells, follow these steps:

Cell Options

Cell margins

☐ Same as the whole table

Top: `0.1"`   Left: `0.08"`

Bottom: `0.09"`   Right: `0.08"`

Options

☑ Wrap text
☐ Fit text

[OK]   [Cancel]

1. Click the cell you want to affect, or select two or more cells.

2. Choose Layout | Table | Properties. Word displays the Table Properties dialog box.

3. Click the Cell tab. Word displays the tab's controls.

4. Click the Options button. Word displays the Cell Options dialog box, shown here.

5. Clear the Same As The Whole Table check box, and then set the top, bottom, left, and right margin distances you want.

6. Select the Wrap Text check box if you want Word to wrap text within the cell. Normally, this is a good idea, but you may need to turn it off for special effects.

7. Select the Fit Text check box if you want Word to change the font size and the spacing to fit the text to the cell, stretching the text if it is short or reducing and compressing the text if it is too long. Normally, this is not a good idea, but you may need it occasionally. (The effect can be subtle when the text is only a little too long for the cell.)

8. Click the OK button. Word closes the Cell Options dialog box, returning you to the Table Properties dialog box.

9. Click the OK button. Word closes the Table Properties dialog box.

11

Creating Table Headings

When you create a table that runs from one page to another, you'll probably want to make the table headings repeat on each page so that the reader can easily grasp the contents of each column. To do so, click in the row (or select multiple rows) you want to repeat, and then choose Layout | Data | Repeat Header Rows. Word makes the Repeat Header Rows button appear pushed-in, so that you can see the setting is on.

If you need to remove table headings, click in the row or select the rows, and then choose Layout | Data | Repeat Header Rows. Word makes the Repeat Header Rows button appear normal again.

Sort Table Data

Word lets you sort the data in a table by any of the table's columns—either by a single column, or by two or three columns in sequence.

 CAUTION   *Word can sort only regular tables, not tables containing merged cells or split cells.*

To sort a table, follow these steps:

1. Choose what you want to sort:
   - ■ To sort the entire table, click anywhere in it.
   - ■ To sort just some rows, select those rows.

2. Choose Layout | Data | Sort. Word displays the Sort dialog box, shown here.

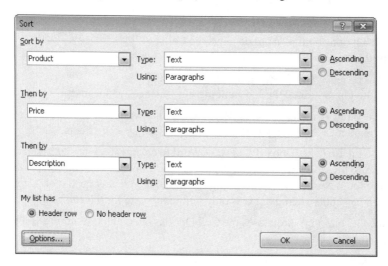

3. At the bottom of the dialog box, make sure that Word has selected the Header Row option button if your table has a row of headings that you don't want to sort. If your table doesn't have headings, make sure the No Header Row option button is selected.

4. In the Sort By area at the top of the dialog box, specify the details of the first sort.
   - ■ In the Sort By drop-down list, choose the field by which you want to sort the table first.

NOTE   *If the table has table headers, the Sort By drop-down list shows the names of the cells in the header row. If the table has no header row, the Sort By drop-down list shows Column 1, Column 2, and so on.*

   - ■ In the Type drop-down list, select the type of sort you want: Text, Number, or Date.
   - ■ In the Using drop-down list, select the items to sort (normally, Paragraphs).
   - ■ Select the Ascending option button to sort in ascending order, or select the Descending option button to sort in descending order.

5. To sort by a second column, select it in the first Then By drop-down list, and then specify the type, using, and order settings.

6. To sort by a third column, select it in the second Then By drop-down list, and then specify the type, using, and order settings.

7. If you need to apply case-sensitive sorting or sort in a different language than your current language, follow these steps:

- Click the Options button. Word displays the Sort Options dialog box, shown here.

- Select the Case Sensitive check box if you want to use case-sensitive sorting.

NOTE *The Separate Fields At options do not apply to sorting within tables.*

11

- If you need to sort in a different language than your current language, choose the sort language in the Sorting Language drop-down list.
- Click the OK button. Word closes the Sort Options dialog box.

8. Click the OK button. Word closes the Sort dialog box and sorts the table (or the rows) you selected.

If you selected some rows in step 1, Word leaves them selected, so you can sort them further if you need to.

Perform Calculations in Tables

If your tables include multiple columns of figures, you may sometimes need to perform calculations in tables. To do so, you can use Word's table formulas. Table formulas are much more limited than the formulas that Excel and other spreadsheet programs provide, but they are enough for straightforward calculations.

CAUTION *Word doesn't automatically update table formulas—so if you change the figures in a table, you will need to update each formula manually. To update a single formula, right-click it, and then choose Update Field from the context menu. To update all the formulas in a table, click the table handle, and then press F9.*

 **Understand How Word Sorts Data**

Word sorts data by records and fields:

- A *record* is one of the sets of information you want to sort—for example, a row in a table that contains the name and address for a customer.

- A *field* is an item of information within a record. For example, in the row containing the customer's details, there may be fields for the customer's title, first name, middle initial, last name, street address (first line), street address (second line), city, state, zip code, and so on.

Word offers three kinds of sorting:

- **Text**   Word sorts punctuation marks and symbols (such as & or !) first, then numbers, and finally letters.

- **Number**   Word sorts symbols first, then letters, then punctuation marks, and finally numbers.

- **Date**   In date order, using any of several date formats.

Word lets you sort in ascending order (from A to Z, from 0 to 9, from early dates to later dates) or in descending order (the opposite).

If two items start with the same letter, Word goes on to the next letter and sorts by that, and so on; if two fields are the same, Word sorts using the next field, etc.

If you want to be able to sort your data effectively, break it up so that each item by which you may ever want to sort is a separate field.

To insert a table formula in a cell, follow these steps:

1. Click in the cell in which you want to place the formula.

2. Choose Layout | Data | Formula. Word displays the Formula dialog box, shown here.

3. In the Formula text box, enter the formula you want.

   - Word automatically suggests a formula depending on the table's layout. For example, if the cell you select in step 1 has figures in cells above it, Word suggests the =SUM(ABOVE) formula; if the cell has figures to the left of it, Word suggests the =SUM(LEFT) formula.

■ You can create simple formulas by referring to the cells in the table as if they were part of a spreadsheet. For example, cell A2 is the cell in the first column and the second row, and cell B3 is the cell in the second column and the third row. Start each formula with an equal sign. For example, =A2+B3 adds cell A2 and cell B3. The formula =A2/B3 divides cell A2 by cell B3.

■ You can either type a formula or assemble it by choosing functions from the Paste Function drop-down list.

■ If the document contains bookmarks, you can paste in a bookmark's name using the Paste Bookmark drop-down list. For example, you can bookmark a value that you need for a formula, and then refer to it by name rather than by table cell.

4. In the Number Format drop-down list, select the number format in which you want to display the formula's result—for example, as a percentage, or with two decimal places.

5. Click the OK button. Word closes the Formula dialog box and inserts the formula in the cell.

Convert a Table to Text

To convert a table back to text, follow these steps:

1. Click in the table. (You don't need to select the whole table.)

2. Choose Layout | Data | Convert To Text. Word displays the Convert Table To Text dialog box, shown here.

3. In the Separate Text With area, select the option button for the character you want to use to separate the data in the table's cells: Paragraph Marks, Tabs, Commas, or Other (you type the character).

4. If you selected the Paragraph Marks option button in step 3, you can decide whether to select or clear the Convert Nested Tables check box. This setting applies only if the table contains one or more nested tables; if so, select the Convert Nested tables check box to have Word convert the nested table to paragraphs, or clear this check box to have Word leave the nested table alone.

5. Click the OK button. Word closes the Convert Table To Text dialog box and converts the table to text as specified.

Create Columns of Text

Tables are great for laying out columns of complex information, but when you need to create snaking, newspaper-style columns, use Word's Columns feature instead. Depending on how far you've gotten with your document, you can either turn existing one-column text into multiple columns, or set up a document to use columns, and then enter the text into them.

You can work with columns in any view, but Word displays them properly only in Print Layout view—so normally you'll want to use this view when working with columns.

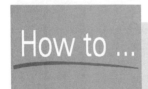 **Use Tables for Quick Sorting and Reformatting**

Tables let you sort data much more finely than regular paragraphs. In some cases, you may choose to convert existing text to a table simply so that you can sort it by any of its columns—or by up to three columns in sequence. After you sort the data into the required order, convert the table back to text.

Tables are also great for reformatting data quickly. For example, say you have many paragraphs of definitions, each of which requires a boldfaced term first, an italicized short definition, and a longer definition. By converting the text to a three-column table, you can quickly apply boldface (or a bold style) to the first column and italics (or an italic style) to the second column. When you convert the table back to text, the formatting remains in place—and you've saved considerable time and effort over applying the formatting manually.

Create Columns Using the Columns Button

To create columns, follow these steps:

1. Choose which part of the document to affect:
   - To turn existing text into columns, select the text.
   - To turn the entire document into columns, click anywhere in it.
   - To turn just part of the document into columns, select that part, even if it consists of nothing but a single blank paragraph.

2. Choose Page Layout | Page Setup | Columns, and then choose the column arrangement from the Columns panel, shown in the illustration on the next page.
   - **One**   Creates a single column. Use this option to return multicolumn text to a single column.
   - **Two**   Creates two even columns.
   - **Three**   Creates three even columns.
   - **Left**   Creates a narrow column on the left and a wider column on the right.
   - **Right**   Creates a wide column on the left and a narrower column on the right.

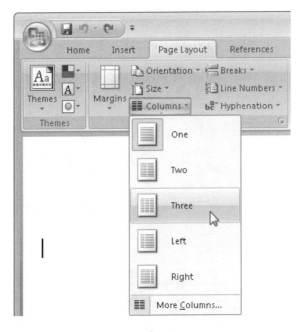

Word applies the column arrangement you choose.

To create more complex columns, or to control the width and spacing of each column, follow these steps:

1. Select the text or document part (as in step 1 of the previous list).

2. Choose Page Layout | Page Setup | Columns | More Columns. Word displays the Columns dialog box (see Figure 11-2).

3. In the Presets area, select the column arrangement you want (see step 2 of the previous list for descriptions).

4. If necessary, use the Number Of Columns check box to increase the number of columns.

5. Select the Line Between check box if you want Word to display and print a vertical line between each pair of columns.

6. In the Width And Spacing area, clear the Equal Column Width check box if you want to be able to create unequal columns. (Word selects this check box if you choose the Two arrangement or the Three arrangement.)

7. Use the Width text box and Spacing text box to set the width and spacing for each column. (Scroll up and down the list if you have more than three columns.)

8. In the Apply To drop-down list, verify that Word has selected the correct part of the document—for example, Selected Text, This Section, Whole Document, or This Point Forward.

11

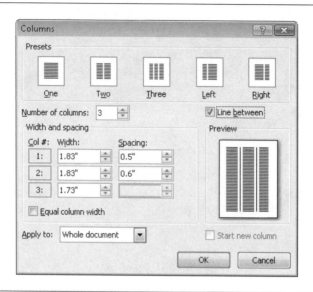

FIGURE 11-2 Use the Columns dialog box to specify exact widths for columns or to add space or lines between them.

9. If you've selected This Point Forward in the Apply To drop-down list, select the Start New Column check box if you want to start a new column layout from this point.

10. Click the OK button. Word closes the Columns dialog box and creates the columns you specified.

Insert and Delete Column Breaks

To start a new column, position the insertion point before the character that will begin the column, and then choose Page Layout | Breaks | Column. Word inserts a column break.

Like paragraph marks, column breaks are normally invisible, but you can display them by choosing Home | Paragraph | Show/Hide ¶.

To delete a column break, place the insertion point before it, and then press DELETE.

Use Different Numbers of Columns in Different Parts of a Document

To use different numbers of columns in different parts of a document, you must put each part in a separate section. See the section "Break a Document into Sections" in Chapter 5 for instructions on creating sections. Alternatively, select the text you want to turn into a section, and apply a different number of columns as described in this section. Word then creates the section for you automatically.

Chapter 12

Create Bookmarks, References, Footnotes, and Indexes

How to...

- Mark parts of a document with bookmarks
- Insert references
- Create footnotes and endnotes
- Create an index
- Create a table of contents, figures, or authorities

In complex documents, you'll often need to mark a part of a document so that you can access it quickly or refer to it. Word's bookmarks let you place marks that you can either move to easily or refer to automatically in text. You can also add references to other items in a document, such as headings.

Complex documents may also need footnotes or endnotes, an index, or a table of contents, a table of figures, or a table of authorities. Word provides features for creating all of these items easily.

Mark Parts of a Document with Bookmarks

Much as you can place a physical bookmark in a paper book, Word lets you place one or more electronic bookmarks in each document. A bookmark can mark either a single point in text—for example, the point between two characters in a word—or a particular section of text that you select.

Set a Bookmark to Mark a Location

To mark a location with a bookmark, you *add* the bookmark. Follow these steps:

1. Choose where to put the bookmark.

    - If you want to mark a single point in the text, place the insertion point at that point.

    - If you want to mark a section of text, or another item (such as a table, a text box, or a graphic), select that item.

2. Choose Insert | Links | Bookmark. Word displays the Bookmark dialog box, shown here with some bookmarks created already using the technique described here.

3. In the Bookmark Name text box, type the name for the bookmark.

Follow these rules:

■ Each name must start with a letter and can be up to 40 characters long.

■ After the first character, the name can use any combination of letters, numbers, and underscores.

■ The name may not contain any spaces or symbols.

> **NOTE** *If you want to change the location of an existing bookmark to refer to the new place or text you chose, click the bookmark's name in the list box.*

4. Click the Add button. Word closes the Bookmark dialog box and adds the bookmark to the document.

Go to a Bookmark

To move to a bookmark, follow these steps:

1. Choose Insert | Links | Bookmark. Word displays the Bookmark dialog box.

2. In the list box, select the bookmark to which you want to move.

> **TIP** *In the Sort By area of the Bookmark dialog box, you can select the Name option button to sort the document's bookmarks alphabetically by name or the Location option button to sort the bookmarks by their locations in the document (first bookmark first, last bookmark last). If you know the name of the bookmark you're looking for, the alphabetical list is usually easiest; but if you're looking for a bookmark by topic, the location list may be more helpful. For special needs, you may also need to select the Hidden Bookmarks check box. Selecting this check box makes Word display the secret bookmarks it uses for maintaining cross-references and similar features. (For example, when you use the Insert | Links | Cross-Reference command to insert a cross-reference, as discussed later in this chapter, Word automatically creates a bookmark to enable it to implement the reference.)*

3. Click the Go To button. Word displays the bookmark's location in the document.

4. Click the Close button. Word closes the Bookmark dialog box.

You can also use the Go To dialog box to move to a bookmark. Unless you've already opened the Go To dialog box for another purpose (for example, to go to a particular page or section), this method of moving to a bookmark is normally slower and more awkward than using the Bookmark dialog box. Follow these steps:

1. Click the Page Number readout in the status bar, or press F5, or choose Home | Editing | Find | Go To. Word displays the Go To tab of the Find And Replace dialog box.

2. In the Go To What list box, select Bookmark.

3. In the Enter Bookmark Name drop-down list on the right side of the dialog box, choose the bookmark's name. (Select the name—you don't need to enter it.)

4. Click the Go To button. Word displays the bookmark's location in the document.

5. Click the Close button. Word closes the Find And Replace dialog box.

12

Display Bookmarks in a Document

Once you've inserted a bookmark in a document, it stays there until you delete it, either deliberately (as described in the next section) or accidentally. Word normally keeps bookmarks hidden, which helps prevent them from cluttering up your documents visually but makes it easy to delete them accidentally. For example, say you create a bookmark in the word "Office." When you select the word "Office" and type "Branch" over it, you delete the bookmark.

To avoid deleting bookmarks accidentally like this, or to avoid creating multiple bookmarks marking the same point in the document, you can make Word display bookmarks. Follow these steps:

1. Click the Office Button, and then click Word Options. Word displays the Word Options dialog box.

2. In the left pane, click the Advanced category, and then scroll down to the Show Document Content area.

3. Select the Show Bookmarks check box.

4. Click the OK button. Word closes the Word Options dialog box.

Word displays a thick I-beam for a bookmark that marks a single point in a document, as shown here.

You can bookmark a point in a document.

Word displays square brackets to indicate a bookmark that encloses text or another object, as in the two examples shown here.

You can place bookmarks around [text] or other objects, such as

 or a picture.

Delete a Bookmark

You can delete a bookmark by selecting the text or object around it and then pressing DELETE or typing over the selection, but the normal way of deleting a bookmark is less destructive of the bookmark's contents or surroundings. Follow these steps:

1. Choose Insert | Links | Bookmark. Word displays the Bookmark dialog box.

2. In the list box, select the bookmark you want to delete.

3. Click the Delete button. Word deletes the bookmark without confirmation.

4. Click the Close button. Word closes the Bookmark dialog box.

Insert References

In a complex document, you'll often need to refer to another part of the same document. While you can retype that part of the document manually, it's easier and quicker to insert a reference—especially if the referenced part of the document may change.

You can insert a reference to a bookmark, to a heading or other paragraph, or to another element. This section shows you how to insert a reference to a bookmark, but the procedure for inserting references to other items is almost the same.

To insert a reference to a bookmark, follow these steps:

1. Create the bookmark as described in the previous section.

2. Position the insertion point where you want the reference to appear. Usually, this will be in a different part of the document from the bookmark.

3. Choose Insert | Links | Cross-Reference. Word displays the Cross-Reference dialog box, shown here with choices made.

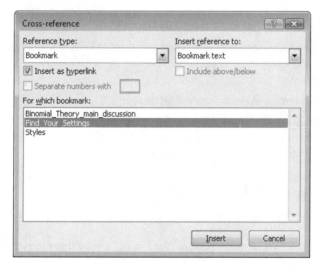

4. In the Reference Type drop-down list, choose Bookmark.

5. In the Insert Reference To drop-down list, choose whether to refer to the bookmark's text, the page number on which the bookmark appears, or another item.

   ■ **Bookmark Text** Select this item to insert the contents of the bookmark where the reference appears. For this to work, create a bookmark that has contents—for example, a word (such as a client's name) or a paragraph. Word then copies the bookmark's contents to the reference. This is a handy way of keeping variable text current throughout a document.

   ■ **Page Number** Select this item to insert the page number on which the bookmark appears. If the bookmark spans two or more pages, Word returns the number of the first page.

12

- **Paragraph Number**   Select this item to include the paragraph number (from a numbered list).
- **Paragraph Number (No Context)**   Select this item to include the paragraph number for this paragraph but not the "context" numbers that show where the bookmarked paragraph appears within a multilevel list. For example, if the bookmarked paragraph is paragraph 1.a., this item gives you **a.** rather than **1.a.**.
- **Paragraph Number (Full Context)**   Select this item to include the paragraph number with its full context from a multilevel list—for example, **1.a.**. If you want to use a different separator character than the one used in the list's numbering, select the Separate Numbers With check box, and then type the character in the text box. For example, you might use a closing parenthesis rather than a period.
  - **Above/Below**   Select this item to have Word include the word "above" if the bookmark appears earlier in the document or "below" if the bookmark appears later in it.

6. For a page number or a paragraph number, select the Include Above/Below check box if you want Word to include the word "above" if the bookmark appears earlier in the document or the word "below" if it appears later.

7. Select the Insert As Hyperlink check box if you want to insert the reference as an item that you can CTRL-click to go to the source bookmark. Such hyperlinks tend to be useful for keeping complex references straight.

8. Click the Insert button. Word inserts the reference.

9. If you need to insert another reference, click in the document, place the insertion point, and then insert the reference using the Cross-Reference dialog box again. Otherwise, click the Close button. Word closes the Cross-Reference dialog box.

Create Footnotes and Endnotes

For academic or other detailed documents, you may need to include footnotes or endnotes:

- **Footnote**   A note placed at the bottom (the foot) of a page that refers to a specific part of the text on that page.
- **Endnote**   A note placed at the end of the document. If the document has sections, you can have endnotes appear at the end of each section or at the end of the whole document.

Word numbers footnotes and endnotes automatically, keeping footnote numbering and endnote numbering separate. Word also automatically adjusts page length to provide space for footnotes, running lengthy footnotes to the next page as needed.

Insert a Footnote

To insert a footnote, follow these steps:

1. Place the insertion point where you want to insert the footnote mark. Normal placement is at the end of the last word to which the footnote refers.

How to ...   **Choose Between Footnotes and Endnotes**

You can use both footnotes and endnotes in the same document, but to make reading easy, it's usually best to choose one or the other.

Footnotes are easier to refer to than endnotes because the reader doesn't need to turn the page to see the note (unless the note runs from one page to the next). However, because footnotes are more visible, they tend to distract the reader's eye more than endnotes—so if you want to provide notes that you expect relatively few readers to read, you may prefer to use endnotes, as they break up the flow of the text less.

Endnotes, which appear together at the end of the document or section, are easier for the reader to browse than footnotes. However, many readers actively dislike having to turn the pages in a book or report to access note material that could easily be displayed on the same page by using footnotes.

When deciding between footnotes and endnotes, also consider note length. If some or many of your notes will be lengthy, endnotes may be a better choice than footnotes. Any footnote that takes up more than a quarter or a third of a page tends to make the layout look awkward, especially if part of the footnote has to flow to the next page.

2. Choose References | Footnotes | Insert Footnote. Word inserts a superscript footnote number or mark at the insertion point and a corresponding footnote number or mark in the footnote area.

■ If you're using Print Layout view, Word displays the footnote area at the bottom of the page, looking as it will when you print it. Here is an example.

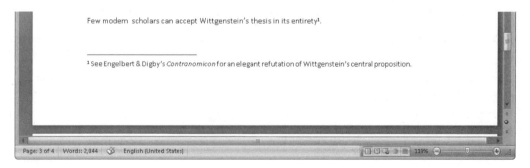

Few modern scholars can accept Wittgenstein's thesis in its entirety[1].

_____

[1] See Engelbert & Digby's *Contranomicon* for an elegant refutation of Wittgenstein's central proposition.

Page: 3 of 4 | Words: 2,044 | English (United States)   110%

12

■ If you're using another view, Word displays the footnote area in the footnote pane, as shown here.

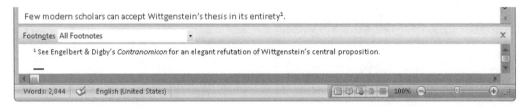

3. Type the footnote (or paste it in). You can also enter other types of content, such as Clip Art or WordArt, but these tend to be less useful in most documents.

4. Return to the main document:

   ■ If you're using Print Layout view, click in the main document.

   ■ If you're using another view, either click the Close button (the × button) or choose References | Footnotes | Show Notes to close the footnote pane, or simply click in the main document pane to continue working with the footnote pane still open.

Insert an Endnote

To insert an endnote, follow these steps:

1. Place the insertion point where you want to insert the endnote mark. As with footnotes, the usual practice is to place the mark at the end of the last word to which the endnote refers.

2. Choose References | Footnotes | Insert Endnote. Word inserts a superscript endnote number or mark at the insertion point and a corresponding endnote number or mark in the endnote area.

   ■ If you're using Print Layout view or Web Layout view, Word displays the endnote area immediately after the current end of the document, with a dividing line in between the two, as shown here.

And that was the last they heard of the notorious critic[iii]...

... or was it?

More next time!

---

[i] For details on McCavity, see the collected works of Eliot.
[ii] Ibid.
[iii] Beckett famously used this word as a term of abuse—at the insistence of the censors.

■ If you're using Draft view or Outline view, Word displays the endnote area in the endnote pane, as shown here.

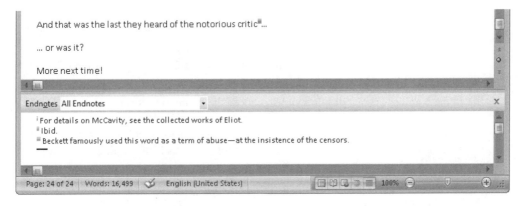

3. Type the endnote (or paste it in). You can also enter other types of content, such as equations or charts, if you need them.

4. Return to the main document:

■ If you're using Print Layout view or Web Layout view, click in the main document.

■ If you're using Draft view or Outline view, either click the Close button (the × button) or choose References | Footnotes | Show Notes to close the endnote pane, or simply click in the main document pane to continue working with the endnote pane still open.

Choose Options for Footnotes and Endnotes

If you simply need to insert footnotes or endnotes as described in the previous two sections, you may find that Word's default placement and numbering of footnotes and endnotes needs no change. But if you want to customize your footnotes or endnotes, follow these steps:

1. If the document has multiple sections, click in the section you want to affect. If you want to affect the whole document, click anywhere in it.

2. Choose References | Footnotes | Footnote And Endnote (click the tiny button at the right end of the Footnotes bar). Word displays the Footnote And Endnote dialog box, shown here.

3. In the Location area, select the Footnotes option button if you want to choose options for footnotes. Select the Endnotes option button if you want to work with endnotes.

12

4. To change where the footnotes or endnotes appear in the document:

- In the Footnotes drop-down list, choose Bottom Of Page or Below Text. Bottom Of Page is the default setting.

- In the Endnotes drop-down list, choose End Of Section or End Of Document. End Of Document is the default setting.

5. In the Format area, choose the number format or custom mark you want for the footnotes or endnotes:

- In the Number Format drop-down list, choose the numbering format you want for the notes. Word offers the formats "1, 2, 3"; "a, b, c"; "A, B, C"; "i, ii, iii"; "I, II, III"; and a series of asterisk, dagger, double-dagger, and other symbols. The default for footnotes is the "1, 2, 3" format. The default for endnotes is the "i, ii, iii" format.

- If you prefer to use a custom note mark, click the Symbol button, choose the symbol in the Symbol dialog box, and then click the OK button. Word enters the symbol in the Custom Mark text box.

- If you chose a numbering format, you can set the starting number in the Start At text box.

- In the Numbering drop-down list, choose Continuous to create continuous numbers throughout the document. Choose Restart Each Page to restart numbering on each page for footnotes. (Restart Each Page is not available for endnotes.) Choose Restart Each Section to restart note numbering at the beginning of each new section.

6. Click the Apply button. Word applies the changes to the notes.

7. Click the Close button. Word closes the Footnote And Endnote dialog box.

Convert Footnotes to Endnotes or Vice Versa

While creating a document, you may find that you need to convert footnotes into endnotes, or convert endnotes into footnotes. Word lets you perform both these tasks easily, and even lets you swap footnotes and endnotes.

To convert footnotes or endnotes, follow these steps:

1. Choose References | Footnotes | Footnote And Endnote (click the tiny button at the right end of the Footnotes bar). Word displays the Footnote And Endnote dialog box.

2. Click the Convert button. Word displays the Convert Notes dialog box, shown here.

3. Select the appropriate option button:

- **Convert All Footnotes To Endnotes** Select this option button to turn all footnotes into endnotes. Any existing endnotes remain endnotes.

- **Convert All Endnotes To Footnotes** Select this option button to turn all endnotes into footnotes. Any existing footnotes remain footnotes.

- **Swap Footnotes And Endnotes** Select this option button to turn footnotes into endnotes and endnotes into footnotes.

4. Click the OK button. Word closes the Convert Notes dialog box and converts the footnotes or endnotes.

5. Click the Close button. Word closes the Footnote And Endnote dialog box.

Display the Footnote Area or Endnote Area

To display the footnote area or endnote area, choose References | Footnotes | Show Notes. If the document contains only footnotes, Word displays the footnote area; if the document contains only endnotes, Word displays the endnote area. If the document contains both footnotes and endnotes, Word displays the View Footnotes dialog box (shown here) so that you can choose which area to display.

Review and Move Among Footnotes or Endnotes

To view a footnote or endnote quickly without displaying the footnote area or endnote area, hover the mouse pointer over the footnote mark or endnote mark. Word displays a ScreenTip showing the note. Complex elements may suffer somewhat, as in the example here, but you can get the general idea.

You can determine the audience's reaction by using the following equation:
$f(x) = a\_0 + \sum (n=1)^\infty (a\_n \cos[n\pi x/L] + b\_n \sin[n\pi x/L])$

the audience went wild (as measured on the Applaudometer[4]).

You can move among footnotes or endnotes in two ways:

- Choose References | Footnotes | Next Footnote to move to the next footnote. To move to the previous footnote, the previous endnote, or the next endnote, choose References | Footnotes | Next Footnote (click the drop-down button), and then choose the appropriate command from the drop-down menu, shown here.

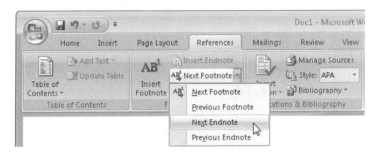

■ Double-click a footnote number or endnote number in the footnote area or endnote area to jump to the corresponding number in the document. Similarly, you can double-click a note number in the document to jump to that note in the footnote area or endnote area.

Create an Index

If you create long reports or similar documents, you may need to create indexes for them. Indexing is a complex task best suited for professionals—but Word makes the process of creating a modest index as simple as possible.

Understand How Indexing Works in Word

To create an index in a Word document, you mark each item that you want to index, inserting a special code in the document that tells Word whether to create a main entry or a subentry. When you're ready to create the index, you give Word the command to do so. After creating the index, you can rearrange your document as needed and update the index with the latest page numbers.

Mark Index Entries and Subentries

To mark index entries, follow these steps:

1. Select the word or phrase from which you want to create an index entry.

2. Choose References | Index | Mark Entry or press ALT-SHIFT-X. Word displays the Mark Index Entry dialog box, shown here, and puts the selected word or phrase in the Main Entry text box.

3. In the Main Entry text box, change the suggested entry if necessary.

4. In the Subentry text box, type the text for any subentry you want to create.

5. In the Options area, choose whether to mark the index entry with a page number, a page range, or a cross-reference:

   ■ **Cross-Reference**   Select this option button if you want to create a cross-reference to another index entry (for example, "saline overdose, *see* salt"). Word inserts the word *See* in italics in the text box to help you create a standard cross-reference. Type the index entry after *See*.

   ■ **Current Page**   Select this option button if you want to display the current page number next to the index entry (for example, "global warming, 483").

   ■ **Page Range**   Select this option button if you want to display a range of pages for this entry rather than a single page number (for example, "glaciers, 23–25"). To use a range of pages, you must define a bookmark spanning the range (see "Set a Bookmark to Mark a Location," earlier in this chapter). After creating the bookmark, select it in the Bookmark drop-down list.

6. In the Page Number Format area, select the Bold check box if you want the page number to appear in boldface. Select the Italic check box if you want the page number to appear in italics. For example, you might use boldface to indicate important mentions of a topic and use italic to indicate charts or illustrations.

7. Click the Mark button to mark this instance of the word or phrase. Click the Mark All button to mark each instance in the document.

8. Word leaves the Mark Index Entry dialog box open to allow you to continue marking index entries. When you want to close the Mark Index Entry dialog box, click the Close button.

Word formats the index entries as hidden text, so they're normally invisible in your documents. To see the index entries, choose Home | Paragraph | Show/Hide ¶. You'll then see each code appear in braces after the term it marks:

Index Entry	Sample Index Code
Standard reference	{ XE "Space Tower" }
Boldface reference	{ XE "Space Tower" \b }
Italic reference	{ XE "Space Tower" \i }
Reference to bookmarked page range	{ XE "Space Tower" \r "Space_Tower_description" }
Cross-reference	{ XE "Space Tower" \t "*See* Landmarks" }

12

 **Mark Index Entries Automatically Using a Concordance File**

Marking index entries manually gives you plenty of control over the process, but it can take a long time. A quicker option is to create a *concordance file*, a file that lists the terms you want to have indexed, and then have Word create the index entries automatically from it.

To create a concordance file, follow these steps:

1. Press CTRL-N. Word creates a new blank document. (You can also create a document based on a particular template if you prefer.)

2. Choose Insert | Tables | Table, and then choose a two-column table from the Table panel. The number of rows doesn't matter, as you can easily add more rows, but make sure no row is left blank.

3. In the first cell of each row, type the word that you want to have indexed. In the second cell, type the index entry itself. For example:

   ```
   anecdotal evidence      evidence, anecdotal
   Thomas McKeown          McKeown, Thomas
   ```

4. Press CTRL-S or click the Save button on the Quick Access Toolbar. Word displays the Save As dialog box. Save the concordance file as a Word document using a name and folder of your choice.

5. Double-click the Office Button, or press CTRL-W. Word closes the concordance file.

To index a document automatically using your concordance file, follow these steps:

1. In the document you want to index, choose References | Index | Insert Index. Word displays the Index dialog box with the Index tab foremost.

2. Click the AutoMark button. Word displays the Open Index AutoMark File dialog box, which is an Open dialog box with a different name.

3. Select the concordance file, and then click the Open button. Word uses the concordance file to index the open document, and then displays a message, such as *420 index entries marked*, in the status bar.

Produce the Index

Once you've marked the entries, you're ready to create the index. Follow these steps:

1. Position the insertion point where you want the index to appear—for example, at the end of the document.

2. Choose References | Index | Insert Index. Word displays the Index dialog box with the Index tab foremost, shown here with choices made.

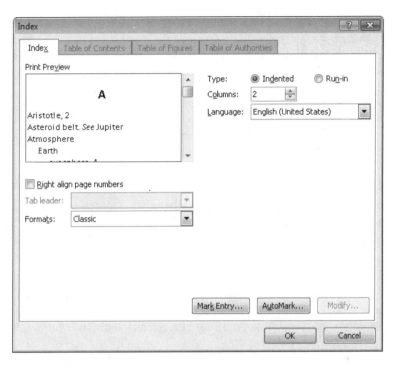

3. In the Type area, choose the type of index to create:

- ■ **Indented**   Select this option button to create a standard index with subentries indented below the main entry. An indented index is easy to read, as each subentry appears on its own line, but takes up more space.

- ■ **Run-in**   Select this option button to create an index in which the subentries are run into the main entry's paragraph, separated with semicolons. Run-in indexes are more compact than indented indexes but tend to be harder to read, especially when entries have many subentries.

4. In the Columns text box, set the number of columns for the index. Two columns are usually best, but you may need to use three columns to cram an index into a modest amount of space.

5. In the Language drop-down list, you can choose the language for the index—for example, English (United States). Word automatically suggests your current language, so normally you won't need to change it.

6. In the Formats drop-down list, choose the format for the index. Your choices are From Template (using the styles in the template attached to the document), Classic, Fancy, Modern, Bulleted, Formal, or Simple. The Print Preview box shows the look of the selected format.

12

7. If you selected the Indented option button, you can choose to right-align the page numbers and apply a tab leader. To do so, select the Right Align Page Numbers check box, and then choose the tab leader characters (dots, dashes, or underlines) from the Tab Leader drop-down list.

8. Click the OK button. Word closes the Index dialog box, repaginates the document if needed, and then inserts the index.

If you chose an index layout using two or more columns, Word creates the index in its own section, using continuous section breaks.

Format an Index

Word automatically applies the styles Index 1 through Index 9 to indexes, using Index 1 for a main entry, Index 2 for a first-level subentry, and so on. You can format the index by changing these styles. Chapter 4 discusses how to work with styles.

Update an Index

After you first create your index, you may find that it needs more entries or subentries, or that you need to change entries.

To delete an existing index entry, choose Home | Paragraph | Show/Hide ¶ to display index codes, select the code, and then press DELETE.

To update an index, right-click anywhere in it, and then choose Update Field from the context menu. Alternatively, click anywhere in the index, and then press F9.

Create a Table of Contents, Figures, or Authorities

To help you make long documents easy to navigate, Word lets you create tables of contents, tables of authorities, and tables of figures.

Create a Table of Contents

A table of contents is a brief overview of a document—normally, a list of the top two or three levels of headings, with page numbers to allow the reader to go directly to any heading. For an example of a table of contents, see the front of this book.

Word creates tables of contents from paragraph styles. If you've used Word's built-in Heading 1 to Heading 9 styles for the headings in a document, you can create a table of contents instantly. If you've used other styles for the headings (or if you want to create the table of contents from paragraphs other than the headings), you'll need to customize the table of contents.

To create a table of contents, follow these steps:

1. Place the insertion point where you want to insert the table of contents—for example, at or near the beginning of the document.

2. Choose Insert | Table Of Contents | Table Of Contents, and then do one of the following:

- Choose a built-in table of contents style from the Table Of Contents panel. Word inserts the table of contents and applies the formatting in the style. Skip the rest of this list.

- Choose Insert Table Of Contents from the Table Of Contents panel. Word displays the Table Of Contents dialog box with the Table Of Contents tab foremost. The Table Of Contents dialog box is the same dialog box as the Index dialog box—except that Word changes the dialog box's title to match the tab displayed.

3. In the Formats drop-down list, select the format you want. Your choices are From Template (using the TOC 1 through TOC 9 styles in the template attached to the document), Classic, Distinctive, Fancy, Modern, Formal, or Simple. The Print Preview box and the Web Preview box show you how the selected format looks.

4. In the Show Levels text box, set the number of heading levels to include. You can set from 1 level (Heading 1 paragraphs only) to 9 levels (Heading 1 through Heading 9 paragraphs).

5. Choose whether to include the page numbers and how to lay them out:

- Select the Show Page Numbers check box if you want to include a page number alongside each heading. Normally, the page numbers are useful.

- Select the Right Align Page Numbers check box if you want the page numbers to be aligned with the right margin, as is standard in most table of contents designs.

- If you select the Right Align Page Numbers check box, choose the tab leader character in the Tab Leader drop-down list. Your choices are "(none)" (having no tab leader), periods, hyphens, or underscores. Periods are the most widely used.

6. Select the Use Hyperlinks Instead Of Page Numbers check box if you want the web version of the table of contents to use hyperlinks instead of page numbers. The hyperlinks are usually more helpful than page numbers.

7. If you want to create the table of contents from styles other than the Heading styles, follow these steps:

- Click the Options button. Word displays the Table Of Contents Options dialog box, shown here.

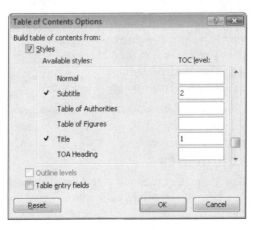

12

- Make sure the Styles check box is selected.

- Use the TOC Level boxes in the Available Styles list box to specify the styles from which you want to create the table of contents and the levels you want to assign them. For example, to use the Title style for the first level of the table of contents and the Subtitle style for the second level, type 1 in the TOC Level box alongside the Title style and 2 in the TOC Level box alongside the Subtitle style.

- Click the OK button. Word closes the Table Of Contents Options dialog box and returns you to the Table Of Contents dialog box.

8. Click the OK button. Word closes the Table Of Contents dialog box and inserts the table of contents at the position of the insertion point.

To update a table of contents, follow these steps:

1. Click the table of contents to display a border around it, as shown here.

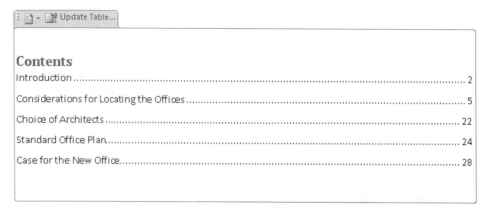

2. Click the Update Table button at the upper-left corner of the border. Word displays the Update Table Of Contents dialog box, shown here.

3. Select the Update Page Numbers Only option button if you don't want to include any changes to headings (or other styles you've used) in the table of contents. Otherwise, select the Update Entire Table option button to update both page numbers and styles.

4. Click the OK button. Word closes the Update Table Of Contents dialog box and updates the table of contents.

Create a Table of Authorities

A *table of authorities* is a list of the sources used for a legal document or scholarly work (such as a thesis). Word lets you create a table of authorities easily once you've marked the citations that you want to include in the table.

Mark the Citations for a Table of Authorities

To mark the citations for a table of authorities, follow these steps:

1. In the document, select the first item for which you want to create a citation.

2. Choose References | Table Of Authorities | Mark Citation. Word displays the Mark Citation dialog box, shown here with choices made. Word automatically displays the text you selected in step 1 in the Selected Text box and the Short Citation text box.

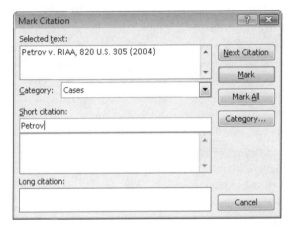

3. If necessary, format the text in the Selected Text box as needed for the citation. You can use keyboard shortcuts such as CTRL-B (boldface) or CTRL-I (italics), or you can select the text, right-click, choose Font, and then work in the Font dialog box.

4. Edit the text in the Short Citation text box to produce the shortened name by which you will refer to the authority (for example, the plaintiff's name or main author's name).

12

5. In the Category drop-down list, select the category to which the authority belongs: Cases, Statutes, Other Authorities, Rules, Treatises, Regulations, Constitutional Provisions, or one of the numbered categories (8 through 16) that appear further down the list. You can change a category name by clicking the Category button and working in the Edit Category dialog box (shown here).

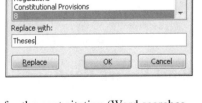

6. To mark each citation for this authority, click the Mark button. Alternatively, click the Mark All button to mark all the citations at once.

7. Click the Next Citation button to make Word search for the next citation (Word searches for identifying text such as "v." and section marks). Continue marking the citations found.

8. When you've finished marking citations, click the Close button. Word closes the Mark Citation dialog box.

Generate the Table of Authorities

To generate the table of authorities from the citations you've marked, follow these steps:

1. Position the insertion point where you want to insert the table of authorities (for example, at the end of the document).

2. Choose References | Table Of Authorities | Insert Table Of Authorities. Word displays the Table Of Authorities dialog box with the Table Of Authorities tab foremost.

3. In the Category list box, select the All item if you want to include all authorities. To include just one category, select it by name.

4. Select the Use Passim check box if you want Word to mark authorities that have five or more references with *passim* (meaning "throughout the document") rather than giving each page reference. (Your course advisor or guidelines should tell you whether to use "passim" or not in your table of authorities.)

5. Select the Keep Original Formatting check box if you want to preserve the formatting used for the references. Usually, this is a good idea.

6. In the Formats drop-down list, choose the format you want for the table of authorities: From Template (using the styles in the template attached to the document), Classic, Distinctive, Formal, or Simple.

7. In the Tab Leader drop-down list, choose the tab leader character to use. Your choices are "(none)" (having no tab leader), periods, hyphens, or underscores. Periods are the most widely used.

8. Click the OK button. Word closes the Table Of Authorities dialog box and inserts the table of authorities.

To update a table of authorities, right-click anywhere in it, and then choose Update Field from the context menu.

Create a Table of Figures

To create a table of figures—essentially, a list of the figure captions in a document—you must first apply captions to the figures using Word's captions feature. These captions can save you time and effort because Word automatically updates the numbering for you.

You can also use Word's captions for tables or equations. This section assumes that you're using figures, but the steps are almost identical for tables and equations.

Insert Figure Captions

To insert figure captions, follow these steps:

1. Insert the figure that you will caption, and then select it.

2. Choose References | Captions | Insert Caption. Word displays the Caption dialog box, shown here.

3. In the Label drop-down list, make sure that Word has selected Figure. (For tables, choose Table; for equations, choose Equation. To number other items, click the New Label button, type the item's label in the New Label dialog box, and then click the OK button.) Word enters your choice in the Caption text box, along with the next number in the automatic sequence (for example, Figure 1 for the first figure).

4. If you want to exclude the label from the caption, select the Exclude Label From Caption check box. For example, if you exclude the label "Figure," Word captions the first figure "1" rather than "Figure 1."

5. Type the rest of the figure's caption in the Caption text box. For example, you might type a colon followed by some text describing the figure's content or meaning.

6. In the Position drop-down list, choose where to position the caption in the document— for example, Above Selected Item or Below Selected Item.

7. If you need to customize the caption numbering (for example, to include the chapter numbers), follow these steps:

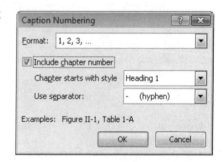

■ Click the Numbering button. Word displays the Caption Numbering dialog box, shown here.

■ In the Format drop-down list, select the numbering format: 1, 2, 3; a, b, c; A, B, C; i, ii, iii; or I, II, III.

■ Select the Include Chapter Number check box if you want to include the chapter number (giving numbering such as "Figure 1-14"). In the Chapter Starts With Style drop-down list, select the style that marks the start of each chapter (for example, Heading 1). In the Use Separator drop-down list, choose the separator character— hyphen, period, colon, em (long) dash, or en (short) dash.

■ Click the OK button. Word closes the Caption Numbering dialog box.

8. Click the OK button. Word closes the Caption dialog box and applies the caption to the figure.

Create the Table of Figures

Once you've captioned your figures, you can create a table of figures quickly. Follow these steps:

1. Position the insertion point where you want to insert the table of figures.

2. Choose References | Captions | Insert Table Of Figures. Word displays the Table Of Figures dialog box with the Table Of Figures tab foremost.

3. In the Formats drop-down list, choose the format for the table of figures. Your choices are From Template (using the styles in the template attached to the document), Classic, Distinctive, Centered, Formal, and Simple. The Print Preview box shows the look of the selected format for printing. The Web Preview box shows the look for creating a web page.

4. In the Caption Label drop-down list, select the caption label you want to include: "(none)," Equation, Figure, or Table.

5. Select the Include Label And Number check box if you want to include the figure (or table, or equation) label and number. Usually, this information is needed, but for special purposes, you may want to omit it.

6. Select the Show Page Numbers check box if you want to include a page number alongside each caption. Normally, the page numbers are useful.

7. Select the Right Align Page Numbers check box if you want the page numbers to be aligned with the right margin. (This option is not available for the Centered format.)

8. If you select the Right Align Page Numbers check box, choose the tab leader character in the Tab Leader drop-down list. Your choices are "(none)" (having no tab leader), periods, hyphens, or underscores. Periods are the most widely used.

9. Click the OK button. Word closes the Table Of Figures dialog box and inserts the table of figures in the document.

Once you've inserted the table of figures, you can CTRL-click an entry in it to jump to the figure in the document.

Update a Table of Figures

To update a table of figures, follow these steps:

1. Right-click anywhere in the table, and then choose Update Field from the context menu. Word displays the Update Table Of Figures dialog box, shown here.

2. Select the Update Page Numbers Only option button if you don't want to include any changes to captions or figures themselves. Otherwise, select the Update Entire Table option button to update both page numbers and captions.

3. Click the OK button. Word closes the Update Table Of Figures dialog box and updates the table of figures.

Chapter 13

Blog and Create Web Pages with Word

How to...

- Create blog entries from Word
- Understand saving directly to an intranet site or Internet server
- Choose Web Options to control how Word creates web pages
- Understand HTML, round tripping, and web file formats
- Save a Word document as a web page

In this chapter, you'll learn how to use Word's web capabilities. First up is one of Word's most popular new features—the ability to create and publish blog entries directly from Word. After that, you'll learn how to save documents directly to intranet servers and Internet servers—and why you may sometimes be better off *not* saving files directly to such servers.

You'll then find out how to choose suitable options for creating web pages, learn which of Word's web file formats is best for which purposes, and save documents as web pages.

Blog from Word

If you have (or want) your own *weblog*, or *blog* for short, you're probably eager to learn about easy ways to create your blog posts. Various blog services provide online templates that you can use when your computer is connected to the Internet, but these don't work when your computer is offline.

Find Out Whether Word Supports Your Blogging Service

At this writing, Word supports the blogging services listed in Table 13-1.

If you haven't yet chosen a blogging service, and you want to blog from Word, choosing a service from this list makes the most sense. The free services are supported by advertising, which gives your blog a less professional feel—so if you're planning to take your blog seriously, paying the relatively modest fees for an advertising-free service may be preferable.

Service	URL	Comments
Blogger	http://www.blogger.com	Free, but you must create a Google account (Google owns Blogger)
WordPress	http://www.wordpress.com	Free
Windows Live Spaces	http://spaces.live.com	Free; blogging is part of the "space" or personal site that you create on this community networking site
TypePad	http://www.typepad.com	Paid (various pricing plans); free 30-day trial
Community Server	http://www.communityserver.com	Paid (various pricing plans)
Microsoft Windows SharePoint Services	(URL depends on your company)	If your company has a SharePoint site, you may be able to create a blog on it—but probably only for work purposes.

TABLE 13-1 Blogging Services Supported by Word

Get Set Up for Blogging

The easiest way to get set up for blogging is to create a new blog post. This causes Word to walk you through the registration process. Follow these steps:

1. Click the Office Button, and then click New. Word displays the New Document dialog box, with the Blank And Recent item selected in the Templates pane on the left.

2. In the Blank And Recent area in the middle of the dialog box, click the New Blog Post item.

3. Click the Create button. Word displays the Register A Blog Account dialog box, shown here.

4. If you want to register now (which is easiest as long as you have an Internet connection), click the Register Now button. Word displays the New Blog Account dialog box, shown here.

NOTE *If you click the Register Later button, Word prompts you to register the next time you create a new blog post or go to publish an existing document by clicking the Office Button, highlighting the Publish item, and then choosing Blog.*

5. Click the Refresh List link to make Word download the latest list of supported blogging services.

6. In the Blog drop-down list, select your blogging service. This example uses Blogger, one of the most widely used blogging services, as an illustration. The procedure for other blogging services varies depending on the service, but each is easy to follow.

7. Click the Next button. Word displays a dialog box with options for the blogging service. The next illustration shows the New Blogger Account dialog box.

13

Despite the "new account" the dialog box mentions, you're not creating a new account with the blogging service. What's new is that you're setting your existing account up to work with Word.

8. Enter your details for the account. For example:

   ■ Type your account name for the blogging service in the User Name text box.

   ■ Type your password for the blogging service in the Password text box.

   ■ Select the Remember Password check box if you want Word to store the password for you so that you don't need to enter it when you post. Storing the password is convenient but poses a small security risk in that anybody who can log on to your Windows user account can post to your blog. (This security risk is small as long as you are the sole user of your Windows user account and you have a password you haven't told anyone else.)

   ■ If your blogging service supports your publishing pictures, you may be able to publish them from Word. However, this works only for some blogging services at this writing. To find out, click the Picture Options button, click the Refresh List link in the Picture Options dialog box (shown here), and then see if the Picture Provider drop-down list lists your blogging service. If your blogging service appears, select it. If the only options you see are "None – Don't Upload Pictures" and My Own Server, you probably will not be able to publish pictures from Word; select the "None – Don't Upload Pictures" item. Click the OK button. Word closes the Picture Options dialog box and returns you to the New Account dialog box.

9. Click the OK button. Word displays the dialog box shown next, warning you that other people may be able to see the information you send to your blogging service.

10. Select the Don't Show This Message Again check box, and then click the Yes button. Word closes the dialog box and attempts to register your account. If it succeeds, Word displays a message box such as the one shown here.

11. Click the OK button. Word closes the dialog box and displays the blog post document ready for writing in Web Layout view, with just the Blog Post tab and Insert tab displayed on the Ribbon, as shown here.

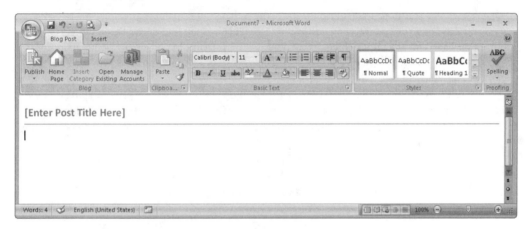

Create a Blog Post

If you've just set up your first blog account, as described in the previous section, you'll have a blog post document open and ready to create. If not, start creating a post by following these steps:

1. Click the Office Button, and then click New. Word displays the New Document dialog box, with the Blank And Recent item selected in the Templates pane on the left.

2. In the Blank And Recent area in the middle of the dialog box, click the New Blog Post item.

3. Click the Create button. Word creates the post and displays it.

13

Set Up a Windows Live Spaces Account for Blogging from Word

To set up a Windows Live Spaces account for blog publishing, you must first enable the E-mail Publishing option on the blog. Follow these steps:

1. Open Internet Explorer (or your preferred web browser) and log on to your space.

2. Click the Options button. The browser displays the Options screen.

3. In the left pane, click the E-mail Publishing item. The browser displays those settings.

4. Select the Turn On E-mail Publishing check box.

5. Type your "From" e-mail address—the address that your e-mail program is using to send mail. (If you're in doubt, send yourself a message, and then find the address in the From line.) You can enter up to three e-mail addresses if you're using different computers.

6. Type a secret word in the Secret Word text box.

7. Optionally, choose photo albums to which you want to post photos.

8. Select the Save Entries As Drafts option button if you want to post the blog entries as drafts. Select the Publish Entries Immediately option button if you want to post the entries right away.

9. Click the Save button at the bottom of the window to save the addresses.

Now you can set Word up to publish to your Windows Live Spaces blog.

You can now create the post by using standard Word techniques you've learned earlier in this book. Start by clicking in the "[Enter Post Title Here]" placeholder and typing the title of your post, as shown here.

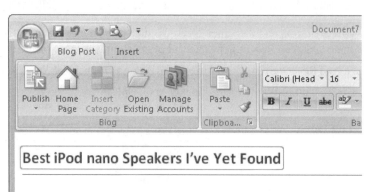

Then click below the line and type the text of the document.

You can apply any formatting options on the Blog Post tab, and you can insert any of the objects on the Insert tab (shown here). However, you may lose some formatting and objects when you publish the post to your blog. It's a good idea to publish a test post using the formatting and objects you may want to use before you invest too much time in them.

Save the document as you normally would, as a document on your hard disk. You may be tempted to create the whole document without saving, and then post it to the blogging service, but saving any material that's worth keeping is a much safer approach.

Publish to Your Blog

When your blog post is ready, publish it to your blog. Follow these steps:

1. If the post document contains unsaved changes, press CTRL-S or click the Save button on the Quick Access Toolbar to save them.

2. Choose Blog Post | Blog | Publish (click the top part of the Publish button, not the drop-down part). Word connects to the blogging service and publishes the post on it. If publishing is successful, Word displays a confirmation bar across the top of the post, as shown here.

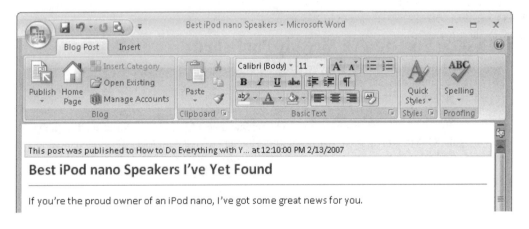

3. To verify that the post appears as you intended, choose Blog Post | Blog | Home Page. Word opens an Internet Explorer window showing your blog's home page.

If you want to publish your post document as a draft, putting it in your blog's Drafts folder rather than actually publishing it to your blog, choose Blog Post | Blog | Publish | Publish As Draft. (Click the drop-down part of the Publish button to display the Publish panel.)

Publish a Document That's Not Set Up as a Blog Post

As you've seen, Word displays the Blog Post tab when you create a new document based on the New Blog Post template. But you can also publish to your blog a copy of an existing document that you didn't originally set up as a blog post.

To publish such a document, follow these steps:

1. Open the document.

2. Click the Office Button, highlight or click the Publish item, and then click Blog. Word creates a new blog post document and inserts the content of the document into it.

3. Click in the "[Enter Post Title Here]" placeholder and type the title for the post.

4. Verify that the rest of the content looks okay, and that it's not missing any vital element it used to contain.

5. Choose Blog Post | Blog | Publish, and then publish the document as usual.

When you publish an existing document to a blog like this, you probably don't need to save the contents of the blog post document that Word creates for you. If anything goes wrong with this document, you can simply repeat the Office Button | Publish | Blog command to create a new copy of the original document.

Edit a Blog Post You've Already Published

Word even lets you edit a blog post you've already published. This capability is great for taking care of omissions, unfortunate phrases, or errors.

To edit a blog post, follow these steps:

1. If you don't already have a blog post open, create a new blog post (as described in the section "Create a Blog Post," earlier in this chapter) to make the Blog Post tab available.

2. Choose Blog Post | Blog | Open Existing. Word displays the Open Existing Post dialog box, shown here.

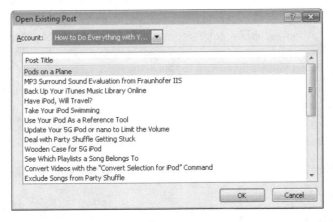

3. In the Account drop-down list, select the blog account. (If you have only one blog account, Word will already have selected it.) Word displays the list of posts for that account.

4. In the list box, click the post you want to open, and then click the OK button. Word opens the blog post in a new document.

5. Edit the document as required, and then choose Blog Post | Blog | Publish. Word republishes the post, and then displays a confirmation bar to tell you that it has done so.

Manage Multiple Blog Accounts

To manage your blog accounts, choose Blog Post | Blog | Manage Accounts. Word displays the Blog Accounts dialog box, shown here.

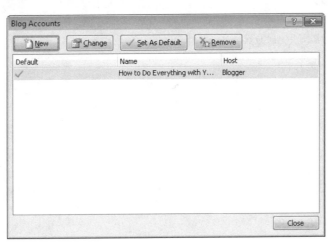

13

From the Blog Accounts dialog box, you can take the following actions:

- **Create a new account**   Click the New button. Word displays the New Blog Account dialog box. Follow through the procedure described earlier in this chapter.

- **Modify an existing account**   Select the account in the list box, and then click the Change button. Word displays the account's dialog box, which offers the same settings as the dialog box that you used to set up the account.

- **Remove an account**   Select the account in the list box, and then click the Remove button. Word removes the account without confirmation.

- **Set your default account**   Once you've set up two or more accounts, decide which is the default account. Select the account in the list box, and then click the Set As Default button.

When you've finished working in the Blog Accounts dialog box, click the Close button. Word closes the dialog box.

Choose Which Account You Post To

Once you've set up multiple blog accounts, Word displays an Account readout below the title of each blog post. To choose which account you're publishing to, click the readout, and then choose the account from the resulting drop-down list, as shown here.

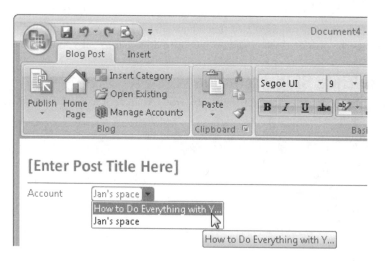

Choose the Category for a Post

If your blogging service lets you create categories and assign them to posts, Word makes available the Insert Category button in the Blog group on the Blog Post tab. To assign a post to a category, choose Blog Post | Blog | Category, and then choose the category from the Category drop-down list that Word adds to the post.

Understand Saving Directly to an Intranet Site or Internet Server

Word can store files directly on a web server, a File Transfer Protocol (FTP) server, or a server running Microsoft's SharePoint Services. This capability can be very useful for working with intranet sites, because you can open a page on an intranet server directly in Word, edit or update the page, and then save it. To open a file from a server, you need what's called *read permission*; to save a file to a server, you need *write permission*.

NOTE *The technology for opening files from and saving files to web servers is called Web Digital Authoring and Versioning, or WebDAV. Sometimes it's also called Web Sharing.*

If you have a fast and reliable Internet connection, you can work with files on Internet servers (as opposed to intranet sites) as well. You *can* also work with files on Internet servers across slower or less reliable connections, but the results tend to be less satisfactory. The problem is that if Word is unable even temporarily to write data to the server, it may be unable to save a file. If worst comes to worst, you may lose any unsaved changes in the file.

For this reason, it's usually best not to work directly with files on Internet servers; even fast and usually reliable Internet connections can suffer glitches severe enough to cost you work. Instead, use Windows Explorer or another tool to download a copy of any file you need to open in Word. Then work with the file on your local disk, where you can save changes instantly as often as necessary. When you've finished making changes to the file, or when you've created a new file that you want to place on the Internet server, upload the file. This way, you keep a copy of the file on your local disk at all times, which will help you avoid losing any data.

You can access an intranet server or Internet server via Internet Explorer or another web browser, a third-party graphical FTP client (or even the command-line FTP client built into Windows Vista and Windows XP), or a common dialog box (for example, the Open dialog box or the Save As dialog box). But the most convenient way to access a server is to create a network place using a wizard.

To launch the wizard:

- **Windows Vista**   Use the Add Network Location Wizard. Follow these steps:

    1. Choose Start | Computer. Windows displays a Computer window.

    2. Click the Map Network Drive button on the toolbar. Windows displays the Map Network Drive dialog box.

    3. Click the Connect To A Web Site That You Can Use To Store Your Documents Or Pictures link. Windows launches the Add Network Location Wizard.

- **Windows XP**   Use the Add Network Place Wizard. Follow these steps:

    1. Choose Start | My Network Places. Windows displays the My Network Places folder.

    2. Click the Add A Network Place link in the Network Tasks pane.

13

Once you've launched the wizard, follow its steps to create the network. Choose the Custom Network Location option (in Windows Vista) or the Choose Another Network Location option (in Windows XP), which allows you to specify the address of a web site or FTP site.

Choose Web Options to Control How Word Creates Web Pages

To control how Word creates web pages, choose options in its Web Options dialog box. (The other Office applications have their own Web Options dialog boxes, but the settings you choose in one application don't affect the other applications.)

To display the Web Options dialog box, follow these steps:

1. Click the Office button, and then click Word Options. Word displays the Word Options dialog box.

2. In the left panel, click the Advanced category, and then scroll down to the General area (almost at the bottom of the dialog box).

3. Click the Web Options button. Word displays the Web Options dialog box.

Choose Options on the Browsers Tab

The Browsers tab of the Web Options dialog box, shown here, lets you specify the types of browsers for which you want to make the web page work properly.

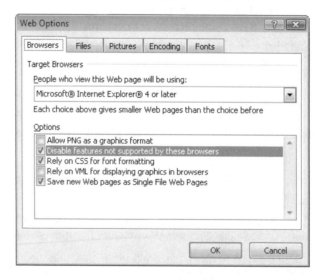

Select the lowest expected version of browser in the People Who View This Web Page Will Be Using drop-down list. (The default setting is Microsoft® Internet Explorer 4 or Later, which should safely cover most Internet users.) Word automatically selects and deselects the options in the Options box to match that browser's needs. You can also select and deselect check boxes manually to suit your needs:

- ■ **Allow PNG As A Graphics Format** Select this check box to allow web pages to use the Portable Network Graphics (PNG) format. PNG is a new format, and Internet Explorer versions before version 6 can't display it.

- ■ **Disable Features Not Supported By These Browsers** Select this check box to prevent Word from including features that browsers of the chosen caliber do not support. These features include read-only recommendation and some encryption settings; most are not a major loss for normal web pages.

- ■ **Rely On CSS For Font Formatting** Select this check box to use Cascading Style Sheets (CSS) for font formatting.

- ■ **Rely On VML For Displaying Graphics in Browsers** Select this check box to use Vector Markup Language (VML; a text-based format for vector graphics) for displaying graphics.

- ■ **Save New Web Pages As Single File Web Pages** Select this check box to make Word save new web pages using the Single File Web Page format by default. (You can override this setting manually.)

Choose Options on the Files Tab

The Files tab of the Web Options dialog box includes the following check boxes:

- ■ **Organize Supporting Files In A Folder** Select this check box to make Word place the supporting files in a subfolder of the folder that contains the page rather than in the same folder as the page. Using a subfolder tends to be neater and easier, especially when you need to move the page.

- ■ **Use Long File Names Whenever Possible** Select this check box to make Word use long filenames if possible when saving files to a web server. You may want to clear this check box to force Word to use short (eight-character) names, which are compatible with a wider range of web servers.

- ■ **Update Links On Save** Select this check box to make Word automatically update hyperlinks in the page when you save it. Updating the links helps prevent the page from containing broken links.

- ■ **Check If Office Is The Default Editor For Web Pages Created In Office** Select this check box to make Word see if it's the default editor for web pages that Office applications create. If you use the Office applications to create most of your web pages, you'll probably want to select this check box. This check box is selected by default but is a matter of preference. If you prefer to use another web editor than Word, clear this check box to prevent Word constantly warning you about a choice you know you've made.

13

■ **Check If Word Is The Default Editor For All Other Web Pages** Select this check box if you want Word to check if it's the web editor for all web pages other than those created by other Office applications. If you use another web editor (for example, Dreamweaver), clear this check box.

Choose Options on the Pictures Tab

On the Pictures tab of the Web Options dialog box, you can select the screen resolution at which you expect most viewers will view your web pages. The default is 800 × 600 resolution, which is a good choice for making sure that anybody on the Internet can view the pictures. If you're creating web pages for a specific audience—for example, cutting-edge computer professionals, or your colleagues in an office equipped with new computer hardware—you may want to choose a higher resolution, such as 1024 × 768 or 1280 × 1024. This setting changes the resolution at which Word creates the web page; it doesn't change the actual resolution of the monitor, which remains as the user has set it.

You can also specify the number of pixels per inch on the web page. The default is 96 pixels per inch and is normally the best choice; the other available settings are 72 pixels per inch and 120 pixels per inch.

Choose Options on the Encoding Tab

On the Encoding tab of the Web Options dialog box, you can select the type of encoding to use for the web page—for example, Western European (Windows) or Unicode (UTF-8)—and decide whether to always save web pages in the default encoding.

Choose Options on the Fonts Tab

On the Fonts tab of the Web Options dialog box, you can choose the character set, proportional font, and fixed-width font for your web pages. The default character set for a U.S. English installation of Office is English/Western European/Other Latin Script, and you'll seldom need to change it unless you need to create, say, Arabic or Japanese pages. On the other hand, you may want to change the fonts in the Proportional Font drop-down list and the Fixed-Width Font drop-down list to change the visual effect your pages have.

After choosing options, click the OK button. Word closes the Web Options dialog box, returning you to the Word Options dialog box. Click the OK button to close this dialog box as well.

Understand HTML, Round Tripping, and Web File Formats

For creating web content, Word and the other Office applications use Hypertext Markup Language (HTML), a formatting language that's extensively used and that's understood more or less perfectly by all modern web browsers. HTML uses *tags*, or codes, to specify how an item should be displayed. For example, if you apply an <H2> tag to indicate that some text is a level-two heading, any browser should recognize the tag and apply the appropriate formatting to the heading.

Word's Standard HTML Tags and Custom Tags

Word automatically applies all necessary tags when you save a document in one of the HTML formats. Roughly speaking, the tags break down into two separate categories:

- Standard HTML tags for coding those parts of the file—the text and its formatting—that a web browser will display.

- Custom, Office-specific HTML tags for storing document information and application information. For example, when you save a document in Single File Web Page format or Web Page format, Word saves items such as the author's name and the last author's name, creation date, and VBA projects (in macro-enabled documents) using custom HTML tags.

Word's custom tags should be ignored by web browsers, which don't care about document items such as the name of the person who last modified the document or the application that created the file. These tags are used for *round tripping*—saving a document or template with all its contents, formatting, and extra items (such as VBA code) so that Word can reopen the file with exactly the same information and formatting as when it saved the file.

HTML as a "Native" File Format

Saving files without losing the information they contain is something that any well-designed application should normally do as a matter of course, but in most cases, applications that create rich content (as opposed to, say, basic text) have historically used proprietary formats for saving their contents rather than HTML. For example, Word used to be able to save its documents only in the Word Document format. When Word first gained the capability to create HTML files, it wasn't able to round-trip fully: the HTML files Word produced contained only a subset of the data saved in the Word Document format, and if you reopened such an HTML file in Word, most of the non-content items would be missing.

But Word 2007 and the other Office 2007 applications support HTML as a "native" format—a format that can save all Word features—alongside their previous native formats. This means that you can save documents in HTML instead of the Word Document format, without losing any parts of those documents.

Understand Word's Three Web File Formats

Word can save web pages in three file formats: Single File Web Page, Web Page, and Web Page, Filtered. All three file types use Office-specific HTML tags to preserve all of the information the file contains in an HTML format.

Single File Web Page Format

The Single File Web Page format creates a web archive file that contains all the information required for the web page. This doesn't seem like much of an innovation until you know that the Web Page format (discussed next) creates a separate folder to contain graphics. Files in the Single File Web Page format use the .mht and .mhtml file extensions.

In most cases, you'll find the Single File Web Page format the better choice for saving complete Word files, because it creates files that you can easily distribute.

Web Page Format

The Web Page format creates an HTML file that contains the text contents of the document, together with a separate folder that contains the graphics for the document. This makes the web page's HTML file itself smaller, but the page as a whole is more awkward to distribute, because you need to distribute the graphics folder as well.

Word creates the folder automatically and assigns it the web page's name followed by _files. For example, a web page named Web1.htm has a folder named Web1_files. Files in the Web Page format use the .htm and .html file extensions.

Web Page, Filtered Format

The Web Page, Filtered format saves the Word document's content in HTML format but does not save the Office-specific information. The result is a web page that can be read by Word or by any web browser.

This format does not allow round-tripping, and normally you shouldn't use this format for saving documents that you want to treat as Word documents. Instead, save your documents in the Word Document format, and then save a document in this file format when you want to create from it a web page for posting on a web site or an intranet site.

Save a Word Document as a Web Page

After choosing the appropriate web options for Word and learning the essentials of HTML and the available file formats, you're ready to save an existing document as a web page.

Put the Web Page Preview Command on the Quick Access Toolbar

Before you save a document as a web page, it's a good idea to use Web Page Preview to make sure the page will look okay. Microsoft chose not to include Web Page Preview on the Office button menu or on the Ribbon, so you need to add it to the Quick Access Toolbar before you can use it. To do so, follow these steps:

1. Click the Customize Quick Access Toolbar button (the small button at the right end of the Quick Access Toolbar with the horizontal line and down-pointing arrow), and then choose More Commands from the drop-down menu. Word displays the Customize category in the Word Options dialog box.

2. In the Choose Commands From drop-down list, select the Commands Not In The Ribbon item.

3. In the left list box, select the Web Page Preview command, and then click the Add button. Word adds the command to the right list box.

4. Click the OK button. Word closes the Word Options dialog box and adds the command to the Quick Access Toolbar. You can then click the button to issue the command.

Use Web Page Preview to Preview the Document

To preview the document, click the Web Page Preview button on the Quick Access Toolbar. Word creates a temporary file in your *%userprofile%*\AppData\Local\Temporary Internet Files\ Content.MSO\WordWebPagePreview\ folder, and then displays the page in your default browser (for example, Internet Explorer).

Check the web page, and then close the browser tab or window. If the page needs changing, make the changes, and then use Web Page Preview again to verify them.

Don't worry about the page's title at this point—Word automatically generates a title from the document's Title property. You can give the page a different title when you save it as a web page.

Save as a Web Page

To save a Word document as a web page, follow these steps:

1. Open the document.

2. Click the Office Button, and then click Save As. Word displays the Save As dialog box.

3. In the Save As Type drop-down list, choose Single File Web Page, Web Page, or Web Page, Filtered, depending on which type of file you want to create. (See "Understand HTML, Round Tripping, and Web File Formats," earlier in this chapter, for an explanation of the differences between the file types.) The bottom part of the Save As dialog box displays extra controls for creating web pages, as shown here.

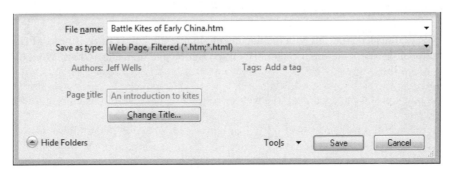

4. Check the title (if any) assigned to the web page:

  ▪ If there is a title, it appears in the Page Title text box.

  ▪ The title is displayed in the browser's title bar when the browser loads the page.

13

■ To change the title, click the Change Title button. Word displays the Set Page Title dialog box (shown here). Type the text for the title, and then click the OK button.

5. Choose the folder in which to save the document, and specify the filename.

 As discussed earlier in this chapter, Word lets you save directly to an intranet or Internet server. But usually it's safer to save the document to a local or network drive and then transfer it to the server via other means, such as FTP.

6. Click the Save button. Word saves the document.

■ If you chose the Web Page, Filtered format, Word displays the following dialog box to warn you that saving the document in this format will remove Office-specific tags and you will lose some features. Click the Yes button if you want to proceed. Word then saves the document.

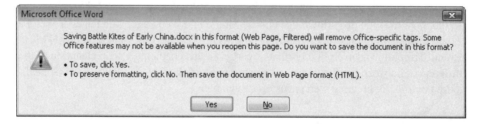

7. If you've finished working with the document, double-click the Office Button, click the Close button (the × button), or click the Office Button and then click Close. Word closes the document.

You can now transfer the document to a web server or simply view it in its current folder using a browser.

Chapter 14

Create Forms to Collect Data

How to ...

- Create a form
- Protect a form against unwanted changes
- Set up a form so that it prints only the form data
- Fill out a form someone else has created

In this chapter, you'll learn how to create forms with Word to streamline the collection of data—for example, in business situations.

A form is a document or template that contains content controls (or fields) in which a user enters information. You set up the form ahead of time so that the areas the user needs to fill in contain suitable content controls. For example, you can use a text box for textual information such as each of the user's names, a drop-down list to allow the user to choose a preset item from a set, or a date picker to let the user select the appropriate date from a calendar.

You can then protect the form so that the only action the user can take is to fill in the fields rather than messing with the structure of the form. You can even make Word print only the information the user entered in the form, rather than the preset information in the form itself. This is useful when you create a Word form to enable people to easily complete preprinted forms.

You may also need to fill out a form that someone else has created. If you know how forms work because you've created forms yourself, you'll find filling out a form child's play.

Create a Form

Before you create a form, you should first plan what type of information the form will collect. Once you've done that, create the document or template in which you'll build the form. You then add text and other content, together with the content controls necessary for the types of content that the user will enter. Content controls are straightforward to use, but you can make them even easier by changing their default text to explanations of exactly what the user must do to complete the form.

Plan What the Form Will Do

Normally, it's best to start by planning what the form will do. Establish the following:

- What information will the form contain to explain its purpose and contents to the user?
- Which fields will the form contain for the user to fill in information?
- Which fields are compulsory, and which are optional?
- Which fields will require validation or other checking?
- Which fields will require explanation beyond the information on the form?

If you're creating a form to put an existing process online, you may have a paper form from which you can start. This can be a great way to start, even though the online version of a form need have little visual similarity to its paper-based original. Otherwise, you may want to draft a rough version of the form, either on paper or in a drawing program.

Decide Between a Document and a Template

You can create a form using either a document or a template. Usually, a template is the better choice for three reasons:

- The user can start a new document based on the template, fill in the document, and then save it in a suitable location (for example, a Forms folder on the network) without opening the underlying template.

- There's no risk of the user altering the template inadvertently, as they may do with a document unless you protect it or make it read-only.

- When a user opens a document, no other user can open it. But if the user creates a new document from a template, this problem doesn't arise.

However, you can also use a document, provided that you protect it with a modify password (see Chapter 18) to force each user to open a copy of the document rather than the document itself. If you plan to have users open the form from Word's Open dialog box, a document is preferable, because it appears in the Open dialog box when one of the "Word Document" filters is applied (for example, All Word Documents, Word Documents, or Word Macro-Enabled Documents), whereas a template does not. (The user must choose a filter such as All Word Templates or All Files to display templates in the Open dialog box.)

Start the Form Document or Template

With your plan in place, start the form document or template. Follow these steps:

1. Create a new template or document as usual. For example:
   - Click the Office Button, and then click New. Word displays the New Document dialog box.
   - Select the template on which you want to base the new template or document.
   - In the Create New area, select the Template option button if you want to create a template. Otherwise, select the Document option button.
   - Click the Create button in the New Document dialog box or the OK button in the New dialog box. Word creates the template or document.

2. Save the template or document. For example, click the Save button on the Quick Access Toolbar, and then use the Save As dialog box to save the file.

3. Add information about the form to the template's or document's properties. For example:
   - Click the Office Button, highlight or click Prepare, and then choose Properties. Word displays the Document Properties bar.

14

- Enter information in fields such as Title, Subject, and Comments to make sure that whoever looks at the form's properties will understand its purpose.
- Click the Close button (the × button). Word closes the Document Properties bar.

4. Enter the text and create the layout of the form. For example:

- Type the form's name, explanation, and any other text.
- Insert any graphics needed (such as your company's logo).
- Create any tables needed for laying out the fields.

5. Save the form again—for example, click the Save button on the Quick Access Toolbar.

Add the Developer Tab to the Ribbon

To work with form fields, you must add the Developer tab to the Ribbon. Follow these steps:

1. Click the Office button, and then click Word Options. Word displays the Word Options dialog box.

2. In the Popular category, select the Show Developer Tab In The Ribbon check box.

3. Click the OK button. Word closes the Word Options dialog box and adds the Developer tab to the Ribbon, as shown here. The Controls group contains the controls you'll use for the form.

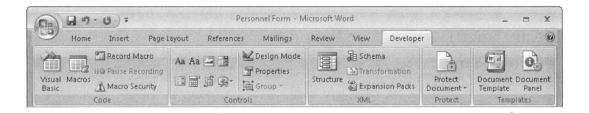

Switch to Design Mode

Before placing controls on your form, switch to Design mode by choosing Developer | Controls | Design Mode. Design mode is for laying out forms and working with content controls. When the document or template is in Design mode, Word makes available some commands that are not available in normal mode.

You can place content controls in a form while in normal mode (as opposed to Design mode), but the full range of commands are not available—so normally it's better to use Design mode.

Add Content Controls to the Form

Word provides seven main types of content controls, together with "legacy" (older) form controls that were used in earlier versions of Word. The legacy controls are included mainly for backward compatibility with older versions of Word. You can still use the legacy controls, but unless you want older versions of Word to be able to use your forms, you'll do better to use the content controls. This book does not discuss the legacy controls.

Table 14-1 provides an overview of the content controls.

Content Control Name	Description	Use This Control When
Text	A box in which you can enter only text.	You require text with no formatting.
Rich Text	A box in which you can enter text and format it using basic formatting (such as bold and italic).	You require text with formatting (sometimes or always).
Picture Content Control	A box in which you can place a picture.	You need to insert a picture.
Combo Box	A text box at the top, in which you can type a new entry, with a drop-down list from which you can select an existing entry.	You need to let users select one of several preset choices but also let them enter custom items of their own.
Drop-Down List	A drop-down list from which you can select an existing entry.	You need to let users select one of several preset choices. Users cannot add custom items.
Date Picker	A pop-up calendar panel from which the user can pick a date or time.	You need users to enter a date accurately in a particular format (for example, 26 June 07).
Building Block Gallery	A drop-down panel from which the user can pick any of various kinds of building blocks—for example, preset tables or equations.	You need users to insert a specific type of content from a building block gallery.

Table 14-1   Word's Content Controls for Forms

Add a Content Control to Your Form

The general procedure for adding a content control is as follows:

1. In the document, click where you want the control to appear.

2. Choose Developer | Controls, and then click the control you want to add. For example, to add a rich-text box, choose Developer | Controls | Rich Text.

3. If necessary, change the placeholder text for the control by selecting the placeholder text and typing over it. For example, the placeholder text for a rich text box is "Click here to enter text"—straightforward enough, but in many cases, more specific text (such as "Type your first name here") is more helpful.

4. Change the properties for the control. Different controls have different properties, which the following sections discuss.

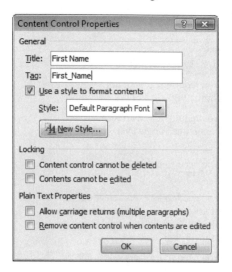

5. With the control selected, choose Developer | Controls | Properties. Word displays the Content Control Properties dialog box for the control.

   ■ The properties vary according to the content control and its capabilities. This section discusses the properties that are common to most or all content controls, using the Content Control Properties dialog box for a text box as an illustration.

   ■ For coverage of the properties that are unique to a particular control, see the following sections on the individual controls.

6. In the Title text box, type the title for the content control. This is the text that appears in the tab at the top of the control when the user selects it, as in this example (where the title is "First Name").

7. In the Tag text box, type the name for the tag. The tag is the text that appears in the beginning and ending tags for the content control in Design mode. In this example, the tag is "First_Name."

8. In the Locking area, choose locking properties:

   ■ **Content Control Cannot Be Deleted**   Select this check box if you want to prevent users from deleting the content control. Once you've placed the content control to your satisfaction, locking the control against deletion is usually a good idea.

   ■ **Contents Cannot Be Edited**   Select this check box if you want to prevent the user from editing the control's contents. This option can be helpful when you need to provide users with a partly completed form that includes set entries they must not change, but normally you will not need to use this option.

 *When you select the Contents Cannot Be Edited check box, the user can still delete the content control unless you select the Content Control Cannot Be Deleted check box as well.*

9. For any control except a picture content control, select the Use A Style To Format Contents check box if you want to apply a style to the control's contents. Choose the style in the Style drop-down list. If necessary, you can click the New Style button and use the Create New Style From Formatting dialog box to create a new style for the control, but usually, it's better to use an existing style (as long as one is suitable).

10. Choose other properties for the control as appropriate. See the following sections for coverage of the properties specific to certain controls.

11. Click the OK button. Word closes the Content Control Properties dialog box and applies your choices to it.

Delete a Content Control

To delete a content control, right-click it, and then choose Remove Content Control from the context menu. You can also click the content control's tab and then press DELETE.

Insert a Rich Text Box

Use a rich text box when you need the user to be able to enter text and format it using basic formatting (such as bold and italic). If you need text without formatting, use a text box, discussed in the next section.

To insert a rich text box, follow these steps:

1. Place the insertion point at the appropriate spot in the document.

2. Choose Developer | Controls | Rich Text. (Rich Text is the upper-left control in the Controls group. Hover the mouse pointer over a control to display a ScreenTip showing its name.) Word inserts a rich text box, as shown here.

Work Experience: [Click here to enter text.]

3. With the insertion point still in the rich text box, choose Developer | Controls | Properties. Word displays the rich text box's Content Control Properties dialog box, shown here with some properties chosen.

14

NOTE *Instead of choosing Developer | Controls | Properties to open the Content Control Properties dialog box, you can right-click the control, and then choose Properties from the context menu.*

4. Choose general options as discussed in the section "Add a Content Control to Your Form," earlier in this chapter.

5. In the Rich Text Properties area, select the Remove Content Control When Contents Are Edited check box if you want Word to remove the content control

when the user starts entering their own text in place of the instructions or placeholder text. Normally it's best to leave this check box cleared (as it is by default) so that the user's custom content is placed in the content control, where you can manipulate it as needed.

6. Click the OK button. Word closes the Content Control Properties dialog box and applies your changes.

Insert a Text Box

A text box is good for gathering items of text that don't need formatting—for example, a user's first or last name or an address item.

To insert a text box, follow these steps:

1. Place the insertion point at the appropriate spot in the document.

2. Choose Developer | Controls | Text. Word inserts a text box, as shown here.

3. With the insertion point still in the text box, choose Developer | Controls | Properties. Word displays the text box's Content Control Properties dialog box, shown here with some properties selected.

4. Choose general options as discussed in the section "Add a Content Control to Your Form," earlier in this chapter.

5. In the Plain Text Properties area, choose text box–specific options:

   ■ **Allow Carriage Returns (Multiple Paragraphs)** Select this check box if you want users to be able to insert a carriage return in the text box by pressing ENTER so that the text box can contain two or more paragraphs. In most cases, you'll want to make sure that this check box is cleared, but you may need to use it on occasion.

   ■ **Remove Content Control When Contents Are Edited** Select this check box if you want Word to remove the content control when the user starts entering their own text in place of the instructions or placeholder text. Normally it's best to leave this check box cleared (as it is by default) so that the user's custom content is placed in the content control, where you can manipulate it as needed.

6. Click the OK button. Word closes the Content Control Properties dialog box and applies your changes.

Insert a Picture Content Control

You can use a picture content control to
let the user insert a picture in the form.
To insert a picture content control, follow
these steps:

1. Place the insertion point at the
   appropriate spot in the document.

2. Choose Developer | Controls |
   Picture Content Control. Word
   inserts a picture content control,
   as shown here.

   Picture:

3. If necessary, resize the picture content control.
   Click the control to display sizing handles and a
   rotation handle, as shown here. You can then resize
   the control either proportionally (by dragging
   a corner handle) or in a single dimension (by
   dragging a side handle). You can also rotate the
   control, although this is rarely useful.

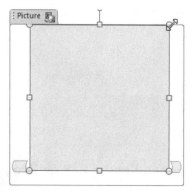

4. With the insertion point still in the text box, choose
   Developer | Controls | Properties. Word displays the
   text box's Content Control Properties dialog box,
   shown here.

Content Control Properties

General

Title:

Tag:

Locking

☐ Content control cannot be deleted

☐ Contents cannot be edited

OK   Cancel

14

NOTE *Word automatically assigns the word "Picture" as the title and tag for the picture
content control, even though this word does not appear in the Title text box and Tag text
box in the Content Control Properties dialog box for a picture content control. Because
of this default title and tag, you may not need to assign a title and tag manually.*

5. Choose general options as discussed in the section "Add a Content Control to Your Form," earlier in this chapter. There are no options that are specific to picture content controls.

6. Click the OK button. Word closes the Content Control Properties dialog box and applies any changes you have made.

When you turn off Design mode, the picture content control appears as shown next. When the user hovers the mouse pointer over the picture placeholder, Word displays a ScreenTip prompting them to click to insert a picture. When the user clicks, Word displays the Insert Picture dialog box.

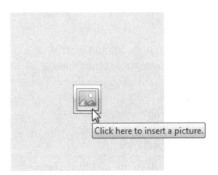

Insert a Combo Box or Drop-Down List

A combo box lets the user either choose a preset entry from the drop-down list or type a custom entry in the text box at the top. A drop-down list does not have the text box at the top, and so restricts the user to choosing a preset entry. This difference aside, the two controls work in the same way, so this section explains both.

To insert a combo box or drop-down list and populate it with preset entries, follow these steps:

1. Place the insertion point at the appropriate spot in the document.

2. Choose Developer | Controls | Combo Box or Developer | Controls | Drop-Down List. Word inserts a combo box, as shown here, or a drop-down list.

How did you hear about Acme Dynamics?   Choose an item.

3. With the insertion point still in the combo box or drop-down list, choose Developer | Controls | Properties. Word displays the control's Content Control Properties dialog box, shown here with some properties selected.

4. Choose general options as discussed in the section "Add a Content Control to Your Form," earlier in this chapter.

5. In the Drop-Down List Properties area, set up the preset choices for the combo box or drop-down list. Follow these steps:

   ■ To add an entry, click the Add button. Word displays the Add Choice dialog box, shown next. In the Display Name text box, type the text you want the user to see in the drop-down list. Word automatically enters the same text in the Value text box, which is for the text that the combo box or drop-down list returns when you retrieve the contents of the form. Normally, you'll want to use the same text, but if necessary, you can enter different text in the Value text box.

   ■ To remove an entry, select it in the list box, and then click the Remove button.

   ■ To modify an existing entry, select it in the list box, and then click the Modify button. Word displays the Modify Choice dialog box, which has the same controls as the Add Choice dialog box. Change the display name, the value, or both, and then click the OK button.

14

■ The list box shows the entries in the order in which you entered them. To change the order, select the entry you want to move, and then click the Move Up button or Move Down button, as appropriate.

6. Click the OK button. Word closes the Content Control Properties dialog box and applies your changes.

When you turn off Design mode, Word displays the combo box or drop-down list with the first entry showing. You can then click the drop-down arrow and choose from the list, as shown here. In a combo box, the user can also type a custom entry.

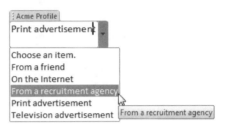

Insert a Date Picker

A date picker lets the user easily select a date (and time, if necessary) from a calendar-style control. Because the date picker contains real dates, the user should be able to choose a valid date without making mistakes that occur in manual calendaring—for example, scheduling a business appointment for a holiday.

To insert a date picker, follow these steps:

1. Place the insertion point at the appropriate spot in the document.

2. Choose Developer | Controls | Date Picker. Word inserts a date picker, as shown here.

3. With the insertion point still in the date picker, choose Developer | Controls | Properties. Word displays the date picker's Content Control Properties dialog box.

4. Choose general options as discussed in the section "Add a Content Control to Your Form," earlier in this chapter.

5. In the Date Picker Properties area, choose date-picker options:

■ **Display The Date Like This**   In this list box, select the date format, date and time format, or time format you want.

■ **Locale**   In this drop-down list, you can select the locale for the date and time. You will seldom need to change the default choice, which shows your system locale—for example, English (United States).

- ■ **Calendar Type** In this drop-down list, you can select the calendar type. You will seldom need to change the default choice, Western.

- ■ **Store XML Contents In The Following Format When Mapped** In this drop-down list, you can choose how Word stores the date and time information. Normally, the default format, Date And Time (xsd:dateTime), is the best choice.

6. Click the OK button. Word closes the Content Control Properties dialog box and applies your choices.

When you turn off Design mode, you can click the date picker to display its border, and then click the drop-down button to display the picker panel from which you choose the date. If the date picker's format includes a time, as in the example here, you can adjust it by typing.

Insert a Building Block Gallery

If you need the form's users to be able to insert building blocks, insert a building block gallery. Follow these steps:

1. Place the insertion point at the appropriate spot in the document.

2. Choose Developer | Controls | Building Block Gallery. Word inserts a building block gallery content control, as shown here.

3. With the insertion point still in the building block gallery content control, choose Developer | Controls | Properties. Word displays the date picker's Content Control Properties dialog box, shown here with some properties selected.

4. Choose general options as discussed in the section "Add a Content Control to Your Form," earlier in this chapter.

5. In the Document Building Block Properties area, choose the gallery and category:

   - ■ **Gallery** In this drop-down list, choose the gallery that contains the objects you want the user to be able to add. Your choices include AutoText, Equations, Quick Parts, Tables, Custom 1 through Custom 5, Custom AutoText, Custom Equations, Custom Quick Parts, and Custom Tables.

14

■ **Category**   In this drop-down list, choose the category of items within the gallery you selected. Your choices depend on the gallery. For example, when you select Tables in the Gallery drop-down list, the Category drop-down list offers the choices "(All Categories)," Built-In, and General.

6. Click the OK button. Word closes the Content Control Properties dialog box and applies your choices.

When you turn off Design mode, Word displays the prompt for the building block gallery content control. You can click the content control to display its border, and then click the drop-down button to display the gallery and select an item.

Protect a Form Against Unwanted Changes

Once you've created a form, you'll probably want to protect it so that users can fill it out but cannot delete or otherwise alter its contents. To do so, follow these steps:

1. Choose Developer | Protect | Protect Document | Restrict Formatting And Editing. Word displays the Restrict Formatting And Editing pane, shown here with choices made.

2. Select the Allow Only This Type Of Editing In The Document check box, and then choose Filling In Forms in the drop-down list. Selecting this item allows everyone to use form features (filling in fields) but perform no other editing.

3. Click the Yes, Start Enforcing Protection button. Word displays the Start Enforcing Protection dialog box, shown here.

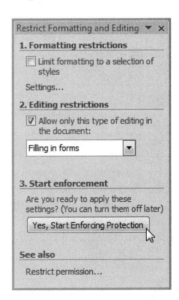

4. Choose how to protect the document:

   ■ **Password**   Select this option button to protect the document with a password but no encryption. This gives moderate protection, but someone could edit the document and remove the password. Type the password in the Enter New Password text box and the Reenter Password To Confirm text box.

   ■ **User Authentication**   Select this option button to authenticate users by user name. Word encrypts the document and enables the Restricted Access feature. Authentication requires the use of Information Rights Management (IRM), discussed in Chapter 18.

5. Click the OK button. Word closes the Start Enforcing Protection dialog box, applies the protection, and displays details of the protection and your permissions in the Restrict Formatting And Editing pane, as in this example.

6. Click the Save button on the Quick Access Toolbar. Word saves the document.

Set Up a Form So It Prints Only the Form Data

In many cases, when you create a form, you'll want users to print the full form—all the material you entered to create the layout of the form, and all the data the user has entered. This type of form works well when you need to create a printout that looks the same way the form looks on screen. If this is what you need, you don't need to take any special action in the form template, because Word prints the full form by default.

For other forms, however, you may want to print just the data the user has entered in the form—for example, because you've set up the Word form to collect the data required to complete a preprinted form. To set up a form to print just the data, follow these steps:

1. Open the form (if it's not already open) and click in it.

2. Click the Office Button, and then click Word Options. Word displays the Word Options dialog box.

3. In the left panel, click the Advanced category, and then scroll down to the When Printing This Document area.

4. The When Printing This Document bar contains a drop-down list that shows the document or template these settings will affect. Verify that the drop-down list shows the form's name (it should, because you clicked in the form in step 1).

5. Select the Print Only The Data From A Form check box.

6. Click the OK button. Word closes the Word Options dialog box.

7. Click the Save button on the Quick Access Toolbar. Word saves the change to the form.

Once you've created and protected a form, open a copy of it and fill it out. Verify that each of the content controls works in the way you intended, and that your experience using the form matches the experience you want a "real" user to have.

Fill Out a Form Someone Else Has Created

When you need to fill in a form that someone else has created, you'll have no problems. Follow these general steps:

1. Start a new document based on the form. For example, if the form is set up as a template on your computer, click the Office Button, and then click New, select the template in the New Document dialog box, and then click the Create button.

2. Fill in the form by proceeding from field to field. Type text in text boxes or rich text boxes; select items from combo boxes or drop-down lists; choose pictures in picture content controls, and so on.

3. Save the form by clicking the Save button on the Quick Access Toolbar, choosing a folder and assigning a name, and then clicking the Save button.

4. If necessary, print the form by clicking the Office Button and then clicking Print, choosing any relevant print settings in the Print dialog box, and then clicking the OK button. If the form's designer set up the form to print only the data rather than the entire form, you may need to select a particular paper tray that's loaded with the preprinted form (or insert the preprinted form in the printer manually).

5. Close the form.

Chapter 15

Use Fields to Streamline Documents

How to...

- Understand what fields are and when to use them
- Know what fields look like and how they behave
- Insert fields in a document
- Edit a field
- Update fields automatically when you print
- Lock fields to prevent them from being changed

This chapter shows you how to streamline your documents by using Word's fields. Fields provide a flexible and powerful way to insert information—anything from dates and times to page references—in your documents and have Word update it automatically for you.

Fields can seem awkward or even forbidding at first, because you can't normally see them in your documents—so when a field changes automatically to show updated information, the effect can be unsettling.

This chapter starts by explaining what fields are and what you can do with them in your documents. It then shows you how to make all fields visible all the time so that you'll always know what's a field and what's not. After that, you'll learn how to insert various kinds of fields, set options for fields, update fields automatically, and even lock fields to prevent them from being updated.

Understand What Fields Are and When to Use Them

In Word, a *field* is a code that you insert in a document. The field code tells Word to insert some specific information at that point.

For example, when you create headers and footers, you may insert the "Page X of Y" building block that tells Word to insert the current page number for X and the total number of pages for Y: Page 1 of 9 for the first page, Page 2 of 9 for the second page, and so on. When you add a page to the document, Word adjusts the value of Y accordingly, so the readout becomes "Page 1 of 10" and so forth.

Understand the Fields That Word Provides

Here are examples of the wide variety of fields that Word provides. For more details, see Table 15-1, later in this chapter.

- **Document Information** In many documents, you'll need to insert information about the document itself. For example, in a header or footer, you may include page numbers, the document's filename or title, the author, or the date when the document was last saved. Word maintains all this information (and much more) for each document, updating much of the information each time you save the document.

- **Links and References** Word includes various fields for retrieving information from the same document or from other documents.

- **User Information**   Word automatically saves some information about you—or about the Windows user who's currently logged in—in each document. Word gets the user information from the User Name text box and the Initials text box in the Popular category of the Word Options dialog box (click the Office Button, and then click Word Options).

- **Date and Time**   Word retrieves date and time information from Windows, which gets the information from your computer's hardware clock.

Know What Fields Look Like and How They Behave

The best way to get started with fields is to insert a field so that you can see what it looks like and how it behaves.

Insert a Date and Time Field

Start by inserting a field so that you can see it. Follow these steps:

1. Press CTRL-N. Word creates a new document.

2. Type some sample text: **The office party will take place on**.

3. Choose Insert | Text | Date And Time. Word displays the Date And Time dialog box, shown here.

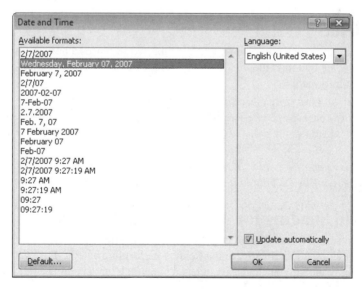

4. In the Available Formats list box, select the date format you want to use.

5. Select the Update Automatically check box. This setting makes Word insert the date (or time) as a field rather than as text that's correct at the moment you insert it.

15

6. Click the OK button. Word closes the Date And Time dialog box and inserts the date or time as a field. The document displays the field's result, so it shows the date in the format you chose. Here is an example.

> The office party will take place on Wednesday, February 07, 2007.

7. Type a period to complete the sentence.

See How Word Displays Fields

Fields normally appear as normal text (or other standard objects, such as graphics) in a document, so you can't instantly see what's a field and what's not. To help you identify fields, Word's default behavior is to apply shading to a field when you select it.

If you hover the insertion point over any part of the field, Word highlights the whole field, as shown here.

> The office party will take place on Wednesday, February 07, 2007.

If you move the insertion point to just before or just after the field by using the arrow keys or other navigation keys, Word applies field shading, as shown here.

> The office party will take place on Wednesday, February 07, 2007.

Update a Field

If you click the field or move the insertion point within it, Word places a border around it, together with an Update button at the top, as shown here. Click the Update button to update the field with the latest information.

> Update
>
> The office party will take place on Wednesday, February 07, 2007.

You can also update a field by right-clicking it and choosing Update Field from the context menu, or by clicking in it (or placing the insertion point in it) and pressing F9.

Turn On Field Shading for All Fields All the Time

For many documents, you'll find it more helpful to have every field shaded all the time. That way, you can avoid unintentionally affecting a field by performing an edit. For example, because Word's highlighting is subtle, you can easily delete a paragraph that contains a field without noticing the field at all.

To change field shading, follow these steps:

1. Click the Office Button, and then click Word Options. Word displays the Word Options dialog box.

2. In the left panel, click the Advanced category, and then scroll down to the Show Document Content area.

3. In the Field Shading drop-down list, choose the setting you want:

    ▪ **Never**   Word never displays field shading. Use this setting if you find field shading distracting.

    ▪ **Always**   Word always displays shading on every field. The shading makes fields easy to see (and to avoid deleting accidentally) and so is usually helpful. The disadvantage is that field-heavy documents have a gray patchwork effect.

    ▪ **When Selected**   This is Word's default behavior: Word displays shading only when you select a field. This setting has a strange effect, as the shading suddenly appears when you click a field or the insertion point reaches a field, but it helps you identify fields while you're working.

4. Click the OK button. Word closes the Word Options dialog box and applies the shading you chose.

Toggle Between Field Codes and Field Results

When you insert a field in a document, Word normally displays the field's *result*—the information the field produces—rather than the field's code itself. In the previous example, Word displays the date that the field returns.

Sometimes you may need to look at the field codes rather than the results. For example, if a field seems to be producing an unexpected result, you might need to check which information it's supposed to provide.

To display the field codes for a single field, right-click the field, and then choose Toggle Field Codes from the context menu. Word displays the codes, as in this example.

The office party will take place on { DATE \@ "dddd, MMMM dd, yyyy" }.

To switch back to the field results, right-click the field again, and then choose Toggle Field Codes from the context menu once more.

If you need to display field codes for all the fields in a document, follow these steps:

1. Click the Office Button, and then click Word Options. Word displays the Word Options dialog box.

2. In the left panel, click the Advanced category, and then scroll down to the Show Document Content area.

3. Select the Show Field Codes Instead Of Their Values check box.

4. Click the OK button. Word closes the Word Options dialog box and displays the codes.

To switch back to field results, repeat this process, but clear the Show Field Codes Instead Of Their Values check box.

15

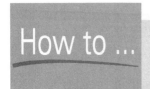

Print Field Codes Instead of Field Results

Word normally prints field results rather than field codes. If you need to print field codes (for example, to see which fields a document uses), follow these steps:

1. Click the Office Button, and then click Word Options. Word displays the Word Options dialog box.

2. In the left panel, click the Advanced category, and then scroll down to the Print area.

3. Select the Print Field Codes Instead Of Their Values check box.

4. Click the OK button. Word closes the Word Options dialog box.

5. Print the document.

6. Return to the Word Options dialog box and clear the Print Field Codes Instead Of Their Values check box unless you want to print field codes next time as well.

Insert Fields in a Document

Word uses fields for a wide variety of purposes. In many cases, you'll use a field without realizing that you're doing so. For example, when you insert a header that includes page numbers, Word uses a field for the page number. The field tells Word to insert the page number for that particular page. If you insert a "Page 2 of 15" readout in a header or footer, Word uses two fields—one for the current page number, the other for the total number of pages in the document.

Understand the Categories of Fields That Word Provides

Word divides its fields up into the nine categories explained in Table 15-1.

Insert Fields Using the Field Dialog Box

As mentioned in Table 15-1, Word provides tools for inserting many of the most widely useful fields in your documents quickly and easily. You've met some of these tools (such as the Header And Footer Tools section of the Ribbon) earlier in this book; you'll meet other tools (such as the Mail Merge tools) in later chapters.

However, you can also insert any field by using the Field dialog box. The advantage of the Field dialog box is that you can use the full range of options for any field, which lets you set the field up exactly as you want it. The disadvantage is that you need to know at least the basics of using fields in order to use them effectively.

Category	Description	Examples
Date And Time	Fields that enter a date or time in the document. You can choose among different dates (such as when the document was created, last saved, or last printed) and use various formats. You can insert some of these fields by using the Date And Time dialog box.	The CreateDate field inserts the date the document was created. The Date field inserts the current date.
Document Automation	Fields that you can use to automate elements in documents, move to a different part of the document, or run a macro.	The GoToButton field moves the insertion point to the specified bookmark. The MacroButton field runs the specified macro.
Document Information	Fields that enter information drawn from the document's properties. You can insert some of these fields quickly from the Insert	Text	Quick Parts	Document Property submenu.	The Author field inserts the author's name. The FileName field inserts the document's filename. The DocProperty field lets you insert the full set of document properties.
Equations And Formulas	Fields that enter equations and formulas. Normally, you insert equations using the Insert	Symbols	Equation panel.	The Eq field lets you insert a custom equation.
Index And Tables	Fields used for index entries, indexes, tables of contents, tables of authorities, and tables of figures. Normally, you insert these fields by using the commands in the Table Of Contents group, the Captions group, the Index group, and the Table Of Authorities group on the References tab of the Ribbon.	The XE field marks an index entry, and the Index field tells Word to insert an index.
Links And References	Fields used for inserting linked information and references. You can insert the most widely useful of these fields by using the commands in the Links group and the Header And Footer group on the Insert tab of the Ribbon.	The IncludePicture field inserts a picture from the specified file. The StyleRef command inserts the text from the paragraph with the specified style—for example, so that you can include the current Heading 1 title in a header or footer.
Mail Merge	Fields used for setting up mail-merge documents. Normally, you insert these fields by using the commands on the Mailings tab of the Ribbon.	The AddressBlock field inserts an address block consisting of the main address fields. The Fill-in field prompts the user to insert custom text during a mail merge—for example, to personalize each letter to the recipient.

Table 15-1   Word's Nine Categories of Fields, with Examples

15

Category	Description	Examples
Numbering	Fields that implement numbering automatically for lists, page numbers, and other items. Normally, you use these fields via other tools, such as Word's list-numbering features or the Header And Footer tools.	The Page field inserts the current page's number. The Seq field allows you to set up custom numbering sequences.
User Information	Fields that enter the user's name, initials, or address. (You can change this information in the Popular category in the Word Options dialog box.)	The UserName field inserts the user's name. The UserAddress field inserts the user's address.

Table 15-1   Word's Nine Categories of Fields, with Examples (*Continued*)

This section shows you the essentials of inserting fields using the Field dialog box. The example uses a date field, which is easy to grasp but offers enough options and settings to let you see how to choose advanced settings.

To insert a field, follow these steps:

1. Position the insertion point where you want the field's result to appear.

2. Choose Insert | Text | Quick Parts | Field. Word displays the Field dialog box. In the Categories drop-down list, Word may select the "(All)" item (as shown here) or the category of field you used last.

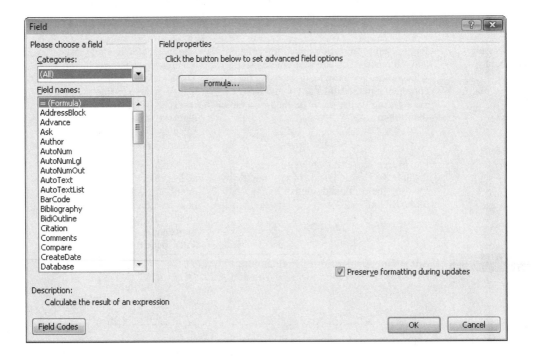

3. In the Categories drop-down list, select the category of field you want to insert. Word displays the fields in the category and selects the first field in the Field Name list box. This example uses the Date And Time category. Refer to Table 15-1, earlier in this chapter, for details of the categories.

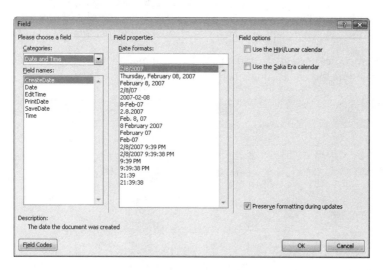

4. In the Field Names list box, select the field you want to use.

- ■ Word displays a description of the field near the lower-left corner of the dialog box.

- ■ In the center section of the dialog box, Word displays the field properties and formatting available for the selected field. For the SaveDate field shown here, there are only field properties.

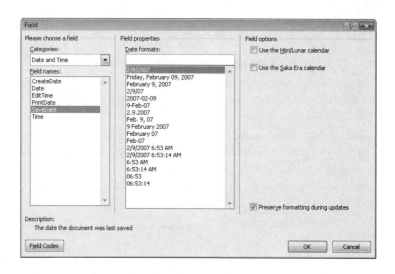

15

■ In the right-hand section of the dialog box, Word displays field options and the Preserve Formatting During Updates check box.

NOTE

The dialog box contents discussed here are typical for most fields. However, for other fields, Word displays different controls suitable to the field. For example, when you select the Index field in the Field Names drop-down list, the Field Properties area contains only the Index button, which you click to display the Index dialog box.

5. Choose properties or options for the field. For example, for the SaveDate field, choose the date or time format, as shown here.

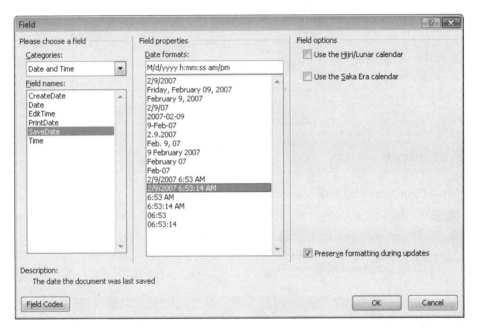

6. In the Field Options area, choose any options that you want to apply to the field.

■ Depending on the field, the options may be common or specialized. The top two options for the SaveDate field are international, letting you use different calendars for calculating the date.

■ Most fields include the Preserve Formatting During Updates check box. Select this check box if you want Word to retain the field's formatting when you update the information in a field.

7. Click the OK button. Word inserts the field in the document and displays the field's result.

View Field Codes in the Field Dialog Box and Access Advanced Options

If you looked at the Field dialog box earlier in this section, you probably noticed the Field Codes button. You can click this button to display the Advanced Field Properties area of the dialog box instead of the Field Properties area, Formatting area, and Field Options area. The Advanced Field Properties area shows the field codes that represent the field and options you've chosen, as in the following illustration.

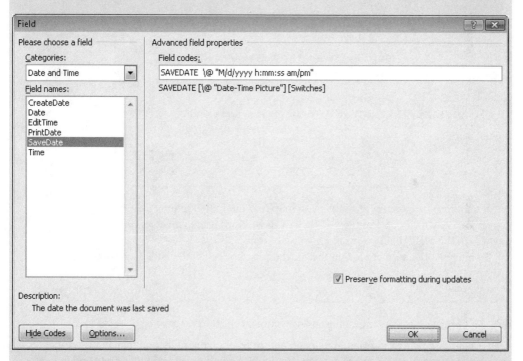

When you click the Field Codes button, Word also displays the Options button at the bottom of the Field dialog box. You can click this button to display the Field Options dialog box, in which you can set *switches* (options) for the field. The exact contents of the Field Options dialog box depends on the field you're using, but the Field Options dialog box shown next is fairly typical. To add a switch to the field, select the switch in the list box, and

15

then click the Add To Field button. When you've finished choosing switches, click the OK button. Word closes the Field Options dialog box.

If you become expert with fields, you may find the Field Options dialog box a convenient way to set up complex fields. For most Word users, however, the regular controls in the Field dialog box are easier and faster.

To return to the normal view in the Field dialog box, click the Hide Codes button.

Edit a Field

To edit a field that you've inserted in a document, right-click the field, and then choose Edit Field from the context menu. Word displays the Field dialog box, showing the field and the options currently set for it.

Edit the field as needed, and then click the OK button. Word closes the Field dialog box and updates the field in the document with the changes you made.

Update Fields Automatically When You Print

As you saw earlier in this chapter, you can update any field manually by selecting it and then clicking its Update button (or by right-clicking the field and then choosing Update Field from the context menu). To update all the fields in the document, select the entire document (press CTRL-A or choose Home | Editing | Select | Select All) and then press F9.

 ## Insert Fields Manually

If you insert the same type of field code so frequently in your documents that you learn all its ins and outs, you may prefer to insert the field code manually by typing it rather than using the Field dialog box or other conventional means.

To insert a field code, follow these steps:

1. Place the insertion point where you want the field.

2. Press CTRL-F9. Word inserts a pair of field braces and positions the insertion point between them.

3. Type the details of the field.

Even though the field braces may appear to be regular braces, they're in fact special. If you type the braces instead of pressing CTRL-F9, you get normal text rather than a field code.

Instead of updating fields manually, you can have Word update fields automatically for you before you print. This automatic updating tends to be very useful for making sure that your documents are up-to-date.

To set Word to update all the fields in a document each time you print it, follow these steps:

1. Click the Office Button, and then click Word Options. Word displays the Word Options dialog box.

2. In the left panel, click the Display category. Word shows the Display options.

3. Select the Update Fields Before Printing check box.

TIP *If your document contains linked data (for example, a chart linked from an Excel workbook), you may also want to update this data before printing. To do so, select the Update Linked Data Before Printing check box in the Display category in the Word Options dialog box.*

15

4. Click the OK button. Word closes the Word Options dialog box.

Now, each time you tell Word to print, Word automatically updates all the fields in the document.

Why Word Thinks a Document "Contains Unsaved Changes" When You Haven't Changed It

Have you ever opened a document, printed it, and then gone to close it—only to find Word asking you if you want to save changes? You *know* you haven't made any changes…but Word has.

When this happens, normally the culprit is Word automatically updating a field, such as a page number or linked content, when you issue the Print command. So usually, when you close the document, you'll want to save the changes that Word has made to it.

Lock Fields to Prevent Them from Being Changed

Normally, you'll want all the fields in a document to be updatable, so that you get all the latest information when Word updates fields automatically before printing or when you update the entire document. However, in some cases, you may want to lock a field to prevent Word from updating it along with the other fields in the document.

To lock a field, place the insertion point in the field (for example, click in the field), and then press CTRL-F11. Word dims the left part of the Update button (the document with the red exclamation point) to indicate that this command is not available. Similarly, if you right-click the field, the Update Field command appears dimmed on the context menu.

To unlock a locked field, place the insertion point in the field, and then press CTRL-SHIFT-F11. Word restores the graphical parts of the Update button to indicate that the command is available.

Sometimes, you may need to turn a field into regular text so that it can no longer be updated. To do so, you unlink *the field from its source. To unlink a field, click in it, and then press CTRL-SHIFT-F9.*

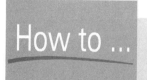

Move Quickly Through the Fields in a Document

Word provides three ways of moving quickly through the fields in a document:

- **Press F11 or SHIFT-F11**   Press F11 to move to the next field of any type. Press SHIFT-F11 to move to the previous field of any type.

- **Browse by Field**   Click the Select Browse Object button (or press CTRL-ALT-HOME), and then select the Browse By Field item from the Select Browse Object panel. You can then press CTRL-PAGE DOWN to move to the next field of any type or CTRL-PAGE UP to move to the previous field. You can also click the Next button and Previous button below the vertical scroll bar.

- **Use the Go To page of the Find And Replace dialog box**   To move among fields of the same type, follow these steps:

1. Double-click the Page readout in the status bar, or press F5. Word displays the Go To tab of the Find And Replace dialog box.

2. In the Go To What list box, select Field, as shown here.

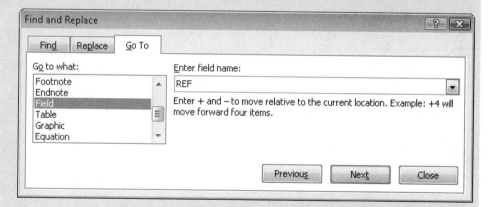

3. In the Enter Field Name drop-down list, select the field type.

4. Click the Previous button to move to the previous field of that type, or click the Next button to go to the next field of that type. To move in larger jumps, enter a + number to move forward or a – number to move back. For example, +5 moves forward five fields, and –5 moves back five fields.

5. You can click in the document to edit it, leaving the Find And Replace dialog box open. When you've finished using the Find And Replace dialog box, click the Close button.

15

Chapter 16

Mail Merge Letters and Much More

How to...

- Plan and start a mail merge
- Create the main document
- Specify the data source to use for the merge
- Edit the recipient list
- Insert merge fields and text in the main document
- Preview and check the merged documents
- Perform the merge
- Restore a main document to a regular document

This chapter shows you how to perform mail merges to create standardized documents such as form letters, catalogs, envelopes, and labels. You'll learn how to plan a mail merge; create the main document containing merge fields, connect a data source to it, and edit the recipient list; and then preview the merge to identify errors before executing the merge. You'll also learn how to create e-mail messages via merge and how to restore a mail merge main document to a regular Word document.

Mail merges may seem off-putting at first because you must not only learn some new skills but also spend some time and effort setting up your merge documents and data sources. The good news is that once you've put in this time and effort, you can perform mail merges quickly and accurately—not just once, but as many times as needed.

Word 2007 makes mail merges easier than earlier versions of Word because its new Mailing tab on the Ribbon gives you easy access to all the commands you need for standard mail-merge operations. But if you want to use the Mail Merge Wizard, it's still there. To launch the Wizard, choose Mailings | Start Mail Merge | Start Mail Merge | Step By Step Mail Merge Wizard.

Plan and Start a Mail Merge

To perform a mail merge, you need a main document and a data source:

- **Main document** This document contains the standard text, layout, and formatting for the documents. For example, in a mail merge letter, the main document usually contains some degree of static text that won't change from letter to letter, such as the company's name and address, the text of the letter, and the sender's information as well as merge fields for the information that's to be supplied by the data file—the recipient's name and address, their salutation, details of the special offer the computer has selected for them, and so on.

■ **Data source** The data source contains the *records* or data that Word places in the main document to form each merge document. For example, for the mail merge letter just mentioned, the data source would contain the recipients' name and addresses and their preferred salutations. The data source may be an actual file (for example, an Excel workbook) or a database query that returns a particular set of data. Each record usually consists of multiple *fields*—that is, separate items of information. For example, a customer record may have fields for first name, middle initial, last name, each address component, phone number, e-mail address, and so on.

 **Create an Efficient Data Source**

For many mail merges, you'll work with an existing data source—for example, your company's customer database, or an Excel workbook or Word table in which you've stored your clients' details. In this case, you probably won't have any control over how the data source is arranged.

But if you need to create a new data source of your own, follow these guidelines to make it suitable for use with mail merges:

■ **Use a robust file format** Word can use various kinds of data sources, including Excel worksheets, text files, database connections, or your Outlook contacts. If you use Outlook to store contact information, merging from it can be a good solution. Otherwise, either use an Excel workbook or create a new list in Word as described in this chapter, saving the list in the Microsoft Office Address List format (a simple type of Access database).

■ **Divide the data into fields** Normally, you'll do this anyway—but to use your data most effectively, you should divide your data into as many fields as you might ever possibly use. For example, never use a single field for a person's full name. Instead, always have separate fields for first name, last name, and middle initial—together with a separate field for nickname.

■ **Plan your data source for reuse** When you're first performing mail merges, you may be tempted to set up a custom data source for the merge by putting together a list of only the customers you want to include in the merge. For example, you might create a table or worksheet that contains the customer details drawn from your main database. Such manual lists work well in the short term, but in the long term, it's much more effective to tag the customers in the database and then use a query to extract them.

16

Create the Main Document

Your first step in a mail merge is to create the main document.

1. If you have an existing document that you want to use as the main document, open it. Otherwise, create a new document:

   ■ Click the Office Button, and then click New. Word displays the New Document dialog box.

   ■ Choose the template you want to use for the new document, and then click the Create button or the OK button. For example, click the My Templates item, select the template in the New dialog box, and then click the OK button.

2. Choose Mailings | Start Mail Merge | Start Mail Merge, and then choose the document type from the Start Mail Merge panel, shown here.

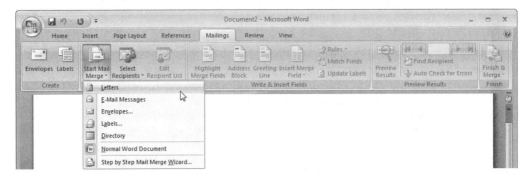

   ■ **Letters** Word switches the document to Print Layout view if it's in any other view.

   ■ **E-Mail Messages** Word switches the document to Web Layout view if it's in any other view.

   ■ **Envelopes** Word displays the Envelope Options dialog box. See the next section for details.

   ■ **Labels** Word displays the Label Options dialog box. See the section after next for details.

   ■ **Directory** Word switches the document to Print Layout view if it's in any other view.

Choose Options for Merged Envelopes

When you choose the Envelopes item on the Start Mail Merge panel, Word displays the Envelope Options dialog box. Figure 16-1 shows the Envelope Options tab of this dialog box on the left and the Printing Options tab on the right.

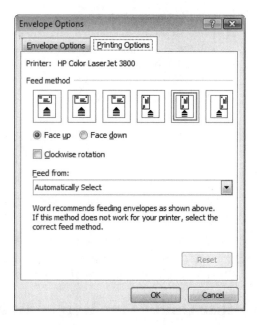

FIGURE 16-1   When setting up a merge for envelopes, you must first choose the envelope size and other options in the Envelope Options dialog box.

On the Envelope Options tab, choose the envelope size and the address fonts:

■ **Envelope Size**   In this drop-down list, choose the size of envelope you'll use—for example, Size 10 for a standard folded letter. The Preview area shows a thumbnail of the envelope's dimensions and layout. If none of the many sizes in the list meets your needs, choose the Custom Size item at the bottom of the list, define a custom size in the Envelope Size dialog box (shown here), and then click the OK button.

■ **Delivery Address**   In this area, click the Font button, and then use the Envelope Address dialog box to set the font formatting you want to use for the delivery address. (The Envelope Address dialog box is the Font dialog box with a different name.) If you want to move the delivery address from its default position shown in the Preview area, change the settings in the From Left text box and the From Top text box.

■ **Return Address**   In this area, click the Font button, and then use the Envelope Return Address dialog box to set the font formatting you want to use for the return address. (The Envelope Return Address dialog box is the Font dialog box with another different name.) If you want to move the return address from its default position shown in the Preview area, change the settings in the From Left text box and the From Top text box.

16

On the Printing Options tab, choose printing options for the envelope:

- **Feed Method** In this area, click the picture that shows the direction and orientation you will use for feeding the envelope. Select the Face Up option button or the Face Down option button to tell Word whether the envelope will be face up or face down. Select the Clockwise Rotation check box if you want to rotate the envelope in any of the right three feed methods by 180 degrees.

- **Feed From** In this drop-down list, you can choose the printer tray that contains the envelopes.

- **Reset** Click this button to restore the Feed Method and Feed From settings to their default settings for your printer.

When you've finished choosing options, click the OK button. Word closes the Envelope Options dialog box, and you're ready to select the data source for the mail merge.

 *The Printing Options tab of the Envelope Options dialog box makes setting up an envelope as easy as possible—but it's still a good idea to test printing a few envelopes to make sure you've chosen suitable options for your printer before printing an entire merge of envelopes.*

Choose Options for Merged Labels

When you choose the Labels item on the Start Mail Merge panel, Word displays the Label Options dialog box, shown here, so that you can specify the type of label you're using.

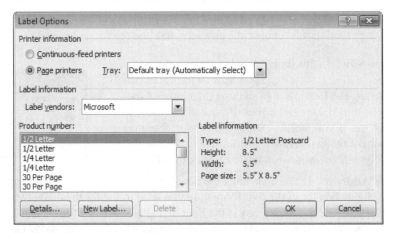

In the Printer Information area, choose the Continuous-Feed Printers option button if your printer prints labels from a continuous roll. If you are not printing from a continuous roll, select the Page Printers option button, and then choose the paper tray that holds the labels in the Tray drop-down list.

In the Label Information area, specify the type of label:

- **Label Vendors** In this drop-down list, select the make of label you're using—for example, Microsoft, Avery US Letter, or Office Depot. Word displays this vendor's set of products in the Product Number list box.

■ **Product Number** In this list box, select the label by description or number. For example, read the label-type number on the label box, and then click the matching number. The Label Information readout shows the type, height, width, and page size of the labels you've selected.

■ **Details** If you need to see further details of the label type's setup, click the Details button. Word displays the Information dialog box for the selected label type. Click the OK button when you're ready to close the dialog box.

■ **New Label** If your label type doesn't appear in any of the lists, follow these steps:

1. Click the New Label button. Word displays the Label Details dialog box, shown here with settings chosen.

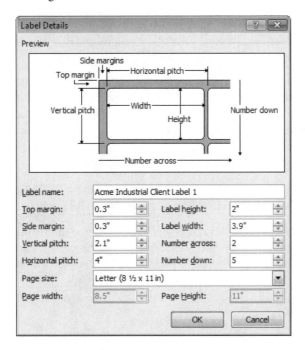

2. In the Label Name text box, type the name you want to assign the label.

3. In the Page Size drop-down list, choose the size of sheet the labels come on. If necessary, use the Page Width text box and Page Height text box to specify a custom size.

4. In the Top Margin text box, set the distance from the top of the sheet of paper to the top of the first label.

5. In the Side Margin text box, set the distance from the left edge of the sheet of paper to the left edge of the first label.

6. In the Label Height text box, set the height of each label.

16

7. In the Label Width text box, set the width of each label.

8. In the Number Across text box, set the number of labels across the sheet of paper.

9. In the Number Down text box, set the number of labels down the sheet of paper.

10. If the Number Across setting is more than 1 and there's a gap between labels, use the Horizontal Pitch setting to indicate where the second and subsequent labels start across the page. For example, if there's a 0.1-inch gap between labels and the labels are 3.9 inches wide, set the horizontal pitch to 4 inches.

11. If the Number Down setting is more than 1 and there's a gap between labels, use the Vertical Pitch setting to indicate where the second and subsequent labels start down the page.

12. Click the OK button. Word closes the Label Details dialog box, changes the Label Vendors drop-down list setting to Other/Custom, and displays the name you entered in step 2 in the Product Number list box.

When you've chosen your label type, click the OK button. Word closes the Label Options dialog box and sets up the document as a table with cells the right size for the labels you chose, so the Table Tools section appears on the Ribbon. However, the table cells have no borders, and you won't see the gridlines unless Word is set to display them (choose Layout | Table | View Gridlines to toggle the gridlines on or off).

You're now ready to select the data source for the mail merge.

Specify the Data Source to Use for the Merge

After you've chosen the type of merge document you're creating, you specify the data source. Choose Mailings | Start Mail Merge | Select Recipients, and then choose the appropriate item from the Select Recipients panel, shown here: Type New List, Use Existing List, or Select From Outlook Contacts.

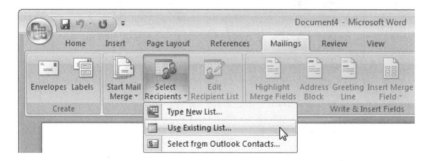

The following sections discuss these three options.

As mentioned earlier in this chapter, it's usually better to use an existing list (or your Outlook contacts, if appropriate) than to create a custom list for a mail merge.

Create a New List for the Mail Merge

To create a new data source for the mail merge, follow these steps:

1. Click the Type New List item on the Select Recipients panel. Word displays the New
Address List dialog box, shown here with one entry created and a second entry underway.

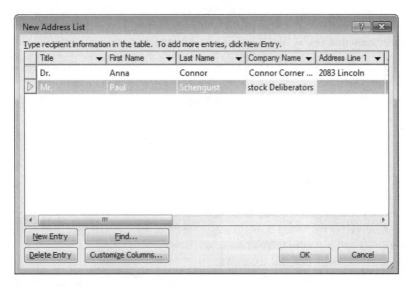

2. Before you enter any data, see whether you need to customize the fields in the record
from Word's default selection of fields. To customize the fields, follow these steps:

■ Click the Customize Columns button. Word displays the Customize Address List
dialog box, shown here.

16

■ To add a field, click the Add button. Word displays the Add Field dialog box, shown here. Type the name for the field, and then click the OK button. Word closes the Add Field dialog box and adds the field to the list.

■ To delete an existing field, select it in the Field Names list box, and then click the Delete button. Word confirms the deletion, as shown here, making sure that you understand that you're also deleting any information contained in the field. (As long as you're setting up the fields before entering the data, however, there's no data yet to lose.) Click the Yes button.

■ To rename an existing field, select it in the Field Names list box, and then click the Rename button. Word displays the Rename Field dialog box. Type the new name for the field, as in the example shown here, and then click the OK button. Word closes the Rename Field dialog box and changes the field's name in the Field Names list box.

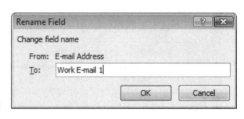

■ To rearrange the order of the fields, click a field, and then click the Move Up button or the Move Down button, as appropriate.

■ When you've finished customizing the fields, click the OK button. Word closes the Customize Address List dialog box, returning you to the New Address List dialog box, where the column headings show the fields as you have set them up.

3. Type the entries in the table. Press TAB to move from one item to the next item.

4. When you press TAB from the last column of the current entry, Word automatically starts a new entry for you on the next line. However, you can also start a new entry manually at any time by clicking the New Entry button.

5. To delete an entry you've created, click anywhere in the entry, click the Delete button, and then click the Yes button in the confirmation dialog box that Word displays.

6. When you've finished adding entries to your list, click the OK button. Word closes the New Address List box and displays the Save Address List dialog box.

7. Type the filename for the data source, choose the folder in which to save it, and then click the Save button. Word closes the Save Address List dialog box and saves the data source.

In the Save As Type drop-down list in the Save Address List dialog box, you'll see that Word describes the data source file type as being "Microsoft Office Address Lists." This is a form of Access database. You can't choose any other file format for data sources you create from Word.

Open an Existing List or Query a Database

If you have an existing list of customers (or other suitable data for your merge) in any widely used format—such as an Excel spreadsheet, a Word document, a text file, or a database—you should be able to use it for the merge.

To open an existing data source or set up a query to a database, follow these steps:

1. Click the Use Existing List item on the Select Recipients panel. Word displays the Select Data Source dialog box.

2. Navigate to the data source, select it, and then click the Open button. Word then attaches the merge document to the data source, prompting you for any decisions along the way.

The details of connecting the merge document to the data source vary depending on the data source. For example, when you choose an Excel workbook as a data source, Word displays the Select Table dialog box, as shown here. Choose the table or range in the list box. Select the First Row Of Data Contains Column Headers check box if the first row contains headers rather than data. Click the OK button. Word closes the Select Table dialog box.

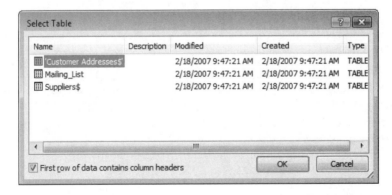

Use Your Outlook Contacts

To use your Outlook Contacts folder as the data source for the mail merge, follow these steps:

1. Click the Select From Outlook Contacts item on the Select Recipients panel. Word displays the Select Contacts dialog box.

2. In the Select A Contact Folder To Import list box, select the contact folder you want, and then click the OK button. Word displays the Mail Merge Recipients dialog box, discussed in the next section, so that you can choose the contacts to use for the mail merge.

16

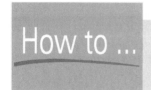

Add a Data Source Folder to Windows' Indexed Locations

If the Select Data Source dialog box includes an information bar saying "Searches might be slow in non-indexed locations," as in the example here, it means that some of the folders in which Windows Vista stores data sources are set not to be indexed. As a result, Windows Vista takes longer to find the data sources in these folders.

If you perform mail merge only occasionally, this may not be a problem. But you may choose to add the data source folders to Windows' indexed locations. To do so, follow these steps:

1. Click the information bar, and then choose Add To Index from the menu that appears, as shown here.

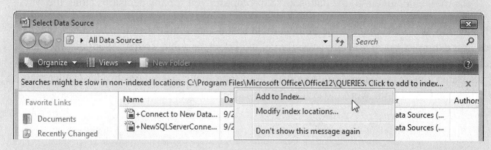

2. Word displays the Add To Index dialog box.

3. Click the Add To Index button, and then authenticate yourself to User Account Control to make this change. (To authenticate yourself, you must either be logged on using an Administrator account or be able to provide an Administrator password when prompted for one.)

Edit the Recipient List

When you connect the data source to the merge document, all the records in the data source become available to you. If you've created a data source especially for this merge, you'll probably want to use all of it. If you're using an existing data source or your Outlook contacts, you'll most likely want to use only some of the records in the data source. For example, if you're using a list of all customers, you might want to write to only those in California, or only those who had bought a particular product.

To edit the recipient list, follow these steps:

1. If you created a new data source or connected to an existing source, choose Mailings | Start Mail Merge | Edit Recipient list. Word displays the Mail Merge Recipients dialog box (see Figure 16-2).

> **NOTE** *If you chose the Select From Outlook Contents item, Word automatically displays the Mail Merge Recipients dialog box for you, so you don't need to display it manually.*

2. Clear the check box for any record you want to exclude.

- Word automatically selects the check box for each of the records in the list.

- You can clear all the check boxes by clearing the check box in the header row; to select all the check boxes again, select this check box.

3. Choose other options as discussed in the following subsections, and then click the OK button. Word closes the Mail Merge Recipients dialog box.

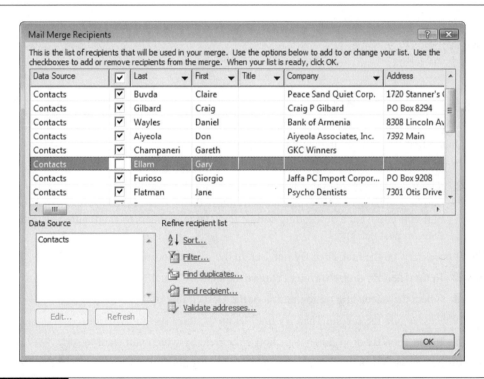

FIGURE 16-2 The Mail Merge Recipients dialog box lets you choose recipients for this mail merge from the list in the data source you connected to the merge document.

Sort the Recipient List

For many mail merges, you may need to sort the recipient list into a particular order. Word lets you perform either a quick sort or a complex sort.

To perform a quick sort, click a column heading once to sort by that column in ascending order. Click the heading again to sort by that column in descending order.

To perform a complex sort, follow these steps:

1. In the Refine Recipient List area of the Mail Merge Recipients dialog box, click the Sort link. Word displays the Filter And Sort dialog box with the Sort Records tab foremost, shown here with settings chosen.

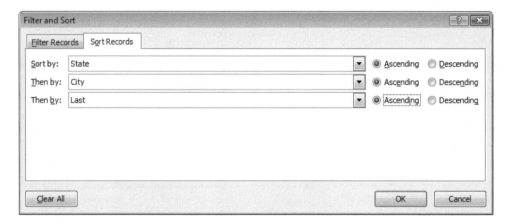

2. On the Sort By line, set up the first sorting criterion:

- In the Sort By drop-down list, choose the field by which you want to sort first.

- Select the Ascending option button if you want an ascending sort (A to Z, small numbers to large numbers, past dates to future dates). Select the Descending option button if you want a descending sort (Z to A, large numbers to small numbers, future dates to past dates).

3. If necessary, on the first Then By line, set up the second sorting criterion:

- In the Then By drop-down list, choose the field by which you want to sort.

- Select the Ascending option button or the Descending option button.

4. If necessary, on the second Then By line, set up the third sorting criterion:

- In the Then By drop-down list, choose the field by which you want to sort.

- Select the Ascending option button or the Descending option button.

5. Click the OK button. Word closes the Filter And Sort dialog box and applies the sorting to the list.

Filter the Recipient List

If necessary, filter the list to see only the records that match certain criteria. Word lets you perform either a quick filter or a complex filter.

To perform a quick filter, click the drop-down arrow on a column heading, and then choose the item from the drop-down list. For example, click the City column heading in a typical merge, and then click the city name in the drop-down list.

To perform a complex filter, follow these steps:

1. In the Refine Recipient List area of the Mail Merge Recipients dialog box, click the Filter link. Word displays the Filter And Sort dialog box with the Filter Records tab foremost, shown here with settings chosen.

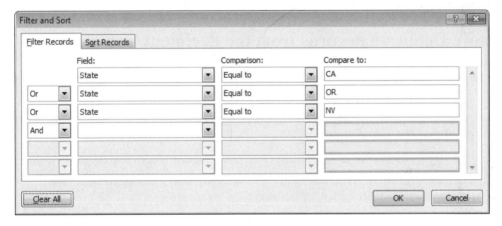

2. On the top line, set up the first filter:

■ In the Field drop-down list, select the field that you want to evaluate.

■ In the Comparison drop-down list, choose the comparison: Equal To, Not Equal To, Less Than, Greater Than, Less Than Or Equal, Greater Than Or Equal, Is Blank, Is Not Blank, Contains, or Does Not Contain.

NOTE *The Is Blank comparison means that the field in the record must be blank (not have any contents) for the criterion to match. The Is Not Blank comparison means that the field must have some contents.*

■ In the Compare To text box, type the value with which you want to compare the field's contents. For example, you might compare a State field to CA, OR, NV, or another state abbreviation, as in the example. If you choose the Is Blank comparison or the Is Not Blank comparison, Word makes the Compare To text box unavailable, because you do not need to enter comparison text.

16

3. To add a second filter, choose And or Or in the first column, and then use the Field drop-down list, Comparison drop-down list, and Compare To text box to set up the comparison as explained in the previous step.

   ■ **And filter**   Choose And if you want to select records that match both or all of two or more criteria. For example, you might filter for customers in a particular city who had bought a particular product.

   ■ **Or filter**   Choose Or if you want to select records that match one criterion or another. For example, you might filter for customers in either Los Angeles or Las Vegas.

4. Add a third, fourth, or further filter as needed.

5. Click the OK button. Word closes the Filter And Sort dialog box and applies the filter to the records in the data source.

Remove Duplicate Records from the Recipient List

Depending on your data source, you may need to check for and remove duplicate records to make sure that no recipient appears twice. To check for duplicate records, follow these steps:

1. In the Refine Recipient List area of the Mail Merge Recipients dialog box, click the Find Duplicates link. Word analyzes the records in the data source and then displays the Find Duplicates dialog box.

2. Clear the check box for each duplicate entry you want to exclude from the mail merge.

3. Click the OK button. Word closes the Find Duplicates dialog box and removes the excluded records from the list for the merge.

Search for a Particular Entry in the Recipient List

To search for a particular entry in the recipient list, follow these steps:

1. In the Refine Recipient List area of the Mail Merge Recipients dialog box, click the Find Recipient link. Word displays the Find Entry dialog box, shown here.

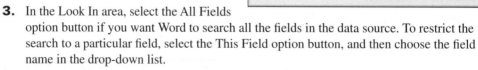

2. In the Find text box, type the text you want to find—for example, a last name.

3. In the Look In area, select the All Fields option button if you want Word to search all the fields in the data source. To restrict the search to a particular field, select the This Field option button, and then choose the field name in the drop-down list.

4. Click the Find Next button. Word searches for the text.

   ■ If Word finds a match, it highlights the entry in the Mail Merge Recipients dialog box, leaving the Find Entry dialog box open. You can then click the Find Next button to find the next instance.

■ If Word finds no match, or no further match, it displays the message box shown next. Click the OK button to close the dialog box.

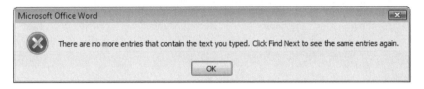

5. Click the Cancel button. Word closes the Find Entry dialog box.

Validate the E-mail Addresses in the Recipient List

If your company subscribes to an address-verification service, such as CorrectAddress from Intelligent Search Technology or the Stamps.com service from the U.S. Postal Service, you can validate addresses in your mail merge against a database by clicking the Validate Addresses link in the Refine Recipient List area of the Mail Merge Recipients dialog box.

If your computer is not set up to use an address-verification service, clicking this link produces a dialog box that offers to show you information on the services available.

NOTE *If your data source changes frequently and you spend a while setting up your merge, it may be a good idea to refresh the data that Word has pulled from the data source. To do so, select the data source in the Data Source list box in the Mail Merge Recipients dialog box, and then click the Refresh button. Word retrieves the latest data.*

Insert Merge Fields and Text in the Main Document

Once you've chosen your data source and (if necessary) edited down the list of recipients, you're ready to insert merge fields and text in the main document. This example uses a letter, but the process is similar for other types of merge documents.

Type any unchanging text that the main document requires. For example, for a customer service letter, you might enter some text that applies to all the customers included in the merge.

Position the insertion point where you want the first merge field, and then insert it in one of the following ways.

Insert an Address Block

To insert an address block (for example, the customer's name and address), follow these steps:

1. Position the insertion point where you want the address block to appear in the document.

2. Choose Mailings | Write And Insert Fields | Address Block. Word displays the Insert Address Block dialog box, shown here.

   ■ The Preview box displays the address block in its current form.

16

■ You can move among the records by clicking the buttons. For example, click the Next button to display the address for the next record, or type a record's number in the Record Number box and press ENTER to move to that record.

First   Previous   Record Number   Next   Last

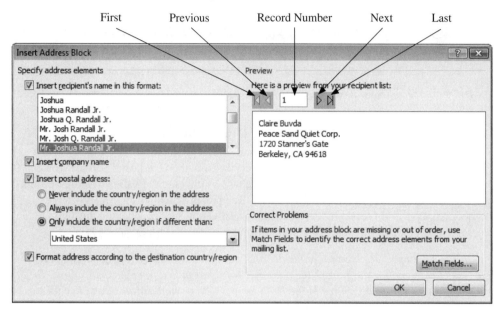

3. In the Specify Address Elements area, set up the address block the way you want it:

■ **Insert Recipient's Name In This Format**   Select this check box to include the recipient's name, as you'll often want to do. In the list box, select the name format you want to use.

■ **Insert Company Name**   Select this check box to include the company's name.

■ **Insert Postal Address**   Select this check box if you want to include the postal address, as you would for a typical mailing. If you include it, choose whether to include the country or region by selecting the Never Include The Country/Region In The Address option button, the Always Include The Country/Region In The Address option button, or the Only Include The Country/Region If Different Than option button. The last option button is usually the best choice; when you select it, choose the country in the drop-down list.

■ **Format Address According To The Destination Country/Region**   Select this check box if you want Word to apply country- or region-specific address conventions to the address. (For example, some countries place the equivalent of the zip code before the city.)

4. If elements in the address appear in the wrong order, you may need to change the field matching. Follow these steps:

■ Click the Match Fields button. Word displays the Match Fields dialog box.

- In the Required For Address Block area, select the matching field in each drop-down list, or select "(not matched)" from the bottom of the drop-down list to indicate that there is no match for the item.

- If you'll need to use the same field matching again with this data source, select the Remember This Matching For This Set Of Data Sources On This Computer check box.

- Click the OK button. Word closes the Match Fields dialog box and rearranges the address information in the Insert Address Block dialog box accordingly.

5. Click the OK button. Word closes the Insert Address Block dialog box and inserts the address block in the document as an <<AddressBlock>> merge field, as shown here.

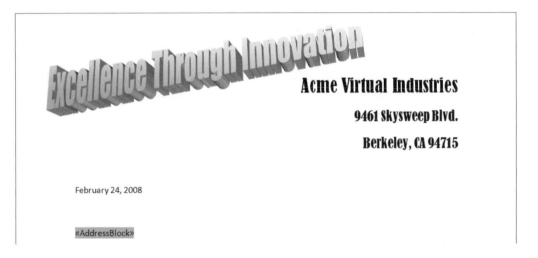

Insert a Greeting Line

To insert a greeting line (for example, for a letter), follow these steps:

1. Position the insertion point where you want the greeting line to appear in the document.

2. Choose Mailings | Write And Insert Fields | Greeting Line. Word displays the Insert Greeting Line dialog box, shown here. The Preview box displays the address block in its current form, and you can move among the records by clicking the blue buttons or typing the record number in the text box and pressing ENTER.

16

3. In the Greeting Line Format area, use the three drop-down lists to set up the greeting format you want to use—for example, **Dear Mr. Jones,** or **To Bill:**.

4. In the Greeting Line For Invalid Recipient Names drop-down list, choose the greeting you want to use when the name isn't available—for example, **Dear Sir Or Madam,** or **To Whom It May Concern:**.

5. If the names in the greeting appear wrong, click the Match Fields button, and then use the controls in the Match Fields dialog box to remap the fields, as discussed in step 4 of the previous list.

6. Click the OK button. Word closes the Insert Greeting Line dialog box and inserts the greeting line as a <<GreetingLine>> merge field in the document.

Insert Other Merge Fields

Word provides the Insert Address Block dialog box and the Insert Greeting Line dialog box to help you insert the two most common sets of fields required for mail merges—but for most merges, you'll also need to insert fields manually. To do so, follow these steps:

1. Position the insertion point where you want the field to appear in the document.

2. Choose Mailings | Write And Insert Fields | Insert Merge Field, and then choose the merge field from the list. The list shows all the merge fields available in the data source. Word inserts the merge field between chevrons—for example, a merge field named City appears as <<**City**>>.

To see at a glance where all the merge fields in a document are, choose Mailings | Write And Insert Fields | Highlight Merge Fields. Word applies field shading to all merge fields. Issue the command again if you want to turn the field shading off.

Save the Main Document

Once you've finished laying out your main document, save changes to it so that you can use it in the future, either to perform further instances of the same merge or as the basis for a new merge document.

Preview and Check the Merged Documents

When you've laid out the merged document, preview the merge before you merge the data into it. To preview the merge, choose Mailings | Preview Results | Preview Results. Word merges data from a record in the data source into the main document so that you can see whether the data appears as it should. For example, in the next illustration, Word has merged in the address block and greeting line.

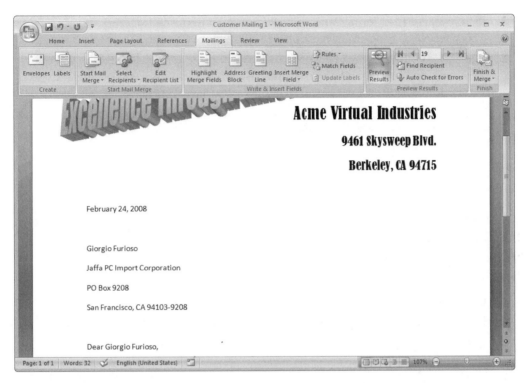

Use the record-navigation buttons in the Preview Results group on the Mailings tab to navigate from record to record, examining how the data looks once it's in place. For example, click the First Record button to move to the first record, or type a record number in the Go To Record text box and press ENTER to go to a specific record.

You can also access a particular record by choosing Mailings | Preview Results | Find Recipient and using the Find Entry dialog box to search for the record.

Rather than examine all of the records in the merge manually, you can have Word check for errors for you. To do this, follow these steps:

1. Choose Mailings | Preview Results | Auto Check For Errors. Word displays the Checking And Reporting Errors dialog box, shown here.

2. Choose the option button for the action you want to perform:

    ■ **Simulate The Merge And Report Errors In A New Document**   Select this option button to make Word produce a new document containing a list of errors without actually creating a merge document. If there are no errors, Word displays a message box telling you so.

16

■ **Complete The Merge, Pausing To Report Each Error As It Occurs** Select this
option button to run the merge but have Word stop at each error. This approach lets you
see each error in context, which can be more helpful than seeing the error list in a report.

■ **Complete The Merge Without Pausing. Report Errors In A New Document** Select
this option button if you want to run the merge and have Word produce a new document
containing a list of errors.

3. Click the OK button. Word closes the Checking And Reporting Errors dialog box and
performs the action you requested.

If your preview of the merge identifies any errors, fix them. Depending on the error, you may
need to change the merge fields in the main document or fix problems with the source data.

Perform the Merge

Once your merge is ready, you can run the merge and create the documents. You have three
choices, which the following sections explain:

■ Create individual documents that you can edit as needed before printing

■ Merge directly to a printer, so you get printed documents

■ Merge directly to e-mail, creating e-mail messages

Create Individual Documents

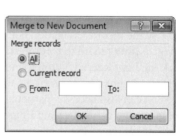

To create individual documents, follow these steps:

1. Choose Mailings | Finish | Finish And Merge | Edit
Individual Documents. Word displays the Merge To
New Document dialog box, shown here.

2. Choose which records to merge:

■ **All** Select this option button to merge all the records.

■ **Current Record** Select this option button to merge just the current record. This
option is useful for producing a single merge document after you've corrected a
record that produced an unusable result.

■ **From** Select this option button, and enter the start and end values in the text boxes,
to run part of the merge.

3. Click the OK button. Word closes the Merge To New Document dialog box and runs the
merge you specified.

4. Review the resulting merge document and make any changes needed.

5. Press CTRL-S or click the Save button on the Quick Access Toolbar, and then save the
merge document.

You may want to print all or part of the merge document you have created.

Merge Directly to a Printer

To merge directly to a printer, producing printed documents rather than a Word document that you can save, follow these steps:

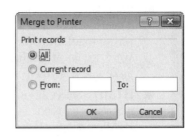

1. Choose Mailings | Finish | Finish And Merge | Print Documents. Word displays the Merge To Printer dialog box, shown here.

2. Choose which records to print:

   ■ **All**   Select this option button to print all the records.

   ■ **Current Record**   Select this option button to print just the current record. This option is useful for printing a single document after you've corrected a record that produced an unusable result.

   ■ **From**   Select this option button, and enter the start and end values in the text boxes, to print documents for just some of the records.

3. Click the OK button. Word closes the Merge To Printer dialog box and runs the merge you specified. Provided that the printer is online and functional, Word prints your documents.

Merge Directly to E-mail Messages

To merge directly to e-mail messages, follow these steps:

1. Choose Mailings | Finish | Finish And Merge | Send E-mail Messages. Word displays the Merge To E-mail dialog box, shown here.

2. In the To drop-down list, select the field in the data source that contains the e-mail address.

3. In the Subject Line text box, type the subject line you want to give the e-mail messages.

4. In the Mail Format drop-down list, choose the e-mail format you want to use:

   ■ **Attachment**   Select this item to send the Word document as an attachment to an e-mail message. An attachment is a good way of making sure the Word document transfers successfully without losing formatting, but it has two disadvantages. First, many people are reluctant to open unsolicited Word documents because they may contain macro viruses or other malware. And second, many people will not bother to open e-mail attachments at all.

16

- ■ **Plain Text**   Select this item to send the text of the Word document in a plain-text e-mail message (a message that uses text only without formatting). Plain text is a good way of transferring text information, but any formatting that you have applied to the Word document will be lost—so if you use Plain Text, you should run a test first to make sure that you have laid out your message in a suitable way.

- ■ **HTML**   Select this item to send the Word document's contents as a formatted e-mail message. This is often the best choice provided that the recipient has chosen to receive HTML messages. If the recipient has chosen to receive text-only messages (for example, because HTML messages can pose a threat to privacy), they will see a version of the message with HTML codes rather than formatting. The result is hard to read.

5. In the Send Records area, choose which records to send.

- ■ **All**   Select this option button to send all the records.

- ■ **Current Record**   Select this option button to send just the current record. This option is useful for producing a single e-mail message after you've corrected a record that produced an unusable result.

- ■ **From**   Select this option button, and enter the start and end values in the text boxes, to run part of the merge.

6. Click the OK button. Word activates or launches your e-mail program, creates the messages, and sends them.

Restore a Main Document to a Regular Document

To restore a mail merge document to a regular document, follow these steps:

1. Open the document.

2. Choose Mailings | Start Mail Merge | Start Mail Merge | Normal Word Document.

3. Click the Save button on the Quick Access Toolbar to save the document.

Chapter 17

Use Outlines and Create Master Documents

How to...

- Create an outline
- Create outline numbered lists
- Create master documents

Short documents are easy to navigate—especially if you have one of the monster displays that are gradually becoming more and more affordable. But once a document grows to more than a dozen or so pages long, you'll likely find you spend too much time scrolling through it trying to find the part you need to work on next.

Word's outlining tools can save you a lot of time. Outline view lets you collapse a document to different numbers of heading levels so that you see only those levels. This allows you to focus on the structure of your document and easily move sections of text up and down the document. You can also expand the text and subheadings under any heading as needed. And you can apply multilevel list formats to documents that need complex numbering.

If you're creating truly large documents, or documents that your colleagues need to work on at the same time as you edit them, you may want to use master documents. A *master document* is a document that contains two or more subdocuments. You and your colleagues can open the subdocuments independently of each other without needing to worry about permissions, sharing, or revision marks.

Create an Outline

When you're creating any long document, you can usually save time and effort by outlining it, either from the start or as you work on the document.

Understand the Basics of Outlines

In Word, an outline uses ten levels of "importance," Level 1 (highest) through Level 9 (lowest) for headings, and Body Text for the rest. Word maps the nine heading levels to the built-in heading styles Heading 1 through 9: Heading 1 has Level 1 importance, Heading 2 has Level 2, and so on. Any paragraph that doesn't have one of the heading levels has the Body Text level.

The easiest way to work with outlines is to use Word's built-in heading styles. For example, if you're creating a book-length document, you might use Heading 1 style for the chapter titles, Heading 2 style for the first-level headings, Heading 3 style for the second-level headings, and so on. Under normal circumstances, you will not need to use all nine heading levels Word provides—for a conventional document, having more than four or five levels of headings becomes confusing, especially for readers. But for complex documents, having extra heading levels available for special uses can be helpful.

If you need or prefer to use your own styles instead of the built-in heading styles, you can assign heading levels to your styles as needed. For example, in a template for a newsletter, you might assign Level 1 importance to a style named Story Lead, Level 2 importance to a style named Subhead 1, and Level 3 importance to a style named Subhead 2. You can also customize the heading levels for the built-in heading styles if necessary. For example, in a book template, you might assign Level 1 importance to a style named Chapter Title, Level 2 importance to the Heading 1 style, Level 3 importance to the Heading 2 style, and so on.

Start an Outline

You can start an outline either from an existing document or by creating a new document. In fact, if you've used Heading styles in your document, you've already created an outline in it, even if you've never viewed the outline.

To use an existing document, open it. To use a new document, create one—click the Office Button, click New, select the document type in the New Document dialog box, and then click the Create button.

To start working with the outline, click the Outline View button on the status bar or choose View | Document Views | Outline. From the keyboard, press ALT, W, U in sequence. Word displays the document in Outline view and adds the Outlining tab to the Ribbon, as shown here. The Outlining tab appears in the first position on the Ribbon, before the Home tab, unlike most of the other extra Ribbon tabs.

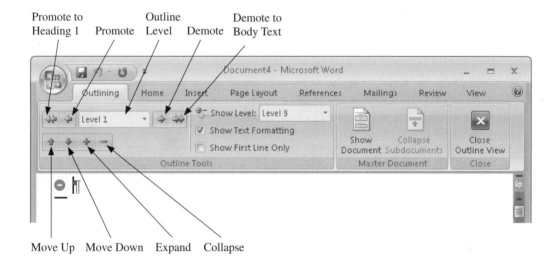

Promote to Heading 1   Promote   Outline Level   Demote   Demote to Body Text

Move Up   Move Down   Expand   Collapse

NOTE   *When you create a new document and then switch to Outline view, Word automatically applies the Heading 1 style to the first paragraph in the document, on the assumption that you want to create an outline.*

17

Start Creating the Outline Headings

To start creating the outline in a new document, type the text of the first heading, and then press ENTER.

When the document is in Outline view and you press ENTER at the end of a paragraph, Word continues the current style to the next paragraph rather than applying the style for the following paragraph specified in the current style's definition. For example, a Heading 1 style normally has a body-text style, such as Body Text or Normal, specified for the following paragraph, because a heading is typically followed by body text. But when the document is in Outline view, Word makes the following paragraph Heading 1 as well on the assumption that you need to enter more headings in the outline.

Change the Heading Level

To change the heading level, click in the paragraph and then

■ Press TAB or choose Outlining | Outline Tools | Demote to demote the paragraph to the next level—for example, from Heading 1 style to Heading 2 style. Word displays the lower level of heading indented in Outline view, as shown here, even if the actual style has no indentation.

■ Press SHIFT-TAB or choose Outlining | Outline Tools | Promote to promote the paragraph to the next level—for example, from Heading 3 style to Heading 2 style.

■ Choose Outlining | Outline Tools | Demote To Body Text to demote the paragraph to body text. Word displays a body paragraph with a gray dot before it, as shown here.

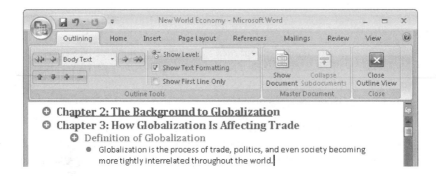

■ Choose Outlining | Outline Tools | Promote To Heading 1 to promote the paragraph to Heading 1 style.

NOTE *TAB and SHIFT-TAB are the easiest keyboard shortcuts for demoting and promoting, respectively. However, you may find on some installations of Word that pressing TAB does not work like this. You can also press ALT-SHIFT-→ to demote the current paragraph or ALT-SHIFT-← to promote it.*

A plus sign (+) next to a heading indicates lower-level headings or body text below the heading, as with the "Chapter 3" heading and the "Definition of Globalization" subheading here.

⊕ **Chapter 3: How Globalization Is Affecting Trade**
    ⊕ Definition of Globalization
      ● Globalization is the process of trade, politics, and even society becoming more tightly interrelated throughout the world.
      ⊖ Historical Background
      ⊖ Globalization Going Forward

Expand and Collapse Headings

Double-click the plus sign to expand or collapse the heading section. Here is the same section collapsed by double-clicking the plus sign next to the "Chapter 3" heading. The shaded underline starts at the indentation level of the first subheading, so you can tell whether it is the next level of subheading or a lower level.

⊕ **Chapter 3: How Globalization Is Affecting Trade**

A minus sign indicates that no lower-level headings or body text lies below the heading, as in the "Historical Background," "Globalization Going Forward," and "Chapter 4" headings shown here.

⊕ **Chapter 3: How Globalization Is Affecting Trade**
    ⊕ Definition of Globalization
      ● Globalization is the process of trade, politics, and even society becoming more tightly interrelated throughout the world.
      ⊖ Historical Background
      ⊖ Globalization Going Forward
  ⊖ **Chapter 4: Disturbing Developments in Trade Balances**

TIP *To expand or collapse more than one heading section at a time, select the part you want to expand or collapse, and then click the Expand button or the Collapse button.*

Set Outline View's "Show" Options

The right half of the Outline Tools group on the Outlining tab contains three options that let you control how Outline view displays the document:

■ **Show Level**   In this drop-down list, select the lowest level of headings to display. The choices are Level 1, Level 2, and so on to Level 9, and All Levels (which includes body text). For example, select Level 3 to display the top three levels of headings, hiding all the lower levels. Once you've set the level, you can display lower-level headings within a heading section by double-clicking the plus sign next to the heading. Similarly, you can collapse displayed headings by double-clicking the plus sign next to the heading above them.

■ **Show Text Formatting**   Select this check box if you want Word to display font formatting on text. The formatting can help you distinguish the levels of heading easily. Clear the check box to make Word display all the text in the same font (your default font), which usually lets you see more of the document (unless your headings use fonts smaller than your default font). The next illustration shows part of an outline with formatting turned off.

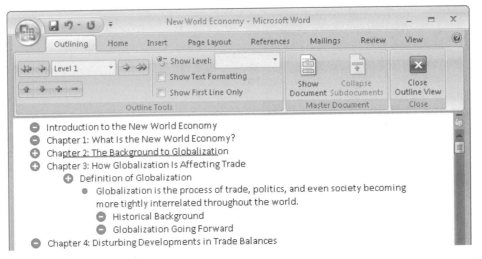

■ **Show First Line Only**   Select or clear this check box (or press ALT-SHIFT-L) to toggle between showing entire paragraphs of body text and showing only the first line of each paragraph, followed by an ellipsis (…) to show that Word has truncated it. Showing only the first line helps you get an overview of a section without having to scroll up and down the document.

Outline view and the Document Map both provide a collapsible outline of a document, so using both at once seems like overkill. However, when you're wrestling with a long outline, you may find the Document Map useful for moving quickly from one part of the outline to another without having to collapse, expand, or scroll the outline in the main pane. (To toggle the display of the Document Map, choose View | Show/Hide | Document Map.)

Select, Promote, and Demote in Outlines

Once you've displayed the parts of the outline that you want to see, you can work in Outline view much as in other views—but you must watch out for a few things.

Click the plus sign next to a heading to select that heading and all its subheadings and text. You can then promote, demote, copy, move, or delete that entire heading section. When you promote or demote a heading whose subheadings are selected, you promote or demote the subheadings by the same amount as the heading. So if you promote a Heading 2 paragraph while the three Heading 3 paragraphs below it are selected, you end up with a Heading 1 paragraph with three Heading 2 paragraphs below it.

To select just a heading that has subheadings and text, expand the contents (if they are collapsed), and then select the heading by using other selection means than clicking the plus sign. For example, CTRL-click the heading to select its paragraph, or click in the selection bar (the invisible vertical bar to the left of the text of the document). You can then promote, demote, or otherwise change that heading without affecting its subheadings. (If you delete the heading, its subheadings join the previous heading of the same level as the one you deleted.)

Click the minus sign next to a heading to select only that heading.

Demoting a heading to body text by clicking the Demote to Body Text button makes Word apply Normal style to the paragraph. If you don't use the Normal style for body text, apply the appropriate style (for example, Body Text) to the heading instead of clicking the Demote to Body Text button. Provided that the style has the Body Text outline level, applying the style stops Word from including the paragraph as a heading in the outline.

Reorder Paragraphs in the Outline

In Outline view, you can quickly rearrange the order of headings and paragraphs:

1. Display the headings or paragraphs you want to reorder. Either use the Show Level drop-down list on the Outline Tools panel of the Outlining tab to display the headings, or double-click the plus signs to the left of headings to expand or collapse them manually.

2. Select the headings or paragraphs you want to move:
   - Click a plus sign to select a heading and its subordinate headings and text.
   - Drag in the selection bar (or drag in the document) to select multiple heading sections.

3. Click the Move Up button or the Move Down button to move the selection up or down the outline. Each click moves the selection by one displayed item (a heading or a paragraph). For faster progress, drag the selection up or down (see Figure 17-1).

Apply Formatting in Outline View

You can apply styles and most formatting in Outline view, but you won't see the formatting if you've turned off Show Text Formatting. Word prevents you from displaying the Paragraph dialog box in Outline view, because you can't see most of the formatting that it provides.

17

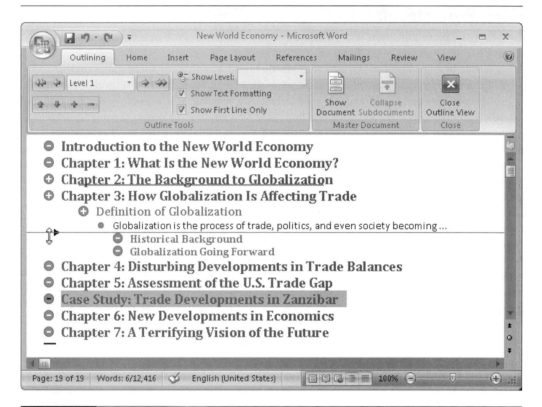

FIGURE 17-1   The quickest way to move selected headings and paragraphs up and down your outline is to drag the symbol until the destination line reaches the right place.

Print the Outline of a Document

To print the outline of a document, follow these steps:

1. Open the document, and then switch to Outline view.

2. Expand or collapse the document so that it shows only the headings (and paragraphs, if necessary) that you want to print.

3. Click the Office Button, and then click Print. Word displays the Print dialog box.

4. Choose any printing options needed (for example, multiple copies), and then click the OK button.

Create Outline Numbered Lists

For some documents, you may want to create an outline numbered list using either the Heading styles or with custom headings.

Apply an Existing Multilevel Numbered List Format

To apply an existing multilevel numbered list format, follow these steps:

1. Select the text you want to turn into the list. If you haven't yet created the list, click in the paragraph where you want the list to start.

2. Choose Home | Paragraph | Multilevel List, and then choose the list format from the Multilevel List panel (shown here).

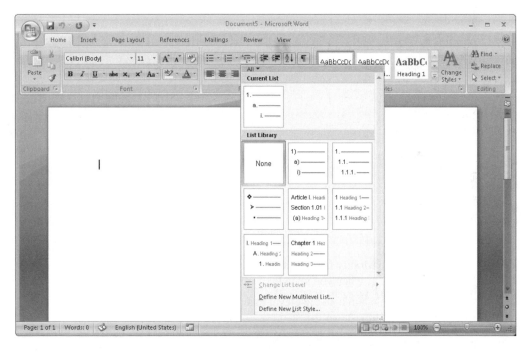

Create a Custom Outline Numbered List

If none of Word's built-in multilevel formats is suitable for your list, you can create a custom multilevel list format. To do so, follow these steps:

1. Select the text you want to turn into the list. If you haven't yet created the list, click in the paragraph where you want the list to start.

2. Choose Home | Paragraph | Multilevel List | Define New Multilevel List. Word displays the Define New Multilevel List dialog box.

17

3. If the button in the lower-left corner is the More >> button, click it. Word displays an extra panel at the right of the dialog box, so you see the full dialog box, as shown here. Word also changes the More >> button to a << Less button that you can click to hide the extra section of the dialog box again.

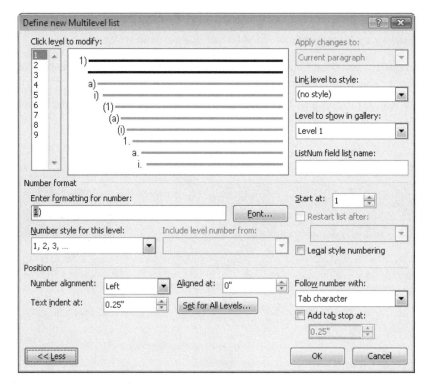

4. In the Click Level To Modify list box, select the list level you want to change. Word selects the first level, 1, when you open the Define New Multilevel List dialog box.

5. If you need to link this numbered list level to a particular style, select the style in the Link Level To Style drop-down list.

6. Use the controls in the Number Format area to specify the number format.

■ In the Number Style For This Level drop-down list, select the number format you want to use—for example, "1, 2, 3," "i, ii, iii," or "A, B, C."

■ To include the number from the previous level (or a higher level), choose the level from the Include Level Number From drop-down list. (This drop-down list is unavailable for the first level because there's no level above it.) For example, if Level 1 uses "1, 2, 3" numbering and Level 2 uses "a, b, c" numbering, applying Level 1 in the Include Level Number From drop-down list to Level 2 changes the Level 2 numbering to 1a, 1b, and so on.

■ Word displays the number formatting you've chosen in the Enter Formatting For Number text box. Type any changes for the text of the format into this text box. For example, you might edit the "A)" format to "Section A)" so that each instance of the number included the word "Section."

■ To specify font formatting, click the Font button. Word displays the Font dialog box. Choose the font, font style, size, and any extras (such as color or effects), and then click the OK button.

■ To customize the numbering, use the Start At spinner to change the starting number. If you want to restart numbering after a certain level, select the Restart List After check box and choose that level in the drop-down list. (The Restart List After controls aren't available for the first level in the list, because there's no higher level.)

■ Select the Legal Style Numbering check box if you want to use legal-style numbering (changing any roman numeral to an Arabic numeral—for example, 1.1.1 instead of I.1.1).

7. Use the controls in the Position box to customize where the number appears.

■ In the Number Alignment drop-down list, choose Left, Centered, or Right.

■ In the Aligned At text box, choose the position at which to align the number.

■ In the Text Indent At text box, set the indent position for the text.

■ In the Follow Number With drop-down list, select the character to include after the number: a tab, a space, or nothing. If you choose a tab, you can select the Add Tab Stop At check box and set the distance at which to place a tab stop.

8. Click the OK button. Word closes the Define New Multilevel List dialog box and applies the list style to the selected text.

Close Outline View

To close Outline view and return to your previous view, choose Outlining | Close | Close Outline view. Alternatively, click one of the other view buttons on the status bar.

Work with Master Documents

This section shows you how to work with master documents, which are useful for long projects. You'll learn what master documents are, how to create them and work with them, and even how to restore a master document to a "normal" document.

Understand What a Master Document Is and When to Create One

A *master document* is a document that contains two or more component documents called *subdocuments*. The contents of the subdocuments appear in the master document, which acts as a container for them. Usually, you put almost all the text and other content in the subdocuments,

17

although you can also enter text in the master document as needed. For example, the master document might contain introductory text to the document as a whole.

You and your colleagues can open the subdocuments independently of each other without needing to worry about permissions, sharing, or revision marks (topics which are explained in greater detail in Chapter 10). You can also edit the master document when you need to make changes to it as a whole—for example, rearranging the subdocuments that make up the master document, making edits to all the subdocuments at once (for instance, checking spelling or replacing terms), or printing the document.

Pros, Cons, and Known Problems with Master Documents

Master documents can save you plenty of time and effort, but they suffer from known problems, and you should make the decision about whether to use master documents with your eyes open.

Even if you use Word's new XML-based file format (with the .docx file extension), which is more robust than the older binary format, master documents may become corrupt. The more complex a master document is, or the more changes you make to it or its subdocuments, the more likely it is to suffer corruption. The problem is that you won't find out that a master document is suffering corruption until it's too late to do anything about it.

If you decide to create a master document for a project, protect your work by keeping plenty of backups that will enable you to reconstruct the master document with minimal effort and loss of content if the document gets corrupted.

To keep a master document manageable, follow these guidelines:

- Use the Word Document (.docx) format. Use the Word 97–2003 format only if some of your colleagues still use an earlier version of Word and haven't installed the conversion filters for the Word 2007 Word Document format.

- Break your document up into a manageable number of subdocuments. Usually it's best to have between 5 and 20 subdocuments. Having more than 20 subdocuments may increase the risk of corruption occurring.

- Keep your master document and all its subdocuments in the same folder so that you can back up the entire document project easily—and make those backups.

- Save the master document frequently while working with it. In particular, save the master document after creating, inserting, merging, or splitting subdocuments, because these operations cause major changes to the subdocument files.

Create a Master Document

A master document is like an outline on steroids. You can turn an existing document into a master document or start by creating a master document in a new document. For example, you might find that a project you've been working on has now grown too long or complex to be contained in a single document, or that you and your colleagues need to be able to edit different parts of it simultaneously. Or, if you're organized enough to know that a project you're embarking on will need a master document, you can start the master document from scratch.

You can also create a master document from existing component documents. For example, you might create a master report document from ten existing documents, each of which contains a chapter of the report.

Create a Master Document from an Existing Document or a New Document

To create a master document from an existing document or a new document, follow these steps:

1. Create a folder in which to store the master document and its subdocuments.

   - This step isn't absolutely necessary but it's heavily recommended for file management, backup, and your sanity. Word automatically creates the subdocuments in the same folder as the master document.

   - If you're creating the master document from an existing document, copy that document into this folder.

2. Open the document you'll use:

   - If you're using an existing document, open it.

   - If you create a new document, base it on the template you use for this type of document. Save the document in the folder you created in step 1.

> NOTE   *Word uses the same file format for the subdocuments as you use for the master document.*

3. Click the Outline View button on the status bar. Word displays the document in Outline view, adds the Outlining tab to the Ribbon, and displays the Outlining tab. If the document is blank, Word automatically applies Heading 1 style to the first paragraph.

4. Create the heading structure of the document.

   - Each subdocument must start with the same level of heading. For most projects, it's easiest to make each subdocument into a Heading 1 section. (For huge projects, you may need to use a lower level of heading for each subdocument.)

   - If you're using an existing document, make sure that it has headings of the right level. If you're creating a new document, type the headings that you will turn into the subdocuments.

17

5. Select the headings to turn into subdocuments.

  ■ Use the Show Level drop-down list to collapse the outline to the level of the subdocument headings (for example, Level 1) so that you can easily select the headings.

  ■ Make sure that the first heading in the selection is a subdocument-level heading.

6. Choose Outlining | Master Document | Show Document. Word displays the previously hidden controls in the Master Document group, as shown here.

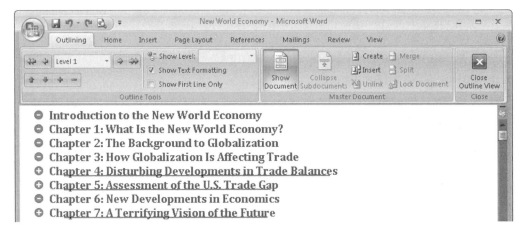

7. Click the Create button. Word turns each of the subdocument headings into a separate subdocument. Word displays a subdocument icon in the selection bar to indicate the start of each subdocument, and encloses each subdocument in a gray box, as shown here. Word adds a blank paragraph between each subdocument.

8. Click the Save button on the Quick Access Toolbar or press CTRL-S to save the master document.

Word automatically saves the subdocuments in the same folder as the master document. Word automatically assigns each subdocument a filename based on the heading with which the subdocument starts. If any filename will clash with an existing file (for example, because two headings are the same), Word automatically increments the filename.

NOTE   *Word doesn't change the subdocument filenames when you edit the headings from which those names are derived. So a subdocument's filename may sometimes be completely different from the related heading. This doesn't matter: Word keeps track of the subdocument names, so you don't need to.*

Create a Master Document from Existing Component Documents

If you already have component documents that will provide the content for the master document, create the master document like this:

1. Create a folder in which to store the master document and its subdocuments.

2. Move the subdocuments into this folder. This step isn't strictly necessary, but having all the subdocuments in the same folder as the master document is usually helpful.

3. Create a new document using the same template that the subdocuments use, and then save it in the folder.

4. If the subdocuments don't all use the same template, open each in turn and apply to it the template that you're using for the master document.

5. Click the Outline View button on the status bar. Word adds the Outlining tab to the Ribbon and displays it.

6. Choose Outlining | Master Document | Show Document. Word makes the Master Document tools available.

7. Choose Outlining | Master Document | Insert. Word displays the Insert Subdocument dialog box. This is a standard Open dialog box with a different name.

8. Select the document, and then click the Insert button. Word inserts the document as a subdocument in the master document. Word displays a subdocument icon in the selection bar to indicate the subdocument's start and encloses the subdocument in a gray box to indicate that it is a separate unit.

9. If necessary, collapse the subdocument by choosing Outlining | Master Document | Show Level | Level 1 (or another appropriate level) so that you can more easily navigate around the master document.

10. Position the insertion point, and then repeat steps 7 through 9 to insert the other documents.

11. Press CTRL-S or click the Save button on the Quick Access Toolbar. Word saves the master document.

17

View the Master Document

As you saw earlier in this chapter, you use Outline view to create a master document, so your first sight of the master document is in Outline view. This is the view you use to manage the master document and its subdocuments—and there are a couple of extra view choices for master documents than there are for plain outlines.

The first choice is whether to display the subdocument structure of the master document or just its content. You switch between the two views by clicking the Show Document button.

When the Show Document button is "pushed in" (so that it appears darker), Word displays a gray box around each subdocument and marks the start of each with a subdocument icon in the upper-left corner, as shown here.

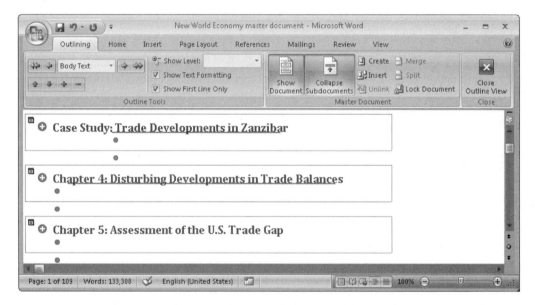

When the Show Document button is not pushed in, Word displays two section breaks around each subdocument, as shown next. The first section break marks the start of the subdocument and the second its end. Between one subdocument and the next are two section breaks: a section break marking the end of the subdocument, then the empty paragraph that Word inserts between subdocuments, then the section break marking the start of the next subdocument.

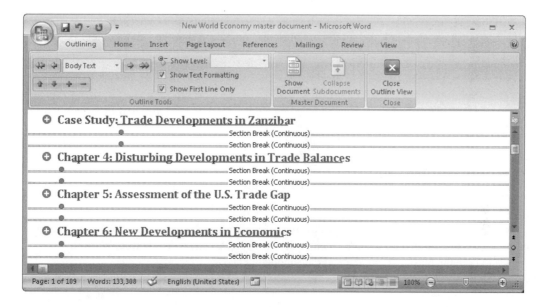

Expand and Collapse Subdocuments

When you're viewing the subdocument structure of the master document, you can expand and collapse the subdocuments. The terms can be confusing, because this expanding and collapsing is different than those for outlines.

With the subdocuments expanded, as they are when you create or insert subdocuments, the text of each subdocument appears in the master document, either collapsed to the level of headings you've set or in full. Here is an example.

17

With the subdocuments collapsed, each subdocument appears as a hyperlink, and a padlock icon appears beneath the subdocument icon, indicating that the subdocument is locked. Here is an example.

When you choose Outlining | Master Document | Collapse Subdocuments, Word may prompt you to save changes to the master document, as shown here. Click the Yes button. Word saves changes to both the master document and the subdocuments.

When the subdocuments are collapsed, you can CTRL-click a hyperlink to open the subdocument. The idea is that once you've created the master document and arranged the subdocuments as needed, you collapse the subdocuments and then use the master document to access the subdocument you want to work with.

Work with Subdocuments

Once you've split your master document up into subdocuments, you can use the master document to arrange and manage the subdocuments.

Add a Subdocument to a Master Document

To add an existing document to the master document as a subdocument, follow these steps:

1. If you want to be able to back up your master document and all its subdocuments easily, use Windows Explorer to move the existing document to the same folder as the master document.

2. Position the insertion point at the blank paragraph between two existing subdocuments.

3. Choose Outlining | Master Document | Insert. Word displays the Insert Subdocument dialog box, which is a standard Open dialog box given a different name.

4. Navigate to the appropriate folder, select the document, and then click the Open button. Word inserts the document as a subdocument.

If Word displays a dialog box such as that shown here, telling you that a style exists in both the subdocument and the master document and inviting you to rename the style in the subdocument, click the Yes button. If Word displays the dialog box again, click the Yes To All button. Renaming the style removes the problem of having a particular style name in the subdocument refer to different formatting than does the same style name in the master document.

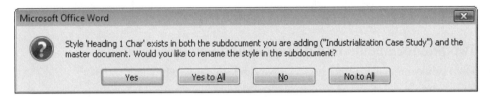

Remove a Subdocument from a Master Document

When you remove a subdocument from a master document, Word unlinks the subdocument from the master document. The subdocument's content stays in the master document (unless you delete the content manually), and the subdocument file stays in its current folder (again, unless you delete it manually).

To unlink a subdocument from the master document, follow these steps:

1. Click anywhere in the subdocument you want to unlink. (You don't need to select the subdocument—just click anywhere in it.)

2. Choose Outlining | Master Document | Unlink. Word deletes the link, leaving the content in position.

If you don't delete the content or make it part of another subdocument (see the section "Join Two Subdocuments into a Single Subdocument," later in this chapter), the content becomes part of the master document file.

Split a Subdocument into Two Subdocuments

One problem you'll often encounter is that a subdocument grows too long for easy handling, or your colleagues need to work on different parts of it at the same time. The solution to both problems is to split the subdocument into two or more subdocuments.

To split the subdocument, follow these steps:

1. Open the master document (if it's not already open).

2. Choose Outlining | Master Document | Show Document if necessary to display all the controls in the Master Document group.

17

3. Choose Outlining | Master Document | Expand Subdocuments if necessary to expand the subdocuments.

4. In the subdocument you want to split, select the headings and paragraphs that you want to split into a new subdocument. The easiest way to do this is to either promote an existing heading to the subdocument level, or create a new heading at the appropriate point in the subdocument.

5. Choose Outlining | Master Document | Split. Word creates a new subdocument.

6. Press CTRL-S or click the Save button on the Quick Access Toolbar. Word saves the new subdocument in the same folder as the master document, creating a filename from the first part of the subdocument's opening heading.

Join Two Subdocuments into a Single Subdocument

To join two subdocuments together into a single subdocument, follow these steps:

1. Open the master document (if it's not already open).

2. Choose Outlining | Master Document | Show Document if necessary to display all the controls in the Master Document group.

3. Choose Outlining | Master Document | Expand Subdocuments if necessary to expand the subdocuments.

4. Choose Outlining | Outline Tools | Show Level | Level 1 so that you see only the first-level headings. Alternatively, collapse each of the subdocuments you want to join.

5. Select the subdocuments you want to merge. You can select by dragging in the selection bar, but often the easiest way is to click at the beginning of the first subdocument, and then SHIFT-click at the end of the second subdocument.

6. Choose Outlining | Master Document | Merge. Word merges the subdocuments together into the first subdocument.

7. Press CTRL-S or click the Save button on the Quick Access Toolbar. Word saves the master document and saves all the contents of the merged subdocument in the file that contained the first of the subdocuments you merged.

Word doesn't delete the file for the other subdocument; that file retains its existing name and remains in the project folder, so you can return to it later if necessary. (If you don't need this file, delete it manually.)

Lock a Subdocument to Prevent Changes

Sometimes, you may need to lock a subdocument to prevent others (or even yourself) from making changes to it from within the master document. For example, you might lock a subdocument once it's finalized and approved.

Subdocument locking works only from within the master document. It does not prevent anyone from opening the subdocument directly from Word (for example, via the Open dialog box). If you need to prevent all changes to the document, use one of the means of protection discussed in Chapter 18.

To lock a subdocument, click in it, and then choose Outlining | Master Document | Lock Document. Word adds a lock symbol to the upper-left corner of the subdocument, as shown in the upper subdocument here, and the Lock Document button takes on a pushed-in lock when the subdocument is selected.

To unlock the subdocument again, click in it, and then choose Outlining | Master Document | Lock Document. Word removes the locking and the lock icon.

How to ...   Rename a Subdocument

The best way to handle subdocuments is to leave their management strictly to Word once you've created them from the master document or added them to it. But you may sometimes need to rename a subdocument manually. When you do so, you must remove the subdocument from the document, rename it, and then reinsert it—a complex procedure best avoided if possible.

If you rename or move a subdocument manually using Windows Explorer, Word doesn't know that the subdocument's name or path has changed. When you try to expand the master document, Word can't find the subdocument. Usually, when this happens, you'll see a message such as the following, which allows you to proceed without the document or cancel the expansion. However, it is also possible that your master document may become corrupted.

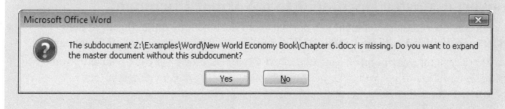

Edit the Master Document and Subdocuments

You can edit either the master document or individual subdocuments. When you make edits to a subdocument through the master document, Word saves the edits in that subdocument. The master document file contains only text that appears in the master document but not in any of the subdocuments.

You can open a subdocument in any of these ways:

- **When subdocuments are expanded** Double-click the subdocument's icon in the upper-left corner of its subdocument box.

- **When subdocuments are collapsed** CTRL-click the document's link in the master document.

- **At any time** Use a standard means of opening the document—for example, click the Office Button, and then choose the document from the Recent Documents list; or press CTRL-O, and then use the Open dialog box; or double-click the document file in a Windows Explorer window.

Once the document is open, you can edit it as you would any other document. The only difference is that, if you opened the subdocument from the master document, Word returns you to the master document when you close the subdocument.

If one of your colleagues has the subdocument open when you try to open it, Word displays the File In Use dialog box. See the section "Share Documents with Your Colleagues via a Network" in Chapter 10 for a discussion of your options when this happens.

Add Headers and Footers to a Master Document

To use headers and footers in a master document, you put them in the master document itself rather than in the subdocuments. Each subdocument can have its own headers and footers, but these appear only when the subdocument itself is open or when you print the subdocument—they don't appear in the master document, even if the master document has no headers or footers of its own.

To add a header or footer to a master document, open the master document and expand the subdocuments. You can then choose Insert | Header And Footer | Header or Insert | Header And Footer | Footer, and then work as described in the section "Add Headers and Footers to Your Documents" in Chapter 5.

Convert a Master Document to a Normal Document

You can convert a master document to a normal Word document by unlinking all of the subdocuments. Once you've done this, it's best to save the document under a different name.

Chapter 18

Protect Your Valuable Documents

How to...

- Understand Word's security features
- Protect a document with a password
- Protect a document with encryption
- Implement read-only protection
- Apply access restrictions to a document
- Apply editing and formatting restrictions
- Apply a digital signature to a document
- Remove sensitive or personal information from a document

Whether you work at home or in a company or organization, you'll probably have documents you need to protect against prying eyes. This chapter introduces you to the features that Word provides for protecting your documents and shows you how to use them.

Understand Word's Security Features

Word provides eight features that you can use to secure your documents. Table 18-1 provides a brief overview of these features, giving a brief explanation of each and indicating its purpose. You'll learn the details of the features in the rest of this chapter.

Protect a Document with a Password

To keep unauthorized users out of your documents, you can apply Open passwords and Modify passwords to them:

- **Open password**   The user must enter the password to open the document at all.
- **Modify password**   The user can open the document in read-only format without a password. To open the document for editing, the user must supply the password.

To protect a document with a password, follow these steps:

1. Click the Office button, and then click Save As. Word displays the Save As dialog box.
2. Click the Tools button (to the left of the Save button), and then choose General Options from the pop-up menu. Word displays the General Options dialog box.
3. To apply an Open password, type it in the Password To Open text box.
4. To apply a Modify password, type it in the Password To Modify text box.
5. Click the OK button. Word displays the Confirm Password dialog box.
6. Type the password in the Reenter Password To Open text box or the Reenter Password To Modify text box, and then click the OK button. Word closes the Confirm Password dialog box and the General Options dialog box.

Feature	Brief Explanation	Purpose
Open Password	Requires a password for opening a document.	Prevent colleagues from opening a document they shouldn't.
Modify Password	Requires a password for opening a document in read-write mode rather than read-only mode.	Enable colleagues to read but not alter a document.
Encryption	Requires a password to decrypt the document.	Prevent colleagues who don't have the password from opening the document. More secure than an Open password.
Read-Only Protection	Recommends to the person opening the document that they do so in read-only mode.	Request colleagues to open a document as read-only unless they need to save changes.
Editing and Formatting Restrictions	Restricts the user to performing only some actions—for example, enforces the use of change tracking.	Limit the actions your colleagues can take in a document.
Access Restrictions	Allows only approved users to open a document or take other actions with it.	Define which users can take which actions with a document. For example, you can allow some people to read a document and others to edit it.
Digital Signature	"Signs" the document electronically to indicate that it has not changed since being signed.	Mark a document as being verifiably final.
Document Inspector	Removes sensitive or personal information from a document.	Clean up a document before distributing it.

TABLE 18-1   Word's Security Features

7. Click the Save button. Word displays the Confirm Save As dialog box, warning you that you are overwriting an existing file.

8. Click the Yes button. Word closes the Confirm Save As dialog box and the Save As dialog box, and saves the document with the password you specified.

The next time you open the document, Word displays the Password dialog box, prompting you for the password. The next illustration shows the Password dialog box for an Open password on the left and the Password dialog box for a Modify password on the right.

As you can see, for a Modify password, the Password dialog box includes a Read Only button that you can click to open the document in read-only mode. You can then change the

18

document (depending on other forms of protection used) and save the results under a new name. You can't save changes to the original document.

To remove the password, open the General Options dialog box again, delete the password, and then save the document again. As before, you'll need to overwrite the existing file.

Protect a Document with Encryption

An Open password or a Modify password offers only weak protection, because you (or anyone else) can easily find password-cracking utilities on the Internet. To protect a document more securely, you can encrypt it. To do so, follow these steps:

> **Encrypt Document**
>
> Encrypt the contents of this file
>
> Password:
>
> ••••••••
>
> Caution: If you lose or forget the password, it cannot be recovered. It is advisable to keep a list of passwords and their corresponding document names in a safe place. (Remember that passwords are case-sensitive.)
>
> OK   Cancel

1. Click the Office button, and then choose Prepare | Encrypt Document. Word displays the Encrypt Document dialog box, shown here.

2. Type a strong password in the Password text box.

3. Click the OK button. Word displays a Confirm Password dialog box.

4. Type the password in the Reenter Password text box, and then click the OK button. Word closes the Confirm Password dialog box and applies the encryption.

5. Click the Save button on the Quick Access Toolbar. Alternatively, press CTRL-S. Word saves the document.

To create an effective password, use at least six characters, and make them a mix of uppercase- and lowercase, numbers, and symbols (for example, ! or @). Never use a real word as a password, no matter which language it is from.

Implement Read-Only Protection

Encryption provides effective protection for your important documents, but other documents may need a lesser degree of protection. Word's weakest form of protection is read-only protection, which you can set to recommend to your colleagues that they open a document in a read-only format so that they can't save changes to the original document.

When you implement read-only protection, Word displays a message box like that shown next when someone goes to open the document. You can see the weakness: The user can simply click the No button to open the document with full editing privileges.

> Microsoft Office Word
>
> Staff Protocols should be opened as read-only unless changes to it need to be saved. Open as read-only?
>
> Yes   No   Cancel

To implement read-only protection, follow these steps:

1. Click the Office button, and then click Save As. Word displays the Save As dialog box.

2. Click the Tools button (to the left of the Save button), and then choose General Options from the pop-up menu. Word displays the General Options dialog box.

3. Select the Read-Only Recommended check box.

4. Click the OK button. Word closes the General Options dialog box, returning you to the Save As dialog box.

5. Click the Save button. Word closes the Save As dialog box and saves the document.

When you open a document in read-only mode, Word displays "(Read-Only)" in the title bar to remind you. You can make changes freely—but you can't save them to the original document. Instead, click the Office Button, click Save As, and then specify a different filename or folder.

 Don't rely on read-only protection to keep unwanted changes out of your documents. Always back up such documents so that you can quickly recover from unwanted changes.

Apply Editing and Formatting Restrictions

As you saw in the previous section, a read-only recommendation gives your document minimal protection. If you want more protection, you can apply editing and formatting restrictions to the document, as described in this section.

For example, you may allow your colleagues to insert comments in a document but not otherwise change it. Or you may enforce change-tracking to make sure that nobody edits the document without their changes being tracked. You can even prevent your colleagues from changing the document at all.

To apply editing and formatting restrictions, follow these steps:

1. Choose Review | Protect | Protect Document, and then choose Restrict Formatting And Editing from the drop-down menu, as shown here. Word displays the Restrict Formatting And Editing pane (see Figure 18-1).

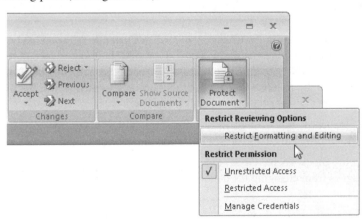

18

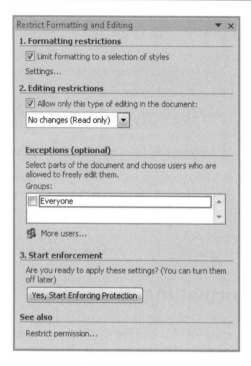

FIGURE 18-1 **FIGURE 18-1** Use the Restrict Formatting And Editing pane to limit the damage your colleagues can inflict on your documents.

2. If you want to restrict your colleagues to applying only styles you choose, follow these steps:

■ Select the Limit Formatting To A Selection Of Styles check box.

■ Click the Settings link. Word displays the Formatting Restrictions dialog box (see Figure 18-2).

■ Use the check boxes in the Checked Styles Are Currently Allowed list box to specify which styles your colleagues may use. Click the All button to select all the check boxes; click the None button to clear all the check boxes; or click the Recommended Minimum button to make Word select the most widely used styles. For greater control, select or clear the check boxes manually.

■ Select the Allow AutoFormat To Override Formatting Restrictions check box if you want AutoFormat to be able to apply formatting. Normally, this is not a good idea.

■ Select the Block Theme Or Scheme Switching check box if you want to prevent your colleagues from changing the document's theme or color scheme.

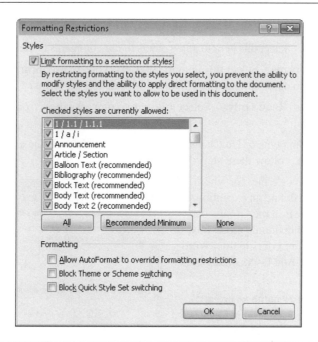

FIGURE 18-2 By applying formatting restrictions, you can ensure that your colleagues use only the styles you approve.

- Select the Block Quick Style Set Switching check box if you want to prevent your colleagues from changing the Quick Style Set applied to the document.

- Click the OK button. Word closes the Formatting Restrictions dialog box. Depending on the restrictions you chose, Word may warn you that the document may contain formatting or styles that aren't allowed, as shown here. Click the Yes button if you want Word to remove them; click the No button if you prefer to deal with them manually yourself.

3. If you want to apply editing restrictions to the document, select the Allow Only This Type Of Editing In The Document check box, and then choose which type in the drop-down list:

18

- **Tracked Changes**   Select this item to force everyone to use tracked changes (revision marks).

- **Comments**   Select this item to allow others to use comments but no other editing tool.

- **Filling In Forms**   Select this item to allow everyone to use form features (filling in fields) but no other editing. See Chapter 14 for details on forms.

- **No Changes (Read Only)**   Select this item to prevent others from making any changes.

4. If you chose Comments or No Changes (Read Only), you can define exceptions for parts of the document. Follow these steps:

- If the person or group for whom you want to define an exception doesn't appear in the Groups list box or the Individuals group box, click the More Users button. Word displays the Add Users dialog box, shown here.

- Type each user name or group name, using the example formats shown below the text box, and separate the names using semicolons. Click the OK button. Word closes the Add Users button and adds the users and groups to the Exceptions area, as in this example.

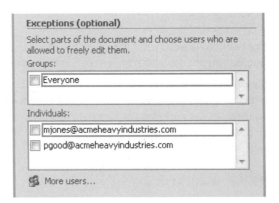

- Select the area you want the user or group to be able to edit, and then select the user's check box or group's check box in the Exceptions area. Repeat this process as needed to assign other areas that each user or group can edit.

- To check which parts of the document a user or group can edit, move the mouse pointer over the user's name or group's name, and then click the drop-down arrow that appears. Use the Find Next Region This User Can Edit command to move through the user's permitted regions one by one, or use the Show All Regions This User Can Edit command to view all the regions at once. If necessary, use the Remove All Editing Permissions For This User command to revoke the user's current permissions.

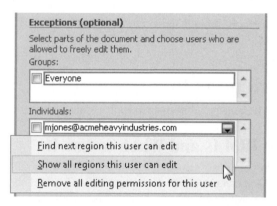

5. Click the Yes, Start Enforcing Protection button. Word displays the Start Enforcing Protection dialog box, shown here.

6. Choose how to protect the document:

- ■ **Password** Select this option button to protect the document with a password but no encryption. This gives moderate protection, but someone could edit the document and remove the password. Type the password in the Enter New Password text box and the Reenter Password To Confirm text box.

- ■ **User Authentication** Select this option button to authenticate users by user name. Word encrypts the document and enables the Restricted Access feature (see the next section). Authentication requires the use of Information Rights Management (IRM), discussed later in this chapter.

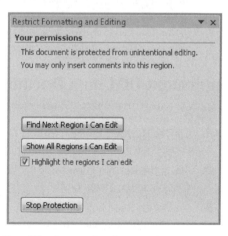

7. Click the OK button. Word closes the Start Enforcing Protection dialog box, applies the protection, and displays details of the protection and your permissions in the Restrict Formatting And Editing pane, as in this example.

18

8. Click the Save button on the Quick Access Toolbar. Word saves the document.

You can now use the Find Next Region I Can Edit button and Show All Regions I Can Edit button to find the parts of the document you can change. Select the Highlight The Regions I Can Edit check box if you want these areas highlighted so that you can identify them more easily.

To remove the restrictions, click the Stop Protection button in the Restrict Formatting And Editing pane, type your password in the Unprotect Document dialog box, and then click the OK button.

Apply Access Restrictions to a Document

For heavy-duty protection, you can apply Information Rights Management (IRM) to your documents.

Understand What IRM Is and When to Use It

IRM is typically used in corporate, government, and military situations rather than in small businesses or homes—but you can use it anywhere you have an Internet connection. IRM requires authentication to determine whether a particular user is allowed to access a particular document or take another action with it. Authentication is normally provided by a corporate server, but Microsoft also provides a free trial service that uses a Windows Live ID (the credential formerly known as Microsoft Passport).

To set up IRM with this free trial service, choose Review | Protect | Protect Document | Restricted Access, and then follow through the Service Sign-Up Wizard that Word launches. The main steps involve you providing your Windows Live ID (or signing up for a Windows Live ID if you don't already have one), creating a rights-management certificate for that Windows Live ID, and downloading the certificate to your computer.

Always remember that IRM is no panacea: Even if you turn off printing and copying, anyone determined to copy a document can do so by using traditional means: Capture it screen by screen on the computer by using PRINT SCREEN or ALT-PRINT SCREEN, or a more sophisticated screen-capture utility; photograph it on screen; type it into another document or program; dictate it into their iPod or other digital-audio player; or simply write down valuable information on paper. Even if you were to guard against all of the above, someone could simply memorize key information and reproduce it later.

Implement IRM on a Document

To apply access restrictions to the active document, follow these steps:

1. Choose Review | Protect | Protect Document | Restricted Access. Word displays the Permission dialog box, shown in Figure 18-3 with some choices made.

2. Select the Restrict Permission To This Document check box. Word enables the other controls in the dialog box.

3. Add to the Read box the name of anyone who may read the document but not change, copy, or print it. Add to the Change box the name of anyone who may read, edit, and save changes to the document, but again not print it. Use these techniques:

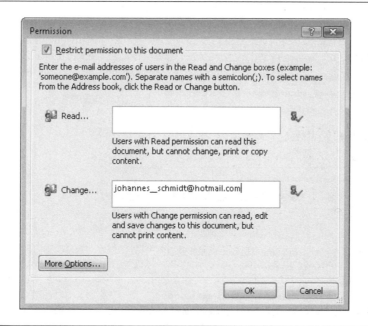

FIGURE 18-3 The Permission dialog box lets you apply Information Rights Management to a document to give it comprehensive protection against the excesses of your colleagues.

- To add users by name, type their e-mail addresses in the box. Separate each address with a semicolon.

- To add users from the Address book, click the Read button or the Change button, as appropriate, and then use the Select Names dialog box to select the names. When you click the OK button, Word closes the Select Names dialog box and adds the names to the box.

4. To implement further restrictions, click the More Options button. Word displays the larger version of the Permission dialog box (see Figure 18-4).

5. Make sure the Restrict Permission To This Document check box is selected. (Word selects this check box if it was selected in the smaller version of the Permissions dialog box.)

6. In the The Following Users Have Permission To This Document list box, set up the list of users:

- To add a user, click the Add button, use the Add Users dialog box to specify the names using the techniques described in step 3, and then click the OK button.

- To remove a user, click their name in the list box, and then click the Remove button.

18

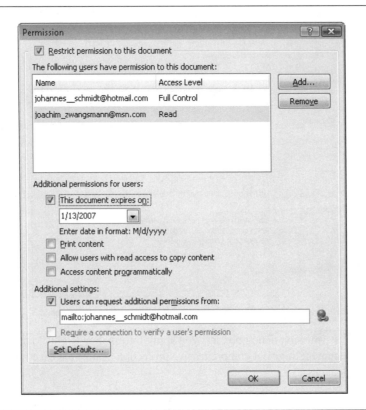

FIGURE 18-4 To implement more detailed permissions, use the larger version of the Permission dialog box.

7. In the Additional Permissions For Users area, decide whether to allow other permissions:

- **This Document Expires On**   To give the document an expiration date, select this check box, and then click the drop-down arrow on the date box and choose the date from the panel.

- **Print Content**   Select this check box if you want the users to be able to print the document.

- **Allow Users With Read Access To Copy Content**   Select this check box if you want users who can read the document but not edit it to be able to copy content from the document and paste it elsewhere. Normally, this is not a good idea—but there are exceptions.

- **Access Content Programmatically**   Select this check box if you want users to be able to access the document's content via programming tools such as Visual Basic for Applications, Visual Basic, or Visual C#. For example, your company's IT department might need such access.

8. If you want users to be able to request additional permissions for the document, select the Users Can Request Additional Permissions From check box, and then enter a hyperlink to the appropriate URL.

■ For example, you might enter a **mailto:** hyperlink to your e-mail address.

■ You can type a hyperlink manually or click the Insert Hyperlink button at the right end of the text box, and then use the Edit Hyperlink dialog box to set up the link.

9. If you want Word to authenticate the user each time they open the document, select the Require A Connection To Verify A User's Permission check box. Depending on the implementation of IRM, this check box may not be available.

10. If you want to use the permission settings you've chosen here as your default settings for all Office documents to which you apply permissions, click the Set Defaults button. Word displays the confirmation dialog box shown next. Click the OK button.

11. Click the OK button. Word closes the Permission dialog box, applies the permissions, and displays a Restricted Access bar below the Ribbon, as shown here. You can click the Close button (the × button) to close this bar.

12. Click the Save button on the Quick Access Toolbar to save the document.

Open a Document That Has Permissions Applied

If you've applied permissions to a document yourself, you'll know that the document requires user authentication. But if someone else has applied permissions to a document, you may not know—or you may know that the document has permissions applied (for example, because it's in a protected folder) but not whether you have permission to read or change the document.

If you try to open a protected document on a user account that doesn't have IRM installed, Word prompts you to get credentials for the IRM service, as shown here. Click the Yes button.

18

Word may display the following Microsoft Office dialog box warning you that the document has restricted permissions.

If you don't have permission for the document, and the document is configured so that you can request permissions, Word offers you the opportunity to do so, as shown next. If you want to request the permission, click the Yes button. Word launches the appropriate program. For example, if the permissionholder has provided a mailto hyperlink, Word launches Outlook or your default mail program and starts an e-mail message in it.

Instead of requesting permission, you can click the Change User button, which displays the Select User dialog box (shown next) so that you can supply other credentials for opening the document.

Apply a Digital Signature to a Document

Normally, you sign a (paper) check to authenticate its validity to the recipient (and, in due course, to your bank). Similarly, you can apply a digital signature to a Word document to authenticate its validity.

If your computer already has one or more digital IDs installed, you're ready to go; skip ahead to the section "Apply a Digital Signature." If not, you must first set Word up to use a digital signature, as described in the next section.

This feature can be useful for determining whether a document has been changed since the digital signature's holder applied the signature, but because digital signatures are neither widely used nor widely accepted at this writing, applying a digital signature to a Word document doesn't always have the intended effect.

Set Word Up to Use a Digital Signature

To set Word up to use a digital signature, follow these steps:

1. Open a Word document that has been saved. (If you start from a new document, Word will prompt you to save the document.)

2. Click the Office Button, click or highlight Prepare, and then click Add A Digital Signature. Word displays the Microsoft Office Word dialog box shown here, warning you that "evidentiary laws may vary by jurisdiction" and that Microsoft "cannot warrant a digital signature's legal enforceability."

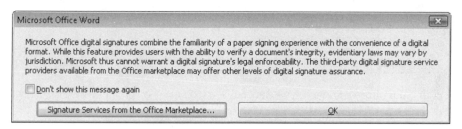

3. Select the Don't Show This Message Again check box (unless you want to see this message each time you go to apply a digital signature), and then click the OK button. Word displays the Get A Digital ID dialog box, shown here.

4. Choose how to get a digital ID:

   ■ **Get A Digital ID From A Microsoft Partner**   Select this option button and click the OK button to open a browser window to the Digital Signing page on the Microsoft web site. Here, you will find a variety of services that provide digital signatures. Most provide a trial of their paid services.

18

■ **Create Your Own Digital ID**   Select this option button and click the OK button to display the Create A Digital ID dialog box, shown next. Type the details of your ID, and then click the Create button. Word creates the digital ID, installs it, and then displays the Sign dialog box. Go to step 3 in the next section.

NOTE   *A digital ID you create yourself via the Create A Digital ID dialog box is useful only for testing. It has no authentication and is worthless in the real world.*

Apply a Digital Signature

To apply a digital signature to a document, follow these steps:

1. Finalize the document, and save any unsaved changes to it.

2. Click the Office Button, click or highlight Prepare, and then click Add A Digital Signature. Word displays the Sign dialog box, shown here.

3. In the Purpose For Signing This Document text box, type a description of why you're signing the document.

4. If your computer has two or more digital IDs installed, and the Signing As group box shows the wrong signature, click the Change button, choose the correct certificate in the Select Certificate dialog box, and then click the OK button.

5. Click the Sign button. Word closes the Sign dialog box, applies the digital signature, and then displays the Signature Confirmation message box, shown here, warning you that changing the document will render your signature invalid.

6. Select the Don't Show This Message Again check box if you can dispense with this message box in future, and then click the OK button. Word closes the message box and displays the Signatures pane, shown here.

7. Close the document. (You don't need to save changes—Word has already saved them for you.)

Remove Sensitive or Personal Information from a Document

Before you distribute a document, you may want to remove sensitive or personal information from it for security.

In the past few years, several major governments have embarrassed themselves by releasing files that inadvertently contained information they weren't supposed to, such as hidden revision marks or metadata in Word documents. Word's Document Inspector helps to make sure you don't join the governments in the red-face parade.

To run the Document Inspector and remove such information, follow these steps:

1. If the document contains unsaved changes, click the Save button on the Quick Access Toolbar (or press CTRL-S) to save it.

2. Click the Office Button, highlight or click Prepare, and then click Inspect Document. Word displays the Document Inspector (see Figure 18-5).

3. Select the check box for each type of data that you want to scan the document for:

   ■ **Comments, Revisions, Versions, And Annotations** These four items are easy to miss when you're finalizing a document, as revision marks can be hidden, and comments and annotations may appear only as hard-to-see markers in the text. Versions are a bit different: Word 2007 doesn't support versions, but a Word document created in an earlier version of Word may contain them. (A *version* in this sense is a different edit of the same document. You can store multiple versions in the same document file and switch from one to another.)

   ■ **Document Properties And Personal Information** A document can contain information such as your name, your manager's name, and custom document properties.

   ■ **Custom XML Data** The document may contain XML tags and mappings that you don't want to share outside your company.

   ■ **Headers, Footers, And Watermarks** If you're working in Draft view or Outline view, it's easy to forget to check the headers or footers in a document. You may also need to remove a watermark such as DRAFT before distributing a document.

   ■ **Hidden Text** Hidden text is often useful for hiding boilerplate items that don't apply to the current document, for inserting extra information that can be added only if required, and other such purposes. Normally, it's best to remove all hidden text before distributing a document.

18

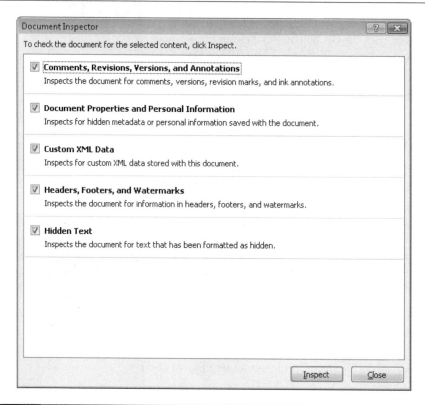

FIGURE 18-5   Use the Document Inspector to identify hidden content or metadata that you might want to remove before distributing a document.

4. Click the Inspect button. Word inspects the document for the items whose check boxes you selected, and displays the results, providing a Remove All button for each category found.

5. Click any of the Remove All buttons to remove all instances of those items.

6. If necessary, click the Reinspect button to reinspect the document.

7. Click the Close button. Word closes the Document Inspector dialog box.

8. Double-check your document to make sure that removing the items hasn't had unintended consequences. If all is well, save the document.

Appendix

Keyboard Shortcuts

As you've seen throughout the book, Word supports many keyboard shortcuts for invoking commands from the keyboard rather than navigating through the menus. You can save a lot of time and effort in your work by memorizing and using the keyboard shortcuts for the actions you take frequently, but unless your job is wildly varied, you won't need to learn all the keyboard shortcuts—there will be many shortcuts you use so seldom that they would save you hardly any time even if you memorized them.

This appendix presents Word's keyboard shortcuts by category.

■ This list contains most of the keyboard shortcuts that are widely useful. It omits a few highly esoteric keyboard shortcuts.

■ Some of the keyboard shortcuts have the same effect in the other Office applications as well, but others have different effects—so don't apply Word's shortcuts rashly to vital documents in other applications.

NOTE   *You can also navigate the Word user interface by pressing* ALT *and then pressing the navigation letters that Word displays in boxes. This method of navigation can be very useful and fast, but it is somewhat different from keyboard shortcuts, and this appendix does not list the navigation keypresses.*

■ For a quick-reference list of essential keyboard shortcuts, see the inside back cover of the book.

NOTE   *Some actions have multiple keyboard shortcuts for historical reasons: Microsoft introduced new keyboard shortcuts for actions but didn't remove key combinations that users knew from older versions of the software. Some keyboard shortcuts cater to users with different keyboard layouts. For example, most keyboard shortcuts that use* F11 *or* F12 *are duplicated with shortcuts that don't use* F11 *or* F12, *because some keyboards don't have the* F11 *and* F12 *keys.*

Action	Keyboard Shortcut
Creating and Displaying Documents	
Create a new default document	CTRL-N
Close the active window or exit the application	ALT-F4
Close the active document window	CTRL-F4, CTRL-W
Open, Save, and Print Documents	
Display the Open dialog box	CTRL-O, CTRL-F12, CTRL-ALT-F2
Display the Save As dialog box	F12

Action	Keyboard Shortcut
Save the active document	CTRL-S, SHIFT-F12, ALT-SHIFT-F2
Display the Print dialog box	CTRL-P, CTRL-SHIFT-F12
Move and Resize Windows	
Restore or maximize the active document window	CTRL-F10
Restore the active document window	CTRL-F5
Switch to the next application window	ALT-TAB
Switch to the previous application window	ALT-SHIFT-TAB
Maximize or restore all open document windows	ALT-F10
Restore all maximized document windows	ALT-F5
Split the active window	CTRL-ALT-S
Remove the current split from the active window	CTRL-ALT-C
Move Among Windows, Panes, and Dialog Boxes	
Switch to the next window	CTRL-F6
Switch to the previous window	CTRL-SHIFT-F6
Switch to the next pane in a clockwise direction	F6
Switch to the next pane in a counterclockwise direction	SHIFT-F6
Toggle between a modeless dialog box and the document	ALT-F6
Change Views	
Switch to Draft view (Normal view)	CTRL-ALT-N
Switch to Print Layout view	CTRL-ALT-P
Switch to Outline view	CTRL-ALT-O
Toggle Print Preview on or off	CTRL-ALT-I
Move the Insertion Point	
Go back to the previous, second-previous, or third-previous edit	SHIFT-F5 OR CTRL-ALT-Z (from one to three times)
Move one character to the left	←
Move one character to the right	→
Move up one line	↑
Move down one line	↓
Move to the start of the current paragraph or previous paragraph	CTRL-↑
Move to the start of the next paragraph	CTRL-↓

Action	Keyboard Shortcut
Move to the start of the next word (if there is one) or the end of the current word	CTRL-→
Move to the start of the current word (if the insertion point is within a word) or the start of the previous word	CTRL-←
Move to the start of the current line	HOME
Move to the end of the current line	END
Move to the start of the document	CTRL-HOME
Move to the end of the document	CTRL-END
Move down one screen of text (the amount that fits in the window at its current size)	PAGE DOWN
Move up one screen of text	PAGE UP
Move to the next page	CTRL-PAGE DOWN
Move to the previous page	CTRL-PAGE UP
Apply Formatting	
Display the Font dialog box	CTRL-D, CTRL-SHIFT-F
Toggle boldface on or off	CTRL-B
Toggle italics on or off	CTRL-I
Toggle underline on or off	CTRL-U
Toggle word underline on or off	CTRL-SHIFT-W
Toggle double underline on or off	CTRL-SHIFT-D
Apply hidden formatting	CTRL-SHIFT-H
Increase the font size in steps	CTRL-SHIFT->
Decrease the font size in steps	CTRL-SHIFT-<
Increase the font size by one point	CTRL-]
Decrease the font size by one point	CTRL-[
Toggle the display of nonprinting characters	CTRL-SHIFT-8 OR CTRL-*
Cycle through the case of letters	SHIFT-F3
Apply all caps formatting	CTRL-SHIFT-A
Apply small caps formatting	CTRL-SHIFT-K
Apply a default superscript	CTRL-SHIFT-+ (plus)
Apply a default subscript	CTRL-=
Remove all manual character formatting	CTRL-SPACEBAR
Apply Symbol font	CTRL-SHIFT-Q

Action	Keyboard Shortcut
Cut, Copy, and Paste	
Copy the current selection to the Clipboard	CTRL-C, CTRL-INSERT
Paste the current contents of the Clipboard at the position of the insertion point	CTRL-V, SHIFT-INSERT
Cut the current selection to the Clipboard	CTRL-X, SHIFT-DELETE
Copy the screen to the Clipboard as a picture	PRINT SCREEN
Copy the active window to the Clipboard as a picture	ALT-PRINT SCREEN
Display the Paste Special dialog box	CTRL-ALT-V
Copy formatting with the Format Painter	CTRL-SHIFT-C
Paste the formatting only	CTRL-SHIFT-V
Repeat Actions and Invoke Common Tools	
Undo the previous action	CTRL-Z, ALT-BACKSPACE
Repeat the previous action	CTRL-Y, F4
Display the Find tab of the Find And Replace dialog box	CTRL-F
Display the Replace tab of the Find And Replace dialog box	CTRL-H
Display the Go To tab of the Find And Replace dialog box	CTRL-G
Find the next instance of the search term (after using and closing the Find And Replace dialog box)	CTRL-PAGE DOWN
Find the previous instance of the search term (after using and closing the Find And Replace dialog box)	CTRL-PAGE UP
Open the Select Browse Object list	CTRL-ALT-HOME
Display the Insert Hyperlink dialog box	CTRL-K
Run the Spell Checker	F7
Display the Research task pane with the Thesaurus selected	SHIFT-F7
Display the Research pane with information about the clicked word	ALT-CLICK
Display the Word Count dialog box	CTRL-SHIFT-G
Insert Special Characters	
Insert an em (long) dash	CTRL-ALT-– (minus)
Insert an en (short) dash	CTRL-– (minus)
Insert an optional hyphen	CTRL-- (hyphen)
Insert a nonbreaking hyphen	CTRL-SHIFT-- (hyphen)
Insert a nonbreaking space	CTRL-SHIFT-SPACEBAR

Action	Keyboard Shortcut
Insert a line break	SHIFT-ENTER
Insert a page break	CTRL-ENTER
Insert a column break	CTRL-SHIFT-ENTER
Insert a copyright symbol (©)	CTRL-ALT-C
Insert a registered trademark symbol (®)	CTRL-ALT-R
Insert an ellipsis (…)	CTRL-ALT-. (period)
Change the Line Spacing and Alignment	
Apply single spacing	CTRL-1
Apply 1.5-line spacing	CTRL-5
Apply double spacing	CTRL-2
Add or remove one line space	CTRL-0 (zero)
Apply left alignment	CTRL-L
Toggle centering and left alignment	CTRL-E
Toggle right alignment and left alignment	CTRL-R
Toggle justified and left alignment	CTRL-J
Increase the indent by one tab	CTRL-M
Decrease the indent by one tab	CTRL-SHIFT-M
Apply a hanging indent	CTRL-T
Reduce the hanging indent by one tab	CTRL-SHIFT-T
Remove all direct paragraph formatting	CTRL-Q
Review Documents and Create References	
Insert a new comment	CTRL-ALT-M
Insert a footnote	CTRL-ALT-F
Insert an endnote	CTRL-ALT-D
Toggle Track Changes on or off	CTRL-SHIFT-E
Close the Reviewing pane	ALT-SHIFT-C
Mark an index entry	ALT-SHIFT-X
Mark a citation	ALT-SHIFT-I
Mark a table of contents entry	ALT-SHIFT-O
Navigate in a Table	
Move to the next cell	TAB
Move to the previous cell	SHIFT-TAB

Action	Keyboard Shortcut
Move to the first cell in the current row	ALT-HOME
Move to the last cell in the current row	ALT-END
Move to the top cell in the current column	ALT-PAGE UP
Move to the last cell in the current column	ALT-PAGE DOWN
Move the current row up one row	ALT-SHIFT-↑
Move the current row down one row	ALT-SHIFT-↓

Work with Fields

Insert field braces (so you can create a field manually)	CTRL-F9
Update the current field or all selected fields	F9
Toggle between displaying field codes and results	SHIFT-F9
Toggle between displaying all field codes and results	ALT-F9
Unlink the current field or all selected fields	CTRL-SHIFT-F9
Move to the next field	F11
Move to the previous field	SHIFT-F11
Lock the current field or all selected fields	CTRL-F11
Unlock the current field or all selected fields	CTRL-SHIFT-F11
Insert a PAGE field	ALT-SHIFT-P
Insert a TIME field	ALT-SHIFT-T
Insert a LISTNUM field	ALT-SHIFT-L
Insert a DATE field	ALT-SHIFT-D
Update linked information in a source document	CTRL-SHIFT-F7

Work in Outline View

Switch to Outline view	CTRL-ALT-O
Display Heading 1 through Heading 9 levels	ALT-SHIFT-1 through ALT-SHIFT-9
Promote the selected paragraph by one level	ALT-SHIFT-←
Demote the selected paragraph by one level	ALT-SHIFT-→
Demote the selected paragraph to body text	ALT-SHIFT-N
Expand the text under the selected heading	ALT-SHIFT-+ (plus on keypad)
Collapse the text under the selected heading	ALT-SHIFT-− (minus on keypad)
Expand or collapse all text and headings	ALT-SHIFT-A
Move the current paragraph or selected paragraphs up by one displayed item	ALT-SHIFT-↑

Action	Keyboard Shortcut
Move the current paragraph or selected paragraphs down by one displayed item	ALT-SHIFT-↓
Toggle the Show First Line Setting on or off	ALT-SHIFT-L
Launch Help and the Visual Basic Editor	
Launch Help	F1
Display the Visual Basic Editor	ALT-F11
Display the Macros dialog box	ALT-F8

Index

WITHDRAWN